BRYCE 4 f/x and design

R. Shamms Mortier

Bryce 4 f/x and design

© 1999 The Coriolis Group. All Rights Reserved.

All rights reserved. This book may not be duplicated in any way without the express written consent of the publisher, except in the form of brief excerpts or quotations for the purposes of review. The information contained herein is for the personal use of the reader and may not be incorporated in any commercial programs, other books, databases, or any kind of software without written consent of the publisher. Making copies of this book or any portion for any purpose other than your own is a violation of United States copyright laws.

Limits Of Liability And Disclaimer Of Warranty

The author and publisher of this book have used their best efforts in preparing the book and the programs contained in it. These efforts include the development, research, and testing of the theories and programs to determine their effectiveness. The author and publisher make no warranty of any kind, expressed or implied, with regard to these programs or the documentation contained in this book.

The author and publisher shall not be liable in the event of incidental or consequential damages in connection with, or arising out of, the furnishing, performance, or use of the programs, associated instructions, and/or claims of productivity gains.

Trademarks

Trademarked names appear throughout this book. Rather than list the names and entities that own the trademarks or insert a trademark symbol with each mention of the trademarked name, the publisher states that it is using the names for editorial purposes only and to the benefit of the trademark owner, with no intention of infringing upon that trademark.

The Coriolis Group, LLC
14455 N. Hayden Road, Suite 220
Scottsdale, Arizona 85260

480/483-0192
FAX 480/483-0193
http://www.coriolis.com

Library of Congress Cataloging-In-Publication Data
Mortier, R. Shamms.
Bryce 4 f/x and design / by R. Shamms Mortier.
p. cm
Includes index.
ISBN 1-57610-482-6
1. Computer graphics. 2. KPT Bryce. 3. Computer animation. I. Title.
T385.M6687 1999
006.6'9--dc21 99-35765
CIP

Printed in the United States of America
10 9 8 7 6 5 4 3 2 1

President, CEO
Keith Weiskamp

Publisher
Steve Sayre

Acquisitions Editor
Mariann Hansen Barsolo

Marketing Specialist
Beth Kohler

Project Editor
Melissa D. Olson

Technical Reviewer
Nancy Wood

Production Coordinator
Jon Gabriel

Cover Design
Jody Winkler
additional art provided by Brandon Riza

Layout Design
April Nielsen

CD-ROM Developer
Robert Clarfield

Other Titles For The Creative Professional

3D Studio MAX R3 f/x and design
by Jon A. Bell

3D Studio MAX R3 In Depth
by Robert Polevoi

Adobe ImageStyler In Depth
by Daniel Gray

After Effects 4 In Depth
by R. Shamms Mortier

AutoCAD 2000 3D f/x and design
by Brian Matthews

Character Animation In Depth
by Doug Kelly

CorelDRAW 9 f/x and design
by Shane Hunt

Flash 3 Web Animation f/x and design
by Ken Milburn and Janine Warner

Illustrator 8 f/x and design
by Sherry London and T. Michael Clark

Photoshop 5 3D Textures f/x and design
by Geoffrey Smith

Photoshop 5 Filters f/x and design
by T. Michael Clark

Photoshop 5 In Depth
by David Xenakis and Sherry London

This book is dedicated to my mother, who taught me that creativity, respect, and hard work could accomplish miracles.

❧

About The Author

R. **Shamms Mortier**, Ph.D., operates a design studio, Eyeful Tower Communications, in Bristol, Vermont. This facility serves the broadcast and display needs of regional clients. He has written more than 800 computer graphics and animation articles, reviews, and interviews for national and international magazines. He taught computer arts at the college level for 15 years and has had exhibitions of his work (traditional and digital) in local and regional galleries and museums.

Shamms writes a bimonthly column for *TV Technology*, "A Mix of Art and Engineering," that covers videographics. He studied traditional animation techniques with the world-renowned animator David Ehrlich. Shamms received funds from the National Endowment for the Arts and the Boston Film/Video Society to produce his animated film, "The Secret Dreams of Older Men."

He has written 12 books on computer graphics and animation, including books on other MetaCreations products: Bryce 3D, Ray Dream, and Poser. He writes and edits the Komodo Enterprises newsletter for the *Mastering 3D Graphics* and *3D Creature Workshop* subscription Web sites. The *Mastering 3D Graphics* site features his Bryce tutorial column (**http://mastering3dgraphics.com**).

His science fiction novel, *A Convergence of Worlds,* will be published in 2000. All of the environmental graphics and animations for this novel will be rendered in Bryce and posted to *A Convergence of Worlds* Web site. Tutorials devoted to the creation of the novel's graphics will be presented each month on the *3D Creature Workshop* Web site (**www.3dcreatureworkshop.com**).

Shamms can be reached at **rshamms@together.net**.

ACKNOWLEDGMENTS

I wish to thank the following individuals for their assistance in bringing this book to pass:

- The creative minds at MetaCreations, especially the individual programmers who worked on Bryce 4 and Production Manager John Feld
- All of the folks at Coriolis, especially Melissa Olson, Mariann Barsolo, Robert Clarfield, and Jon Gabriel
- All of the artists who contributed to this book (Their names and biographical remarks can be found in Appendix B.)
- David Fugate and Maureen Maloney of Waterside Productions

Thanks to all of you for the extra effort and dedicated participation.

—R. Shamms Mortier

Contents At A Glance

Table Of Contents

INTRODUCTION

Many software developers can only dream of an audience as dedicated as the users of MetaCreations' Bryce. Software does not develop in the absence of user interest and involvement, and thanks to the suggestions and concerns of its users, Bryce has continued to break new ground. With each new update and version, Bryce expands into new and exciting creative territory.

Eric Wenger originally developed Bryce (or KPT Bryce, as it was called then) as a utility for generating scenery art for desktop publishing and print users. Eric has gone on to develop other art applications, leaving Bryce development to a team at MetaCreations. In the time since, what began as an interesting toy has become a high-end, professional tool.

The previous edition, Bryce 3D, was the first to feature 3D animation. Bryce users wanted an application that was not limited to print output. Animation has become a necessary part of the diverse pursuits and enterprises of digital artists. Just browse the Web to see animation in action. But as with all software that has a loyal user-base, the requests for features are more plentiful than the time in which to develop them. However, the latest version of Bryce—Bryce 4—honors MetaCreations' tradition of respecting and rewarding user feedback and adds a wide feature list to this popular (and addictive) creative software.

How This Book Is Organized

This book is organized in the following manner:

- *Chapter 1: A Genesis Of New Worlds*—Bryce 4 contains new features and capabilities that users have long demanded. All of these are described in this chapter.
- *Chapter 2: Model Mania*—Although Bryce lacks many of the modeling features present in other 3D applications, it contains modeling environments that are unique. All of Bryce's modeling options are described in this chapter, with special attention paid to the Terrain Editor.
- *Chapter 3: Materials And Textures*—You would be hard-pressed to find another application—at any price—that allows you to develop materials and textures like those you can generate in Bryce. The process is rather involved however, and this chapter describes it with copious examples.
- *Chapter 4: Scenic Wonders*—This chapter deals with cameras, lights, and the creation and application of environmental effects.

- *Chapter 5: Animation On Demand*—All of Bryce's animation capabilities and methods are described here.
- *Chapter 6: The Color Plates*—The 31 color plates in the "Bryce 4 Studio" are not just eye candy, they are also learning devices. This chapter looks at each plate in detail and describes how specific effects were achieved.
- *Chapter 7: Project Paradise*—Five Bryce projects are described here in step-by-step tutorials. You can find the elements used in their creation on the CD-ROM.
- *Bryce 4 Studio*—These 31 color plates feature the work of the author and eleven other Bryce artists. The plates are examined in detail in Chapter 6.
- *CD-ROM*—Look on the CD-ROM for Bryce projects and other useful goodies.

Who Is This Book For?

Depending on your needs and your expertise, you will find different ways to best use this book as a creative resource. If you see yourself represented in the following list of potential readers, you may want to approach this book in the manner described.

The Seasoned Bryce Professional

Who is the seasoned Bryce professional? Certainly, this includes anyone who has used previous versions of Bryce to develop 2D or 3D art or animations. However, some Bryce pros have used the application to create only a limited range of output, and they remain unfamiliar with many of the software's possible uses. If you consider yourself a professional Bryce user, look over the book to determine which areas might represent new information for you, and focus on those areas. Professionals are always learning—studying how other artists and animators approach the same challenges and achieve different results. For instance, you might find descriptions of textures and materials in this book that hint at opportunities for expanding the way you have applied Bryce's textures and materials in the past. Or perhaps a single new modeling or animation technique will be worth the price of the book. Explore the book as if you were a treasure hunter looking for special gems that twinkle in the dark.

Regardless of your past experience with Bryce, version 4 contains new and upgraded features, so be sure to read Chapter 1. Pay special attention to the projects that explain the use of these new features. When you look at the artwork, consider how you might do it differently. All the artwork represents only a single solution, and it should inspire rather than dictate.

Special Interest Bryce Professionals

If you have used Bryce in the past in any of the following creative areas, use this book to enhance your understanding by approaching your study in the following ways:

- *The Bryce print artist*—If you use Bryce to develop print media, be sure to read Chapters 1 through 4. Pay special attention to the color plates and Chapter 6. Chapter 6 looks at specific areas of each color plate and describes how the results were achieved. Skim the rest of the book as needed.
- *The Bryce game developer*—Bryce is a wonderful tool for developing photorealistic game environments. If you are a game developer, pay special attention to Chapter 1's description of the new features and to Chapter 5's description of animation techniques. Also be sure to read the tutorials in Chapter 7, and examine the approaches used in the projects. Read or skim the rest of the book as needed.
- *The Bryce multimedia producer*—You should cover all the material listed for game developers and also pay special attention to Chapter 4's coverage of the use of lights and cameras. Read or skim the rest of the book as needed.
- *The Bryce film and television producer*—Use this book to enhance your Bryce expertise in all areas, and pay special attention to material that describes the effects possible in Bryce. Remember that Bryce is useful not only as an animation application: Its photorealistic graphics can also make effective backdrops for live footage. With some practice, you can generate amazing titling text in Bryce.
- *The Bryce Web site designer*—Be sure to read Chapter 1's description of new Web features in Bryce 4. Learn to optimize your animations for the Web with the help of Chapter 5. Remember that you can use the latest version of Bryce to embed URL hotspots in a scene. Read or skim the rest of the book as needed.

The New-To-Bryce Professional

Perhaps you have experience with other 3D art and animation applications but have purchased Bryce recently. As you might expect, you can take much of your knowledge of other 3D art and animation software into the Bryce environment. But be cautioned: You should work through both the Bryce documentation and this book (especially Chapter 2) to learn about Bryce modeling in all its guises. Many of Bryce's modeling features cannot be found in other 3D applications, and you need to explore them before you can be considered a Bryce modeling master. (This is especially true of the Terrain Editor.) Study Chapter 3's description of Bryce textures and materials carefully. Bryce is one of the most powerful applications on the market when it comes to creating new textures and materials, but it creates them in an unusual way.

The New 3D Artist And Animator

If you are an artist experienced in traditional media but new to digital art and animation, Bryce may be your first venture into 3D design. Although you may have chosen Bryce because of its affordability or its eye-candy images, you should be aware that Bryce is capable of magical, high-end, environmental effects. You can apply all your traditional media and compositional skills to this new environment, but you also have to master Bryce's tools. Your mastery of these tools will grow in direct proportion to your study and exploration of the software. Read all the Bryce documentation as thoroughly as possible before you use this book. This book will take you from the novice stage to a new level of creative experience and confidence—provided you read it from start to finish. Work through the exercises in every chapter, and when you feel ready, work through them again and modify the parameters.

The Beginning Artist

If you are someone whose love of visual media is just starting to lead you toward creative expression, make use of educational opportunities that will give you a broad base of artistic knowledge rather than obsessing on computer arts. Before developing your computer art and animation skills, you should first have traditional art and animation skills, an understanding of art history, and an appreciation of the visual arts. Then, after you study the Bryce documentation and work through the tutorials, you can use this book to expand your creative potential even further. Work hard, and study long.

The Teacher In The Classroom

If you use computer arts in the classroom—perhaps to teach design or animation—this book will be a tremendous help as both a resource guide and lesson planner. Bryce is especially useful in schools because it includes so much creative design content at an affordable price. After your students are familiar with the Bryce documentation, you can use the tutorials in Chapter 7 as projects that test their skills. Along the way, of course, you will attain a greater mastery of Bryce yourself.

Lovers Of Computer Art And Animation Everywhere

Thanks to television and films, computer art and animation has a wide audience. Not all the members of this audience use digital arts as a creative outlet; some just enjoy the finished product. Most computer users enjoy watching QuickTime or AVI movies and perusing print media for stunning graphics. The CD-ROM that accompanies this book contains animated movies you will enjoy watching regardless of your experience with computer art and animation, and the full-color "Bryce 4 Studio" contains interesting artwork. In addition to its use as a teaching and learning device, this book might find a place on your coffee table or in a waiting room.

The most important thing to remember as you embark on a creative adventure is this: To learn to use creative tools, read all the documentation you can find on the subject and memorize the tools' every nuance. To truly master creative tools, *learn* first. Then dedicate yourself to exploration and play, breaking as many of the rules as possible to see what happens. True mastery is directly related to taking risks at every turn just to see what happens. Master something, and you have been given that most precious gift: a unique style.

Moving On

Okay! It's time to begin. Ladies and gentlemen, start your computers. Get ready to immerse yourself in Chapter 1, which describes the new features of Bryce 4.

1 A Genesis Of New Worlds

This chapter looks at Bryce 4's new features and tools. Many of the new features are subtle, yet they transform Bryce into a wider arena for creating computer graphics and animation.

And The World Was Without Form And Void

The act of creating anything starts with what philosophers call *ex nihilo,* or "out of nothing." Whether you sit in front of a blank canvas or a blank computer screen, the initial challenge is the same: to create something where nothing now exists. How does one take the first steps on a journey of a thousand miles? How does one muster the courage to make the first stroke on canvas or screen?

Although all creative endeavors are similar in terms of creative motivation and the need to take risks, the electronic medium presents a new spectrum of challenges and opportunities for artists. The challenges arise from the need to master tools and processes that have never existed before. But the opportunities are considerable: the magnitude of the audience who will see your work, the tools you can use to defy the laws of physics, the speed and power available to turn your dreams into virtual reality.

MetaCreations' Bryce was born out of a desire to create worlds shaped and populated with photorealistic components. Clouded atmospheres, reflective watery surfaces, striated rock faces, and more became possible with Bryce. Bryce wasn't the first software to offer these capabilities, but it was the first software to do so with an intuitive approach, rather than an engineering approach. Bryce was created for digital artists. As the hardware and software technologies have advanced, Bryce has advanced with them. With Bryce, you don't need to wrestle with the challenge of creating something out of nothing; a few mouse clicks can bring a startling world into view. Of course, mastery of Bryce requires exploration and experimentation, just as any creative medium does.

It is expected that you have already read the Bryce documentation and completed all the tutorials before you use this book. Having done so, you will find this book invaluable for pushing your Bryce work to new heights—creating worlds where none existed before.

What's New In Bryce 4?

Bryce 4 contains enhancements and modifications that experienced Bryce users have requested for a long time. Version 4 also contains major advances and fixes over previous releases. The more experience you have with Bryce, the more you'll be impressed and motivated by Bryce 4. In the following sections, I'll look at the new features and explain why each is important.

New Features And Enhancements

With the following features and enhancements, Bryce 4 adds new creative options for the beginner and professional alike:

- The picture list in the Picture Editor can now contain more than 30 pictures. This provides a number of advantages. You can have more textures on hand to apply to a scene's objects. Textures make an image or animation more interesting and create greater realism. The enhanced Picture Editor also allows you to add more sequential single frames to an existing animation. Working with sequential, single frames allows you to map animated textures to an object, greatly increasing the variety of effects available in animations. And, you can now delete all the pictures in the Picture Editor by pressing Alt (the Apple key on the Mac) when confirming the deletion. This saves you the time of deleting each picture separately.
- View changes made to the Main Controls' Nano Preview are now persistent between visits to the main controls. This saves time because you don't have to reconfigure your customized settings again and again.
- The Scale Pict Size mode works better. No tiling occurs by default, so you can shrink the image. This allows for a better placement of images on targeted picture planes: The images can act as object elements in the background and can be resized.
- An alternate method of aligning objects based on an anchor object has been added to the Align menu in the Edit palette. This feature is helpful when you need to configure alignments using the anchor points of the selected objects as references.
- A new option in the Advanced Motion Lab allows the timeline scale to be shared with the main user interface. This keeps the interface consistent when you craft your animations.
- You can now change the linking (propagation) of multiple selected objects. This speeds up the configuration of linking options for multiple objects.
- The Terrain Editor's Picture tab has been enhanced: You can now copy and paste pictures to and from the Terrain Editor. This speeds up Terrain Editor operations.
- Pressing Shift while pasting finds the terrain that best matches the size of the picture you're pasting. This automated feature saves you a great deal of time when applying images to terrains.

- Clicking and holding down the Load (picture) button now produces a menu of Load options. These include Load Image (the default), Current Terrain, Original Terrain, and a selection of grayscales for use in creating elevated surfaces.
- Triangle-mesh objects no longer display edges as a result of polygon splitting. Groups of triangle meshes now smooth across each other, eliminating a visible seam. The smoothing angle of triangle-mesh objects is now consistent.
- The default media player can be launched to view movies after they've been rendered. This is a time-saver because you don't have to leave Bryce in order to see the animation.
- The main controls' Bump Height values can now be greater or less than 100 or -100. This makes a huge difference in the appearance of textures that require a messier look and also helps to hide bad-geometry anomalies more effectively.
- The Ctrl/Command+click menu now works with only one object, and it does not deselect all the objects if no object was clicked. This makes it easier to select an object from a large group of objects on the screen.
- The Color Picker is now accessible by holding down Ctrl/Command+Alt/Option and clicking the color to edit, which saves time.
- 48-bit dithering has been added as a rendering option.
- A new texture-mapping mode has been added: Object Side. This allows you to do planar mapping—map an image to one side of a selected object.
- Lights now have a new falloff method: Ranged. The Ranged option allows the light to go from full intensity to zero, with no fall-off in between, depending on the Ranged value you set.
- Materials now have a new control: Self Shadows. When you have a complex object in a scene, this option allows the object to cast shadows on itself.
- There is a new texture-mapping control: Repeat Tiling.
- Gamma correction has been added as a rendering option. This allows you to adjust the overall brightness of the image without washing it out.

New Movie Thumbnail Previews

Now you can generate fully rendered thumbnail animation previews in the Nano Preview. Navigating through the preview animation is simple, using a storyboard-style interface that displays each frame separately.

The thumbnail is essentially a Nano-movie preview. When you click on the Play button in the Time palette while holding down Shift, Bryce generates a movie preview (providing you have set up the needed keyframes, of course). After the preview is generated, it plays back at the frames-per-second (FPS) rate you have set for the animation. Hold down Ctrl/Command and click on Play to see the options available for the Movie Preview feature. Movie Preview works very much like the other viewing modes: There's a wireframe view, rendered view, wireframe/rendered view, and now a movie preview view. If you initiate a redraw or render while in Movie Preview, the movie preview disappears and the drawing or rendering begins. If you go back to movie preview without changing anything that affects the animation, the preview begins immediately, without first re-rendering the preview.

The Storyboard option controls what happens when you initiate a movie preview by holding down Ctrl/Command and clicking on Play. If the Storyboard option is enabled, all the frames are shown in a grid as they are rendered. After the rendering is finished, the movie plays in the Nano window. If you click anywhere on the screen as the movie is playing, the movie stops, and you are taken back to the movie preview, where you can explore your animation further. (Hitting Esc or causing a redraw or render closes the movie preview display.) If the Storyboard option is disabled, the movie is generated and played back in the Nano display without the frames first being shown in the grid. You can drag the scrubber to move forward or backward through the animation. If you hold down the left mouse button on a frame, you can drag the mouse and move through the animation while traversing the frame.

You can access the following options for Movie Preview mode by holding down Ctrl/Command and clicking on the Play button:

- *Storyboard*—Described in the preceding section.
- *Frame Outlines*—Enables or disables frame borders in Storyboard mode.
- *Auto Play Loop*—Determines whether the movie plays repeatedly after it has been generated.

- *Auto Play Mode*—Determines whether to play the movie according to the play mode after it is rendered.
- *Line Scrolling*—Scrolls the frame grid a line at a time while in Storyboard mode.
- *Page Scrolling*—Scrolls the frame grid a page at a time while in Storyboard mode.

The preview is generated using the animation's working area (that is, the green area within the timeline). One frame is generated for every tick on the timeline. You can change the frequency of frames in the preview by changing the tick-mark interval.

Import Options

Previous versions of Bryce could import OBJ, DXF, 3DS, and 3DMF formats; support for these formats has been improved. Bryce 4 adds support for a number of other formats as well:

- LightWave LWO and LWS files
- trueSpace COB files
- VideoScape VSA files
- VRML1 WRL files
- Heightfield HF files
- Portable Grayscale Map PGM files
- Ray Dream Studio RDS files
- U.S. Geological Survey (USGS) DEM files
- USGS SDTS DDF files

Support for these formats provides compatibility with virtually every 3D modeling and animation environment. The following import options have been added or enhanced in version 4:

- The 3D Metafile importer now has enhanced material support. This is a welcome addition because the 3DMF format often degrades the look of materials and textures. The 3DMF format is popular among Mac users; OpenGL is the dominant realtime 3D viewing option on Windows (with more OpenGL coming to the Mac as well). See Figure 1.1.
- The 3D Studio MAX (3DS) importer has enhanced material support. This is great news for 3D Studio MAX users who want to use textures developed in that application within Bryce. See Figure 1.2.

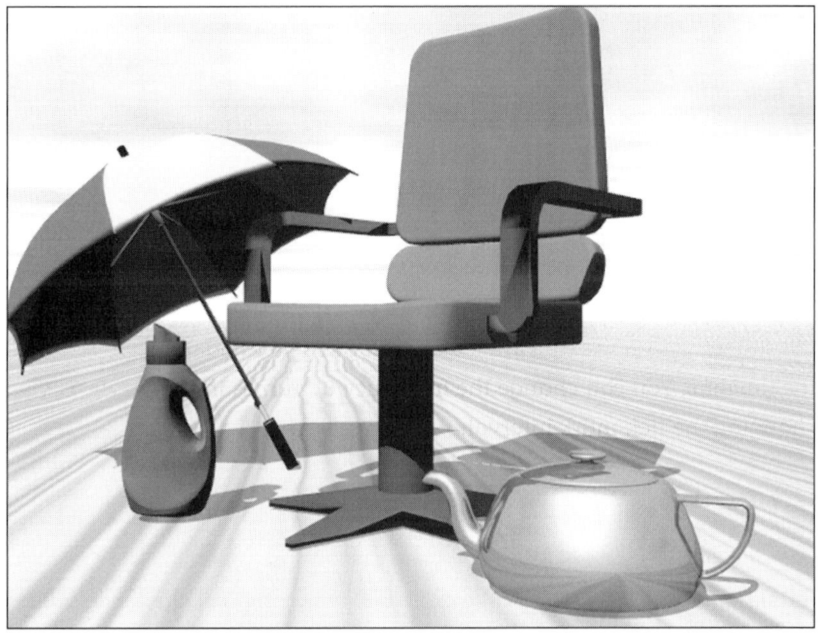

Figure 1.1
3DMF objects imported and rendered in Bryce 4.

Figure 1.2
3D Studio MAX objects imported and rendered in Bryce 4.

- The DXF importer now has enhanced color support. Other 3D applications often save DXF models with custom colors. Although many applications can import and render DXF objects, only Bryce can smooth their facets in an intuitive manner. See Figure 1.3.
- Bryce 4 can import Heightfield HF files (this simple format is used to define heightfields). HF is a binary format developed by Ken Musgrave and RayShade for storing 16-bit square-sized heightfields.

Figure 1.3
DXF objects imported, rendered, and smoothed in Bryce 4.

- The LightWave importer now imports *full* scenes. LightWave scene files are some of the most complex 3D environments in the industry. A LightWave object file often contains object parts that have to be linked in Bryce. In a scene file, everything is already linked. See Figure 1.4.
- Bryce 4 includes a Portable Grayscale Map (PGM) importer. PGM is another format used to import definitions of heightfields (or terrains)

Figure 1.4
LightWave triceratops in a Bryce environment.

into Bryce. This format is fairly popular in the Unix community. Bryce imports both the ASCII and binary PGM formats.

- Bryce 4 includes a Ray Dream Studio (RDS) exporter. The Ray Dream format is ASCII, but texture maps are embedded within it directly. It exports textures, normals, and UV mapping in addition to the material properties. The terrain is converted from a heightfield to a triangle mesh when exported to Ray Dream. See Figure 1.5.

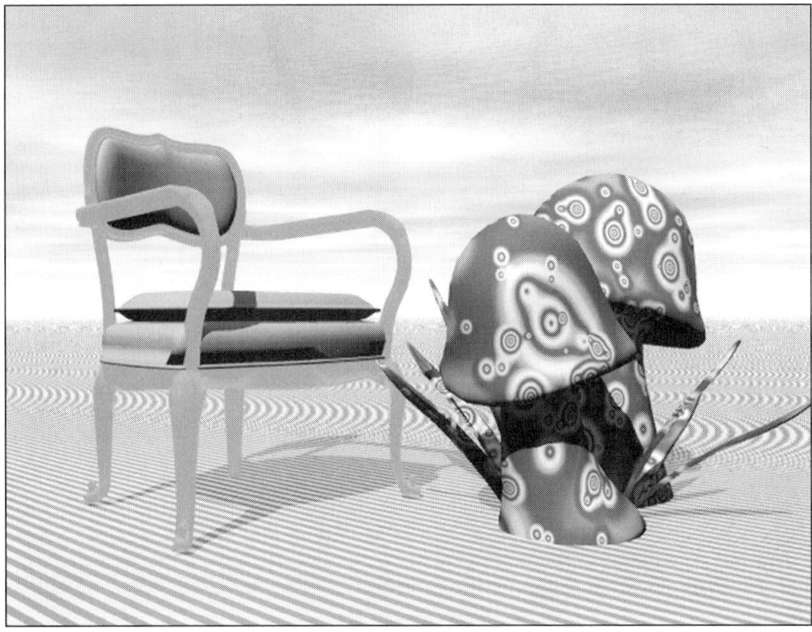

Figure 1.5
Ray Dream objects rendered in Bryce 4.

- Bryce 4 includes a trueSpace (COB) importer. The trueSpace importer supports all versions of trueSpace up to version 4. Material properties are also supported. Of all 3D applications, trueSpace has one of the largest audiences of Windows users, and it offers a number of modeling and effects tools found nowhere else. See Figure 1.6.
- Bryce 4 includes a USGS DEM (DEM) and USGS SDTS (DDF) importer. Bryce can import all forms of Digital Elevation Map (DEM) files, including the new SDTS format that will replace all DEM files eventually. (Bryce is one of the first products to support the new format.) Download a U.S. Geological Survey map from the Internet and you can easily import it into Bryce for realistic texturing and animation of real-world geographical terrains. Imagine importing the terrain map of the Grand Canyon directly from the USGS Web site, applying a preset texture map included with Bryce, and quickly creating a realistic model. Visit the

USGS Web site (**http://ngmdb.usgs.gov/ngmdb/ngm_catalog.ora.html**) to download some samples. See Figure 1.7.

- Bryce 4 includes a VideoScape ASCII (VSA) importer. This is a basic ASCII format that was used by LightWave's predecessor, VideoScape 3-D. Bryce supports this format fully. You can use this format to build basic 3D objects.

Note: *The ability to import and export DEM files opens up new worlds for Bryce users because you can use a number of other applications as DEM modelers for your Bryce work. These include the World Construction Set (Windows 95/98 and NT), World Render 3D (Windows 95/98 and NT), VistaPro (PowerMac and Windows), and Scenery Animator (PowerMac).*

Figure 1.6
trueSpace objects as rendered in Bryce 4.

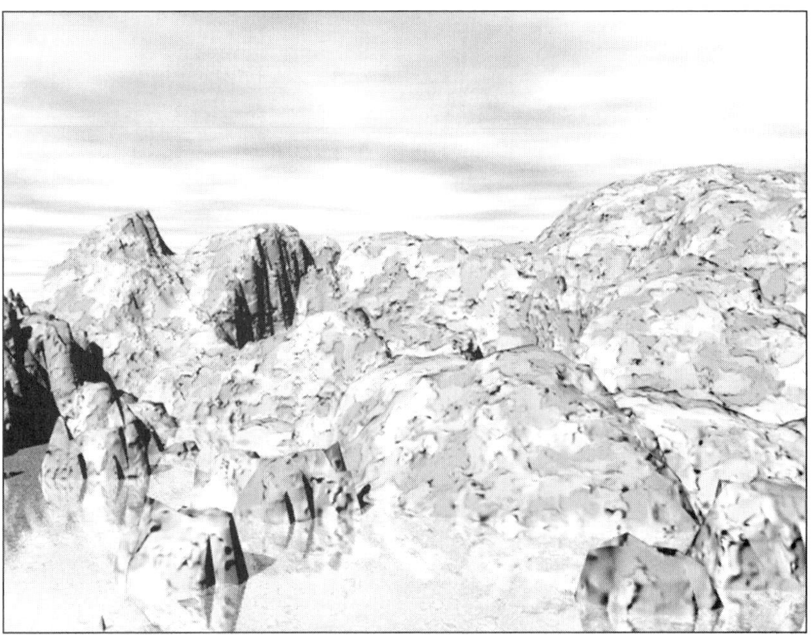

Figure 1.7
A DEM map used as a Bryce 4 terrain.

- Bryce 4 includes a VRML1 (WRL) importer/exporter. This importer supports all the properties within this format that are relevant to Bryce, including cameras, lights, and surface materials and textures.
- Bryce 4 includes a Wavefront OBJ importer. This importer now supports Material Lab material libraries. It imports materials from MTL files referenced in the OBJ file format. See Figure 1.8.

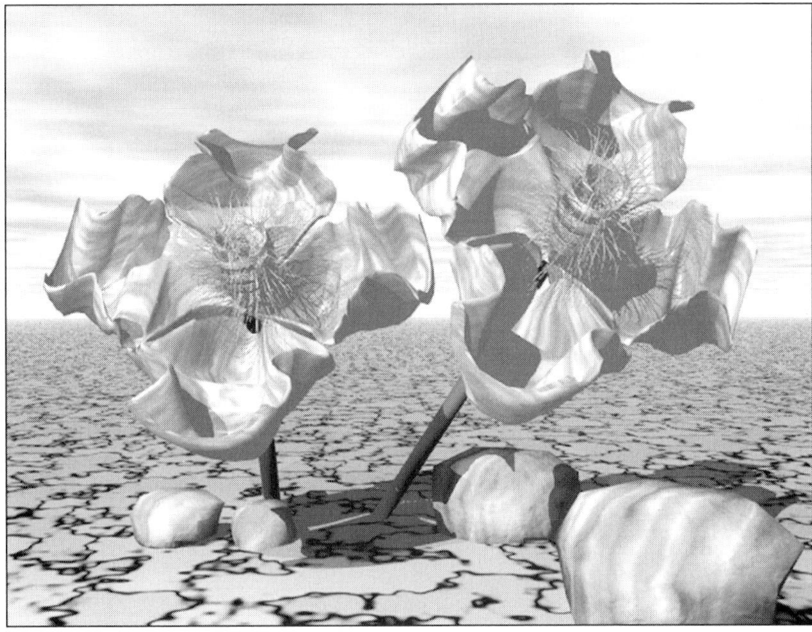

Figure 1.8
Wavefront objects imported by and rendered in Bryce 4.

Export Terrain

The terrain exporter feature was added at the request of users. Previous editions of Bryce could not export terrains. The idea behind the new feature, Export Terrain lab, is to let you control the number of triangles in the mesh object that represents a Bryce terrain and to provide realtime feedback concerning the fidelity of the triangulated mesh. As you decrease the number of triangles, the mesh becomes progressively less detailed until the resemblance to the original terrain disappears completely. Terrain objects that contain many polygons (up to hundreds of thousands of triangles) create very large files on disk, potentially hundreds of megabytes. They consume a lot of memory, and the time required for rendering increases to the point that not even the fastest system can handle them gracefully.

The Export Terrain lab is equipped with shaded and fully textured previews that provide instant feedback regarding the exported object's quality. When you change the selected terrain's polygon count, the results

Note: *Applying a texture can hide imperfections in the mesh and can generate detail, so you can use a lower mesh setting and still wind up with a great-looking object. Of course, the details are fake in terms of the geometry, and you might run into problems such as incorrect shadow casting.*

are shown immediately. This makes it easy to achieve a balance between a terrain that is not detailed enough and a terrain that is so detailed that even a fast system cannot render it quickly.

Two algorithms are provided for customizing the terrain's triangulated mesh:

- *Regular Sampling Of The Terrain*—This algorithm is best for triangulating terrains for use as geometric shapes.
- *Advanced Algorithm*—This algorithm tries to find the best triangulation of the terrain possible with the smallest number of triangles. This is best for making polygonal meshes of fractal or natural-looking terrains. This algorithm may yield unpredictable results on the edges of the Terrain object. It also requires recalculation time, which increases with the number of polygons in the mesh.

To avoid a long delay when opening the Export Terrain lab, the terrain polygon count defaults to 6,000 polygons on a regular terrain and 12,000 on a Symmetrical Lattice Terrain object.

The Export Terrain User Interface

The Export Terrain lab allows you to customize all aspects of the exported Terrain model. See Figure 1.9.

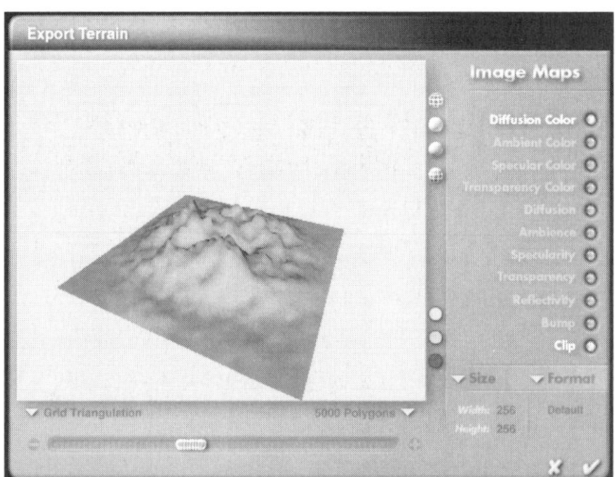

Figure 1.9
Use the Bryce 4 Export Terrain lab to export terrain models.

The Export Terrain user interface provides a large, 3D preview of the triangulated terrain. A menu in the bottom-left corner of the preview lets you choose the preview mode. The options are shaded wireframe, shaded solid, and textured preview. When using the solid and textured previews, you can overlay a wireframe to give you more information about the triangulation. (Toggle the wireframe by pressing *T*.) The bottom-right of the 3D Preview contains a polygon-count readout that tells you how many polygons are contained in the current model. Next to the polygon count is a menu that contains more options, including:

- *Add Polygons*—When using the Advanced Algorithm, this option lets you add polygons if the initial triangulated mesh is not good enough.
- *Clamp Min and Clamp Max functions*—This option is vital when exporting to the MetaStream format (MetaCreations' progressive-geometry streaming-file format).

Below the preview is a slider that controls the polygon count. On the right-hand side of the Export Terrain lab is the Image Maps Control. This control is active only if the terrain has a texture (or color) that differs from the default material assigned to at least one of its material properties. The number at the top of the control indicates the texture map's resolution. You can alter the resolution by using the Size control just below the Texture control. The array of radio buttons lets you select which of the material properties you want to export as a texture map with your terrain. For each material property driven by a texture, a texture map is generated and exported when you exit the Export Terrain lab. You can turn off the textures that you don't require. If any one of the properties is assigned only the default material values, it can not be turned on for texture export. The texture map used for the preview defaults to 256-by-256 pixels in order to avoid delays during the texture generation.

You can activate the Export Terrain feature from the Terrain Editor (Ctrl/Command+D). First, select a 3D format for terrain export. (The 2D formats—DEM, PGM—do not activate the Export Terrain lab for obvious reasons.) After you choose one of the 3D formats, the Export Terrain lab is activated. Within the Export Terrain lab, you set all the terrain's parameters. The terrain mesh is saved to a file when you exit the Export Terrain lab (by clicking the checkmark in the lower right).

The data generated in the Export Terrain lab includes vertices, smoothed normals, UVs (texture coordinates), and texture maps. There are some limitations inherent in some of the 3D formats (for example, DXF does not support smooth normals or UV mapping), but Bryce saves all the supported information about the mesh to the selected file. If the file format does not support texture-map embedding, texture maps are saved as separate images (which are saved to the same location as the mesh file). The image's file names are created by appending the name of the mesh file to the names of the material properties.

Note: *In order to make it easier to work with the data, use file formats that support all the object file data generated by the Export Terrain lab, such as OBJ or VRML.*

Note: *When a terrain is saved to a file that captures only the 2D portion (that is, the image rather than the geometry), all the possible texture maps are generated.*

The Symmetrical Lattice Terrain object is a special case. If the UV information cannot be saved, two texture maps are exported: one for the top portion and one for the bottom portion. You can open these maps in the destination application and map them with top and bottom projections. (This process is automated when you use the LightWave format. LightWave scene files are exported with all the parameters in place. When these files are opened in LightWave, everything is where it should be.)

The keyboard controls for the Export Terrain lab are listed in Table 1.1. Undocumented keyboard controls for the Export Terrain lab are listed in Table 1.2.

Table 1.1 Keyboard controls for the Export Terrain lab.

Shortcut Keys	Control
Enter/Return	OK
Esc	Cancel
Click and drag in the preview	Rotate Camera
Ctrl/Command+click and drag	Zoom camera in and out
G	Switch among triangulation modes
+	Add polygons (move the slider)
-	Remove polygons (move the slider)
Home	Move slider all the way to the left
End	Move slider all the way to the right
*	Adds more polygons (if possible), even when slider is all the way to the right
[	Clamp the minimum value
]	Clamp the maximum value

Table 1.2 Undocumented keyboard controls for the Export Terrain lab.

Shortcut Keys	Control
Alt/Option+click and drag	Move camera without moving the light
Ctrl/Command+Alt/Option+click and drag	Change the light intensity
Ctrl/Command+Shift+click and drag	Change the ambient light intensity
B	Toggle backface culling
C	Toggle culling direction
D	Toggle double-side lighting
N	Toggle normals on and off

Export Formats

Bryce 4 now supports the following 3D file formats for exporting Terrain Objects:

- *AutoCAD (DXF) exporter*—The AutoCAD format is an ASCII format, and it supports simple triangle meshes with a single color. Bryce uses that color as the diffuse color. Most 3D applications (on both Windows and the Mac) support DXF files, so including DXF terrain export in Bryce makes it a useful utility for all other 3D packages.
- *DEM exporter*—To expand Bryce's exporting capacities, a DEM exporter has been added. This exporter creates a 7.5-minute formatted DEM that supports a variable terrain size. The DEM format is ASCII with binary spacing, and it exports the terrain as a full 16-bit heightfield. Bryce does not currently support Latitude and Longitude location-specifiers, so the exported DEM is set to the location of MetaCreations (Santa Barbara, California) as a reference.
- *Heightfield (HF) exporter*—This simple format is used to define heightfields. HF is a binary format used by Ken Musgrave and RayShade for storing 16-bit square shaped heightfields.
- *Infini-D 4 (ID4) exporter*—Terrains are exported to Infini-D's binary format as triangle meshes. All material properties, normals, and UV mappings are exported. Texture mapping is also supported. Bryce creates a Composition surface with all the texture maps and color surfaces and saves each texture map as an image file (PICT on a Mac, BMP on a Windows machine). The Infini-D file contains links to the image files, and Infini-D uses them to find the texture maps. Upon export, the Infini-D file stores a hard-coded path or alias description of the image map's location on disk.
- *LightWave (LWO/LWS) exporter*—Both LightWave objects and scenes are supported. Scene import is as complete as Bryce can handle. The camera, lights, and objects (with their material info) are imported. This exporter addresses triangle meshes with normals, UVs, materials, and textures. LightWave offers astounding animation features, so allowing LightWave to import complex Bryce scenes can greatly reduce rendering time.
- *Portable Grayscale Map (PGM) exporter*—With this popular format, Terrains are exported as an ASCII PGM. This maintains the 16-bit resolution of a Bryce heightfield.

- *QuickTime VR*—Create a QTVR directly from Bryce by exporting an image in this format. Be sure to render using the 360 Panorama Render mode with the QTVR Panorama document setting. You can render a rotated image directly into the QTVR export plug-in. Although you can create a QTVR with *any* image, it won't work as expected unless the source image is properly formatted. There are many QTVR utilities, including a plug-in for After Effects post-production software that allows full QTVR support. QTVR is also a popular format on the Web.
- *VRML1 (WRL) exporter*—The VRML exporter includes triangle meshes with normals, UVs, materials, and textures. VRML is used in multimedia and on the Web for 3D walk-throughs.
- *Wavefront (OBJ) exporter*—This exporter supports normals and UV mappings but not materials or textures. Wavefront is the most-popular format when porting work between MetaCreations' 3D applications (including Poser and Ray Dream).

The Sky Lab

Bryce 4's new Sky Lab lets you control all the sky attributes. Some of the new sky features include spherical clouds and sun/cloud shading effects. You can preview skies quickly and animate them with the integrated preview render and animation controls. The new Sky Lab provides deep and precise access to all the controls that govern sky generation.

The Sky Lab consolidates a set of controls for generating skies. It has its own preview and timeline access as well. Now you can create more complex skies easily. Bryce 4 also includes many new presets. See Figures 1.10 through 1.12.

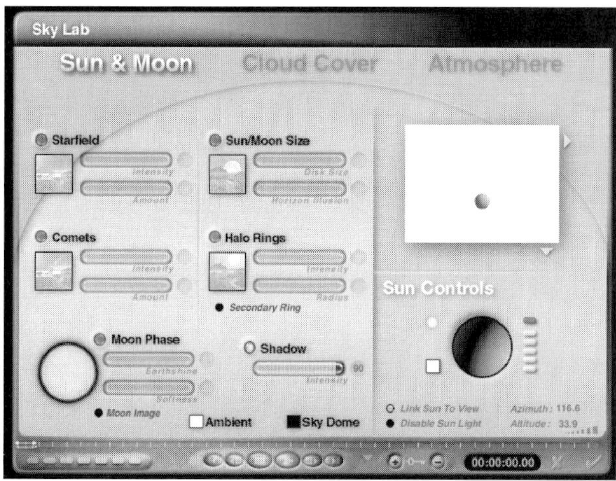

Figure 1.10
The Sun & Moon tab on Bryce 4's new Sky Lab.

Figure 1.11
The Cloud Cover tab on Bryce 4's new Sky Lab.

Figure 1.12
The Atmosphere tab on Bryce 4's new Sky Lab.

New Terrain Editor Features

While working with the Terrain Editor, you can access new terrain-creation modes by clicking on the New button while holding down Ctrl+Shift. There are approximately 30 options. See Figure 1.13.

New Web Features

With the introduction of version 4, Bryce has become extremely Web-friendly. Bryce 4 allows you to create HTML image maps from scenes. It also features RealMovie output that lets you create streaming animations for the Web (the animation starts playing immediately, and the quality improves as the animation finishes downloading). QuickTime VR movies allow you to post navigable scenes on the Internet, and MetaStream output options allow textured terrain export for streaming 3D objects.

Bryce 4 includes new Web functions and ease-of-use features, such as the ability to export scenes to HTML with image-mapped links. New export

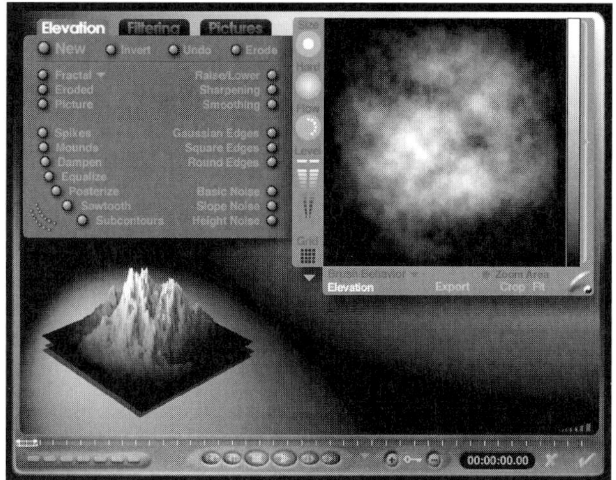

Figure 1.13
One of the modes available in Bryce 4's Terrain Editor.

options include RealPlayer movies and VRML and QTVR for animations and images on the Web. The MetaStream output features allow you to create and stream 3D objects and terrains for use on dynamic 3D Web sites. In addition, the new BryceTalk Web feature creates a forum (from within Bryce) for trading information and URLs. The BryceTalk area features regularly hosted presentations on Bryce, access to technical support personnel, and the ability to post links within the talk area.

Bryce now has a special Links menu that launches your default browser and takes you to the Web link you selected. Bryce 4 can be useful in your Web-related work in a number of other ways:

- *MetaStream (MTS) exporter*—Bryce can export MetaStream files, which allows you to export the terrain model in a variety of resolutions for the Web. MetaCreations provides a plug-in for popular Web browsers that allows you to view and interact with this fully textured model. The visitor to your Web site does not have to wait for the entire model to download. The detail in the model increases progressively as more data arrives.
- *RealMovie (RM) exporter*—This movie format is designed for the Internet. It is streamable in a variety of compression and throughput formats. Bryce 4 can create movies designed for any of these formats.
- *HTML Image Map*—This option generates an HTML page directly from Bryce. Create the scene and set the Web link for the objects you want to use as hot links, and simply export the image as an HTML page. The HTML page is exported using a JPEG file with the same name as the HTML file. Next, load the HTML page into your Web browser and click on a hotspot to take you to that URL.

***Note:** The Export Lab's Clamp Min function allows you to control the minimum number of polygons that must be downloaded before the model displays. The Clamp Max function defines the maximum number of polygons the model can use. You can reset these values with the Reset Clamping command.*

Picture Editor

Bryce 4 allows you to delete all the images by clicking the Delete All button. You can also access Photoshop plug-ins directly; this provides you with the almost-unlimited image effects available through Photoshop filters. Just click on the drop-down triangle in the upper-right corner of the image. Only the color layers of the image are affected. See Figure 1.14.

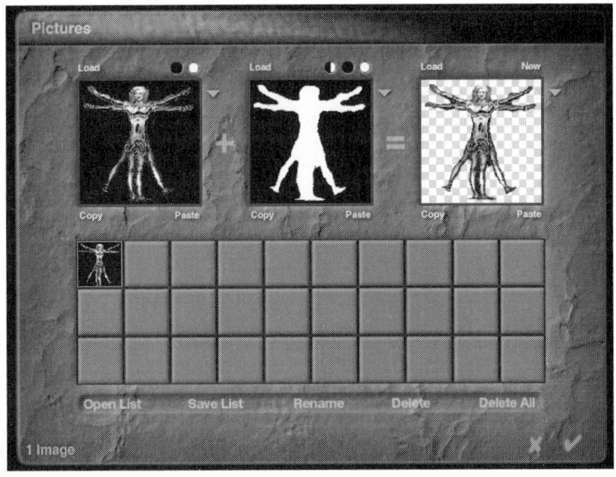

Figure 1.14
Bryce 4's Picture Editor.

Ray Spraying

Ray Spraying is a new method of rendering that is activated by clicking on the spray-can tool on the right-hand side of Bryce's composition window. Use this new tool in wireframe or when the rendered image is displayed. Click and drag the mouse to render the contents below it. This is a tremendous time-saver when you want to preview a small section of the image. Change the brush size and shape by using the number keys: Keys 1 through 5 define a circular brush of varying sizes, and keys 6 through 0 define a rectangular brush. When you use this tool in wireframe mode, a preview render is created. When you use the tool over a previously rendered image, a final render is created.

QuickTime For Windows (PC Only)

At last! The Windows version of Bryce can now create QuickTime movies. Previous Windows versions could create only AVI movies. This option requires the Windows version of QuickTime 3, which includes the necessary DLL.

Hundreds Of Megabytes Of Added Content

Bryce 4 includes a separate CD-ROM that contains an incredible collection of presets, scenes, animations, objects, tutorials, and more. You can find more presets and other goodies online at the Bryce forum. Visit MetaCreations at **www.meatacreations.com** regularly to stay informed about Bryce and other MetaCreations' products.

Moving On

Now it's time to take an in-depth look at some Bryce's modeling features. The next chapter examines importing and exporting models, creating models from primitives and booleans, and the uses of the Terrain Editor. Example graphics are presented throughout.

Model Mania

2

Models are the actors in a Bryce 3D world, whether they are objects, creatures, or terrains. This chapter looks at how you can use a variety of modeling alternatives to their best creative advantage.

Bryce Modeling Categories

Bryce uses several types of models and interacts with those models in a number of ways. A variety of methods are available for generating or acquiring models for your Bryce projects. Among these methods are:

- *Models made from Bryce "primitive" forms*—These include all the 3D forms included in the Create icon bar, shown in Figure 2.1.

  In a sense, Bryce Infinite Planes are primitive objects as well. The Infinite Planes include the Water, Sky, and Ground Planes shown in Figure 2.2.

- *Imported models*—With the introduction of version 4, Bryce finally allows you to import most of the popular 3D-model formats. These include LightWave (LWO, LWS), trueSpace (COB), VideoScape (VSA), VRML1 (WRL), Heightfield (HF), Portable Grayscale Map (PGM), USGS DEM (DEM), and USGS SDTS (DDF). Earlier versions of Bryce supported a number of 3D formats, including OBJ, DXF, 3DS, and 3DMF; support for these formats has been improved.

Figure 2.1
The Create icon bar shows all the Bryce primitive forms. They include (left to right) Terrain, Stone, Symmetrical Lattice, Sphere, Ellipsoid, Squashed Sphere, Torus, Tuboid, Cylinder, Squashed Cylinder, Stretched Cylinder, Cube, Brickoid, Stretched Cube, Pyramid, Squashed Pyramid, Stretched Pyramid, Cone, Squashed Cone, Stretched Cone, Horizontal and Vertical 2D Disk, 2D Picture Object, Horizontal 2D Face, and Vertical 2D Face.

- *Boolean constructs*—Although Bryce lacks the modeling tools found in many other 3D applications, it can use Boolean commands to create models. These commands include Neutral, Positive, Negative, and Intersect. All are activated from the General tab in the selected object's Object Attribute dialog box. See Figure 2.3.

  You can create Boolean constructs by selecting two grouped, intersecting objects and then choosing the appropriate Boolean for each. See Figure 2.4.

- *Terrain Editor*—Without a doubt, you will use Bryce's Terrain Editor to create most of your original models and model elements. Although the module's name suggests that the Terrain Editor is devoted to modeling terrain elements, you can make it do much more than that (as I will describe later in this chapter). See Figure 2.5.

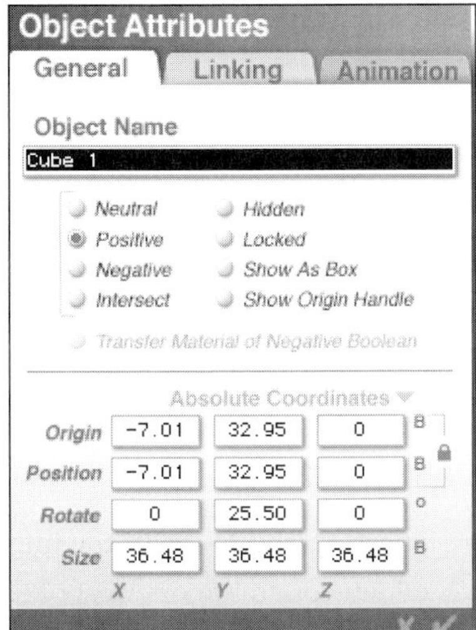

Figure 2.2

(Left) The Water, Sky, and Ground Plane icons as they appear in the Create icon bar.

Figure 2.3

(Right) The Boolean commands are listed on the General tab of the selected object's Object Attributes dialog box.

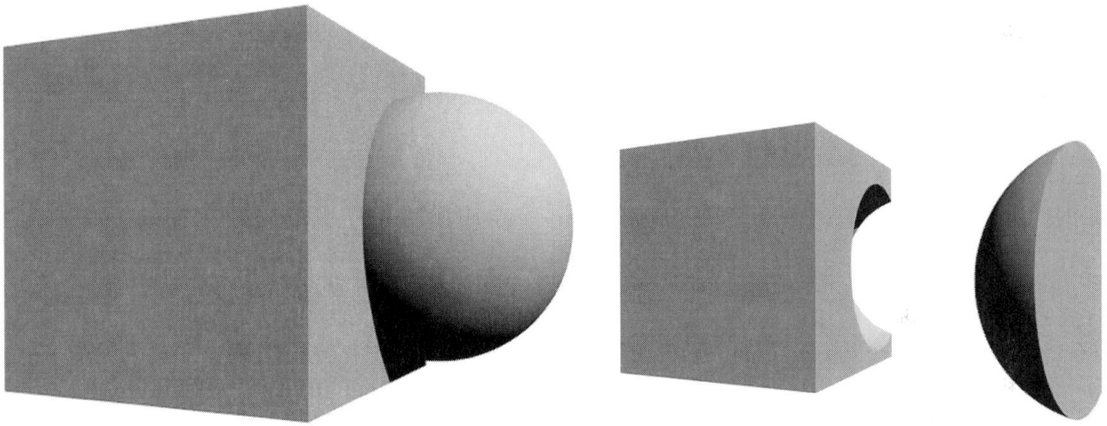

Figure 2.4

From left to right, the sphere has been set to positive, negative, and intersect, creating alternate Boolean constructs. The cube remains as a positive Boolean.

- *Infinite Plane models*—These are one of Bryce's least-documented features. Infinite Plane Models can help you create unbelievable magical effects and scenes. Infinite Planes are also discussed in Chapter 3. This chapter looks at ways you can use Infinite Planes as modeling elements. There are three basic Infinite Planes: Water, Sky, and Ground (see Figure 2.2). Because you can adjust the planes' height and map with any material you like, it doesn't matter which plane is used.
- *Other modeling utilities and CD-ROM collections*—You can use other modeling applications as modeling environments for your Bryce work. I will look at six modeling applications later—Nendo from Nichimen Graphics, Organica from Impulse Software, Amorphium from Play Inc., Scenery Animator from Natural Graphics, Poser from MetaCreations, and Tree Professional from Onyx Software. I will also list a few of the CD-ROM volumes that contain useful models for Bryce work.

Note: *You can transfer the material of the negative Boolean to the hole cut in the positive Boolean.*

Figure 2.5
The Terrain Editor is the core of Bryce's modeling capabilities.

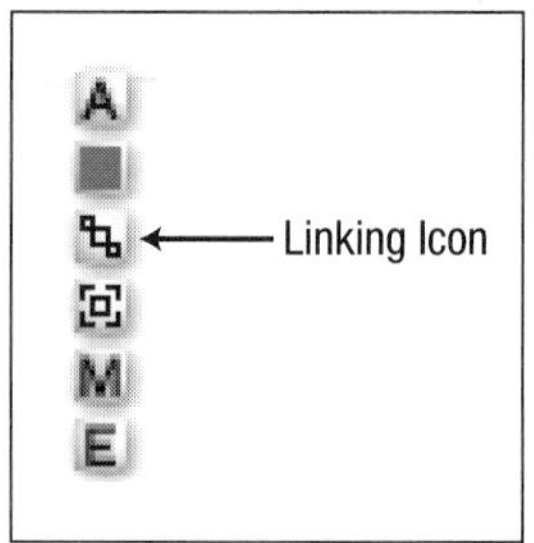

Figure 2.6
The Linking icon in the Object Attributes toolbar makes the target object the parent of your source object. Click on the Linking icon and drag the resulting line to the target object.

First, A Word About Linking

Make sure you are familiar with the documentation when it comes to linking. (I will use the term *linking* a lot in the following text.) Linking object elements is essential in Bryce. It makes the animation of a composited model possible. You accomplish linking by selecting the Linking icon in the Object Attributes toolbar (see Figure 2.6) or by going to the Linking tab in the Object Attributes dialog box and selecting the object's parent from the list. The first method works well when the scene contains only a few objects. When the scene gets cluttered, the second method works best.

Modeling With Bryce Primitives

One of the first things a new Bryce-user does is click on the Sphere icon, which immediately places a 3D sphere in the scene. You can use any of the primitives as standalone objects in Bryce, but that's by no means the end of it. You can also use primitives as parts of more complex models by gluing parts together with the Group command or linking them in a hierarchy.

Primitive Group Modeling

Let's look at how you can use grouped primitives to build a complex stone structure and an intricate building.

Creating A Stone Bridge

You can use Stone primitives to create walls, statues, bridges, and other 3D models. Follow these instructions to create an example of a complex stone-based bridge:

1. Click on the Stone icon to place a stone in the scene. See Figure 2.7. The stone appears with its own material. Don't be concerned with the material for now: Textures and material options are covered thoroughly in Chapter 3.
2. Create five duplicates of this stone and stack them to form a column. Give each stone a slightly different rotation so they do not all look the same. You can also make the stones unique by altering their textures a bit, as covered in Chapter 3. When the column's appearance is to your liking, Shift-select all the rocks and group them into one object (Objects|Group Objects). See Figure 2.8.
3. Use the Multi-Replicate command to generate three copies of the column. Set the X Offset to 75 (you may have to adjust this a bit for your unique stone formation). The idea is to get four duplicated columns, as shown in Figure 2.9.

Note: *Every time you click on the Stone icon, a new stone is added to the scene. The new stone has a random shape, and it uses a different texture than any of the previous stones you have added. If you want all of the stones to look as if they are made of the same substance, select the stone that uses the material you want, and then use the Copy Material command. Click on the other stones in turn and use the Paste Material command.*

Figure 2.7
(Left) The stone bridge begins with the addition of a single stone to the scene.

Figure 2.8
(Right) The six stones are stacked and grouped to form a column.

4. Congratulations! You have created something that computers are good at: a boring, repetitive image. But the natural world clones nothing exactly; no two rocks or leaves are the same. In order to provide a better, more interesting design, you have to adjust the columns so that each has its own personality. Just rotating the columns won't do because it will be instantly apparent that the stones are the same size from column to column. Here's what to do: Select any of the three columns in turn and ungroup them. Then, exchange some of the stones in each stack with stones from the other stacks. You can also resize some of them to create variety. You wind up with a better design and far more viewer interest. When each stack achieves its own personality, re-group to form four separate columns again. See Figure 2.10.

Figure 2.9
(Left) The column is duplicated three times.

Figure 2.10
(Right) The rearranged columns are more distinct after switching some stones around.

5. From the top view, rearrange the columns to enclose a four-cornered area. See Figure 2.11.
6. Now place a cube in the scene. Resize the cube so it can act as a beam that spans the distance between two columns. Copy the material used for the stones to the beam. Make three copies of the beam and place them as shown in Figure 2.12.

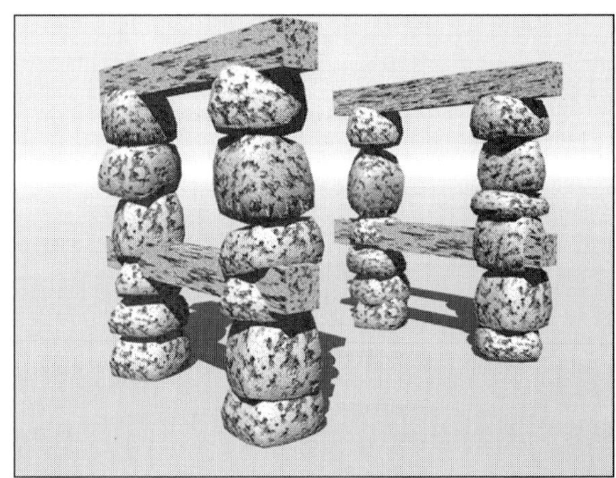

Figure 2.11
(Left) The columns now form the perimeter of a four-cornered space. At this point, the scene occupies less than 1MB of disk space.

Figure 2.12
(Right) Beams add support to the stone bridge.

7. Expand the bridge by grouping everything and placing a duplicate of the original in the scene. Place a rectangular slab on the support beams, resizing the slab so that it spans the distance. Unless you prefer another option, use the Stonewall material from the Rocks & Stones presets for this section of the construct. See Figure 2.13.

Figure 2.13
The finished bridge is perfect for spanning a river, from one bank to the other.

Modeling With Linked Primitives

Before you tackle this project, make sure you understand how to use the Link function. Refresh your knowledge by reading the Bryce documentation again, if necessary. You will use linked primitives to build a simple linked robot. Follow these directions:

1. Place a selection of primitives as shown in Figure 2.14. Work in the front view so that you won't be distracted by perspective distortions.
2. Open each element's Attributes dialog box and choose the Show Origin Handle option. The Origin Handle is a point around which the object rotates. When the Origin Handles of linked objects are placed properly, you can choreograph the objects' behavior in a scene. When animating composite objects, Origin Handle placement is essential (see Chapter 5). Use Figure 2.15 as a guide to placing the Origin Handles for your primitive robot.
3. Now it's time to link the parts. Link the head to the chest and the chest to the pelvis. Link each hand to its lower arm and each lower arm to its upper arm. Link both upper arms to the chest. Link each foot to its

Note: *The entire stone bridge project file is less than 1MB. You can find the file on this book's companion CD-ROM. Look in the OBP folder.*

Note: *Use any material you like. The one displayed in the linked robot is the Warm Gold selection from the Simple & Fast material presets.*

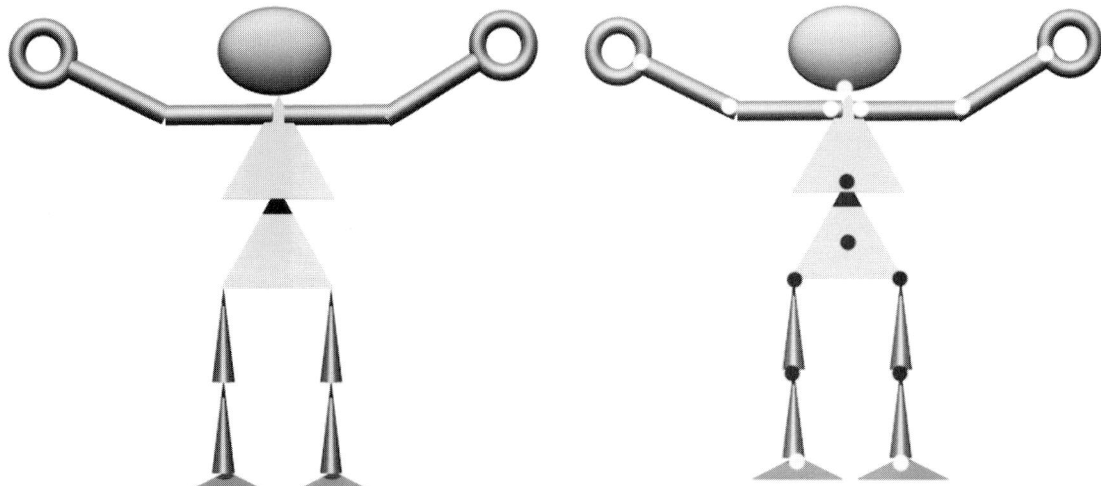

Figure 2.14
(Left) The linked robot begins life as a collection of primitives.

Figure 2.15
(Right) Place the Origin Handles for each element as displayed in this illustration.

lower leg and each lower leg to its upper leg. Link both upper legs to the pelvis. That's it. This is also known as a *Hip-Centric* hierarchy.

If you have followed this procedure correctly, you should be able to click on the pelvis and move the whole model without leaving any part behind. As you can see in Figure 2.16, you can pose the model in any position for your scenes.

Using Imported Models

As you read in Chapter 1, Bryce 4 has added support for many more 3D file formats. When you use an imported model in your Bryce work, there are a few issues to be aware of:

- You will probably have to perform a smoothing operation on the imported model to get rid of the polygonal artifacts. You can accomplish this with the Objects|Edit Object command, which brings up the Smoothing dialog box. Use a default smoothing setting in most cases, although you can explore different values as well. Lower settings set the smoothing angle lower, and higher settings increase it. Depending on the angles on your model, different settings can result in very different looks.
- Some objects contain a tremendous number of polygons, and importing them into Bryce can choke the system. There are two ways to guard against this. First, make sure you have as much RAM as you can possibly afford. 300MB is a good target, and more is better. Second, you can reduce the number of polygons in your object before exporting it from the other 3D application. Many 3D applications

***Note:** The primitive robot model weighs in at less than half a megabyte. You can find the project on this book's CD-ROM. Look in the OBP folder.*

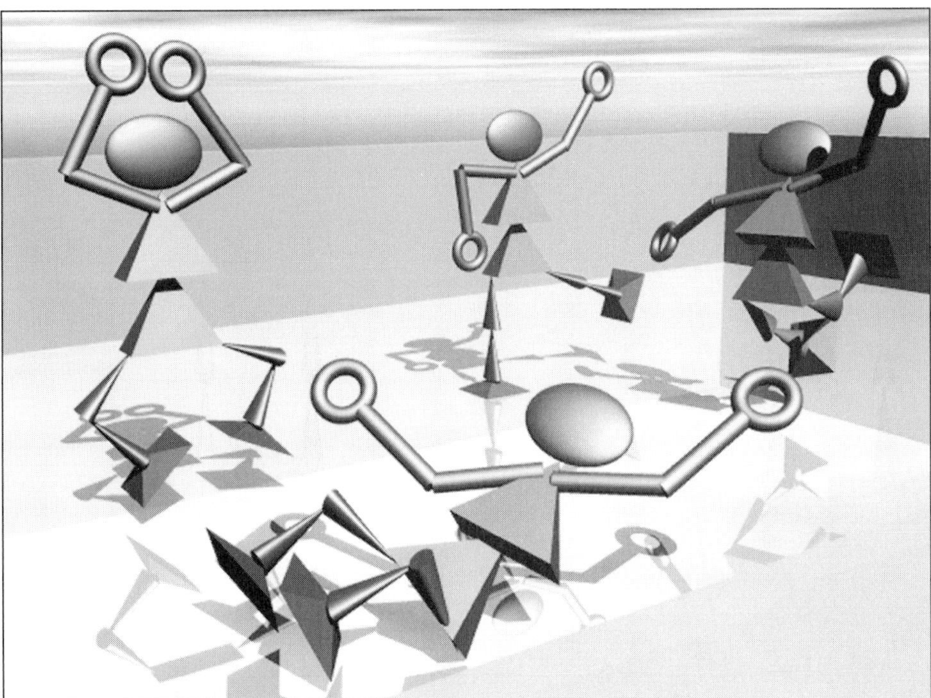

Figure 2.16
You can choreograph the primitive robot by selecting any part and rotating it. Resizing a parent element also resizes its children.

allow you to reduce the number of polygons before exporting, and CD-ROM collections of models often include low- and high-resolution versions of the same model.

- If you have control over the model's export and the model is composed of grouped elements (such as a human or animal figure), be sure to save the model as an object that can be ungrouped. Once in Bryce, you can link the elements for choreography and animation purposes. This also makes sense when you want to apply different textures and materials to the object. Each discrete element can have its own texture. Of course, if you want to use the object as a single-textured item (for example, a marble statue), you can import an object that has no separate grouped elements.
- Imported objects often need a Preview Quality setting of at least 64 in order to be seen clearly. Lower settings are confusing, and they don't provide enough information to allow you to rotate and place the objects as needed.

Note: Be aware that for some rougher organic elements—especially those that use only a color texture—you may want to preserve the faceted, polygonal look. This makes an object look like it has been carved from wood or stone.

Adding Variety To Imported Objects By Stretching

Instead of just using imported objects "out of the can" without altering them, you can use Bryce's Resize/Stretch tool (Figure 2.17) to make them your own. Just select the object and move one of the controls on the Resize/Stretch tool.

Figure 2.17
Pulling on one of the handles of the Edit toolbar's Resize/Stretch tool stretches the selected object in that direction.

When you stretch imported objects, use World Space if the objects haven't been rotated beforehand. Use Object Space if you have rotated the object previously. Using World Space after the object has been rotated causes the object to shear and distort. As you can see in Figure 2.18, you can stretch an imported chair to form a bench. This is just one example of how you can use common stretching to customize an imported object.

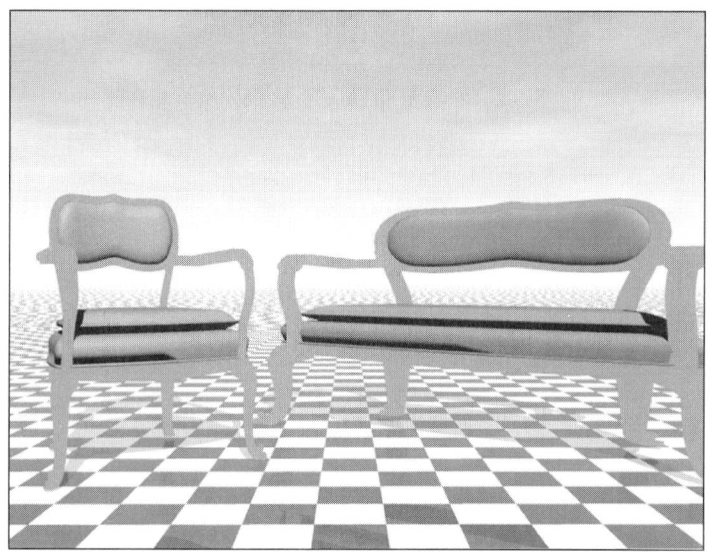

Figure 2.18
The elongated seat on the right was created by stretching the imported chair object on the left.

Adding Variety To Imported Objects By Linking And Moving Parts

Many imported objects come into Bryce grouped; you can modify individual elements separately after using the UnGroup command. Once the object is ungrouped, you can map a different texture to each of the elements, and you can link all the elements in a hierarchy. One thing that most artists forget is that they can move the object's parts and reassemble the object so that it looks like something entirely new. You can also delete various parts of an imported and ungrouped object and use what's left for any purposes you like. You can see that imported objects represent almost infinite resources when you start to design with this in mind. See Figure 2.19.

Creating Models With Booleans

Using a Boolean command assigns a visibility component to a selected object in a group. Boolean assignments are not activated until you make the object part of a group first. Boolean operators are activated by clicking on the appropriate option in the selected object's Object Attributes dialog box. See Figure 2.20.

Note: *You can also drastically alter the appearance of imported objects by mapping them with your own materials and textures. See Chapter 3.*

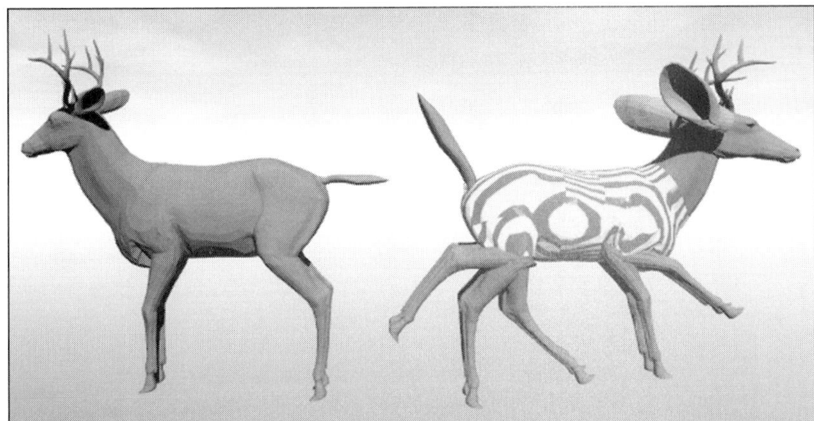

Figure 2.19
After modifying a Zygote deer (exported from Poser) as separate parts, you can wind up with another creature entirely.

Object Attributes
General | Linking | Animation
Object Name
Cube 1
Neutral | Hidden
Positive | Locked
Negative | Show As Box
Intersect | Show Origin Handle
Transfer Material of Negative Boolean
Absolute Coordinates

	X	Y	Z
Origin	-13.38	30.72	14.13
Position	-13.38	30.72	14.13
Rotate	0	-21.50	0
Size	49.33	49.33	49.33

Figure 2.20
The list of Boolean operators appears in the selected object's Attributes dialog box. The options include Neutral (Boolean Off), Positive, Negative, and Intersect.

Sometimes it is easier to create complex models in other applications and then export the model to Bryce. But using Bryce's internal Boolean-modeling operations provides two advantages:

- You can use Booleans to create simple objects within Bryce, saving you the hassle or time commitment involved with working in another application.
- You can animate Bryce Boolean constructs; holes of any shape can appear and move through any object over time (see Chapter 5).

Note: *When using Booleans, it's always best to work in the front, top, and side views without rotating your objects. This provides better control of element placements.*

Creating Boolean Objects From Scratch

Let's investigate Boolean modeling by creating a Curved Chair. Follow the instructions in the next section.

Modeling A Boolean Curved Chair

To create a curved chair using Boolean operations, follow these steps:

1. Create a large cube (See Figure 2.21). Open its Attributes dialog box, and click on Positive in the Boolean options.

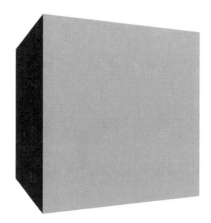

Figure 2.21
The curved chair project begins as a cube.

2. First, you'll create the chair's legs. Create two spheres and elongate them using the resize tool. Use these spheres to cut away the legs by placing them as shown in Figure 2.22. Nothing happens yet because the elements are not grouped. Select Negative in each sphere's Attributes dialog box.

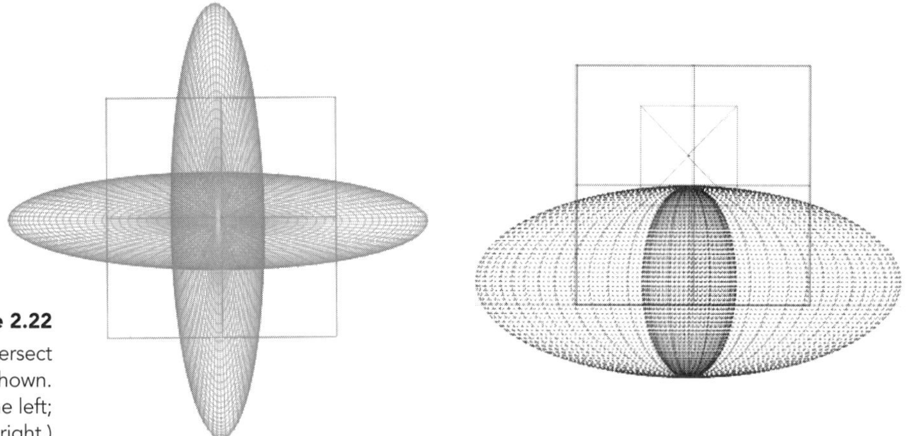

Figure 2.22
Two elongated spheres intersect the bottom of the cube as shown. (The top view is shown on the left; the front view is on the right.)

Note: *When working with Boolean constructs, turn off all shadows. Otherwise, you'll wind up with shadows cast by invisible objects.*

3. Group all three objects, and render for preview. At this stage, your new Boolean object should look like the illustration in Figure 2.23.
4. Now add a cylinder as shown in Figure 2.24. Set the cylinder to Negative. Ungroup all the elements, and group them again.
5. At this stage, your chair should resemble the one displayed in Figure 2.25.

Figure 2.23

The elongated spheres have created the chair's legs by removing portions of the cube.

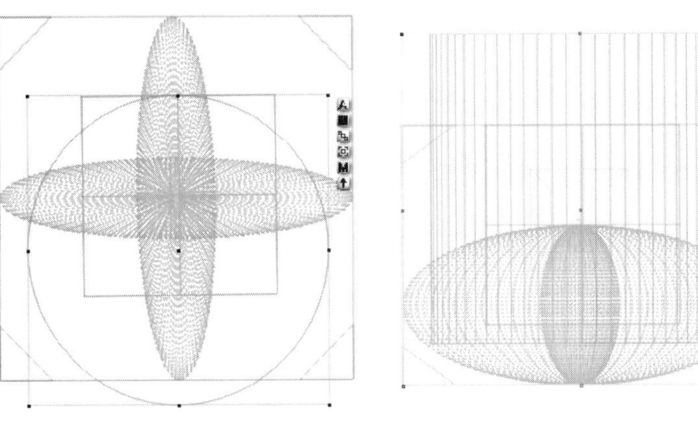

Figure 2.24

The cylinder cuts away space for the seat, revealing the chair's back and arms. (The top view is shown on the left; the front view is on the right.)

Figure 2.25

Once the negative cylinder is in place, the chair has a seat.

6. So far, this makes an interesting chair, but not a very comfortable one. The arms are as high as the back. Ungroup everything and use a negative Boolean cube to cut the arms down to size. The result is shown in Figure 2.26.

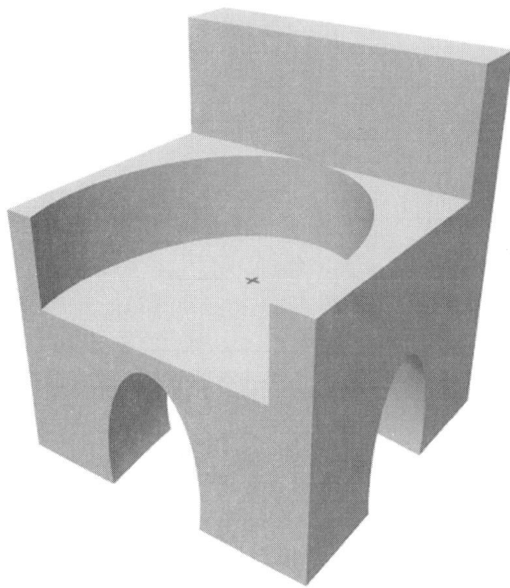

Figure 2.26
The finished Boolean curved chair.

Once you have the basic chair, you can place a flattened sphere on it for a cushion or drill another Boolean cylinder into it to create a pierced chair. See Figure 2.27.

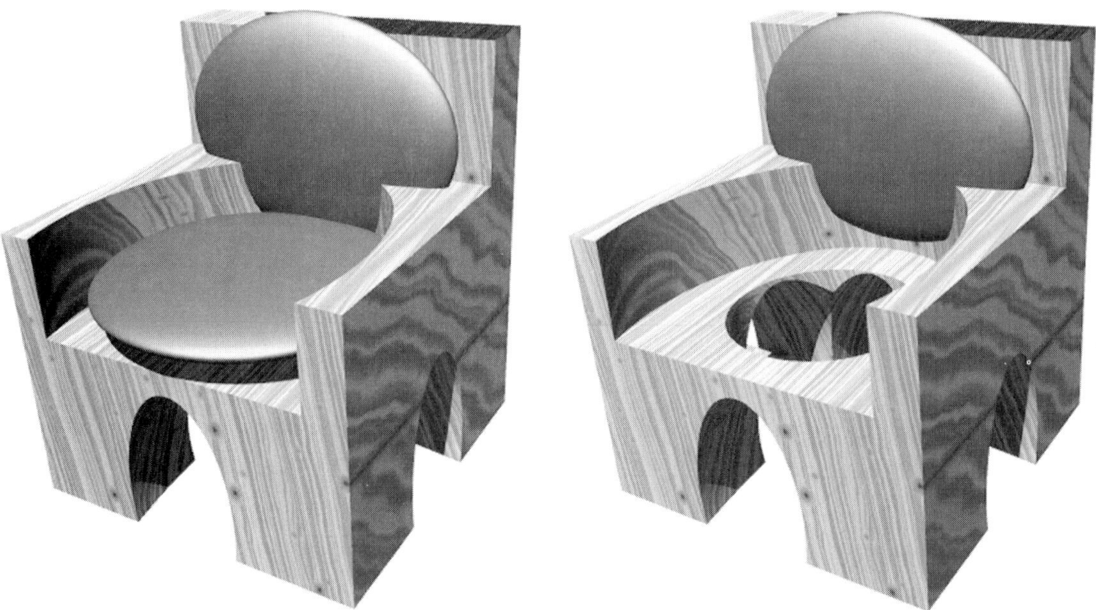

Figure 2.27
Two variations on a theme: A cushioned chair and a pierced chair.

Booleans And Infinite Planes

Few Bryce users realize that they can use negative Booleans to drill through Infinite Planes. The documentation doesn't mention this procedure, even though you can use it to create some startling visual effects.

An Infinite Plane is just another 3D object in Bryce. Its only distinguishing points are that it is infinite along the X and Z axis, and it is commonly mapped to emulate earth, air, or water. Infinite Planes come in two varieties: 2D and 3D. 2D Infinite Planes have no depth factor (Y axis), while 3D Infinite Planes have a user-defined Y-axis depth. Infinite Planes respond to Boolean parameters and controls just as other objects do. See Figures 2.28 through 2.30 for variety of Boolean Infinite Plane examples.

Figure 2.28

A negative Boolean sphere cuts through a rock-surfaced Infinite Plane to reveal a Water Plane beneath. This would be great for developing an animation that shows an object—perhaps a fish—floating by along the Water Plane.

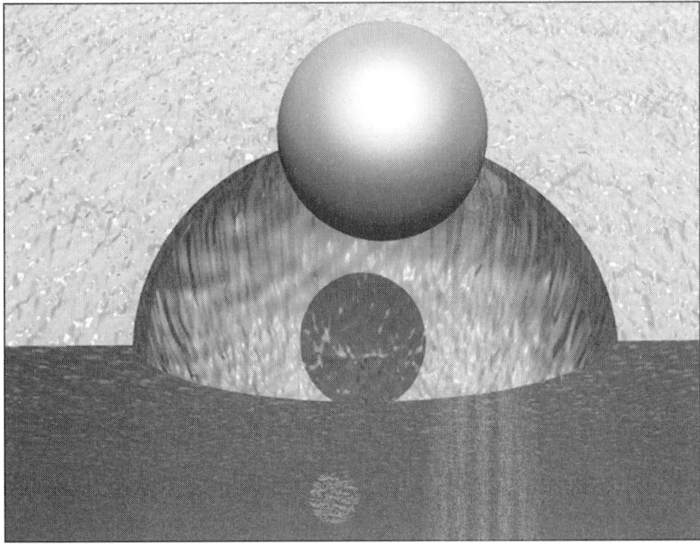

Figure 2.29

A sphere cuts an Infinite Water Plane, while another angled Infinite Plane cuts it as well. The smaller sphere was placed to show the shadowing on the spherical cut.

Figure 2.30
In this image, the Ground Plane is mapped with tiles and assigned a positive Boolean. An upside-down Terrain object is assigned a negative Boolean. The two are grouped to create a jagged hole in the ground. You can create caves using a similar process: Use a terrain to punch a hole in another terrain.

Doing The Impossible

When you work with an Infinite Ground or Water Plane, it is impossible to place terrain on the edge of the horizon: You can never push it back to infinity. There is a way, however, to make infinity come to you. Here's how:

1. Create an Infinite Ground or Water Plane. In its Attributes dialog box, make it a positive Boolean.
2. Create another Infinite Plane. Rotate the second plane so that it cuts through the first plane at the point at which you want a fake horizon. In the second plane's Attributes dialog box, make it a negative Boolean.
3. Group the two planes. Congratulations on achieving the impossible: You have limited the infinite. See Figure 2.31.

Booleans And Imported Objects

Imported objects can take part in any Boolean Group as positive or negative members. This allows you to import stock 3D models and customize them. See Figure 2.32.

Boolean Frames

A Frame is an object with a hole in it that allows things behind the frame to show through. The Frame can be a picture frame, a window, or a more unusual object. Any negative Boolean element grouped with a positive Boolean Frame becomes the cutter. The cutter can be a primitive, an imported object, or a terrain.

Note: *See Chapter 3 for a description of using Boolean objects as 3D paintbrushes.*

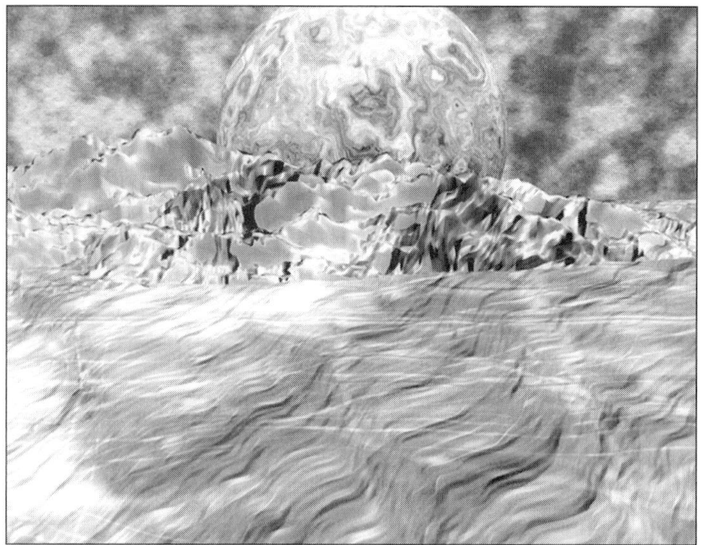

Figure 2.31
Although the Ground Plane used here is infinite, I have created a false horizon by using a negative Boolean Infinite Plane to cut it. The planet has been placed behind the cutting plane. A Terrain object is pushed to the edge to hide its flatness. If you move over the terrain, you will fall off the world (just as the flatlanders predicted).

Figure 2.32
This lion model is from the Zygote collection for Poser. It was exported as a single mesh, so it cannot be ungrouped. If you need only a part of the lion for a scene (perhaps as an architectural element or a chess piece), you can use negative Boolean cubes to cut away the unnecessary elements, as this image displays.

An Unusual Boolean Frame Project

Follow these steps to create a Boolean Frame similar to the one shown in Figure 2.33.

1. Render a Bryce scene that uses a torus as one of its elements. The torus should stand so that its inner space is a perfect circle when seen in the front view.
2. Save the rendering. Create a new document. Place a vertical rectangular plane in the new scene so that it covers the entire image area as seen from the camera view. Map the previously rendered image to this plane.

Figure 2.33
Create this frame by using primitives, planes, and Boolean operators.

3. Place a sphere in the scene so that its seems to fill the hole of the torus on the vertical plane. Set the sphere as a negative Boolean and the plane as a positive Boolean, and group the sphere and the plane.

Now the inside of the torus becomes a window through which you can see anything in the 3D world beyond. See Figure 2.33.

Note: *You should compose the text block in the Terrain Editor from a graphic, and not use real 3D letters. Bryce balks at using Booleans on imported 3D letters.*

Boolean Text

When you need to create 3D text carved into a solid block, use Booleans. Just assign a negative Boolean to the text block and group the text block with a positive Boolean cubic block. See Figure 2.34.

Figure 2.34
Comparable to digital woodburning, Booleans brand letters into the selected object.

Modeling In The Terrain Editor

Bryce is mainly a terrain application, so mastering the design and customization of terrains is crucial to mastering the software. The Terrain Editor is capable of much more than modeling terrains, but you must know how to do that first before you can push the Terrain Editor further. This section assumes that you have a working knowledge of the Terrain Editor's tools and modules. So, if you have not yet explored the Terrain Editor's features by reading and working through the documentation, do that before you read this section.

General Hints And Tips

Bryce's Terrain Editor is one of the most unusual and diverse modeling environments of any 3D software, so it takes a while to learn and master. Some of its features and tools emulate features found in other 3D software modules; other features are found nowhere else. Everyone who uses this modeling environment has secrets for maximizing his or her efforts. It is assumed that you have a working knowledge of the tools and modules contained in the Terrain Editor from your previous study of the documentation. Ideally, you will find a few ideas here you haven't thought of before:

- Use a terrain for natural landscape features and cityscapes. Use a Symmetrical Lattice to design manufactured-looking objects. Why? Because the Symmetrical Lattice object contains an automatic mask that strips away the platform beneath the Terrain object.

- Remember that you can apply various terrain features again and again: click on, hold, and then slide on the feature's buttons. Just clicking on the button applies that feature at full strength. This is especially useful for eroding and then smoothing the terrain.

- To create blades of 3D grass (close to the Camera) or a dense forest of trees (far from the Camera), apply the Basic Noise feature to a terrain between 6 and 12 times. Each time you apply the Basic Noise feature, you increase the number of spikes (or blades). If you are creating grass, give the terrain a color only. If you are creating trees, use a bump map to make it more complex. Duplicate the grassy clump and rotate the copy on its Y axis to give it more body and variety. See Figure 2.35.

- Create a textured brick by starting with a Symmetrical Lattice shaped in the Terrain Editor as a medium-elevation solid block. Apply a small amount of Sawtooth feature to give it texture. (Be sure to watch the preview as you apply filters.) Next, apply a small amount of Erosion to give it a rougher look. The exact amounts are up to you, based on your tastes and your needs. See Figure 2.36.

Figure 2.35
The Terrain Editor's Basic Noise feature created this grass-covered knoll.

Figure 2.36
Textured bricks built in the Terrain Editor.

- Filtering creates unlimited variations on your terrain themes. Draw the Filtering shapes shown in Figure 2.37 through 2.42 to create the Terrain object variations displayed next to them.

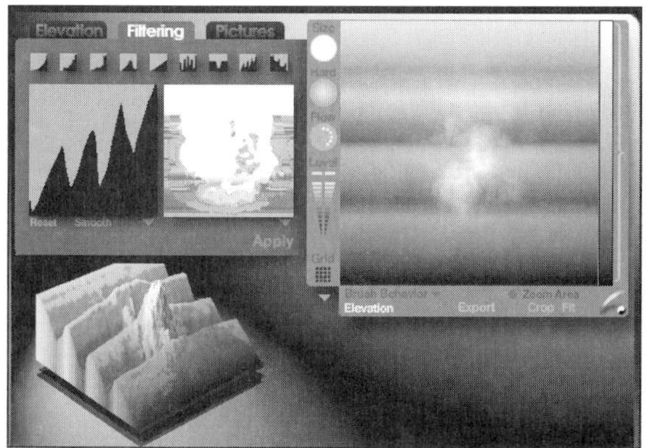

Figure 2.37

Draw the filter shape on the left in the Terrain Editor's Filtering tab to create the terrain shown on the right. The Apply Vertical command was used twice, applying the filter to the terrain's vertical axis. Square Edges were also added.

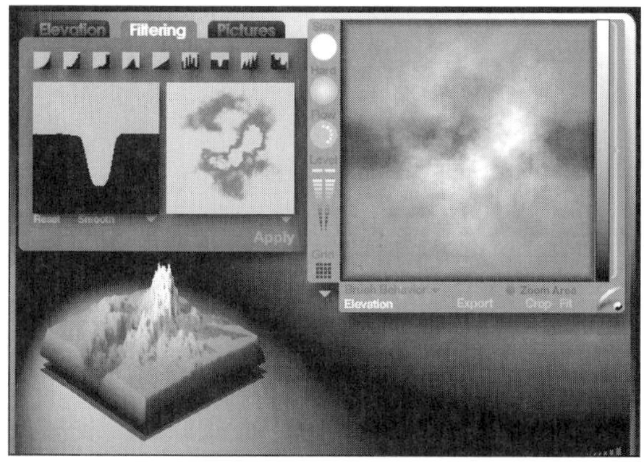

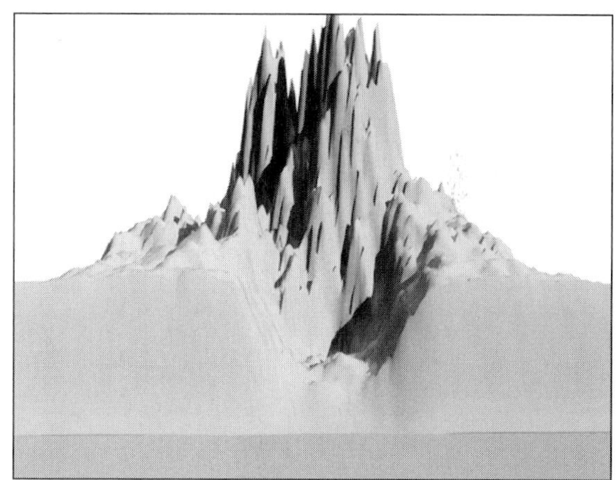

Figure 2.38

Draw the filter shape on the left in the Terrain Editor's Filtering tab to create the terrain illustrated on the right. This shape is great for creating a valley next to the terrain mountain. Apply Vertical was used once.

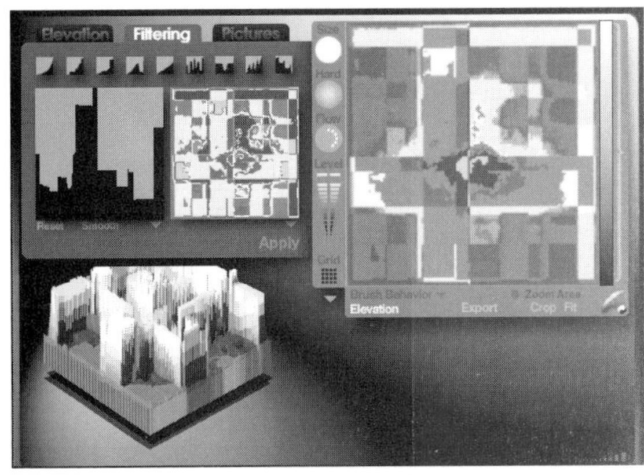

Figure 2.39

Draw the filter shape on the left in the Terrain Editor's Filtering tab to create the terrain illustrated on the right. Apply Vertical and Apply Horizontal was used. This is a spectacular cityscape object.

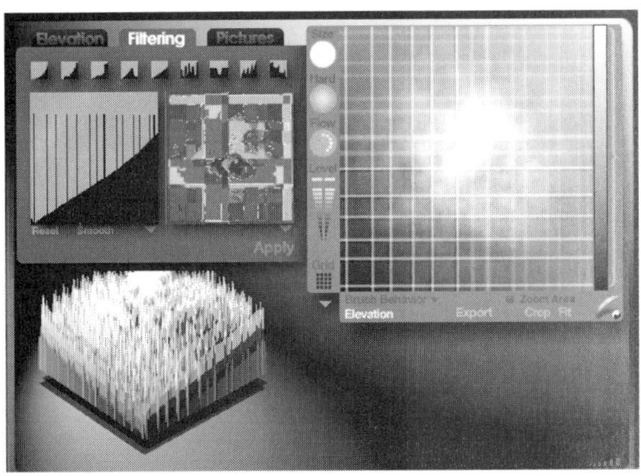

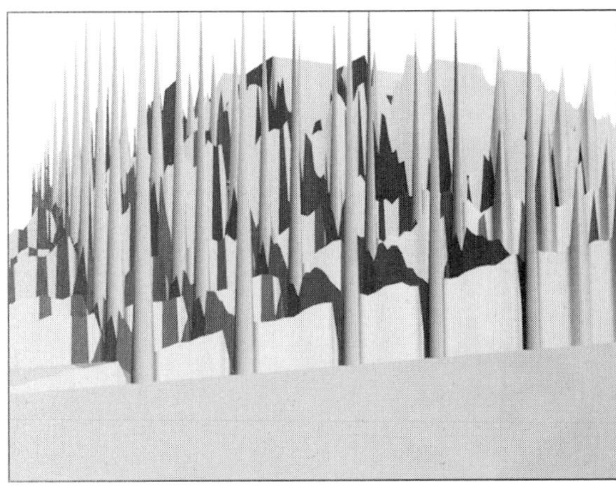

Figure 2.40

Draw the filter shape on the left in the Terrain Editor's Filtering tab to create the terrain illustrated on the right. Apply Vertical Add and Apply Horizontal Add were used. Neat spires or trees are the result.

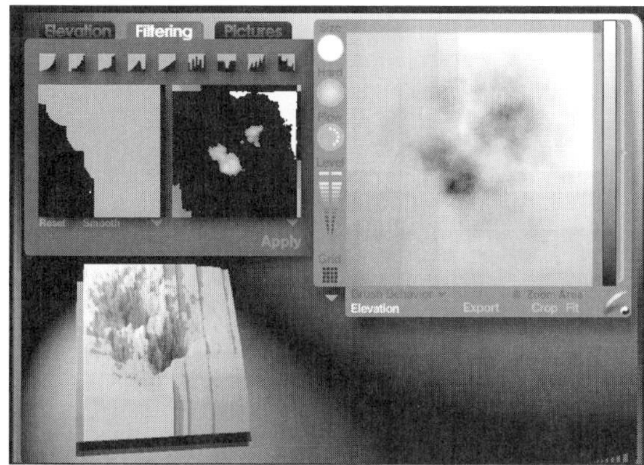

Figure 2.41

Draw the filter shape on the left in the Terrain Editor's Filtering tab to create the terrain illustrated on the right. Apply Vertical and Apply Horizontal were used, along with Invert. The result is this series of bread-loaf hills leading to some sharper features.

Figure 2.42

Here's what the terrain shown in Figure 2.41 looks like after adding a rock material and a sky.

Creating 3D Terrain Height Maps In A Bitmap Application

You can use any application that creates 256-level (8-bit) grayscale bitmaps to create import content for Bryce's Terrain Editor. Let's look at how you can use MetaCreations' Painter for this purpose. You'll use Painter's tools to create two height maps to export to Bryce. (These tutorials require that you own and know how to use MetaCreations' Painter 5. Specifically, you need to be familiar with the use of the Image Hose and Selection Tools.)

Griddy City

In this exercise, you'll use a few of Painter's exclusive tools to create an organized cityscape. Follow these steps:

1. Open Painter 5 and create a new 320-by-240 document at 72 dpi.
2. From the Patterns Listing in the Art Materials menu, select the Checkered pattern. Set the parameters to a Rectangular Pattern of 36 percent.
3. Choose the Effects|Fill option and set the Fill to Pattern. After clicking on OK to apply the fill, you end up with an image like the one in Figure 2.43.
4. Go to Effects|Esoterica and select the Custom Tile option. Configure these parameters: Brick, Blur Radius 1, Blur Pass 0, Thickness 2, Use Grout, Brick Width 12, and Brick Height 16. After clicking on OK to apply the filter, you end up with an image like the one in Figure 2.44.

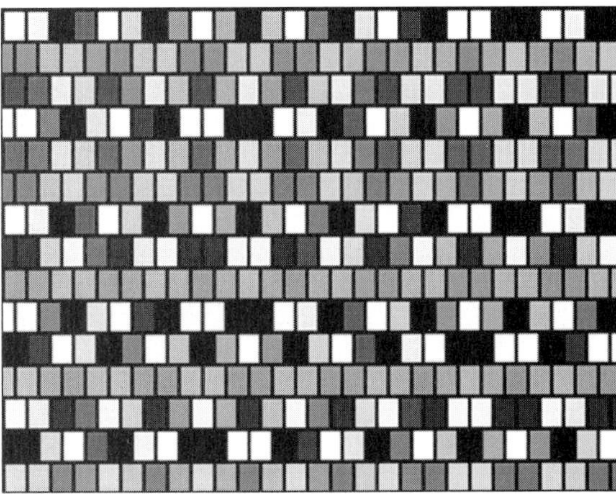

Figure 2.43
(Left) The Checkered pattern fills the image.

Figure 2.44
(Right) The Custom Tile filter is applied to the image.

If you were to create a city terrain from this image, everything would be far too neat and symmetrical to offer any viewer interest. So it's time to randomize this map.

5. After saving the image, close Painter and Open Bryce. Create a Terrain, and go to the Terrain Editor. From the Pictures tab, import the image you just saved from Painter. Use a medium-sized 50-percent gray brush (with Elevation selected) to randomly shrink the elevation of various parts of the image. This adds variety to the otherwise boring terrain. See Figure 2.45.
6. Apply an Office Building II material (from the Wild & Fun materials list) to the Terrain object. Use an Object Mapping of 265. See Figure 2.46 for the result.

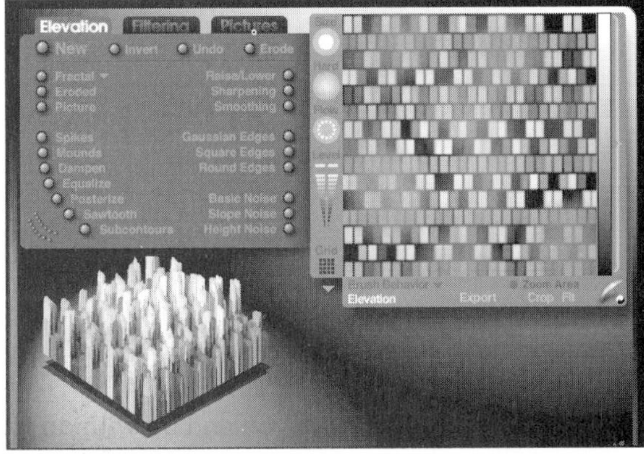

Figure 2.45
Use a medium gray brush to decrease the Elevation of random areas of the image.

Figure 2.46
The finished Griddy City created from the Painter image.

Vegiescape

Any image created in a bitmap application can be turned into a Terrain map, no matter the content. Follow these steps:

1. Open Painter 5 and create a new 360-by-240 document at 72 dpi.
2. Select the Image Hose from the Brush Selection palette. Use the Sushi Nozzle at 100 percent to spray sushi on the image. The image will resemble Figure 2.47.
3. In Bryce, use the Terrain Editor's Picture tab to import the sushi image. Use the Lower slider to decrease the height of the terrain from spires to boulders. See Figure 2.48.

The sushi image creates rounded boulders when used as a Terrain map. See Figure 2.49.

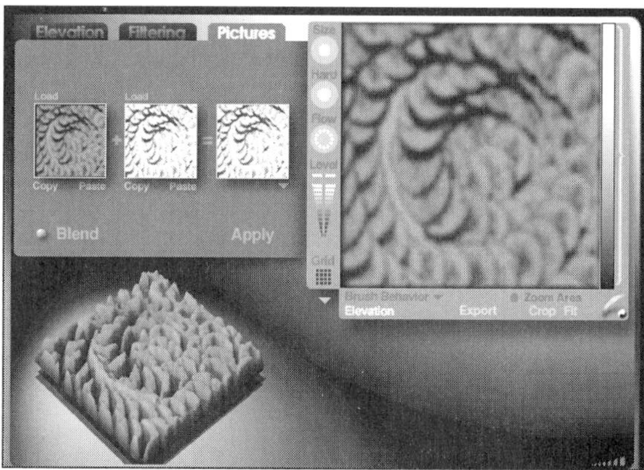

Figure 2.47
(Top Left) Use the Sushi Nozzle with the Image Hose to create an image that resembles this one.

Figure 2.48
(Top Right) The sushi image created in Painter is brought into the Terrain Editor.

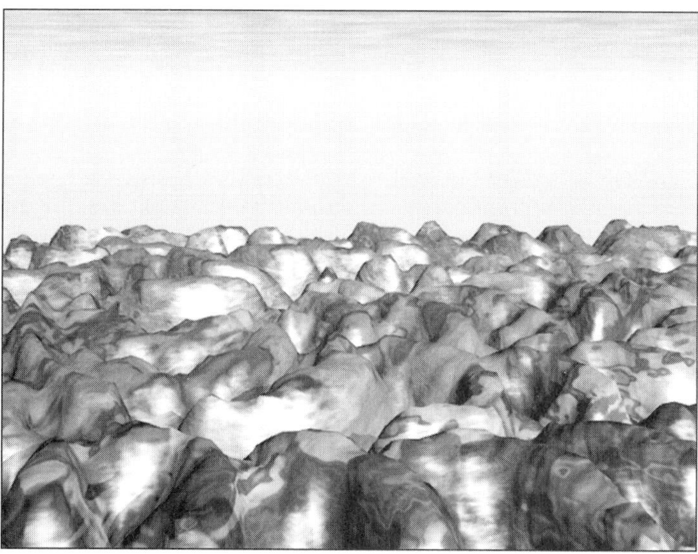

Figure 2.49
(Bottom) These rounded boulders hide the fact that they were generated from an image of spiraling sushi.

Creating Mechanical Elements In The Terrain Editor

You can use the Terrain Editor to create mechanistic object-elements (that is, Terrain objects that look like they were constructed by forces other than those of the natural world). This includes both human and alien constructs. If you follow a few simple rules to set up the basic approach, you can customize the objects in any way you like. Here are some rules to follow:

- Always work with a Symmetrical Lattice; it has automatic drop-out areas when edited in the Terrain Editor that allow you to blend the Terrain object into any other surface. Creating a mechanical object-element from a standard Terrain model is not suggested.
- Start by selecting New, which gives you a blank workspace.

- To create a basic modeling slab in the Terrain Editor, go to the Filtering tab. Make the left box completely black to create a block, and select Apply Vertical. This creates an even block for sculpting.
- Explore the other Filter patterns available with Apply Vertical/Horizontal and Apply Vertical/Horizontal Add. It should take you about 10 minutes to get an intuitive feel for these processes and the resulting model.
- Once you have the basic block, return to the Elevation tab to add other filtering components. Always lower the model's elevation, because the Symmetrical Lattice doubles the height anyway.
- Move the lightness/darkness slider all the way down, and then draw to create holes in the object.
- Straight lines are important for drawing non-organic objects. Hold down Shift while drawing in order to create horizontal and vertical lines.
- Achieve subtle details by painting effects rather than using the Elevation Brush.
- Take care when applying Smoothing because it can distort elements of the model. Lower the height first before applying smoothing.

Follow these rules, and spend time exploring your options and playing. What you get in return is the ability to create complex mechanistic models in the Terrain Editor. See Figure 2.50.

Making Terrain Height Maps In Bryce Itself

Here's some magic that you can use to create height maps from within Bryce itself. Why would you want to do that? Two reasons: First, it's very quick and easy. And second, this method allows you to create height maps that you'd be hard-pressed to match with any other method. There are a few ways to go about this.

The Render Method

What is an *elevation map?* Put simply, a height map is a top view of a terrain or object in which the brightness levels determine the height of elements in the picture. Imagine an aerial photograph in which the mountains are bright and the valleys are dark. However, if the lighting is not correct, translating the top view of a terrain or object into a height map won't work. If the target is lit from the side, strange things happen when the picture is translated into a height map. The lighted side becomes "higher," and the darker side "lower." Follow these steps to explore this method:

1. In a new image, create a series of randomly sized cubes. Place some near the camera, and others farther away.
2. Select the Distance Renderer, and render the image. See Figure 2.51.

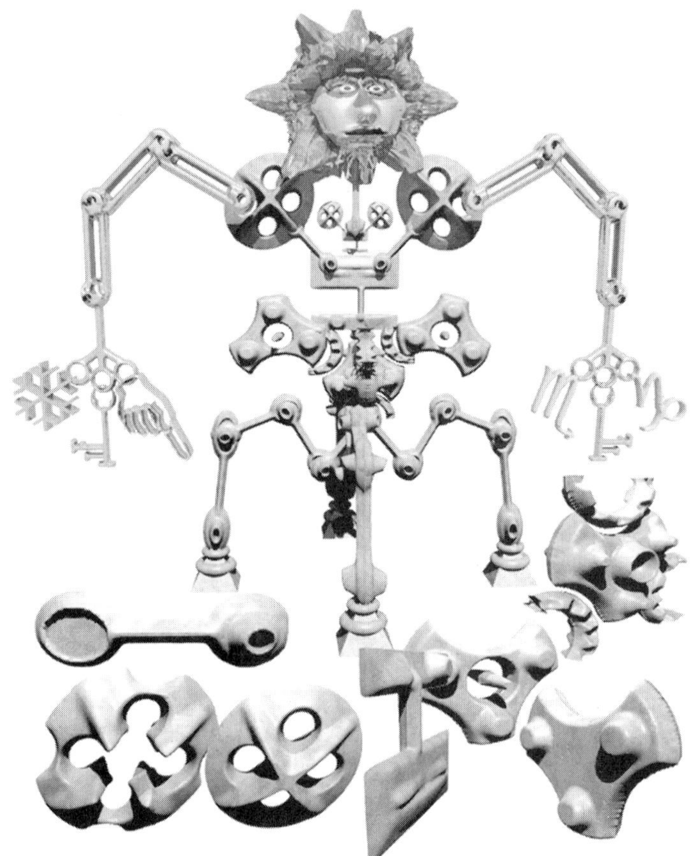

Figure 2.50
The composite figure in the background was constructed using all the Terrain objects shown in the foreground. All the objects were created by following the basic rules previously outlined in the text.

Figure 2.51
Some blocks are closer to the camera than others. With the Distance Renderer, the nearer the object, the darker the grayscale.

3. Save the image, and delete the blocks. Place a Symmetrical Lattice on the screen, and open the Terrain Editor. Create a new map. Then, from the Pictures tab, import the image you just saved as a height map.

Note: *Be sure to turn Perspective Rendering on again before making the final rendering.*

4. What you should see is a rectangular block with rectangular holes in it. The Distance Renderer always works against a white background, and white is translated into maximum height in the Terrain Editor. Click on Invert to create the translated object. Now you have a series of rectangular blocks, perfect for your Bryce cityscape. The black and white squares on the buildings are from a color map, not the elevation map. See Figure 2.52.

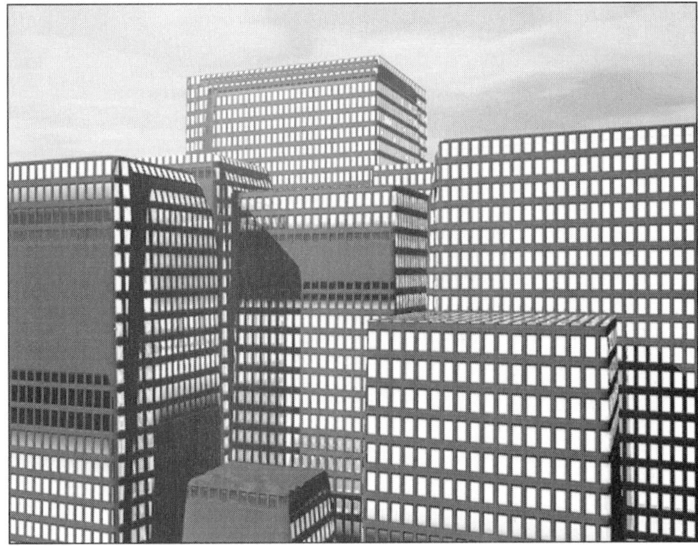

Figure 2.52
The Terrain Edited image has become a 3D construct.

The Snapshot Method

I call this the "snapshot method" of creating a Terrain map. It involves simply taking a snapshot of a screen. Follow these steps:

1. Create a cube and resize it so that its front face fills the screen. Do not rotate the cube.
2. Map any material you like to the cube. Select one that you think might make an interesting height map. Render and save the image. See Figure 2.53.
3. Create a Symmetrical Lattice or a Terrain object, and open the Terrain Editor. Import the image and translate it into a 3D object. See Figure 2.54.

Note: *In the snapshot method, keep the size below 15 percent for the best 3D translations.*

Figure 2.53
This is a close-up of the Etched Rock texture (sized at 10 percent).

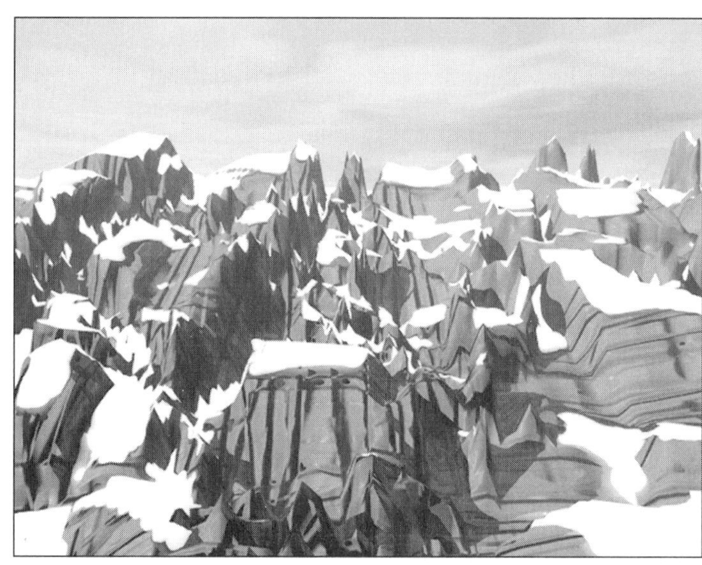

Figure 2.54
The Etched Rock texture is transformed into 3D terrain by the Terrain Editor.

Photoshop Filtered Terrains

Bryce 4 allows you to use your library of Photoshop filters: Access them from the Terrain Editor's Filtering tab.

Using a Photoshop filter on a terrain map allows you to create an infinite number of variations in your model—variations that would be difficult to generate with any other method. When you apply a Photoshop filter to a terrain map, follow these simple guidelines:

Note: *Be aware that some Photoshop filters work only within Photoshop and will not work in Bryce.*

- Avoid filters that add too many small details to the map. Small details translate into too much height variance, making the object too complex.
- In general, stay away from color filters (filters that augment or alter color ranges): Terrain maps are grayscales. An exception would be

adjustment filters that swap color-channel data, because such filters can quickly alter the height map.

- Explore the use of lens flare and cloud filters. These effects translate into interesting terrain features.
- Heighten the contrast of the applied filter, and then tone it down (if needed) with the Terrain Editor's controls.
- Use Photoshop filters with Terrain objects to create natural elements (mountains, canyons, lakes, and so on). Use Photoshop filters with Symmetrical Lattice objects to create manufactured-looking elements.

Filter Suggestions

There are dozens of great filter volumes available for Photoshop and Photoshop-compatible applications, and everyone has a favorite. Here are some that I suggest for use from within the Terrain Editor:

- *Internal Filters*—Photoshop includes dozens of its own filters, many of which are perfect for use as modifiers in the Bryce Terrain Editor. You should explore all of them, although there are some that are especially useful for our purposes. Use any of the Blur filters to tone down the height map, creating smoother features. This can cause fewer distortions than the Terrain Editor's Smooth control. Use Twirl to create beautiful, spiraling terrains. (See Figure 2.55.) Use a Pixelate Mosaic with a cell size of 20 to create interesting blocks useful for urban dwellings. Clouds and Difference Clouds are great for creating rolling hills and mountains. Use Lens Flare to create mountains and volcanoes. Use Craquelure with a depth setting of 10 to create cracked

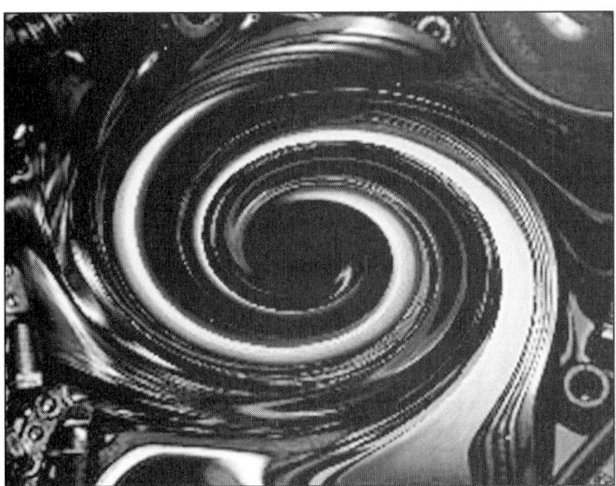

Figure 2.55
On the left is the Twirl-filtered image; on the right is the resulting terrain.

pavement and sidewalks. Select Glass Blocks to create roadways with hilly terrain grids. Use ZigZag Pond Ripples to create rippled areas for water placement. Patchwork creates a height map of square blocks, great for use as a structure's walls.

- *Andromeda Effects*—This large collection contains several volumes of effects filters. For Terrain Editor use, I like the sMulti effect. It creates repeating patterns of parallel areas from any image, leading to unusual and interesting terrain features. See Figure 2.56.

Figure 2.56
On the left is the sMulti filtered image; on the right is the resulting terrain.

- *Eye Candy from Alien Skin*—Another collection of excellent Photoshop filters. Chrome is useful for creating components that resemble human constructs, such as buildings and highways. Jiggle transforms gridded art into more organic forms. The Weave filter creates terrain with a combination of organic and non-organic components. See Figure 2.57.

Figure 2.57
On the left is the Weave-filtered image; on the right is the resulting terrain.

- *Kai's Power Tools 3 and 5 from MetaCreations*—Most Photoshop users have these popular filters. Many of them are excellent for creating 3D map data in the Terrain Editor. Use the Gradient Designer to create topography such as volcanoes and other radial objects. Vortex Tiling creates overlapped walls or gouges, depending on the image content and the use of the Invert command. Spend some time exploring the millions of topographical maps made possible in the Texture Explorer. KPT 5 adds a number of filters that can create complex and bizarre Bryce elements when used in the Terrain Editor. See Figures 2.58 and 2.59.

Figure 2.58
On the left is the Gradient Designer filtered image; on the right is the resulting terrain.

Figure 2.59
This is just one of the countless KPT 5 FraxPlorer models that you can generate by applying this KPT 5 filter from within the Terrain Editor.

- *Pattern Workshop from MicroFrontier (Mac only)*—This filter collection is perfect for designing cityscape elements. The pattern collections come in both color and grayscale, and they include dozens of examples. The result of applying any of these filters is a perfectly symmetrical arrangement of graphic elements on the image. To add variety to the perfection, simply raise or lower areas of the image with the Terrain Editor Elevation brushes. See Figure 2.60.

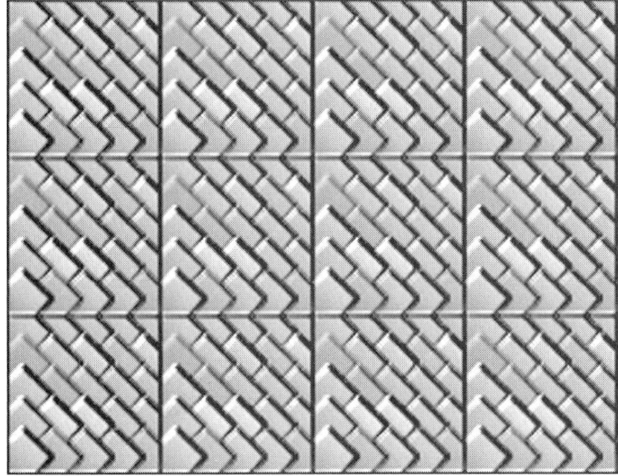

Figure 2.60
On the left is the Pattern Workshop filtered image; on the right is the resulting terrain.

- *Terrazzo from Xaos Tools*—This is one of my all-time favorite Photoshop filters. Using it within the Terrain Editor allows you to create exquisite cityscapes (as long as you add some height variance by using the Elevation Brush on selected areas of the height map first). See Figure 2.61.

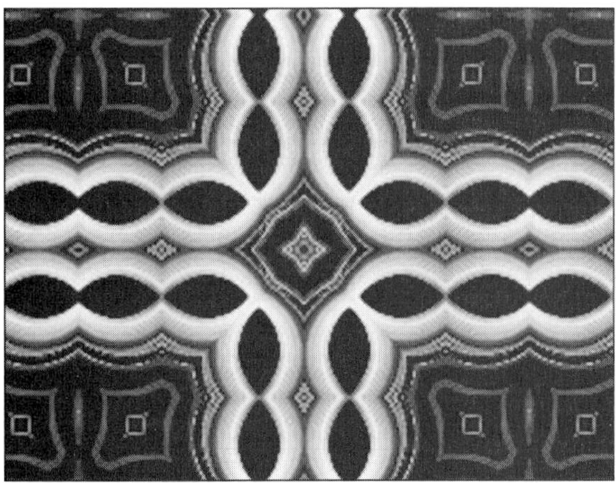

Figure 2.61
On the left is the Terrazzo filtered image; on the right is the resulting terrain.

- *Xenofex from Alien Skin*—Use the Constellation filter to create blobs of light, which translate to 3D mesas in the Terrain Editor. The Baked Earth filter is good not only for creating baked earth, but also for adding roughness to a Terrain object. Lightning creates wonderful Bryce rivers. Just make sure you invert the terrain to get gouges instead of meandering cliffs. (See Figure 2.62.) Little Fluffy Clouds can be customized more extensively than the internal Photoshop Cloud filter, and it creates smoother terrains in Bryce.

Instant Houses

A Bryce scene of nothing but natural-world features can be spectacular, but the same Bryce scene with added creatures or their habitats is even

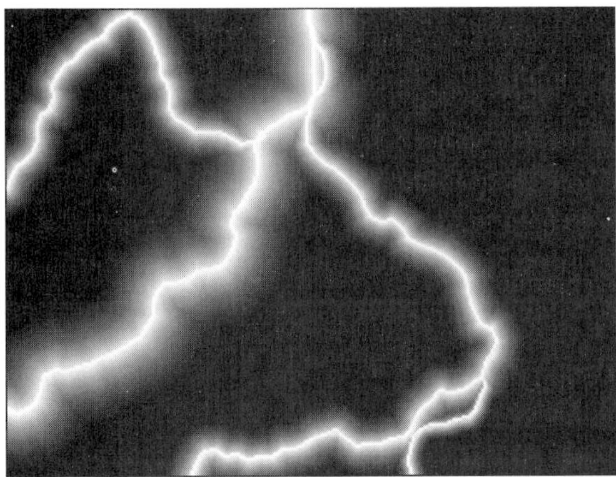

Figure 2.62
On the left is the Lightning filtered image; on the right is the resulting terrain.

more alluring. Adding human or animal elements to your Bryce work connects it to the real world, where nature expresses herself through flora and fauna. It's not always necessary to add human figures to a Bryce scene to hint that someone lives in the vicinity. Often, a dwelling does the trick. Using the Terrain Editor, you can create wonderful dwellings that can be dropped into your worlds. Here's how:

1. Place a Symmetrical Lattice on the screen, and open the Terrain Editor.
2. Click on New. Now click on and drag the Cross Ridges filter. This allows you to center a Cross Ridge in the preview area. When you release the mouse, you see an inverted Cross Ridges model. If you like the model, jump back to the Bryce work screen. If you don't like the model, click on Invert and jump back. See Figure 2.63 for both options.

Figure 2.63
Use the Cross Ridges filter to build a house. The standard Cross Ridges model is on the left; the inverted form is on the right.

3. Use the Cross Ridges filter over and over again to create more complex roofs. Some may resemble cathedrals. See Figure 2.64. You can also explore adding layered square and round edges, as in Figure 2.65.
4. Start a new scene, following the same process just mentioned. This time however, use the Cross Ridges 2 filter. This filter allows you to place Cross Ridges over each other at different parts of the map, creating greater variety that results in palatial constructs. See Figure 2.66.

Figure 2.64
A roof constructed with multiple Cross Ridges filter applications.

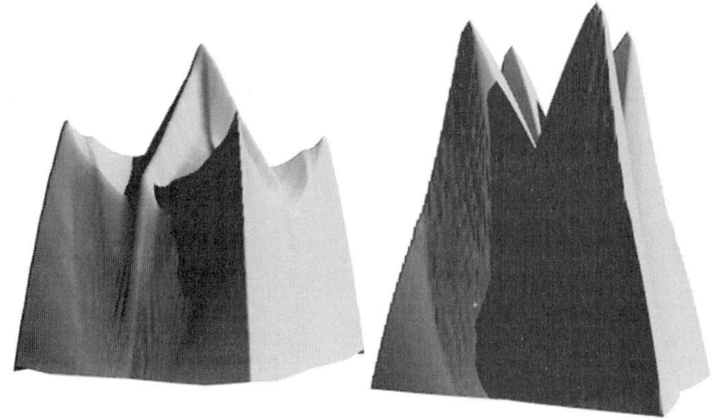

Figure 2.65
More variety is produced when you layer several Square and Round Edges on the same model.

Figure 2.66
Using the Cross Ridges 2 filter in the Terrain Editor creates more complex roof models.

Figure 2.67
The Cross Ridges can emulate a castle when the right materials are applied.

Placing the Cross Ridged object in the proper Bryce setting can create an entire visual history of the scene. See Figure 2.67.

Terrain Exports

Why export a terrain to another format? Exporting a terrain yields two important benefits:

- Other applications offer more options when it comes to scene development, animation tools, textures, and materials. An alternate application may be the best place for your terrain to live.
- Because other applications offer different tools for tweaking the terrain model, you might export the terrain temporarily, only to import it back to Bryce later. This gives you the best of all worlds—literally—and allows you to wind up with the exact terrain models you require.

Infinite Plane Modeling

I have looked at Infinite Planes earlier in this chapter. Even without using Booleans, there are ways you can use Infinite Planes to create some very interesting effects. This is possible because of one Infinite Plane attribute: They can be rotated.

The ability to rotate Infinite Planes allows you to place them so that they intersect. This can create some unexpected optical illusions. In an animation (refer to Chapter 5), a camera can travel from one Infinite Plane environment to another, as if it were crossing the space between different realities. An Infinite Plane has no beginning and no end, so

Note: *Be sure to take advantage of Bryce's excellent Polygon Delimiter when you export terrain models. You seldom need to export a terrain at its full polygon-count to maintain its personality. When you import the terrain within Bryce, the terrain occupies less room, and your system works faster.*

Note: *If you map the planes with a partially transparent material, your infinite hallway will sit in a natural environment, emphasizing the illusion of a hallway that never ends. Also note that you will need a light in this infinite tunnel. Set the light (usually a Radial) to No Falloff.*

creating a construct with more than one always produces bizarre but intriguing visuals (I can't really call it a model, because the dimensions are truly infinite).

To add to Infinite Planes' variety, you can also assign levels of transparency (as you'll see in Chapter 3). This is especially valuable for Sky Planes and clouds. Here are a few experiments to try:

- *Parallel Infinity*—Create a construct with four Infinite Planes, mapped as you like. The construct should be square, with planes for each side and for the top and bottom. Place your camera inside the construct at different points and render to preview the results. If you animate the camera, it will seem as if you are racing down an infinite rectangular hallway. See Figure 2.68.

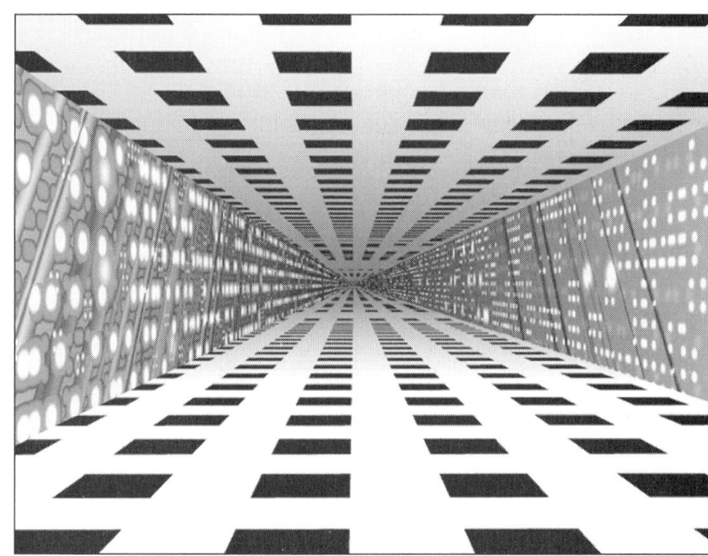

Figure 2.68
No matter how far you travel down this rectangular tunnel, you'll never reach the end.

- *Layered Treats*—Create a stack of horizontally parallel Infinite Planes, each with a 50-percent transparency. Place the camera above them all, looking down at an angle. This is a great way to create layered clouds or water effects. See Figure 2.69.
- *Random Rasters*—Explore the intersections of Infinite Planes that meet at random angles, and discover what visual delights lay in store. There is ample room here for your own personal discoveries and rules.

Figure 2.69
This pyramidal tower is poking through four Infinite Cloud layers, each with a different transparency and size. You can animate each layer to produce thrilling effects. You can use the same process with Infinite Water Planes or with any material you like.

Replacement Modeling

When you import a model that contains grouped elements and ungroup them within Bryce, you avail yourself of one of Bryce's most unusual and spectacular options: Replacement Modeling. You can selectively replace each ungrouped part of the model with one of the Bryce primitive objects, a terrain, a Symmetrical Lattice, or a rock. Depending on the model, this can create simplified variations or intricate complexities. Follow these steps:

1. From within Bryce, import a model that has grouped elements (for example, a Poser model that was saved with its grouped parts linked).
2. Ungroup the model in Bryce and select Show Origin Points from the Attribute dialog box for each part. Move the Origin Points so that they allow you to rotate the parts appropriately. Re-link all the parts in a hierarchy.
3. Replace the model's parts by going to the Replacement Objects menu and selecting an object. See Figures 2.70 and 2.71.

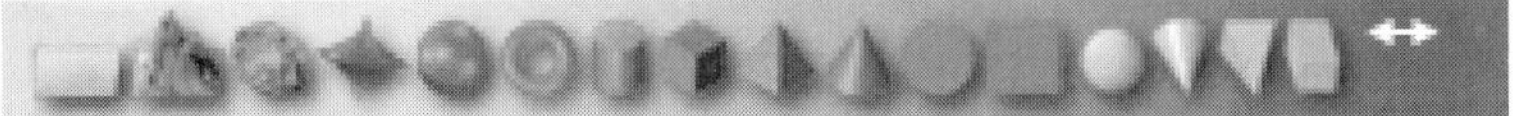

Figure 2.70
The Replacement Objects menu.

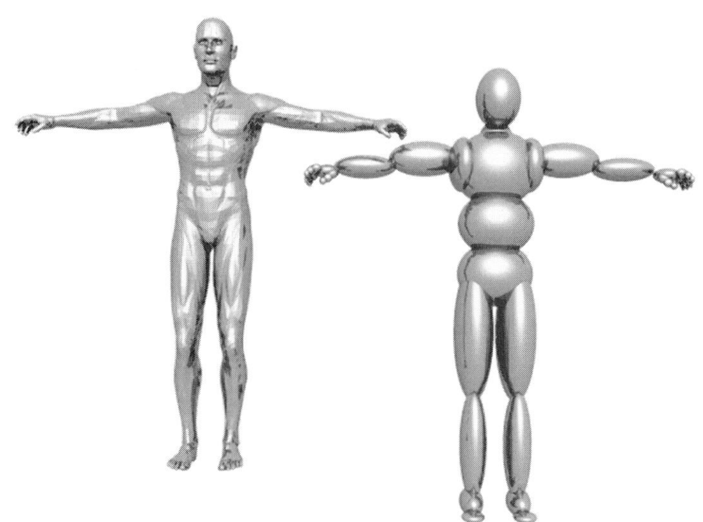

Figure 2.71
The elements of the imported Poser model on the left are replaced with spheres on the right.

The Bionic Model

Here's a way to create a half-human/half-non-human model in Bryce. Follow these steps:

1. From within Bryce, import a Poser model or any human model whose parts are saved as grouped elements.
2. Ungroup the model. Link the arms and legs, moving the Origin Points in the process so that the arms and legs can rotate naturally. Link the head to the chest and the chest to the belly. Link the pelvis to the belly.
3. Select all the parts, and Duplicate the model. Move the cloned model away from the original.
4. Create a rectangular primitive and move it to cover the left side of the model, splitting it exactly in half. Make the rectangular primitive a negative Boolean. Make the model's parts positive Booleans. Group the rectangular, negative Boolean primitive with the half of the model's parts that are covered. Half of the model's body should disappear.
5. Select the cloned model, and use the Replacement Objects menu to replace all the parts with spheres or cubes.
6. Create a rectangular primitive, and move it to cover the right side of the model, splitting it exactly in half. Make the rectangular primitive a negative Boolean. Make the model's parts positive Booleans. Group the rectangular, negative Boolean primitive with the half of the model's parts being covered. Half of the cloned model's body should disappear.

***Note:** If you are doing this with a Poser model, you may want to re-group all the parts of each hand, unless you require complete control of each finger joint.*

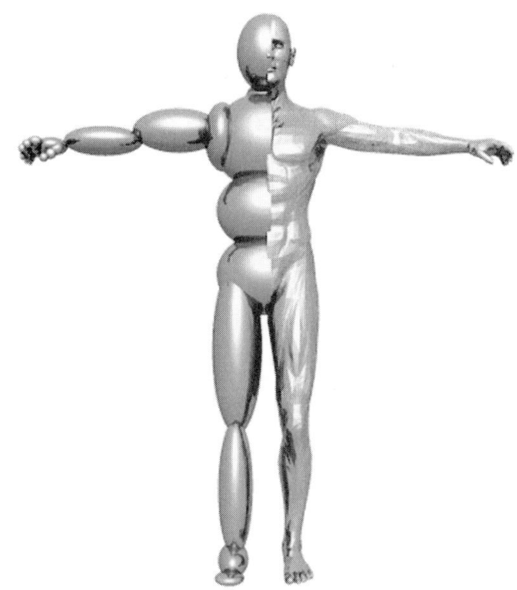

Figure 2.72
The finished bionic model, created using the procedure described.

7. Move the two models together so they join, and link the clone's belly with the original's belly. You'll wind up with a strange hybrid, half-human and half-not. See Figure 2.72.

Important Undocumented Feature

You can use Replacement Modeling in a way that is not documented. If you create models in the Terrain Editor, this information alone is worth the price of this book. Follow these steps:

1. Place a Symmetrical Lattice on the screen, and activate the Terrain Editor.
2. Click on New. This leaves nothing but a red mask in your preview window.
3. Use the painting and/or elevation tools to create some shapes. (The content is not important here, only the process, so create any shapes you like.) Click on the check mark to place the new Symmetrical Lattice object on the screen.
4. As you know, a vertically Symmetrical Lattice object is a mirrored object. The standard way to delete the mirrored bottom portion of the object is to erase it with a negative Boolean cube. Do that now. At this point, you have a Symmetrical Lattice, which has an invisible bottom half. That's fine, but Boolean objects look rather messy on the screen.
5. Here's how to get rid of the mess. With the Boolean Group selected, go to the Replacement Objects toolset at the top of the Edit screen.

Note: *Turn a Symmetrical Lattice object into a non-mirrored object by replacing the Symmetrical Lattice with a Terrain object after you've edited the Symmetrical Lattice.*

Replace the Boolean Group with a Terrain object (*not* a Symmetrical Lattice). A negative Boolean Terrain object replaces the cube.

6. Get rid of the Terrain object by ungrouping and deleting it.

What is left? What you have now is the top half of the Symmetrical Lattice you designed, although it is taller. Reduce the height to your liking. The messy Boolean cube cutter is gone, and you have a standalone 3D model.

Use this technique to create models for trees, huts in a village, or anything else you discover.

Arrays

An Array is a multitude of cloned objects set in a defined 3D pattern. The chairs in an auditorium are an example of a two-dimensional array; they are dispersed along the X and Z axes. Oranges in a crate are an example of a 3D dimensional array; they are dispersed along all three axes. In Bryce, you can create two types of Arrays: Replication and Dispersion. Either type can be 2D or 3D.

Replication Arrays

Replication Arrays start with one object. The object is replicated—or cloned—as many times as you need. As you define the quantity, you also define the clones' relationship to each other in terms of size, position, and rotation. Replication is triggered by the data you enter in the Multi-Replicate dialog box. See Figure 2.73.

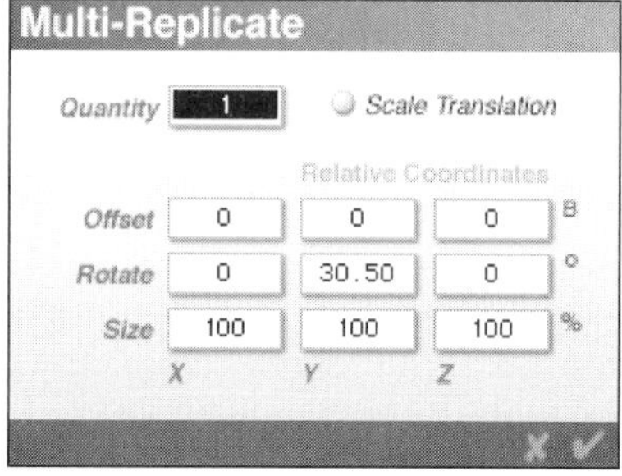

Figure 2.73
The Multi-Replicate dialog box.

Replication Projects

You can construct an infinite number of Arrays. One of the most common applications of an Array is the creation of simple stairs and spiral stairs. Here's how:

1. Create a rectangular block that is square on the front and elongated to about five times the depth of the square on the Z axis.

2. Select the block, and open the Multi-Replicate dialog box. Set Quantity to 12 and X and Y Offset to 20. Accept the default values of 0 for X, Y, and Z Rotation and 100 for X, Y, and Z Size. Click on OK. *Voila!* You have created stairs. See Figure 2.74.

To create spiral stairs, use all the same values except Y Rotation; set that value to 20. See Figure 2.75.

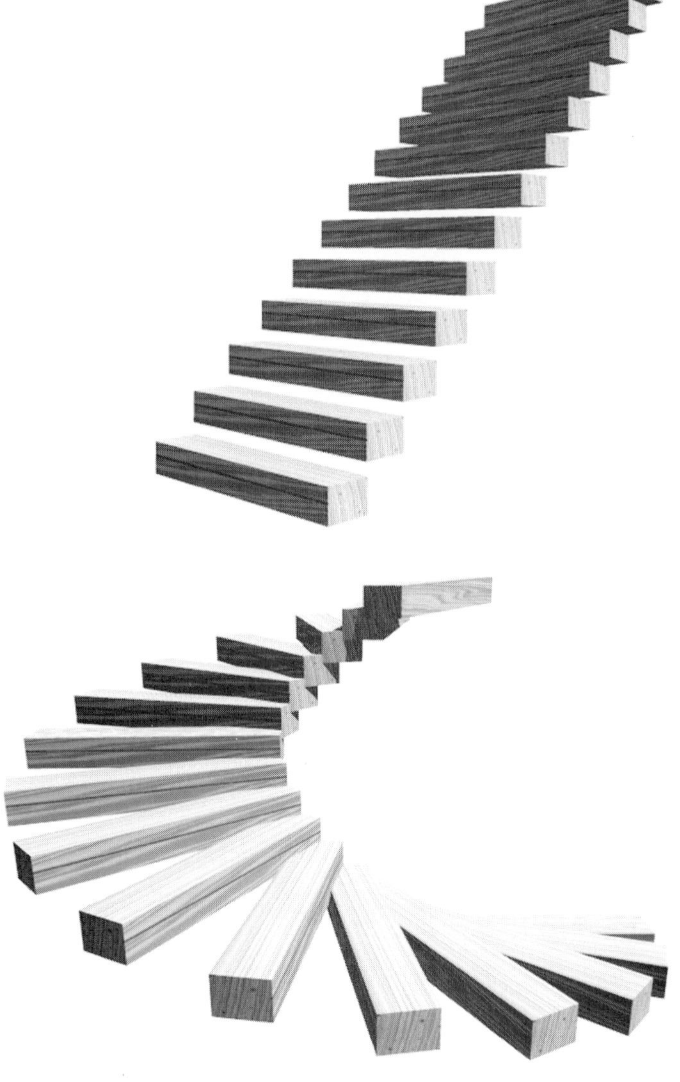

Figure 2.74
Simple stairs created with the Multi-Replicate command.

Figure 2.75
When you use a value other than 0 on the Y Rotation axis, the stairs form a spiral.

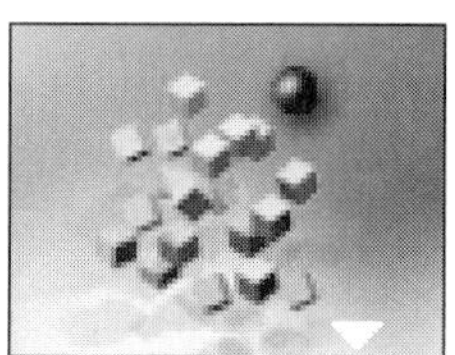

Figure 2.76
The Dispersion tool.

Dispersion Arrays

A Dispersion Array starts with Replication, but all the clones are Replicated in the exact same space as the original object. As you are already aware from your study of the Bryce documentation, Dispersions are activated from the Dispersion tool at the top-right of the Edit screen. See Figure 2.76.

Dispersions are useful for creating chaotic events (such as explosions) and also for creating randomized arrays from a single object. You could, for example, create a meteor field from a single replicated rock by using 3D Rotation Dispersion, or a forest from a single tree by using 2D Size Dispersion. Dispersion adds randomization to a Replication Array. See Figure 2.77.

Figure 2.77
3D Rotational Dispersion applied to the separate elements of the spiral staircase shown in Figure 2.75.

Path Replication

Path Replication is another way to create interesting modeled elements within Bryce, without importing them from other sources. Here's how to create a path-based model:

1. Either import a Path from the Paths Library (found under the Create screen heading), or use the Objects|Create Path command to create your own. Within Bryce, a Path is another object, although it doesn't render. Normally, you use Paths to move the camera in an animation, but you can use them just as well to structure objects.
2. Create a torus, and link it to the Path. Move the torus to one end of the Path.

3. Use the Multi-Replicate command to create 12 cloned tori over the original.
4. Move each torus one by one until you have a chain that covers the Path. Note that when you reshape the Path by pushing and pulling on the nodes, the torus chain is also reshaped. See Figure 2.78.

Figure 2.78
This chain of torus elements was created by using Multi-Replication on a torus linked to a Path.

Important External Modeling Resources

If you need a professional modeling resource, your first option is obviously to have the application whose native format exports directly to Bryce. This means LightWave and Inspire for LWS and LWO exports, trueSpace for COB exports, and so on. But your limited budget might not allow you to purchase another application for its modeling capabilities, or maybe you simply don't want to learn another complex piece of software. In that case, you should be aware that there are alternatives, some of which offer even more options than the high-end 3D applications themselves. (Unless otherwise noted, all the following applications are available for both Windows and the Mac.)

Amorphium

Amorphium from Play, Inc., is one of the most exciting 3D applications to hit the 3D market in years. You might describe it as a realtime, 3D digital-clay-sculpting application, but even that description doesn't do it justice. Amorphium exports LWO, DXF, OBJ, and 3DS formats, making it a perfect modeling utility for Bryce users. Most of the illustrations in this book contain Amorphium components, textured and rendered in Bryce. If you look at the color images in this book's Bryce Studio and read their descriptions in Chapter 6, you will see that many of the objects displayed in those color images were created in Amorphium and exported to Bryce.

Natural Scene Designer

At first glance, you might think that Natural Scene Designer (from Natural Graphics) and MetaCreations' Bryce are competing products. But as a professional, you can't afford to maintain such "either/or" positions concerning software. The question you must always ask is, "Does this software work with my other application in interesting ways?" In the case of Natural Scene Designer and Bryce, the answer is a resounding "yes."

Natural Scene Designer was developed primarily to focus on the import, customization, and export of terrain data and DEMs. Now that Bryce 4 supports the DEM format, Natural Scene Designer is a perfect environment for customizing DEMs before exporting them to Bryce. More than that, Natural Scene Designer also includes a library of super-detailed DEMs that you can import directly in Bryce. Natural Scene Designer's extensive DEM library is of awesome importance to Bryce users. Why spend days downloading DEMs from the Web when all the DEMs you need are available on a CD-ROM? The terrain libraries CD-ROM collection is in Natural Scene Designer format, so you'll have to purchase the application. Once loaded into Natural Scene Designer, however, you can export them as compliant DEMs.

The libraries now include maps for the continental United States and portions of Canada, and more maps are being added.

To export a DEM from Natural Scene Designer to Bryce, follow these steps:

1. Start Natural Scene Designer, and Open a landscape from the 3D Terrain Model CD-ROM.
2. Select File|Export USGS.
3. After the Save USGS dialog box appears, select the directory and enter the file name. Make sure that the name ends with the .DEM extension. Click on the Save button.
4. Start Bryce and import the DEM file created above.

Using Natural Scene Designer with Bryce allows you to create terrains that emulate areas from across North America. See Figure 2.79.

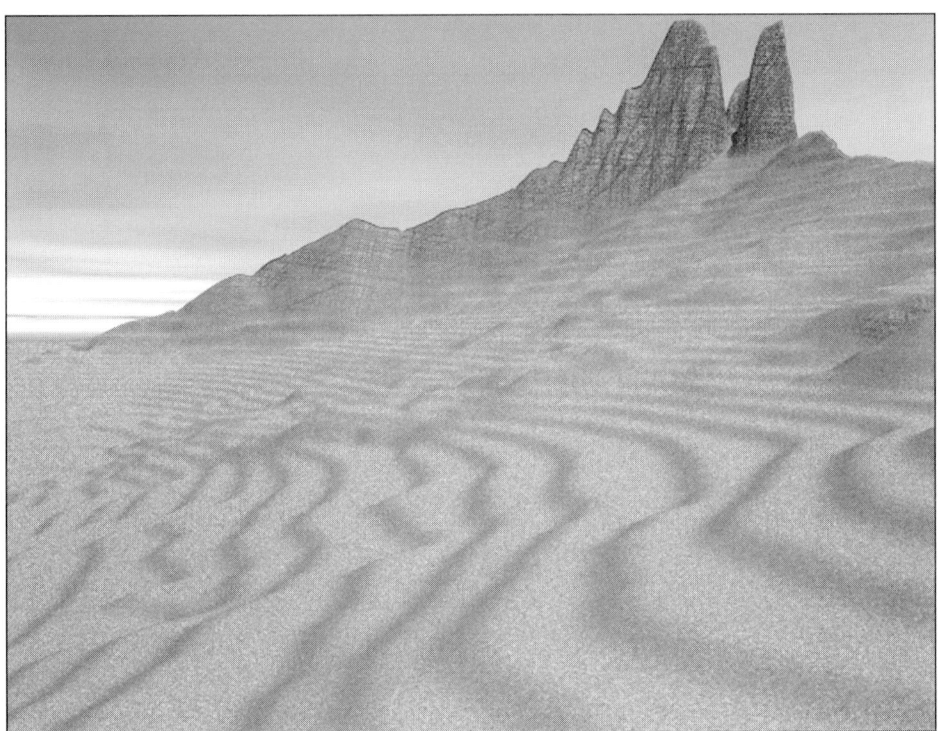

Figure 2.79
This Natural Scene Designer DEM file (representing Lamont, California) has been exported to Bryce and rendered.

Nendo

Nendo from Nichimen Graphics is currently available for Windows only, although a Mac version is under development. Nendo is one of the most intuitive polygonal modelers around. Created with the expertise derived from Nichimen's high-end game modeling software, Nendo allows you to create polygonal models in an interactive 3D environment by manipulating faces, vertices, and edges. When you're done, export the model to a number of formats that Bryce imports. The best thing about Nendo is that it is extremely efficient at optimizing the model's file size.

Organica

Organica from Impulse, Inc., is a "metaball" modeling system. Metaballs are construction objects that can attach themselves to other metaballs in their vicinity. After a metaball model is created, the resulting mesh is saved as a polygonal model. Organica calls its metaball operators "MetaBlocks" because more than spheres are involved. As their name suggests, Organics can be used to create organic-looking 3D models. The two most important formats that Organica exports are 3D Studio (3DS) and LightWave (LWO) models. Organica also exports Wavefront objects (OBJ), but Bryce has an easier time with 3DS and LWO objects than with OBJ objects.

Poser

Bryce can create mesmerizing worlds of wonder, but worlds populated by no animal life soon become sterile and boring places. To add creature content to your Bryce worlds, you need MetaCreations' Poser. Bryce and Poser are the perfect marriage. I can't imagine using Bryce without Poser by its side. To me, both are part of the same creative environment in which each addresses a needed area. Zygote Media Group creates additional Poser models that you can easily import to populate your Bryce worlds. These range from human to animal to fantasy characters.

3D Builder Pro

3D Builder from 3D Construction Company is available for Windows 95/98/NT only. This software gives you another way to create 3D content for your Bryce worlds. By taking two photographs of a subject (from mechanical devices to the human form), you can build almost any 3D object imaginable. By defining the same point in space on multiple views of a target object, you create a 3D matrix of points for use in shaping the object in digital space. 3D Builder's approach to modeling is unusual. As far as complex objects are concerned, this approach can create 3D models much faster than any other method. The output is easily transferred to Bryce.

Tree Professional

Tree Professional from Onyx Software is one of the most useful applications you will find for developing natural-world content for Bryce. Tree Professional is loaded with hundreds of tree pictures that you can map to Bryce Picture Planes. Tree Professional also allows you to create 3D tree models of every type, even alien trees of your own manufacture. Every parameter of the tree is taken into consideration, from the general tree type to specific leaf and stem configurations. The result can be a model much too large for Bryce or any other application, but Onyx has that all figured out. Before the tree is exported, you are given a wide range of parameters to customize in order to create smaller, more manageable files. If Bryce is your main artistic outlet, don't pass up Tree Professional.

CD-ROM Collections To Explore

There are hundreds of CD-ROMs on the market that offer 3D models for Bryce import, especially now that Bryce supports so many 3D file formats. Here are a few that you will find very useful.

LightWave 3D Bug Collection

Use these LightWave models from Dimensional Expressions when your Bryce world demands insect inhabitants. There are several CDs in this collection, and each one offers different varieties of creepy-crawlers.

3D AcuWorlds

The 3D AcuWorlds CD-ROM collection of animals was created by Acuris before there was a Bryce 3D, and the animals' limbs are not articulated for animation. The models make great background figures, however. This CD-ROM may be difficult to find, but if you look hard (especially on the Web), you can secure a copy.

Fantasy Figures

From Epic Software Group, this collection of 3D Studio and LightWave models contains several categories, each including dozens of models. You can ungroup these models for animation.

Replica Tech

There are many CD-ROM model collections from Replica Tech that should be of great interest to Bryce users. There is a complete medieval castle, inside and out, with more than a hundred small items. Replica Tech also markets the Wright Collection, a sample of the work of architect Frank Lloyd Wright. My favorites are the Shark and Dolphin CDs, each with dozens of accurate models that can be animated.

trueClips

Now that Bryce can import the trueSpace model format, don't pass up the trueClips models from Caligari Corporation. There are numerous, high-quality models here for your Bryce rendering and enjoyment.

Newtek

Check the Newtek Web site (**www.newtek.com**) for details on the availability of LightWave model collections. There are dozens of high-quality, LightWave-oriented CDs available from a variety of developers.

All you really have to do is surf the Web to find new postings of available 3D models. Just use a Web search engine to look for the words "3D Models."

Moving On

This chapter explored every possible way you can use Bryce to model objects for your 3D worlds. I also pointed you to other applications as a way to meet your Bryce modeling needs. In the next chapter, I will focus on using materials and textures to assign colorful personalities to your models.

3 Materials And Textures

Two elements define an object's personality. One is the object's structure, and the other is its material—what it is made of. This chapter deals with defining what 3D objects seem to be made of.

The Difference

The substance that an object is made of—its material—is its personality in the world. A ball of rock is as different from a ball of flowers as a ball of water is from a ball of reptilian scales. All the balls may be the same size and shape, but they have different personalities: They react differently to forces, and they are perceived differently as well.

In many applications, the terms *material* and *texture* are interchangeable. In Bryce, they are not. Within Bryce, a *material* is what you apply to an object at the end of the design procedure, and a *texture* is a component of a material. Bryce uses two kinds of textures: Procedural (based on an algorithm or formula) and Picture (based on a bitmap). Bryce includes Materials presets, a collection of simple materials that require no tweaking. A more personal approach to designing materials is to use the Materials Lab and (when required) the Deep Texture Editor.

In this chapter, we will use the Materials Lab to work with both algorithmic and picture texture components in the Materials Lab. We will also look at the Deep Texture Editor.

Materials

You can think of textures as the components of a material. In this section, I'll show you ways you can use the Materials Lab to develop your own material components (from both the internal Bryce algorithms and from imported pictures). To complicate matters just a bit, Bryce allows you to use and design both *Surface* and *Volumetric* materials. I'll show you each kind and explain how they're different.

This chapter details the components and uses of 25 original materials. These materials will enhance the creative potential of your Bryce projects. Bryce will become even more valuable to you once you learn how to create materials yourself. You can also refer to the finished materials included in the CD-ROM's Materials folder.

Note: *Before you work through this chapter, it's vital that you read the Bryce 4 documentation on materials and textures. After you've read the documentation, you're prepared to learn from the material in this chapter.*

Using The Preset Materials

There are thirteen libraries or collections of Material presets: Simple & Fast, Planes & Terrains, Rocks & Stones, Waters & Liquids, Clouds & Fogs, Wild & Fun, Complex fx, Miscellaneous, Glasses, Metals, Volume, Tutorial, and User. You can delete materials from any library, and you can add your own. When you add your own materials, be sure to add them under the appropriate heading.

Simple & Fast

I have many favorites in this collection, including Yellow Gold, Mirror, and the Woods. I suggest you add some simple color presets to those already included: This gives you a way to instantly assign a variety of hues to an object. Yellow Gold renders with absolutely believable clarity, and you can change the material to different metals just by changing the hue of the material's Diffuse and Ambient components (as you will discover). Mirror is the ideal material for water seen from a high altitude, and it renders more quickly than many of the Water presets. I also suggest that you enhance your options by customizing and adding more wood materials to this collection. The simple way to do that is to load one of the Wood presets, and alter its Diffuse and/or Ambient Colors, and perhaps change the Frequency of the algorithmic pattern as well. Then, save the material as a new Wood when you achieve something you like. See Figure 3.1.

EXPERIMENT WITH MATERIALS

Don't truncate your creative potential by using the supplied materials categories too literally. There is nothing to prevent you from assigning an "inappropriate" material to an object. You can assign a water material to a mountain, a metal material to a piece of fruit, or a cloud material to a human figure. Don't let your preconceptions limit your experimentation with materials.

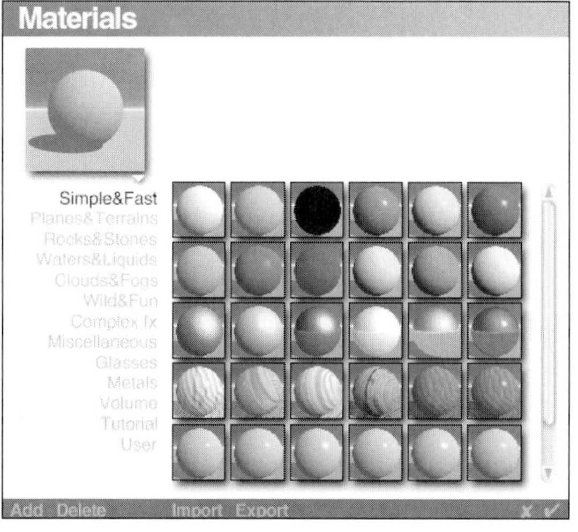

Figure 3.1
The Simple & Fast Materials presets.

Planes & Terrains

The Planes & Terrains collection (shown in Figure 3.2) is designed for use with mountains and Ground Planes. As with any material, you can further customize these materials in the Materials Lab and the Deep Texture Editor. Use the Deep Texture Editor to make subtle alterations in the colorization of a material or to create entirely new materials. Be warned, however, that it takes a lot of exploration to get the hang of this module. Some materials work equally well on both Ground Planes and Terrains; some look good on one or the other, but this is a personal aesthetic judgement call.

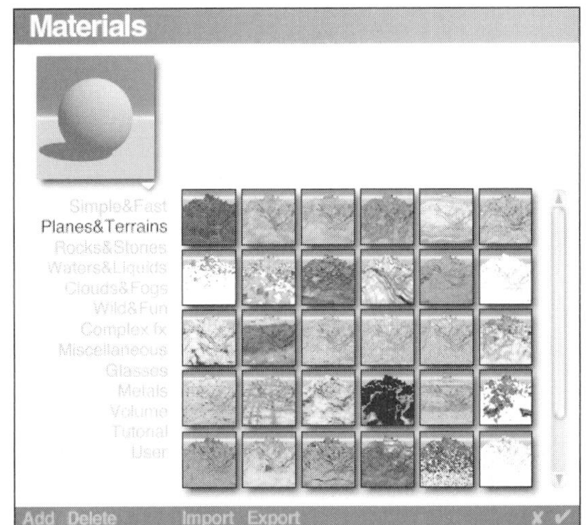

Figure 3.2
The Planes & Terrains Materials presets.

Rocks & Stones

As I described in Chapter 2, stones are special primitive models in Bryce. When you click on the Stone icon and add a stone to a scene, the stone is created with a random stone material (shown in Figure 3.3) and a random shape. You have to alter the material manually if you want the stone to have a different look. Here are some tips for using stone materials on objects:

- Use more detailed and complex materials on stones close to the camera and simpler materials on stones farther from the camera. This provides what computer graphics artists call a realistic Level Of Detail (LOD). The LOD principle is known to visual artists as aerial perspective or atmospheric perspective—the effect of seeing objects through the atmosphere. It simulates the way our eyes perceive the world—objects in the distance are perceived with less intense color and less detail than objects in the foreground. Its discovery is accredited to Leonardo da Vinci during the Renaissance.
- Place stones randomly in your scene to give it a more natural look. Randomize the sizes and orientations. Do not use too many materials, or the scene will appear too busy.
- Before you duplicate or multireplicate a stone, assign a suitable material to it. Consider smoothing the facets carefully (with the Edit Object command), because a stone might look better with sharp, faceted attributes. Stones in water are usually smoother than those eroded by the wind on land.
- Consider using a Terrain Material on a stone to make the stone work as a larger element, such as a cliff or a mountain. Experiment with unconventional materials on stones that are part of an alien or abstract landscape.

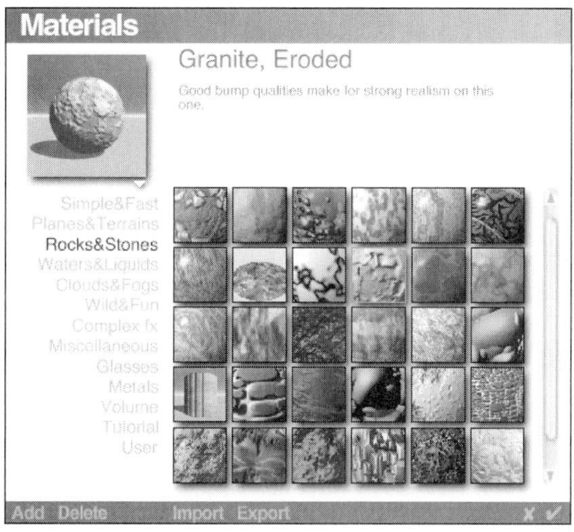

Figure 3.3
The Rocks & Stones Materials presets.

Waters & Liquids

Use waters and liquids as materials for Infinite Water Planes, lakes and pools, water from a faucet, liquids in a glass, or other, more exploratory uses. Waters and liquids usually include varying degrees of transparency and turbulence. Raytraced rendering has to penetrate transparent surfaces, and the math required to compute the turbulence introduces more time in rendering waters and liquids. See Figure 3.4.

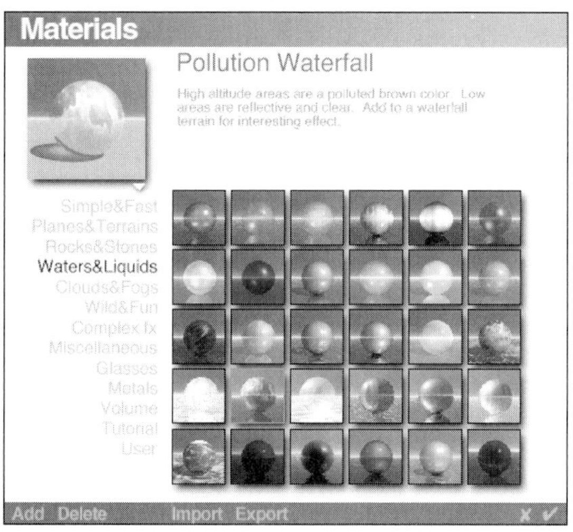

Figure 3.4
The Waters & Liquids Materials presets.

Clouds & Fogs

Think of the Clouds & Fogs presets (shown in Figure 3.5) as a way to enhance the Clouds & Fogs mode settings. You use the Clouds & Fogs settings to define cloud and fog attributes that are applied to Infinite Planes. But these settings are of limited use when you want to develop layers of fog or clouds. You can overcome these limitations by manually placing Infinite Planes in the scene at any height and applying one of the

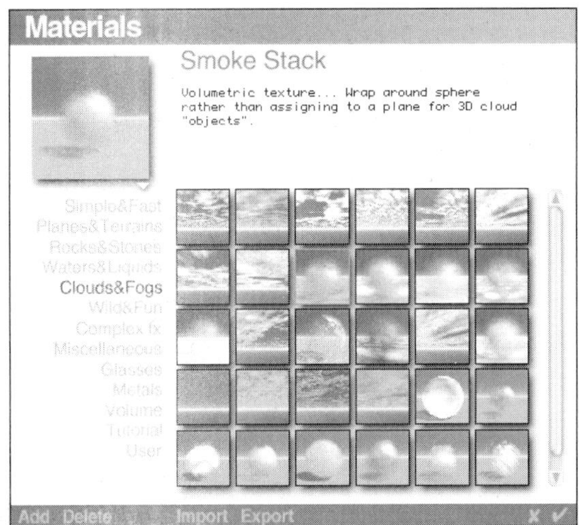

Figure 3.5
The Clouds & Fogs Materials presets.

Clouds & Fogs presets to the Plane. But limiting these materials to this purpose alone will severely limit your creative exploration. Break the boundaries and apply clouds and fog to items not normally made of those materials. For example:

- If your scene contains a human or animal model, duplicate the model and make the duplicate about 25 percent larger than the original. Apply a Cloud or Fog material to the larger model to get an aura of filmy vapor around the model.
- Create several Infinite Cloud Planes, each at a different height. Apply different Sky & Fog presets to each while leaving the sky visible through the layers. By placing the camera above, below, or inside the layers, you can create alternate views of the scene.
- Create a series of spheres emanating from a house's chimney, a train's smokestack, or a vehicle's exhaust pipe. Apply the SmokeStack Cloud material to the spheres.
- To create an explosion in an animation, start by adding a sphere to your scene. This sphere will be the center of the explosion. Make the sphere as small as possible. Apply a cloud material preset to the sphere. In the animation, make the sphere grow until it fills the scene, and then quickly shrink to zero at the last keyframe. Animate the cloud material's size and direction parameters randomly throughout the animation, and perform some test renderings to preview the results. You'll find more information about animation in Chapter 5.

Wild & Fun

Once you've gained experience with Bryce, the Wild & Fun collection of Material presets (shown in Figure 3.6) will certainly contain some of your

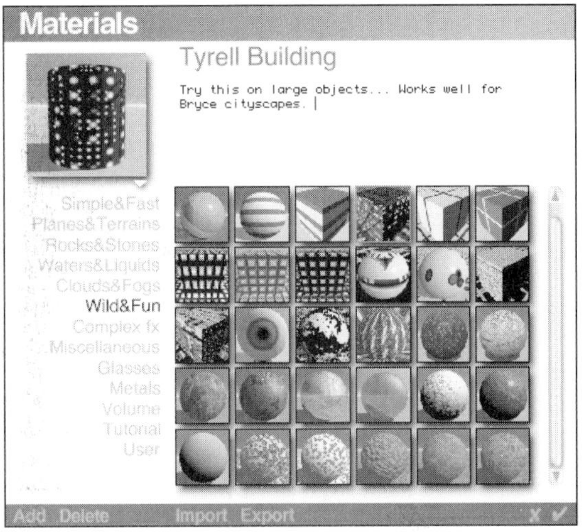

Figure 3.6
The Wild & Fun Materials presets.

favorites. You will likely use these materials as the basis for your own customized materials. Be sure to study how materials in the Wild & Fun collection are constructed in the Materials Lab by applying them to a selected object and doing a test rendering. Some suggestions for the use of these materials include:

- The What Are You Looking At preset is ideal for quickly creating eyeballs for your characters. Just make sure you use Object Space mapping to apply the material to the sphere. (If you need a detailed description of how the Mapping Options differ, see the Bryce documentation.)
- Use Dali Bee Stripes on human or animal models to create "Dali-esque," surreal, semitransparent figures.
- Explore the Tyrell Building material preset as the basis for dark city edifices.
- The Easter Egg Dye #2 preset allows nearly infinite customization, and each offers a new material personality.

Complex fx

The Complex fx collection (shown in Figure 3.7) contains some spectacular organic Materials presets. You can use them straight from the preset or as the basis for your own exploration and customization. Some ideas include:

- Use the Green Lit material on spheres or circular planes to create nebula-like objects in a dark sky. These objects work well when mixed with Star environments.
- Use Fire 1 and Fire 2 for everything from torch flames to fireplaces. Note that Fire 1 needs a dark background in order to be seen; Fire 2 doesn't.

Figure 3.7
The Complex fx Materials presets.

- Use Oily Bronze on a Ground Plane, particularly when you want the look of scorched earth (near a volcano, for instance). This material is also great for dead trees and terrains devoid of vegetation.
- Selene is great for ethereal terrains, such as wispy mountains or the city of Oz.
- Use Disco Kelp as a map for a plane beneath the Water Plane, making sure the Water Plane is semitransparent to give water a swampy look. You can also use the material alone on a Water Plane to create a believable oil spill.
- The I Can't Believe It's Not Fire material excels when you need a material for molten rock.

Miscellaneous

Don't dismiss these materials (shown in Figure 3.8) as throwaways. Some of the most variable presets are included here. (Many are similar to materials in the Rocks & Stones collection, and other organics are thrown in too.) For instance:

- Apply Death Star In Progress to a building or two in an urban scene. It provides an unfinished look.
- Use Foliage I and Foliage II when you need trees in the distance. Just wrap the material to a sphere. Be careful though: The high transparency of this material increases rendering times. Many of the trees in the Objects presets use this material.
- The Pearl Beads material makes a great riverbed or a rocky Maine beach.

Figure 3.8
The Miscellaneous Materials presets.

- Flowing Contortions is the perfect material for giving water a radioactive, polluted look.
- Use Steel Cage when you need a space helmet on a figure or an enclosure that allows you to see inside.

Glasses

The wide selection of glass Materials presets (and the fact that you can customize them further) provides options to fit every possibility. Just remember that the transparency of glasses increases rendering time. See Figure 3.9.

Metals

Metals are one of the most-called-for materials in computer graphics, and this collection of Metals presets (shown in Figure 3.10) includes many of the most requested.

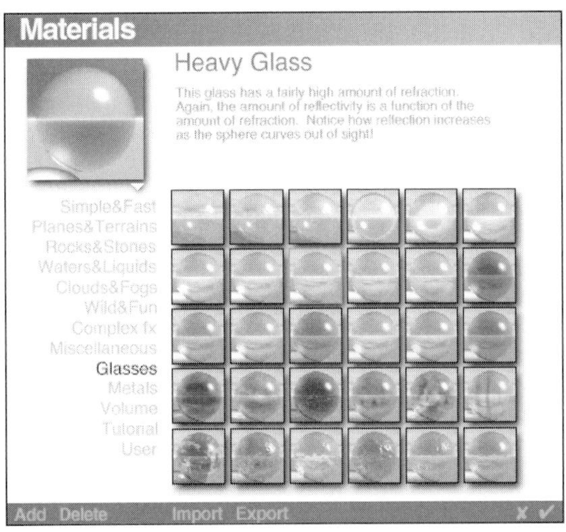

Figure 3.9
The Glasses Materials presets.

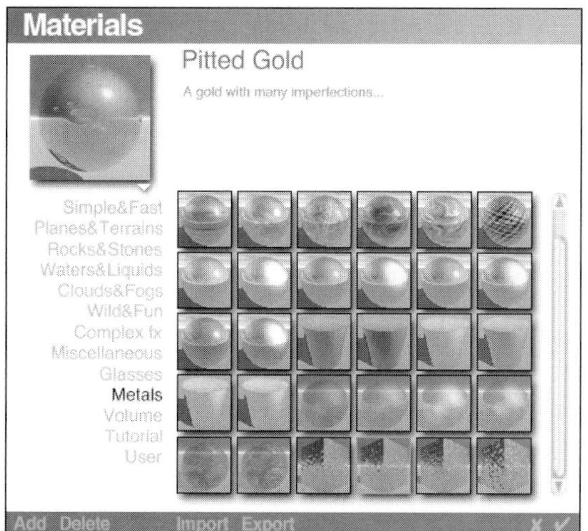

Figure 3.10
The Metals Materials presets.

- Use one of the Christmas Ball presets to create a material that is both metallic and textured.
- Use the Transparent Aluminum Materials when you stack objects on the Z plane, receding along the Z axis. This creates myriad alternate hues, especially in futuristic cities.

Volume

The Volume Materials presets (shown in Figure 3.11) are made specifically for Volumetric objects. A Volumetric object is one in which the material occupies the space defined by the object (unlike a standard Surface object in which the material is simply applied to the object's surface). Volumetric Materials have three dimensions, so keep in mind that they have shadowing and depth. You can use a Volumetric Materials preset as is, or you can customize it for a variety of effects. Some interesting options include:

- Apply the Toxic Slap Clouds material to a sphere to create the cloud surface of a hot planet. Do this on several spheres and animate them for a layered, volatile atmosphere.
- Use Slick and Bumpy for decaying architecture. Simply apply this material to a cube.
- Blood Corpuscles can emulate a squirming mass of microscopic life.
- The Green Rock material is another Volumetric material that suggests decay. Apply the material to a statue, and you achieve instant antiquity.
- Ball Bearings breaks an object into spherical globules that the camera can fly through.

Note: *You can use Boolean objects to act on Volumetric objects, including the Volumetric Materials applied to them. Turn off Transfer Materials from the Negative Object option in the negative Boolean object's Attributes list so the Volumetric Material remains visible.*

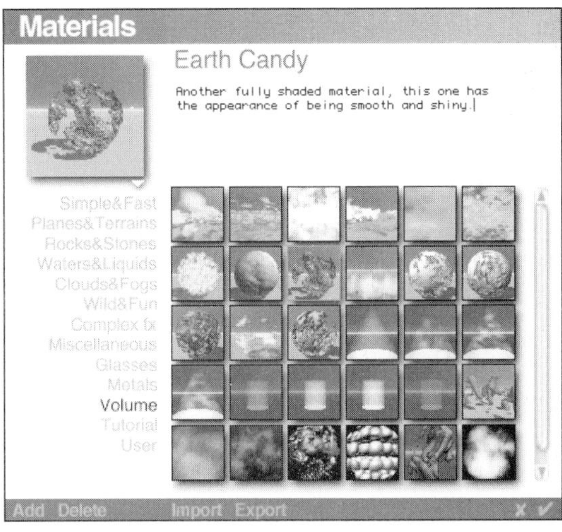

Figure 3.11
The Volume Materials presets.

Volumetric Shading Modes

When you select a Volumetric Material type, three shading modes appear in the Shading Modes list: Flat Shading, Full Shading, and Light Sensitive.

- *Flat Shading*—Flat Shading has no depth.
- *Full Shading*—Full Shading Volumetric Materials are displayed as 3D volumes. Circles become spheres. This allows you to remain aware of the object's dimensionality as you fly through them. Full Shading requires more rendering time.
- *Light Sensitive*—Light Sensitive Volumetric Materials appear only when you shine a light on them, and they take on the color of the light. Light of low-to-medium intensity yields more subtle effects. Objects that use this Shading option can be invisible, materializing only when a light is turned in their direction.

Tutorial

The Tutorial Materials (shown in Figure 3.12) are used for the Bryce tutorials included in the documentation. If you have no use for them, simply delete them. Then you can use the collection to hold customized Materials presets.

User

Use this collection to store your own materials, although you'll also want to save them to another place for a backup. Store your most frequently used materials here while saving all your customized collections outside Bryce for future reference or to trade with other users. See Figure 3.13.

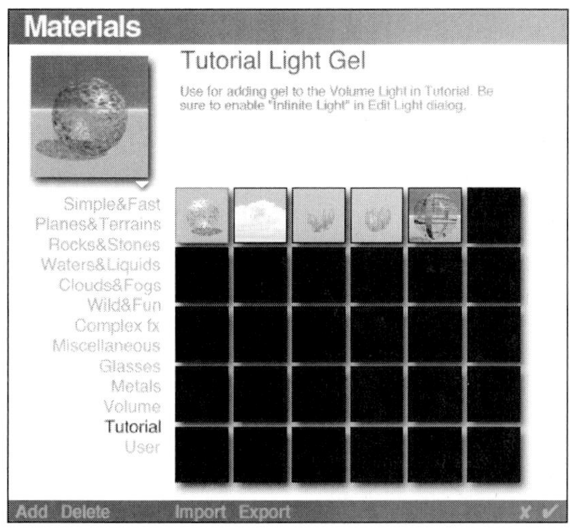

Figure 3.12
(Left) The Tutorial Materials presets.

Figure 3.13
(Right) The User Materials presets.

The Materials Lab

A general principle behind learning a creative discipline is "play equals knowledge." The more you play, the more knowledge you gain. Play is devoid of "making mistakes." In fact, play thrives on exploring unconditionally, with no judgment of the results. Through play, you eventually find things you like, and these results lead you to other explorations and discoveries. Your capabilities grow, and you can repeat processes that lead to known results. This is how the complex becomes simple, and your favorite results become your trademark.

Learning how to create materials in the Materials Lab is a good example of the "play equals knowledge" principle. Begin by simply playing around and seeing what happens when you tweak a control or import a texture. One day, you will realize that you can exactly (or closely) intuit what will result if you do this or that in the Materials Lab. That's when you can claim mastery. You will also realize (especially if you have experience developing materials in other 3D applications) that Bryce's module for developing unusual materials is among the most powerful.

The Materials Lab Roadmap

Your first look at the Materials Lab can be daunting, and might even cause an anxiety attack. After all, it is a complex interface at first sight. But not to worry. With a little knowledge and a lot of exploration, you'll find that the Materials Lab (shown in Figure 3.14) is a friendly and fun place.

The following describes each element that is labeled in Figure 3.14:

A. This is the Materials Preview. You can see the material applied to a primitive object or to the object selected in the Working window. Use the Close-Up option to get a zoomed view.

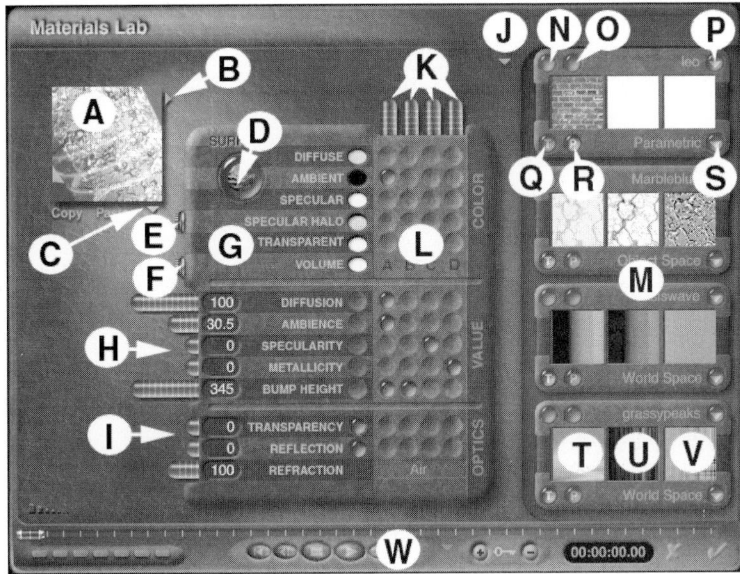

Figure 3.14
The Materials Lab interface. (See the following text for an explanation for each of the elements.)

B. Click here to open the Materials presets collections.

C. Click here to select the primitive object used in the Materials Preview.

D. Clicking here toggles between Surface and Volumetric Materials.

E. Click here to randomize the material. When you have some play time, keep clicking here and see which materials you wind up with. Save the ones you like, or customize further. Randomizing is a simple and useful way to develop hundreds of new materials at one sitting. Randomizing steps you through new patterns.

F. Click here to reset the material to its default attributes.

G. The Material Channels are shown here. You may assign a color or a texture to each of the Material Channels. Four textures, each of which may be either a Procedural or Image Texture, can be used throughout a material. The components of these textures may be refined in either the Deep Texture Editor or the Picture Room.

H. These sliders allow you to control the intensity of an attribute within the material mix.

I. These sliders adjust the Transparency, Reflection, and Refraction Optics Channels. Refraction is the ability of a material to bend light rays. Bryce uses the universal Refraction Index to determine how light is refracted by a material. The refraction controls in Bryce range from 0 to 300. Light rays are bent as they pass through transparent objects. This control would not apply to opaque objects that either bounce the light off or absorb it. See Table 3.1.

Table 3.1 The Refraction settings relate to real-world materials as follows.

Material	Refraction Number
Air	100-plus
Crown Glass	152
Crystal	200
Diamond	242
Emerald	157
Glass	150 through 190
Ice	131
Lapis Lazuli	161
Quartz	155 through 165
Ruby and Sapphire	177
Salt	155 through 165
Topaz	161
Vacuum	100
Water	133

J. Click on this area to add special properties to the material. You can give the material fuzzy edges, or you can translate the material as a light. You can toggle the material's ability to cast and/or receive shadows, and you can alter a number of other features. Objects shaded with the Light mode appear transparent and self-illuminating. All the options on this drop-down list are Shading Modes or Shading Mode modifiers.

K. These Color, Value, and Bump sliders increase or decrease the respective attributes in the textures below the ABCD Channel columns.

L. Placing a button or buttons in the Channel indents means that the information of that specific material quality is taken from the texture data in the related channel (ABCD). The button can be placed to draw data from only one texture (ABC or D) for each channel.

M. These four areas give you a preview of the data in each texture (ABCD). The areas also provide access to controls for customizing each texture.

N. Click on this area to access controls for altering the size, rotation, and displacement of the selected texture.

O. Click on this button on the Texture Source Editor to edit the texture. If you're working on a Procedural Texture, clicking here takes you to the Deep Texture Editor. If you're working on a Picture Texture, you enter the Picture Editor. See the "Using The Picture Editor" section later in this chapter for more information.

P. Click on this area to select a Procedural Texture from one of six categories: Basic, Bump, Clouds, Sand, Rocks, and Psychedelic. Apply them to whatever texture is selected, from *A* to *D*.

Q. Click here to make the texture a Procedural Texture.

R. Click on the Picture Editor button to make the texture a Bitmap Texture.

S. Click here to open the Mapping Options dialog box. Select a mapping type for applying the material to the selected object.

T. This preview represents the Color Map for the Procedural Texture as it relates to the Diffuse and Ambient components.

U. This preview represents the Alpha Map for the Procedural Texture as it relates to the Transparency component.

V. This preview represents the Bump Map (applied with the Bump Map slider) for the Procedural Texture. Procedural Textures are 3D textures that have three different types of output: Color, Alpha, and Bump. Refer to the Bryce user guide for an explanation of how these types of output are used differently by the Material Channels.

   If the texture is a Bitmap Texture, these preview areas represent the Color Map and its associated Alpha (or Transparency) Channel. The type of previews shown depends on whether a Procedural or Image Texture is chosen. The map types are Texture Color, Texture Value (the Alpha Channel for an Image Texture), and Texture Bump. These component headings are the same whether a Procedural or Image Texture are chosen.

W. This area contains the Animation controls. (Animation is covered in Chapter 5.)

Materials Lab Tips

By now, you have no doubt explored the Materials Lab on your own. Here are some important guidelines to remember when you develop customized materials in this environment:

- Be sure to save most of your customized materials to disk rather than to Bryce's internal collections (use the internal collections only for the materials you use most). This opens up more space for materials you create later.
- Use the Random Mapping type to create chaotic and fractal materials.

AB AND ABC CHANNEL MIXING

Bryce offers two magical ways to combine more than one ABCD Channel to create composite mixed materials. Each of these techniques is unique to Bryce 3D. These techniques are named according to the channels they address: AB and ABC. In general, AB mixing allows you to blend the A and B Channels so that the information in each is composited on the selected object in an altitude-sensitive manner. The data in the A Channel is written to the bottom half of the object; the B Channel data is written to the top half. ABC mixes are a little different. The data is written so that a mix of the data from A and B is then mixed with the Alpha Channel data of C.

- Take a picture of the entire scene and save it. Load the saved picture as a Bitmap (Picture)Texture and apply it as a reflection map to an object. You will see the scene reflected in all the objects targeted with the reflection map. This technique, sometimes called *environmental mapping,* is used in many applications as an alternative to raytracing.
- When you use different textures in the Ambient and Diffuse Channels, you create a material that shows one texture (Diffuse based) in light and another (Ambient based) in shadow.
- When a Transparency value is set for a texture, that texture's Alpha Channel determines which areas are transparent. The Transparency slider remains at zero. Applying more transparency makes a greater percentage of the Color Map transparent.
- By setting the Reflection value for a texture, you create reflections mapped to the that texture's Alpha Channel. The reflections appear only in the darker areas of the Alpha Channel. You can create surfaces whose lighter elements are not reflective (for example, a slab of wood that reflects objects placed on it but also allows the grain of the wood to show through).

About The Bump Channel

The Bump Channel in the Materials Lab deserves special attention. This version of Bryce introduces the ability to set the intensity of the Bump Channel to values less than 100 and greater than 100. (The actual limits are now -999.99 and 999.99.) When you set the intensity below -200 or above 200, the dark areas that represent the dents or crevasses in the material are overemphasized. The material starts to look like evenly dented metal or crumpled paper. It's a good idea to use these maximized intensities sparingly in your projects. Otherwise, the materials will compete with the rest of the image content for the viewer's interest.

One way to use the Bump Channel to create materials is to apply a texture to only the Bump Channel while leaving all other Material Channels free of textures. This makes the Bump texture look deeper in the final material, leaving Diffusion and Ambient Channel determinants for hue alone. The Diamond Plate material in the Miscellaneous Materials presets provides an excellent example of how this works. This technique is especially useful when the texture is geometric in nature (that is, straight-edged) rather than organic. Also note the following:

- The dark areas created by depressions in a Bump Map show the texture selected for the Ambience mapping.

- Use a Bump Map that takes its information from a texture other than the one used for the Diffuse and Ambient components. Use this technique to add noise or dirt to an otherwise smooth material.
- Explore the possibility of using negative Bump settings for a different look. When you do this with a text image, the text is embossed into the object.
- If you use a Bump Map that matches the Diffuse or Ambient Channel, another way to create some organic (or chaotic) randomization is to rotate the Bump Map on the Z axis. In order to do this effectively while maintaining the Diffusion and Ambient Channels, use a clone of the original map for the Bump Channel.
- Selecting the Random mapping type always adds a splatter of chaotic elements to a targeted channel. This technique is especially useful in the Bump component: It adds a decayed look to a material (especially when the Bump is lower than -100 or higher than 100).

Using The Deep Texture Editor

Clicking on the Procedural Texture toggle (letter Q in Figure 3.14) and then on the Edit button (letter O in Figure 3.14) takes you to the Deep Texture Editor (shown in Figure 3.15). Use the Deep Texture Editor to work at the most basic level of a texture. The Deep Texture Editor is available from each of the four textures in the Materials Lab.

The Deep Texture Editor is one of the most comprehensive Procedural Texture development tools offered by any 3D application. You can use it to develop textures and materials for other 2D and 3D applications. The following describes each element that is labeled in Figure 3.15:

A. Click on one of these icons to control whether the preview of your customized texture appears applied to a plane, a cube, or a sphere.
B. Click on one, two, or three of these buttons to activate the texture components. A texture can contain up to three components in the Deep Texture Editor. You don't need to use all three components; just one or two will also do the trick.
C. Click here to select from the list of options that will determine how Components 1 and 2 are combined. Read the Bryce documentation for details regarding the influence of each option on the material.
D. Click here to select from the list of options that will determine how Components 2 and 3 are combined. Read the Bryce documentation for details regarding the influence of each option on the material.

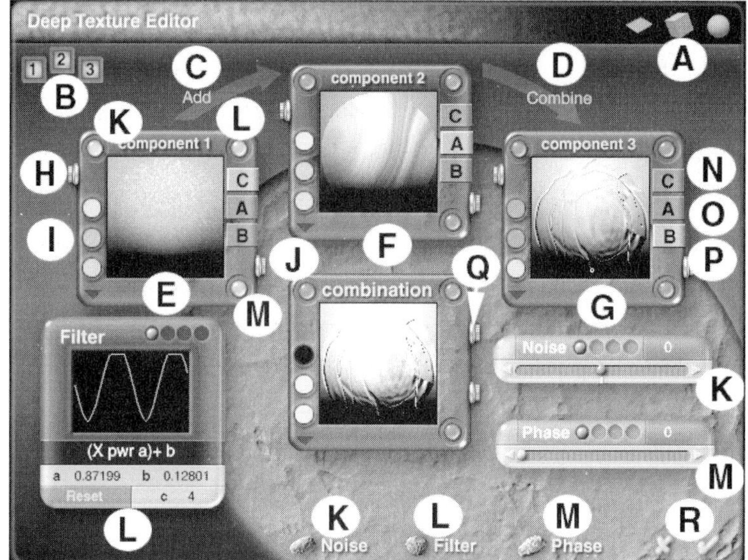

Figure 3.15
The Deep Texture Editor's interface and controls. (See the following text for an explanation for each of the elements.)

E. The Preview and Controls screen for component 1.

F. The Preview and Controls screen for component 2.

G. The Preview and Controls screen for component 3.

H. Each of the Component Preview screens includes this little button on the left. Clicking on this button resets the contents to their defaults. (This can be a lifesaver after you have explored many complex alterations.)

I. These three color pots are featured on the left of each Component screen. Each component in the mix can have up to three colors as its hue element. One of the easiest ways to customize a Material preset is to alter its color elements, which you can do with these color pots.

J. This button is featured in the lower-right of each Component screen. Click on the button, and a new randomized texture appears. You can do this repeatedly until you see something you like.

K. Clicking on this button in any of the Component screens (or on the global button labeled with the same letter) launches the Noise Controller. Move the Noise Controller's slider left or right to control the amount of noise in the targeted Component window. (Noise adds pixelated elements to the texture.)

L. Clicking on this button in any of the Component screens (or on the global button labeled with the same letter) launches the Filter dialog box. Here you can interactively alter the waveform of any Component Texture by moving the mouse in the waveform display. You can also select a different algorithm (formula) for any Component Texture and apply changes to the numeric variables for that texture. If math is not a strong point for you, just play around and see what happens. Learning in the Deep Texture Editor (and especially in the Filter dialog box) comes by doing.

M. Clicking on this button in the any of the Component screens (or on the global button labeled with the same letter) launches the Phase Controller. By moving the Phase Controller's slider left or right, you can alter the amplitude or turbulence of the noise. Refer to the user guide for a more detailed description.

N. Clicking on the *C* in a Component screen causes that Component Texture to control color (hue or other color-channel options are dependent upon your other settings).

O. Clicking on the *A* in a Component screen causes that Component Texture to control the texture's Alpha element (the source of the material's Alpha information). Alpha is used primarily for Transparency modifications.

P. Clicking on the *B* in a Component screen causes that Component Texture to control the material's Bump Map.

Q. This button launches the Deep Texture Editor Component presets, which you can use as a basis for further modification. Your final material is previewed on the combination screen and created from a combination of one, two, or three Component elements. Watch this space carefully to see how each step in the editing process alters the material.

R. Click on the *X* to cancel your modifications and return to the Materials Lab. Click the check mark to accept the modifications and return to the Materials Lab.

Deep Texture Editing

If you have not explored the Deep Texture Editor before, here's a procedure that may help you begin:

1. Select an object, and open the Materials Lab. Place a dot in the Texture A column of the Diffuse Channel. Activate Texture A's source editor. Texture A should be set to Procedural.
2. In the Deep Texture Editor, turn on all three component lights at the upper left. (The lights turn green when you turn them on.)

3. In Component 1, activate only *C* (for Color), and turn *A* (for Alpha) and *B* (for Bump) off. Component 1 now contains only the Color Map data.
4. In Component 2, turn on *A*, and turn off *B* and *C*. Component 2 now contains only the Alpha component.
5. In Component 3, turn on *B*, and turn off *A*. Component 3 now contains only the Bump component.
6. Hit the randomize button on Component 1 as many times as you want, and stop when you see a texture you like.
7. Repeat the process for Component 2.
8. Repeat the process again for Component 3.
9. Go to the curved arrow that connects Component 1 and Component 2. This arrow contains a word that indicates how data from Component 1 is being mixed with Component 2. Click and hold on that word, and a drop-down list of choices appears. (Refer to the Bryce user guide for a further explanation.) Explore each choice, and watch the Combination window for a preview you like.
10. Repeat the process over the curved arrow that indicates how Component 2 is mixing data with Component 3.
11. Explore the Filter window on each component and on the Combination Preview by selecting the appropriate button from the top of the Filter window. By clicking on and dragging in the space in which you see a mathematical curve, you can alter the way that data is filtered in the selected Component or Combination window. You can also click on the name of the math function and select another from the list. Explore the options and watch the preview in the Combination window.
12. Add or subtract noise and alter the Phase in the appropriate control panels. When everything looks interesting, click on the check mark.

In the Materials Lab, tweak the texture you just designed for an original material to customize it further. Click on the check mark and render the scene to preview the material you just created. Deep Texture Editing works on both Surface and Volumetric Textures.

> ***Note:*** *When you activate the Altitude transition formula between two components (with Color activated in each component), the textured material you develop will be height sensitive. The color changes in relation to height. This is how many of the Terrain presets were created.*

Using The Picture Editor

To access the Picture Editor, click on the Image Texture toggle button (letter *R* in Figure 3.14) and then on the Edit Texture Source Editor button (letter *O* in Figure 3.14).

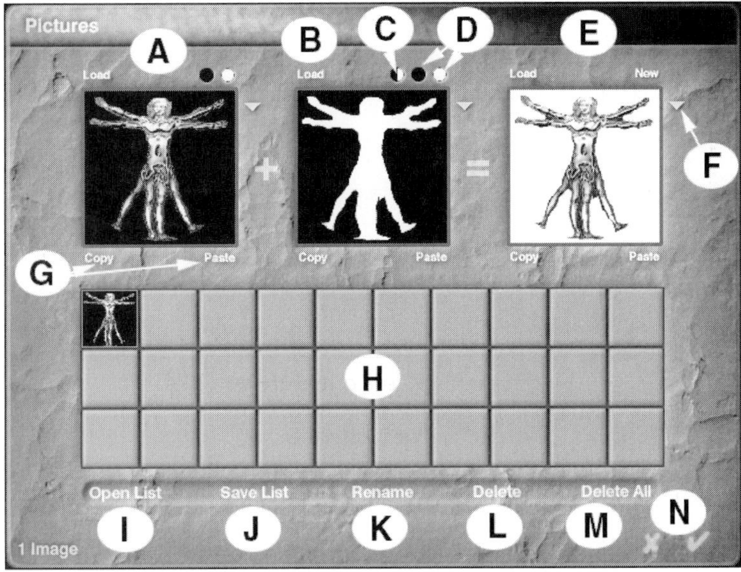

Figure 3.16
The Picture Editor interface. (See the following text for an explanation of the elements.)

You can use the Picture Editor (shown in Figure 3.16) to integrate bitmaps into a material. You can develop a material from a single bitmap, from a combination of up to four bitmaps, or from a combination of bitmaps and Procedural Textures.

You can also use the Picture Editor to apply imported bitmapped graphics to selected objects. In addition, you can integrate bitmaps into the Materials Lab as one (or several) of the ABCD channels, mixing bitmaps and Procedural Textures. The resulting composites greatly expand your ability to create unusual materials. Regarding file formats, here are some important things to remember:

- You can import bitmapped images in any of the common file formats.
- However, you're limited to the PICT (Mac) or BMP (Windows) formats when you create and import an Alpha mask into the Alpha component. Why Bryce enforces this Alpha Map format limitation is unknown.

Details Of The Picture Editor

The following describes each element that is labeled in Figure 3.16:

A. This is the first preview window; it displays the bitmap's image content. Click on the black or white buttons to the right to remove the bitmap and replace it with a black or white image area.

B. This is the second preview window; it displays the Alpha Channel content. The Alpha Channel or mask determines which areas of the bitmap (or picture file) are visible. The white areas of the Alpha mask define visible areas of the bitmap. Image areas under the black area of the Alpha Channel remain masked, or not visible. If the Alpha Channel contains shades of gray, these result in levels of transparency in the mask corresponding to the value of the gray.

C. Click on this black and white button to invert the Alpha Channel.

D. Clicking on one of these eight black or white buttons removes the Alpha Channel content and replaces it with a black or white image area. A black area blocks the entire bitmap from appearing in the final picture. A white image area in the Alpha Channel causes the bitmap to be displayed with no masked areas.

E. This is the final preview window; it shows the completed bitmap (picture based) texture.

F. This toggle-arrow, which appears on the upper right of every preview window in the Picture Editor, is your gateway to unlimited bitmap-based textures. By clicking on this arrow, you can access your Photoshop-compatible plug-ins. You can use Photoshop-compatible plug-ins in the Picture Editor to create thousands of textures (for use as entire materials or as components of materials). I'll have more to say about this a little later in this chapter.

G. Use these buttons to copy the contents from one preview window and paste them into another.

H. This is the Picture Library area, which presents all the bitmaps you have referenced for creating textures in your current document. Click in any empty image box to load a bitmap into the library.

I. Click on this button to open a saved image library.

J. Click on this button to save the current image library for use in other projects.

K. Click on this button to rename an image used in the image library.

L. Click on this button to delete the selected bitmap from the library.

M. Click on this button to delete all the images from the library.

N. Click on this button to cancel or to apply the selected bitmap as a texture and return to the Materials Lab.

Special Considerations For The Picture Editor Alpha Channel

Within the Picture Editor, you can use the Alpha Channel in three ways. The first is to use no Alpha Channel: This places the full-color image (and its background) on the selected object. This is useful for creating a book cover, a hanging painting, or an image on a TV screen (these are only a few examples).

The second option is to copy the color image to the Alpha Channel. This creates areas of transparency where the image is darkest or areas of highest luminance. Use this option to create interesting semitransparent materials on objects.

The third option is to use a bitmap application to create a separate Alpha Channel for the image: This separate Alpha Channel image (which must be saved as a PICT file on Macs or as a BMP file on Windows systems) may outline the image content as a silhouette. Alpha Masks can be created with grayscale values that will create a mask with levels of transparency corresponding to the value of the grayscale. This is the same semitransparent effect described previously for using a color image as an Alpha Mask. Remember that luminance in an image is not dependant upon hue. Loading this separate, two-color image allows you to apply partially transparent bitmapped images to an object. This is vital for mapping human, animal, or any other bitmap image to a 2D plane. In all cases, the Materials Lab's Transparency Channel should get the data from the A, B, C, or D component that contains the bitmap. The Transparency Channel setting should almost always be set to zero (the default). If you use a setting other than zero, you will force more of the image's luminance areas to become increasingly transparent.

Alpha Masks

If you want to remove the background from an imported bitmap, the Picture Editor's second preview window must contain an Alpha Mask that duplicates the silhouette of the image. This allows the final image to be composited as needed. Follow these steps:

1. Open the bitmap in a bitmap application (such as Painter, PhotoPaint, Photoshop, or another suitable application). Using the Magic Wand tool and the Paint Bucket Fill tool (or their equivalents), select the background and fill it with solid 100 percent black.

2. Make the rest of the image (the part you want to appear in Bryce) solid white.
3. Save this image in the same folder as the original bitmap. Make sure that the total pixel size of this image and the original are exactly the same. On a Mac, save the new image as a PICT; on Windows systems, save the file as a BMP.
4. In Bryce, load the full-color bitmap in the first preview window, and load the two-color image you just created in the second preview window (the Alpha Channel window). You can reverse the Alpha Channel by clicking on the black and white button above the Alpha Channel (letter *C* in Figure 3.16).
5. Apply the bitmap to the selected ABCD component in the Materials Lab. Make sure the Transparency, Diffuse, and Ambient Channels are set to the bitmap component. Use either Object or Parametric mapping, whichever works best with the targeted object. Your bitmap is now a material for use in your Bryce document.

Bitmaps As Objects

I already touched on this information in Chapter 2, but it's definitely worth repeating here. Bitmaps can be substituted for 3D objects in your scene when you map them to a 2D plane, especially when their backgrounds are made transparent. Many of the images in this book's color section use this technique. Substituting a bitmap image for a 3D object consumes considerably less memory and makes rendering faster. Bitmapped planes are objects with no depth, so you can't orbit them. Used as background elements, bitmapped planes add variety to your 3D world. The object you should be mapping to in your world should be the 2D Picture Object from the Create toolbar.

Randomizing Bitmap Textures

You can apply random mapping to bitmap textures. This breaks up the identifiable image content but utilizes the color palette of the image, creating randomized variations. You may have to adjust the size of the image (to between -2 and +2 rather than zero) in order to see identifiable parts of the bitmap. Used with this technique, colorful bitmaps provide the greatest texturing possibilities, especially when Symmetrical Tiling is turned on. Follow these steps:

1. With an object selected, open the Materials Lab and activate Component A by placing buttons in the column representing Component

A: Diffuse and Ambient (color), Diffusion and Ambience (value), and Transparency (optics) channels. Click on the *P* (Image Texture) button, and then on the Texture Source Editor button.

2. Load a bitmap. No Alpha Channel is required, so set the Alpha Channel to white. Click on the check mark to apply the changes, and return to the Materials Lab.

3. From the Mapping Options, select Random. This scatters the bitmap's elements across the object. Resize the bitmap in the Transformations palette, if necessary, while keeping an eye on the Nano Preview to see the results. Explore the Symmetrical Tiling function. When you're satisfied with the image, apply the changes and return to your document for rendering.

Creating Bitmap Materials Galore

Matching the quality and variety provided by Bryce's Procedural Textures is quite a challenge, but the Bitmap Texture methods do this and more. Bryce's Procedural Textures are plentiful but limited. However, the number of unusual and startling bitmap-based materials you can develop in Bryce is unlimited. (Or if there is a limit, it is defined only by the number of bitmaps you can access.)

You can create three kinds of bitmap-based materials in Bryce:

- *Materials based on a single bitmapped texture*—Common examples of this type include photographs of real-world materials (for example, wood, bricks, or fungus). This type also includes graphics developed in other applications. These materials might or might not make use of a bitmap Alpha Channel, depending on their use in the document. Customarily, the size of these textures is left at zero in the Materials Lab, so only one instance of the image appears when mapped to the object. You can also use Scale Pict Size under the tiling options to apply only one instance.

- *Materials based on more than one bitmapped texture*—By using this method (and by selecting two or even three Diffuse and Ambient component channels), you can create materials that combine wood and metal, flesh and scales, or any other combination desired. Simply hold down Shift and activate multiple channels for that material. To get the right material, you'll have to explore different size and rotation options after selecting the proper bitmaps. One or more of the bitmap textures can have Transparency applied, generating an even wider variety of results.

- *Materials that mix bitmaps and Procedural Textures*—This results in infinity squared as the potential number of materials you can create. Any of the material's four component channels can contain either a bitmap or a Procedural Texture. There are no rules to limit you; just play around until you generate something you like. The potential for material complexity and variety is enormous.

The Plug-In Method Of Materials Creation

Let's review some of the ways you can use Photoshop-compatible plug-ins in the Picture Editor. I have already described:

- *Using a plug-in or plug-ins to alter the content of the first bitmap channel*—This alters both the hue and Bump component of a texture.
- *Using a plug-in to alter the bitmap-based texture's Alpha Channel*—This alters the areas of the image that are transparent (provided that the transparency is applied to the texture Color component in the Materials Lab).
- *Using plug-ins to control both the original bitmap and the Alpha Channel*—This results in an unlimited number of textures from a single bitmap, without an Alpha Channel.

Even if these were the only methods available, they would be enough. But guess what—there are more! Bryce provides another, tremendously exciting way to create materials using bitmap-based textures, and this method isn't hinted at in the documentation. The results can be startling, and this method opens a door to a new world of material creation options.

Creating An Infinite Variety Of Original Plug-In Textures

Before I describe this method and walk you through several examples, it is vital that you are familiar with the use of Photoshop-compatible plug-ins. The best way to gain this familiarity is to acquire as many plug-ins as you can, load them into the bitmap application you use the most, and take the time to explore the range of their creative use. I'm assuming that most of you have already done that: People who use 3D applications have usually come to them by first immersing themselves in 2D-image creation, and 2D plug-in use is part of that learning curve.

The magical part of this technique is that you do not need to import a single bitmap in order to achieve a final bitmap-based texture. (You get something from nothing.)

Here's why and how it works. In the Picture Editor, letter *D* in Figure 3.16, you see black and white circular buttons. You can find these buttons on the upper-right edge of the first preview window (indicated by letter *A*) and the second preview window (Alpha Channel). The window contains a solid white or solid black bitmap, even if the window had included only the default hermetic man when you open the Picture Editor. It is important that you realize the implications of this: By clicking the black or white circular button over the first preview window or the Alpha Channel preview window, you create a solid black or white bitmap in that texture component place.

You have a solid black or white bitmap, but what next? 2D plug-ins work on bitmaps, regardless of the bitmap's content. You need to understand three types of plug-ins: area-based, media- and deformation-based, and generative-based.

- Area-based Photoshop-compatible plug-ins work on a bitmap after you have selected an area within the image, usually with a Marquee tool. Bryce has no Marquee tools in this version, so you can avoid the use of area-based plug-ins for any texture you might want to generate or customize. Perhaps a future version of Bryce will contain a Marquee selection tool or tools.
- Media-based plug-ins alter the media look of a bitmap. They change a photo into what appears to be a watercolor or an oil painting, or they give it a pen-and-ink or pixelated look. You can apply these plug-ins to solid-color bitmaps, but the results are invisible. Media-based plug-ins need areas of different hues in order to work. Deformation-based plug-ins (such as warp, ripple, and spherize) need something to deform. Deforming a single color bitmap in 2D results in no apparent deformation at all.
- Generative-based plug-ins create something from nothing. They transform a single-color bitmap into a multitude of colors or grays, and they are perfect for use as material-creation tools in the Bryce Picture Editor.

Of these three types of plug-ins, only generative-based plug-ins are useful for the next step in this process.

Useful Bitmap-Texture Creation Plug-Ins

A wide array of generative-based plug-ins is available, and no two digital artists have identical collections. I find a number of Photoshop-compatible plug-ins extremely valuable for use with this texture-creation method:

Note: *Bitmapped textures do not work as Bump Channels, so you have to create Bumps from Procedural Textures. Also note that having a series of alternate single-colored bitmaps available will add more instant colorizing options. An alternate method for colorizing (or tinting) the resulting bitmap is to apply the plug-in to the Alpha Channel alone, keeping the first window black or white in the Picture Editor. Then, back in the Materials Lab, keep Ambient Color set to a hue of your choice while the Ambience Value is set to the bitmap component. Keep the default transparency setting in this case.*

- *Xenofex from Alien Skin Software*—You can use these filters with a white bitmap or with or a multihued bitmap. This collection includes several filters that produce exciting materials in Bryce. Apply them to the first image channel (although applying them to the Alpha Channel can also lead to interesting results). The filters that are especially useful include Baked Earth (especially Big Shiny Pieces, Rock Wall, and Dry Lake Bed), Constellation (especially Oil 'n' Water, Pebbles 'n' Glue, and The Eighth Dimension), Lightning (especially Neon Spaghetti, Twisting Vines, and Raging Rivers), Little Fluffy Clouds (especially Mustard Gas, and Spilled Guts), and Stain (especially Dried Blood, Coffee, and Rust Spots).
- *Kai's Power Tools (KPT) 3 from MetaCreations*—Use the Page Curl filter on an object meant to look like a piece of paper, and it will create the appearance of another piece of paper over the first one. The Gradient Designer includes thousands of spectacular, customizable, multicolored bitmap textures, arranged in a limitless array of patterns. The Spheroid Designer filter creates globular image elements, ranging from eyeballs to clusters of grapes. The Texture Explorer is the single most valuable Photoshop-compatible filter when it comes to developing new bitmap-based textures for Bryce materials, because it allows you to create a nearly limitless number of texture variations.
- *KPT 5 from MetaCreations*—The images created with the Frax4D filter are stunning 3D graphics in themselves. Map the resulting images to picture planes, and make the backgrounds transparent by setting the transparency to the image's Alpha Channel. In your Bryce world, use these images as objects in the distance. Map the images to solid objects to create the look of bitmapped volumetrics. If you need to create rich materials flecked with gold swirls or convoluted distant shapes that emulate energy swirls, use the FraxFlame filter. Use the FraxPlorer filter to create Fractal images as texture maps. The KPT Orb-It filter creates collections of bubbles, and you can use it in Bryce to create bubble effects by mapping to spheres.
- *Knoll Lens Flare Pro from Puffin Designs*—This Photoshop-compatible plug-in creates the most realistic lens flare effects on the planet. Use it with transparency to create floating star objects or against a black background to map a flat vertical sky plane. The flares are commonly mapped to 2D faces, but they can be mapped to any 3D object for unusual effects.

You can find other Photoshop-compatible filters that offer additional bitmap texture-creation capabilities within Bryce. Once you have created a texture, you can continue to use filters to customize it further. The advantage of using this method within Bryce is that the resulting bitmap (when saved as a texture in the Materials library) can be exported to another machine, and the other machine won't need the same filters.

External Bitmap Texture Creation Applications To Lust After

Although dozens of applications are sufficient for creating or customizing bitmaps for use in Bryce, I consider two applications essential for this purpose:

- *Adobe After Effects*—Although many digital artists who use After Effects think of it as a post-production animation tool, it is much more than that. Many of the developers who write Photoshop filters port them to After Effects as animation effects plug-ins. Some developers are exclusively devoted to the creation of After Effects plug-ins, making After Effects as powerful an effects engine as Photoshop. You can use After Effects to create both bitmaps and animations, making this an excellent environment for developing bitmaps that can be imported into Bryce for use as material components. There are hundreds of effects plug-ins available for After Effects that you will find nowhere else.
- *Painter from MetaCreations*—Painter has many notable tools for creating and customizing bitmaps. It offers one tool in particular—the Image Hose—that makes it a perfect utility for Bryce. The Image Hose "sprays" user-selected images on the image. Although an extensive library of Image Hose "nozzles" is available, I find that the foliage nozzles are especially important for Bryce work. Bruce can't add a wide range of flora to a scene, and that makes landscapes seem somewhat lifeless at times. By using Painter's leaves and flowers Image Hose nozzles and importing them into the Picture Editor, you can create large fields of flowers and leafy trees without paying the rendering cost of creating them with imported 3D objects. (Map the bitmaps to flat planes or spheres for a more 3D-looking effect.) As long as the nozzle elements are sprayed on a black background in Painter (and you create an Alpha Channel image using the technique described in the previous section "Alpha Masks"), you can map the Painter image in Bryce with a transparent background.

Note: *For more information on the filters available for After Effects, see my book,* After Effects 4 In Depth, *which is available from The Coriolis Group.*

50 Original Materials

The Materials folder on this book's companion CD-ROM contains 50 original Surface Materials that you can use and customize in Bryce. What follows is a detailed look at each material and some suggestions for its use. Read the descriptions offered here, and be sure to open each material in the Materials Lab to see what the settings look like. Again, learn by playing.

The first 32 materials described here were created with Procedural Textures. When you load these materials from this book's CD-ROM, be sure to look at the settings in the Materials Lab and the Deep Texture Editor.

Alien Tree

Use this material on grouped spheres to create alien-looking foliage on terrains. The material takes a while to render because of its Transparency component. Alien Tree (shown in Figure 3.17) combines the RedGiant and PurpleRock Procedural Textures. This Volumetric Material's transparency causes it to fade toward the bottom of the object, creating the appearance of hanging leaves. Alien Tree doesn't work on terrains or Infinite Planes, and is it best used on imported objects or Bryce primitive objects.

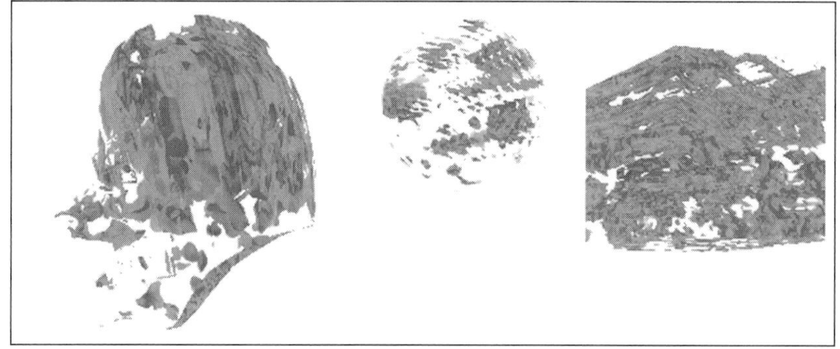

Figure 3.17
The Alien Tree material applied to an imported head, a sphere, and a cube.

Banded Gold

You can use the Banded Gold material (shown in Figure 3.18) on imported objects, primitive objects, terrains, and Infinite Planes. This material is related to the Galvanized Tin material detailed later. The gold bands are height-sensitive, and they blur into a pixelated fog toward the top of the object, looking a lot like a metal cage with frosted glass inside. The Banded Gold material looks more interesting when it is mapped to curved and complex surfaces.

BiGrid 1

The BiGrid 1 material (shown in Figure 3.19) works best when mapped to cubic objects, although you can also use it on imported objects other than

Figure 3.18
The Banded Gold material applied to an imported head, a primitive sphere and cube, a terrain, and an Infinite Plane.

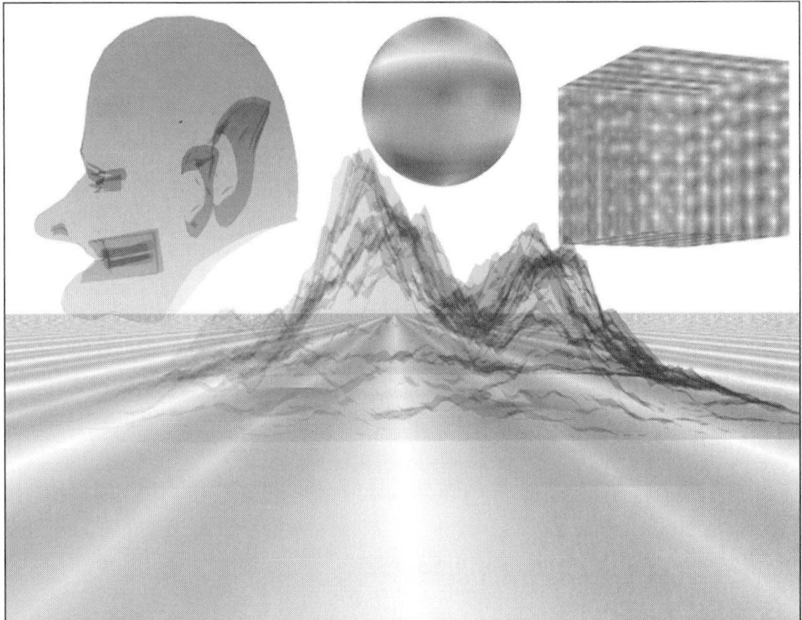

Figure 3.19
The BiGrid 1 material works best when mapped to a cubic object.

cubic primitives, terrains, and even Infinite Planes. When mapped to a terrain, the material creates a 90 percent transparency within the terrain's boundaries. Map this material to a sphere to create an interesting banded planet. This material's design is based on two Gradient Bar Procedurals at different rotations.

BiGrid 2

This variation of the BiGrid 1 material uses different sizes and rotations. Like its cousin, BiGrid 2 works best when mapped to a cubic object. See Figure 3.20.

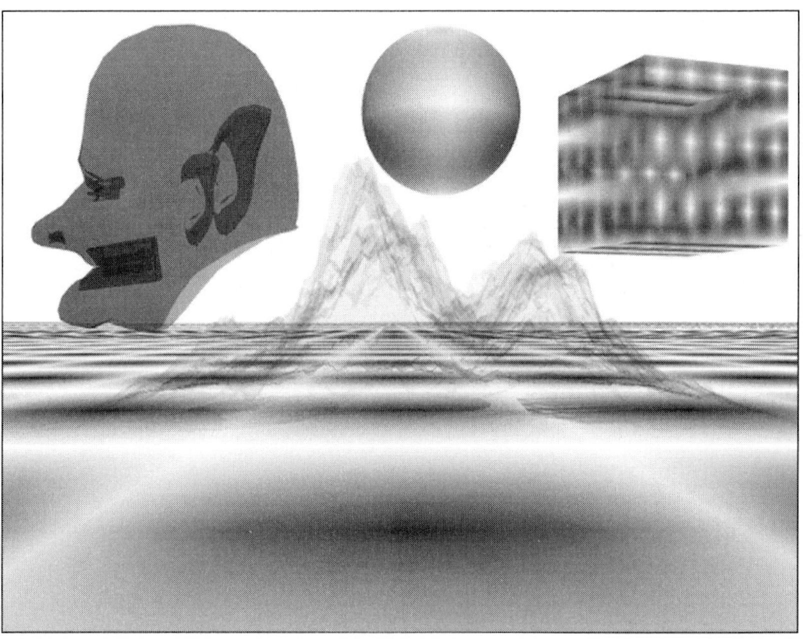

Figure 3.20
The BiGrid 2 material applied to different objects.

Bi-Wood Laminate

The Bi-Wood Laminate material (shown in Figure 3.21) creates the appearance of wood that has a grain running in two directions, which creates an interesting interference patterns. You can map it to imported objects, primitives, terrains, or Infinite Planes with equally interesting results.

Blue Flame

This material modifies the color of the Flame material, creating what looks like blue fire. The Blue Flame material (shown in Figure 3.22) works best when mapped to a sphere.

Cracked Warpaint

This material is composed of three Gradient Vein Procedural Textures, all mapped differently. Although this material (shown in Figure 3.23) works best when mapped to a sphere or an imported model, you can use it with any model type. Use it on an Infinite Plane or other flat surface to create an interesting wood material with a randomized grain.

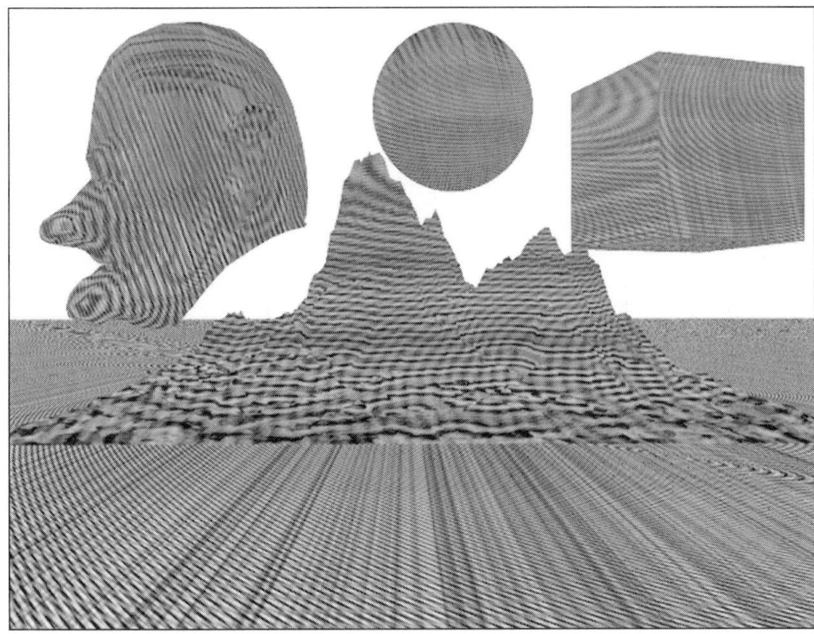

Figure 3.21
The Bi-Wood Laminate material creates intriguing wood patterns.

Figure 3.22
The Blue Flame material can be used on different objects.

Dark Marble

The Dark Marble material is a class act. It looks like the type of marble that would add beauty to a temple column or would serve well as the material in a classic statue or urn. Map it to any type of object. When mapped to an Infinite Plane, Dark Marble creates a dark rocky surface. You can also use it to create believable alien skin and moons. See Figure 3.24.

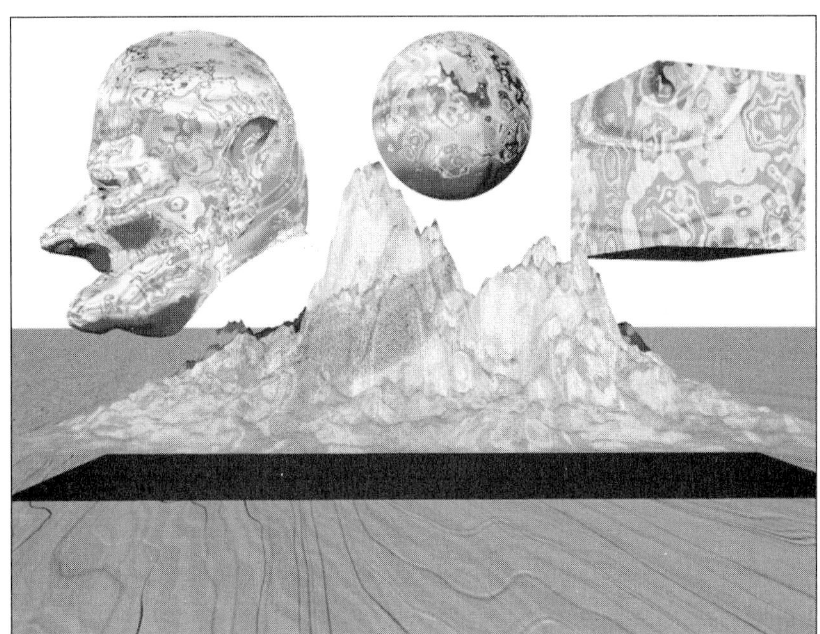

Figure 3.23
The Cracked Warpaint material.

Figure 3.24
The Dark Marble material creates both classic and alien looks.

Decayed Wood

From moldy, blotchy zombie skin to pocked moons, from striated terrains to fungal surfaces, here's a material that suits many purposes. The Decayed Wood material (shown in Figure 3.25) is created with the combination of a Procedural Texture (BlackWhite) and a Bitmap Texture (Mature Wood) from the images on the Bryce 4 CD-ROM.

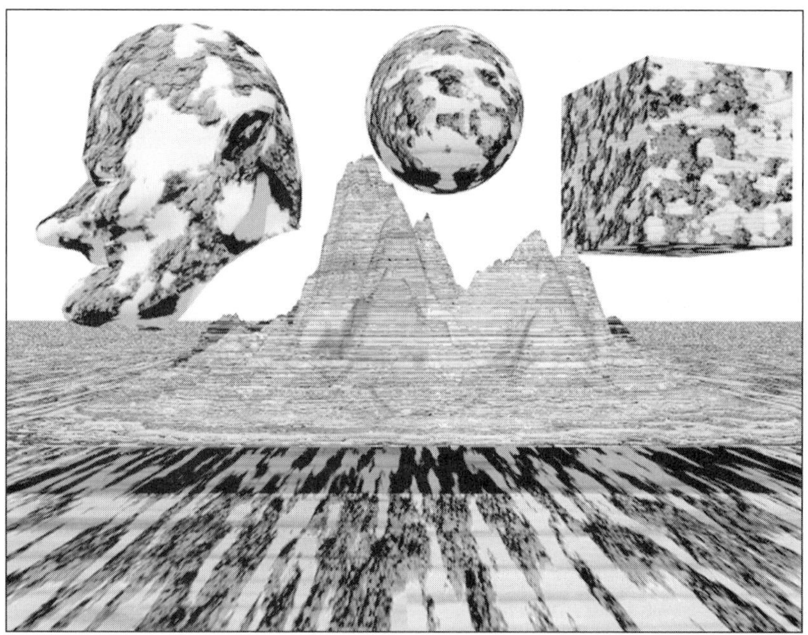

Figure 3.25
The Decayed Wood material looks good on a variety of 3D objects.

DeepSpace

For the best results, map this material to an Infinite Sky Plane or to a 2D Picture object. Placing the camera so that the targeted plane is viewed from a perpendicular angle is also recommended. The DeepSpace material (shown in Figure 3.26) is composed of three Procedural Textures: Nebula, Galaxy, and Stars. The texture was also customized a great deal in the Deep Texture Editor, so be sure to explore the settings.

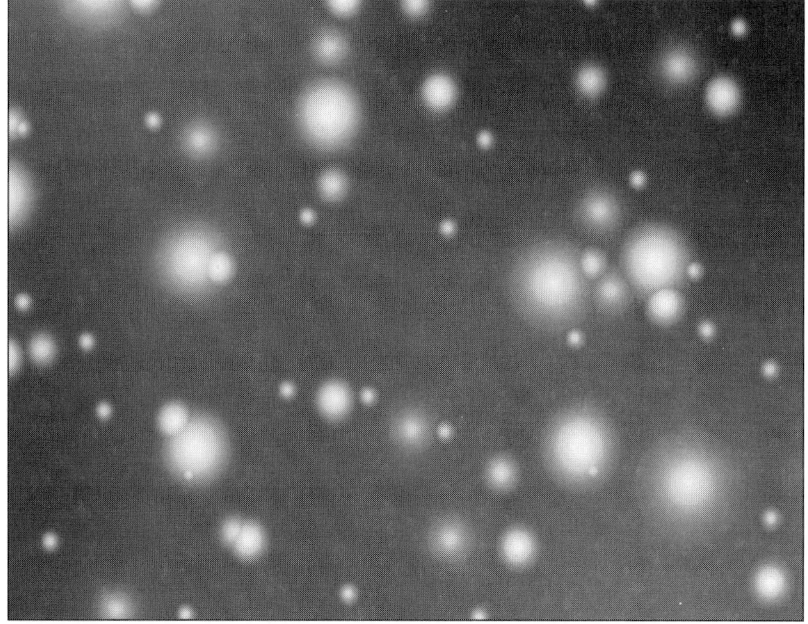

Figure 3.26
The DeepSpace material is just right for cosmic flights of fancy.

ElectroGrid

ElectroGrid is works best when mapped to primitive object surfaces. The material is composed of two Gradient Bar textures: One is Parametric Scale mapped, the other Random mapped. See Figure 3.27.

Figure 3.27
Various objects mapped with the ElectroGrid material.

ElectroSpring

The ElectroSpring material works best when mapped to imported or primitive object types. The ElectroSpring material (shown in Figure 3.28) uses a rotation of the Gradient Bar Procedural Texture to simulate a coiled spring.

Fine Knotwood

Fine Knotwood is a wood material of exceptional quality, featuring dark shadows and gold whorls. Use it for tabletops, sculptures, floors, or anything else that comes to mind. It is a combination of the Mushrooms and Vortex Procedural Textures. See Figure 3.29.

Fog Grid

The Fog Grid material fades to nothing toward the top and bottom of the mapped object. Although Fog Grid works best on spherical objects, it can also yield interesting effects on terrains. You might want to avoid using this material on either cubic objects or on Ground Planes, neither of which show the material at its best. Fog Grid (shown in Figure 3.30) combines three Procedural Textures: Basic Gradient Bar, Structure 21, and Dull Wave.

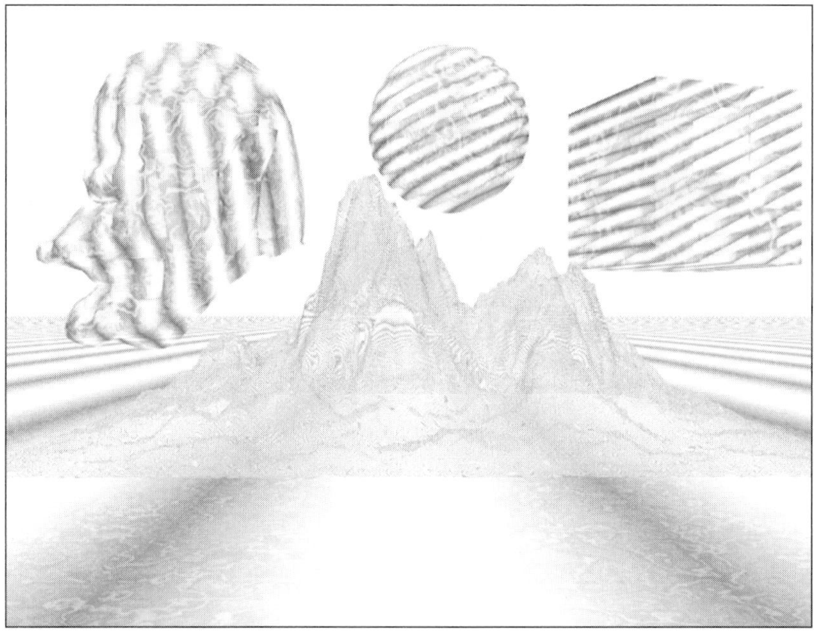

Figure 3.28
The ElectroSpring material adds angled metallic bars to the object's surface.

Figure 3.29
The Fine Knotwood material looks like a dark, rich wood surface.

Galvanized Tin

The Galvanized Tin material, as mentioned previously, is closely related to the Banded Gold material (see Figure 3.18). It features the same look of metal bands enclosing a foggy glass surface. For the best effect, place objects "inside" the object mapped with this material. When using this material on a terrain object, increase the number of bands in the Materials Lab. See Figure 3.31.

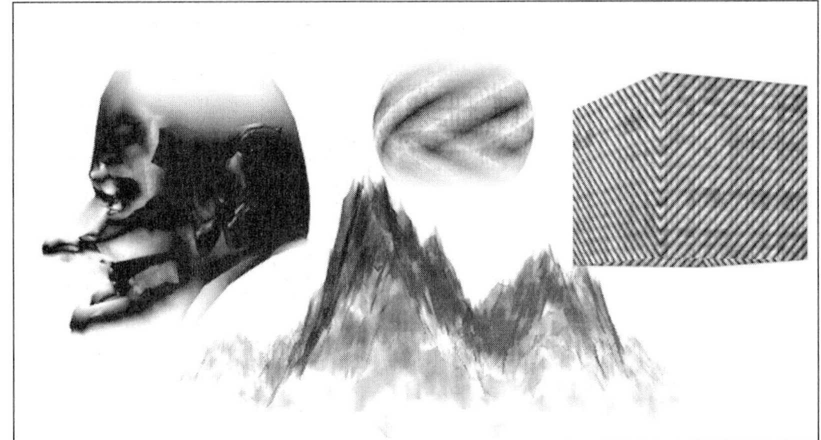

Figure 3.30
Spherical objects and terrains respond best to the Fog Grid material.

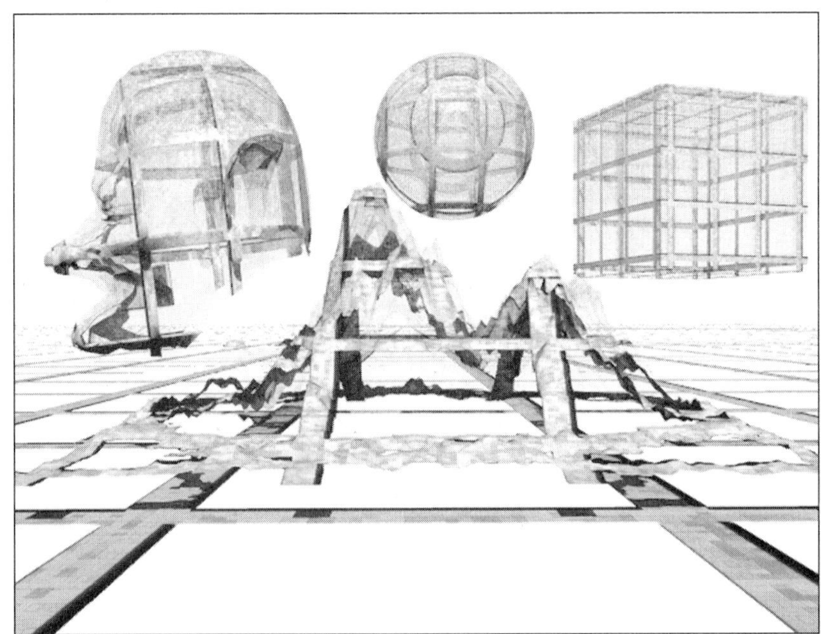

Figure 3.31
The Galvanized Tin material works on all object types, producing different effects for each.

Glow Beads

The Glow Beads material resembles handcrafted beadwork, and it works best on objects that show some curvature. The material (shown in Figure 3.32) was created by combining two Beveled Tile Procedural Textures.

Glowing Coal

The Glowing Coal material is render-intensive, but when you need the effect of a glowing hot surface, it does the trick. The best results are obtained by mapping a rock or terrain, which becomes instantly volcanic. A Ground Plane mapped with this material looks like the surface of a very inhospitable planet. See Figure 3.33.

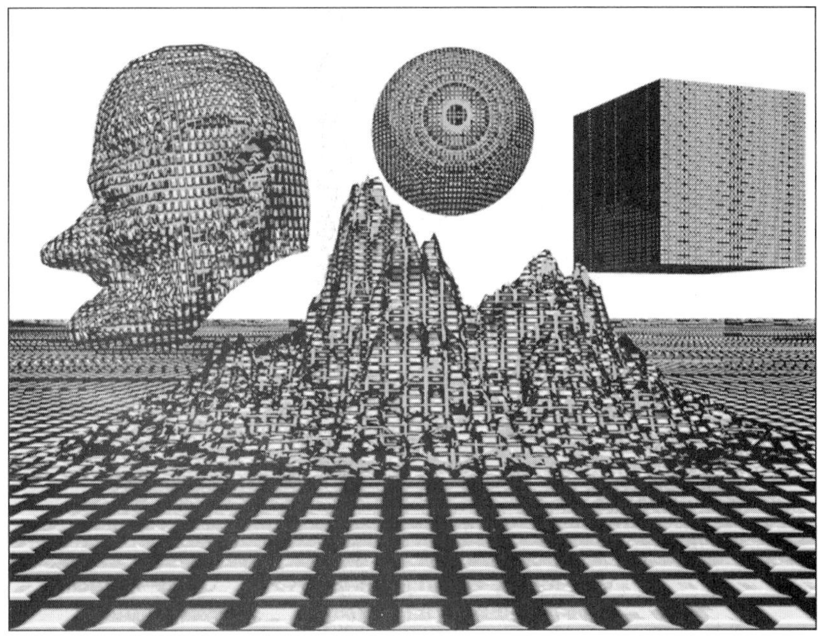

Figure 3.32
Glow Beads works best on objects that have some curvature.

Figure 3.33
The Glowing Coal material creates illusions of heat and charred matter.

GoldPlate

GoldPlate (shown in Figure 3.34) creates sparkling gold separated by dark random veins. It works well on all objects, even Infinite Ground Planes. Use it as a skin material on imported heads. By turning antialiasing off in your renderings, you can make the sparkles in this material more apparent.

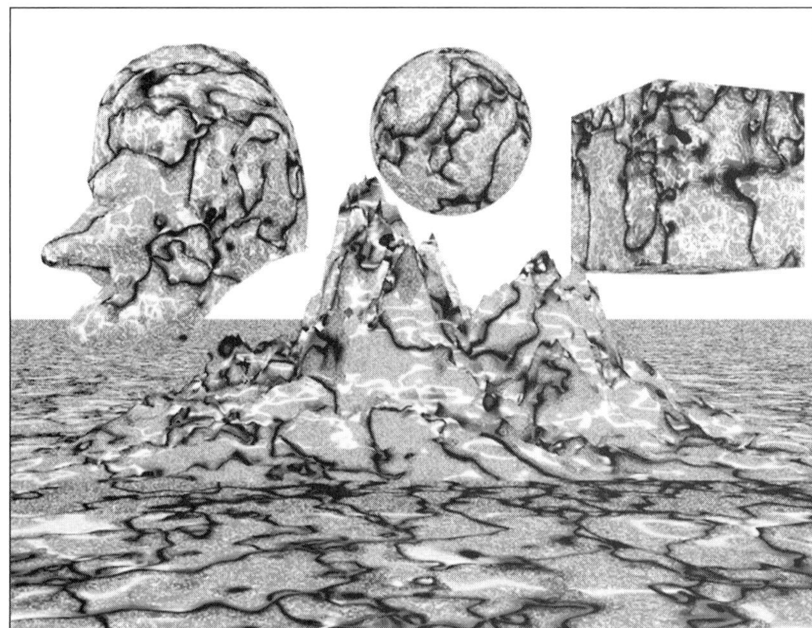

Figure 3.34
GoldPlate creates a sense of richness and joy in your Bryce worlds.

IceKnobs 1

This material combines a grid of blocks and swirling, random icy patterns. The effect resembles an overworked air conditioner or a leaky radiator. IceKnobs 1 works well on primitive objects and Infinite Planes; it doesn't work as well on imported objects or terrains. Be prepared for long render times when you map this material to terrains and Infinite Planes. See Figure 3.35.

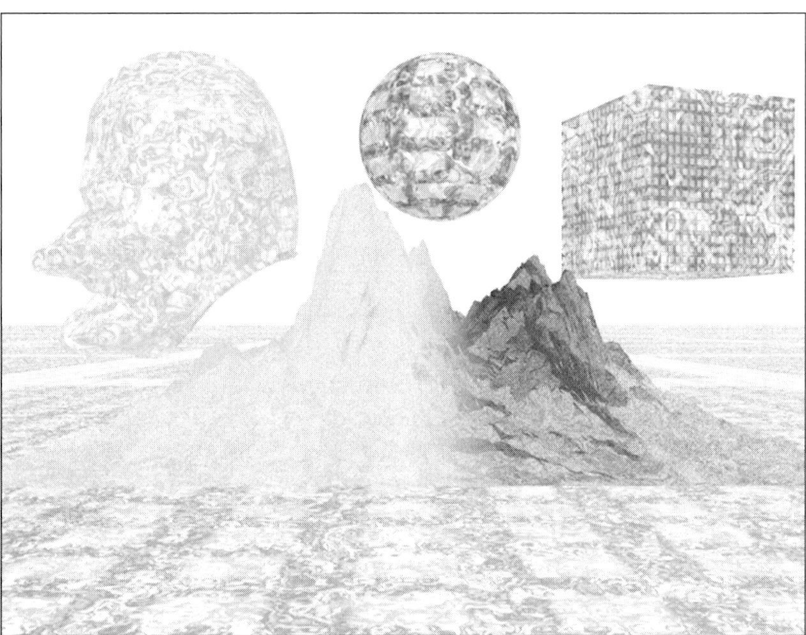

Figure 3.35
IceKnobs 1 freezes the viewer in place.

IceKnobs 2

This material offers subtle variations on IceKnobs 1. See Figure 3.36.

Mecho 1

Mecho 1 is best described as a material with the look of a colorful circuit board. It works best on cubic objects and terrains, and to some extent on Infinite Planes. This would be an interesting material to use on a robot or a building. See Figure 3.37.

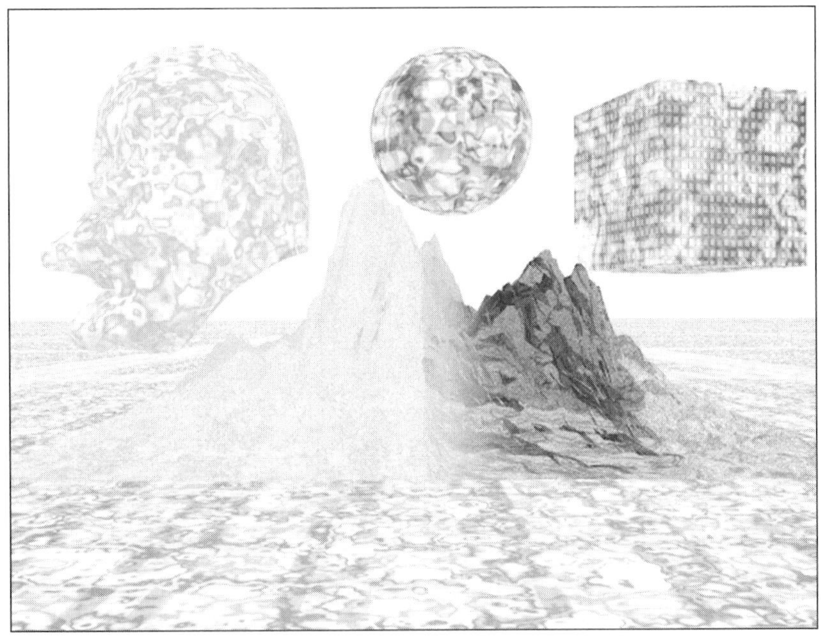

Figure 3.36
IceKnobs 2 subtly tweaks some of the attributes of IceKnobs 1.

Figure 3.37
Mecho 1 is a colorful circuit board material.

Old Brick

To use this material, you must have the Brick Bitmap Texture from the Bryce 4 CD-ROM. The Old Brick material works best on primitive objects and on Infinite Planes. Avoid using it on imported objects unless you change the mapping options to Object Mapping. The Old Brick material combines a bitmap with Procedural Textures to produce the look of pavement or of a randomized brick wall. See Figure 3.38.

Figure 3.38
Use Old Brick to emphasize the decaying nature of an urban environment.

Old Mosaic

This material is a combination of the Yellow Stroke and Beveled Tiles Procedural Textures. Old Mosaic creates the look of old mosaic tiles interrupted by fungus. Use it on walls and buildings, although it maps well to any object type. See Figure 3.39.

PatternBar

The PatternBar material looks best when mapped to primitive objects. Do not use it on Infinite Planes unless you alter the mappings to World Space. Even then, it does nothing special to an Infinite Plane. This material creates a geometric look. See Figure 3.40.

Phagus

The Phagus material looks like a combination of fog and rotted meat. Although it works to varying degrees on any object, it looks best on primitives and imported objects. This material provides an example of using

Figure 3.39
The Old Mosaic material adds a decomposed and time-worn look to objects.

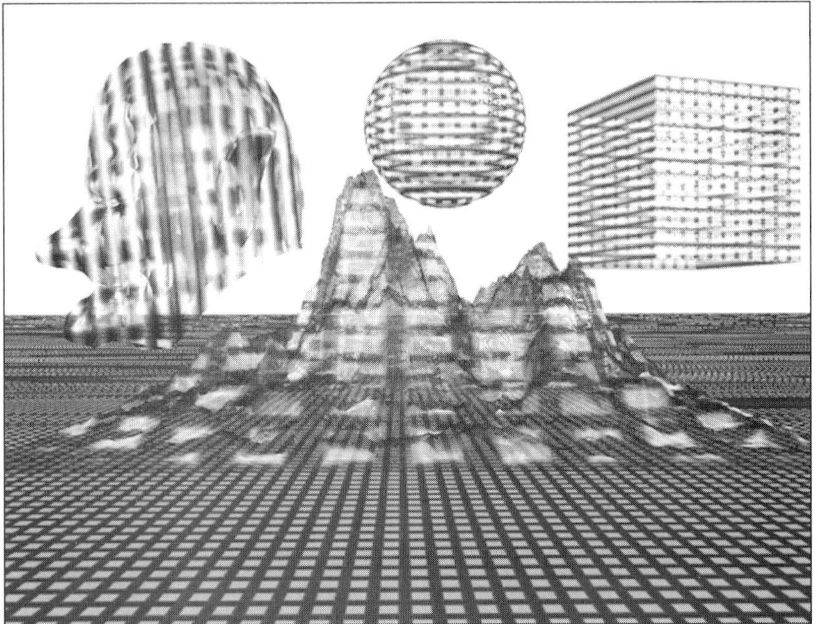

Figure 3.40
The PatternBar material looks best when mapped to primitive objects.

one Procedural Texture (GreyStone 5, in this case) to create a unique material. See Figure 3.41.

Pineapple

Although the Pineapple material (shown in Figure 3.42) maps well to any object, the results differ depending on the object selected. I suppose it is named after its color component: a pineapple yellow. It works very well on imported objects, helping to define their shape.

Figure 3.41
The Phagus material uses just one Procedural Texture.

Figure 3.42
The Pineapple material maps well to all object types.

RockPox 1

Here's a bumpy rock texture with streaks of red—perfect for a menacing alien being. The RockPox 1 material works well (and looks much the same) on any object. You will find this material especially useful for rocks and terrains. See Figure 3.43.

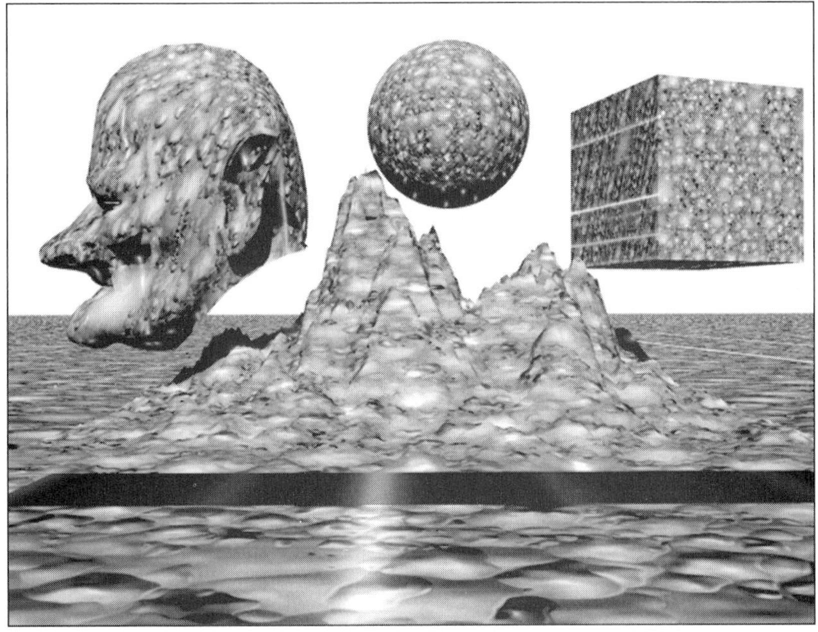

Figure 3.43
The RockPox 1 material has a strong Bump component that emphasizes its chaotic nature.

Figure 3.44
SnowPlane is especially valuable for mapping terrains and Infinite Planes.

SnowPlane

Terrains and Infinite Planes are the best targets for this material. Unlike other snow and ice Material presets, this one looks grainy, as if the snow is still fresh. Use it to develop a deep-winter scene. See Figure 3.44.

StoneWall

Here's an all-procedural material that has a randomized stone look. Use it for walls, buildings, caves, statues, or other suitable objects. When used on terrains, the look is more like slabs of dried mud. See Figure 3.45.

TotalNet 1

Created from the RedLayers and Beveled Tiles Procedural Textures, this material looks like a red net laid over a yellow surface. Although it works well on all object types, it looks a little too mechanical on cubic primitives. See Figure 3.46.

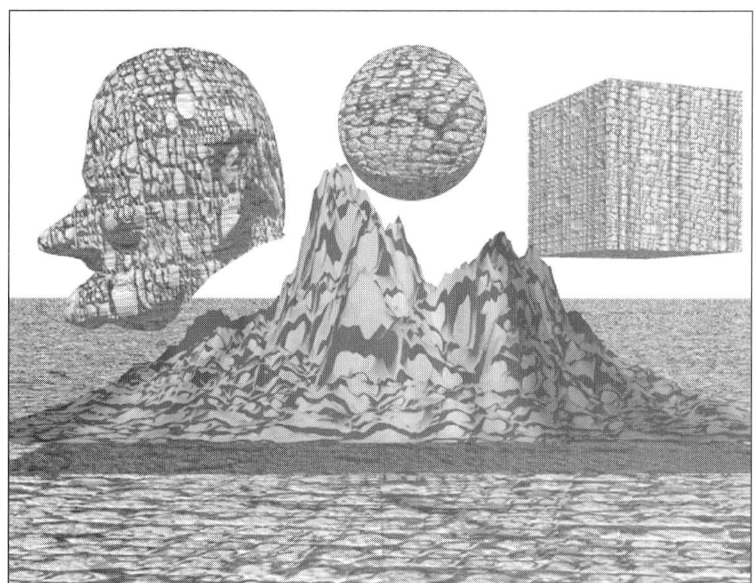

Figure 3.45
The StoneWall material creates a believable randomized stone look.

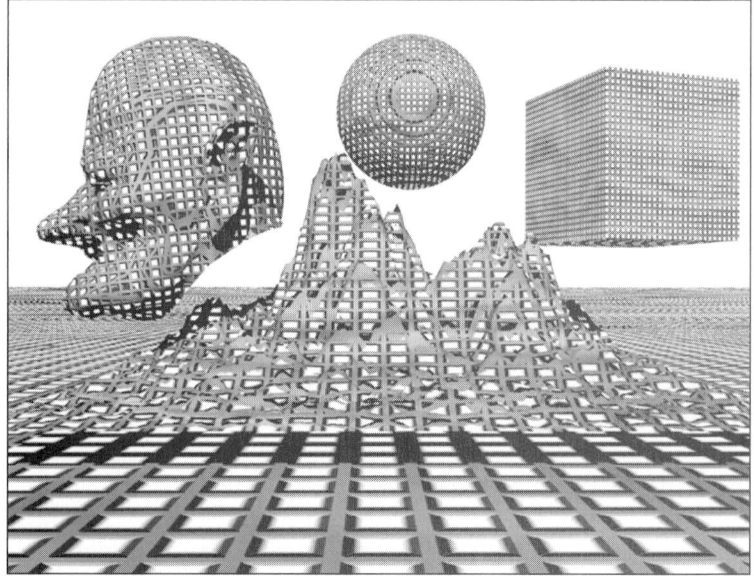

Figure 3.46
The TotalNet 1 material takes on the appearance of a fishnet.

Vegetative 1

The Vegetative material takes on a slightly different look when mapped to different object types. On terrains, it looks like dense underbrush. On Infinite Planes, it looks like a dark green matte. It is a green material speckled with brownish streaks. See Figure 3.47.

WildWeave

WildWeave (shown in Figure 3.48) was developed from the Gradient Bar and Sin Weave Procedural Textures. It shows its woven nature most when mapped to a primitive object (and least when mapped to a terrain).

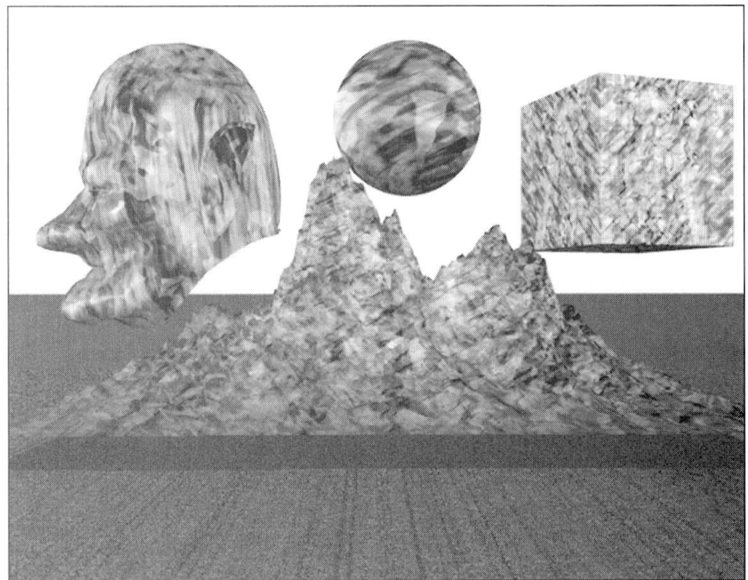

Figure 3.47
The Vegetative 1 material makes a terrain look overgrown with underbrush.

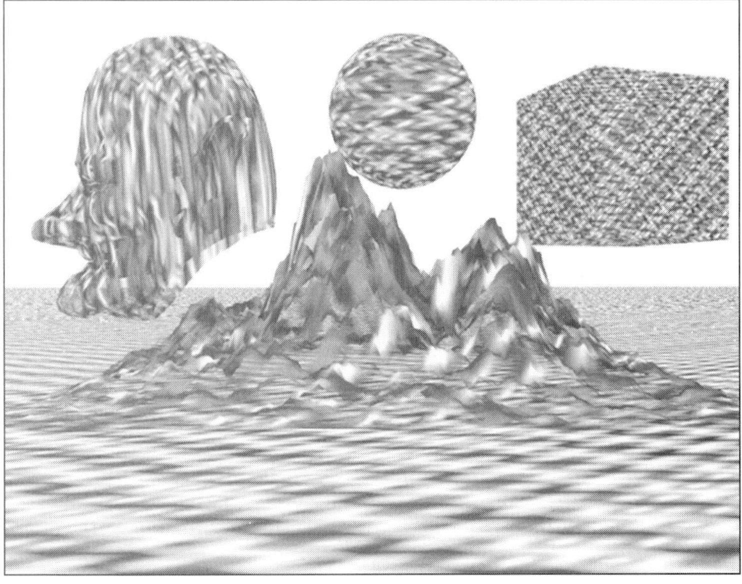

Figure 3.48
Multicolored woven strands form the textural basis of the WildWeave material.

> ***Note:*** *The following materials were created using KPT Gradient Designer. The P in their names is a reminder that they were generated with plug-ins.*

Plug-In-Based Materials

The following materials were created using the plug-in method described in the section "The Plug-In Method Of Materials Creation." Please remember that the images shown display only the bitmap content as it appears when using the bitmap as an image-based component in a material. You can create more complex materials by combining any of these bitmaps with other bitmaps or Procedural Textures in other channels.

P_Burst

The P_Burst material features a sunburst gradient. Use it as a tiled pattern or on a planar object to emulate a sun in the sky. On a terrain, explore both Object and Parametric mapping. See Figures 3.49a and 3.49b.

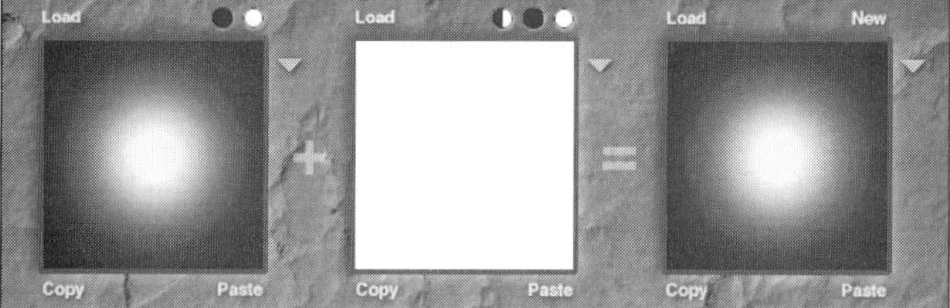

Figure 3.49a
The Picture Editor interface with the Sunburst Gradient in place.

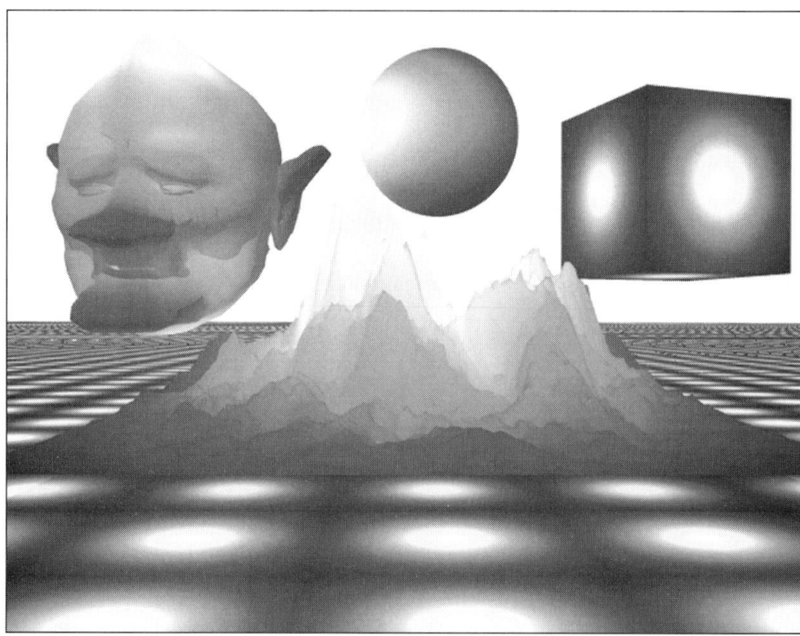

Figure 3.49b
The result of applying the P_Burst Gradient as a surface material created using the bitmap technique.

P_Carnival

P_Carnival is a mix of strong hues. Map it to an object to give it a splash of joyous color. Use World Top or World Mapping when mapping this material to an Infinite Plane. See Figures 3.50a and 3.50b.

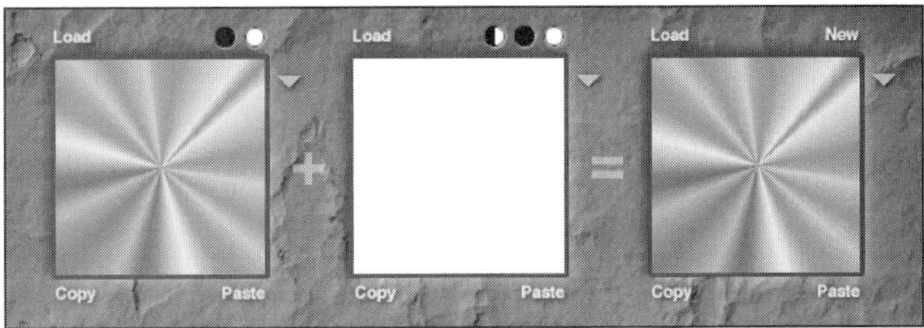

Figure 3.50a
The Picture Editor interface with the P_Carnival Gradient in place.

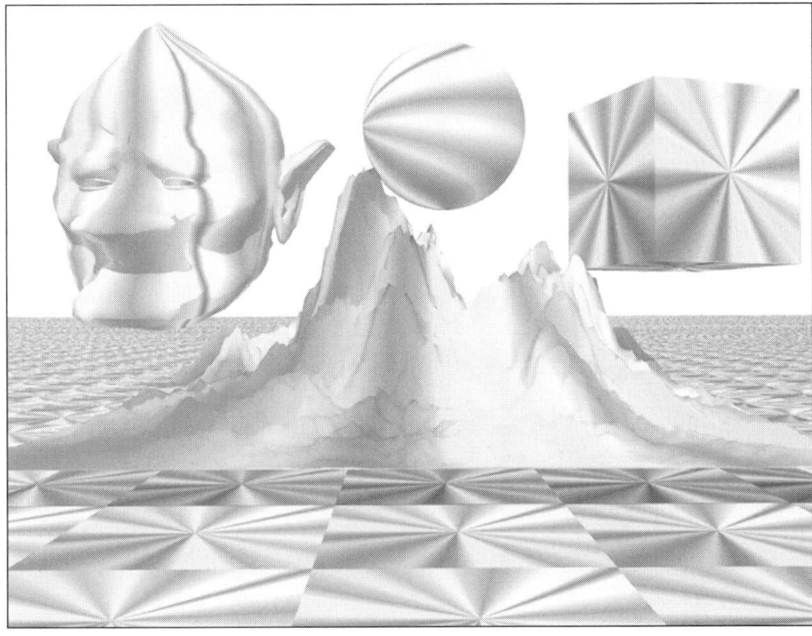

Figure 3.50b
The result of applying the P_Carnival Gradient as a Bitmap Material.

P_Cloth

This gradient is useful when you need a tablecloth or a bedspread in your picture. It can be mapped to any object. See Figures 3.51a and 3.51b.

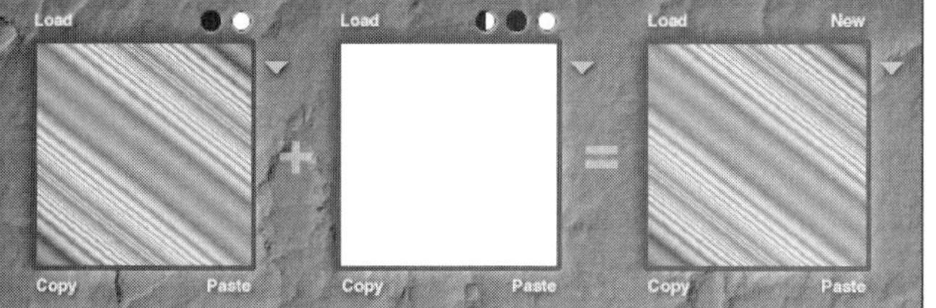

Figure 3.51a
The Picture Editor interface with the P_Cloth Gradient in place.

Figure 3.51b
The result of applying the P_Cloth Gradient as a Bitmap Material.

P_Parquet

Need a Parquet floor? Just map P_Parquet as a Parametric map to a cube, or as a World Top map to an Infinite Plane. See Figures 3.52a and 3.52b.

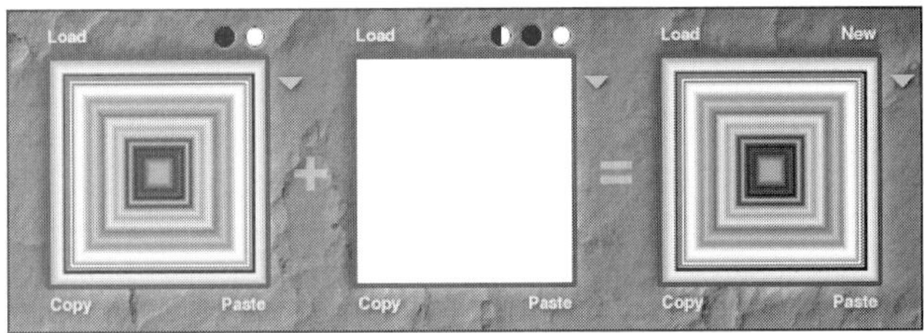

Figure 3.52a
The Picture Editor interface with the P_Parquet Gradient in place.

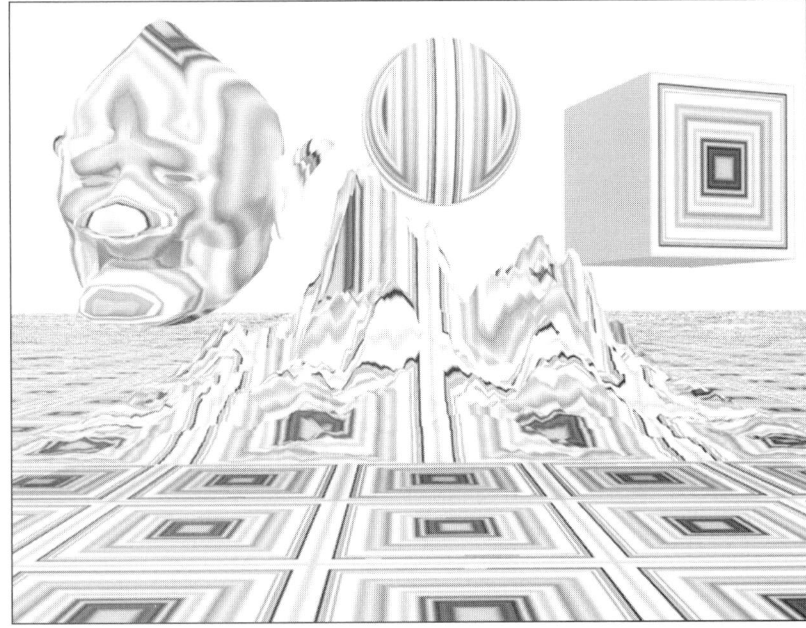

Figure 3.52b
The result of applying the P_Parquet Gradient as a Bitmap Material.

P_Signal

This Bitmap Gradient Material emulates the color-bar test pattern seen on television. Use it to lend a rainbow of color to any object. See Figures 3.53a and 3.53b.

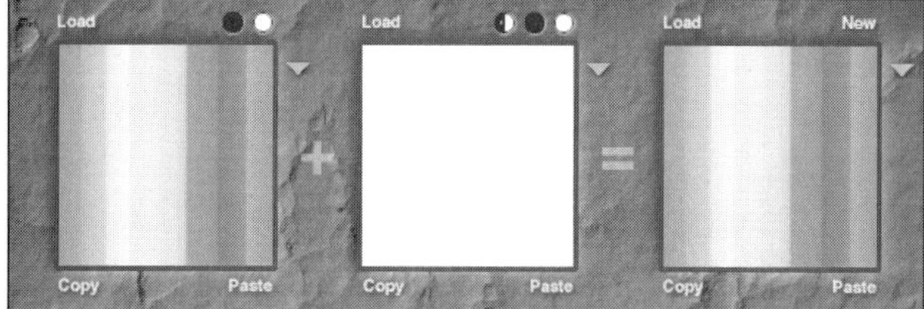

Figure 3.53a
The Picture Editor interface with the P_Signal Gradient in place.

Figure 3.53b
The result of applying the P_Signal Gradient as a Bitmap Material.

P_Berry

Use this material to add berry-colored patterns to any object. It works best on flat surfaces, but you can also use it with transparency to map a curtain in a room. See Figures 3.54a and 3.54b.

Note: *The following eight materials were created using KPT Texture Explorer. The P in their names is a reminder that they were generated with plug-ins.*

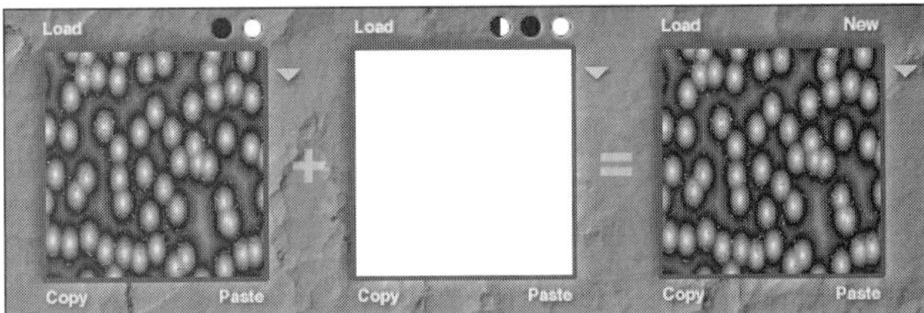

Figure 3.54a
The Picture Editor interface with the P_Berry texture in place.

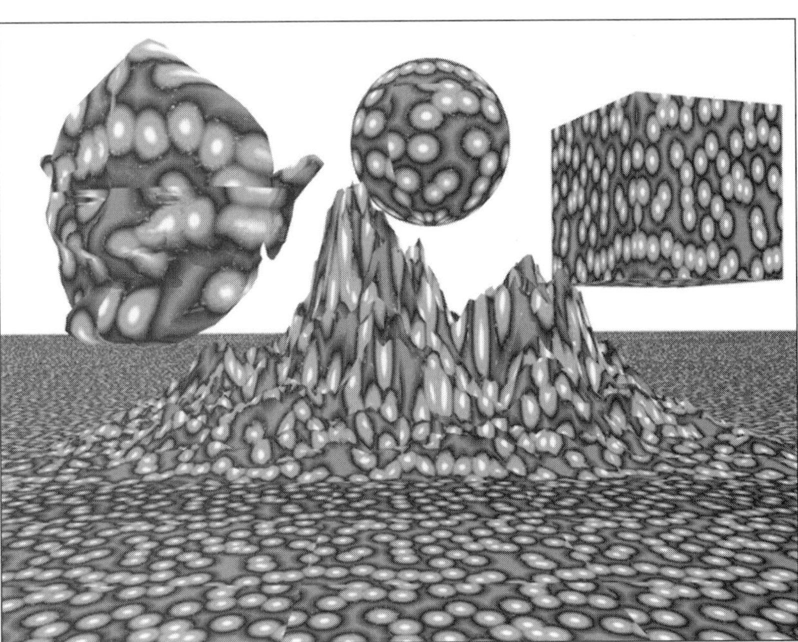

Figure 3.54b
The result of applying the P_Berry texture as a Bitmap Material.

P_Hot 1

This is a fire material. You can use it as a tile or in combination with other fire materials to produce a series of effects. See Figures 3.55a and 3.55b.

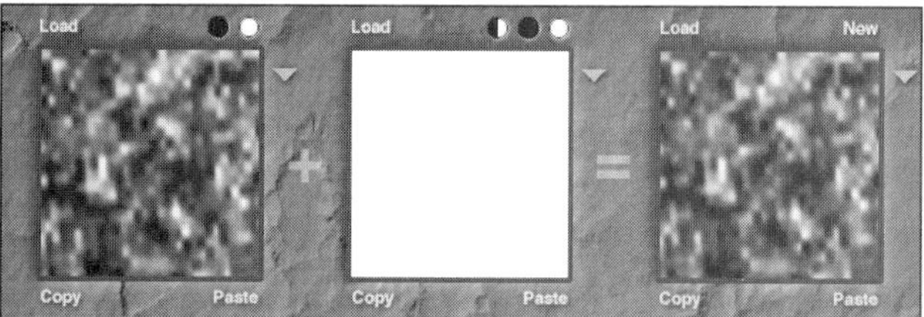

Figure 3.55a
The Picture Editor interface with the P_Hot 1 texture in place.

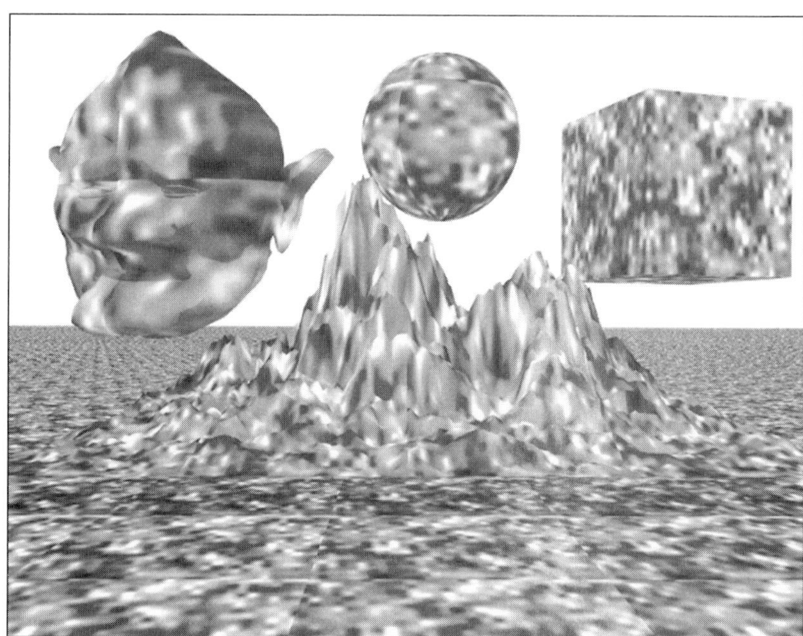

Figure 3.55b
The result of applying the P_Hot 1 texture as a Bitmap Material.

P_Hot 2

Here is an alternate fiery material. See Figures 3.56a and 3.56b.

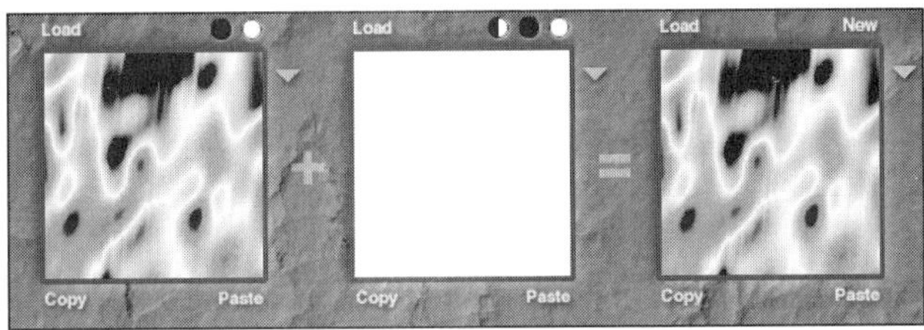

Figure 3.56a
The Picture Editor interface with the P_Hot 2 texture in place.

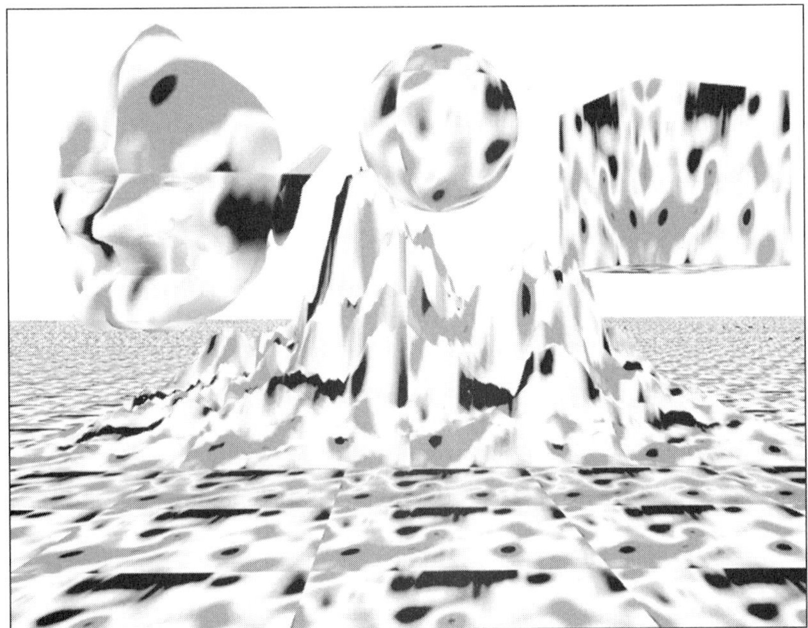

Figure 3.56b
The result of applying the P_Hot 2 texture as a Bitmap Material.

P_PCock

This material has a definite peacock-like coloring. Use it as one texture in a more complex material mix. See Figures 3.57a and 3.57b.

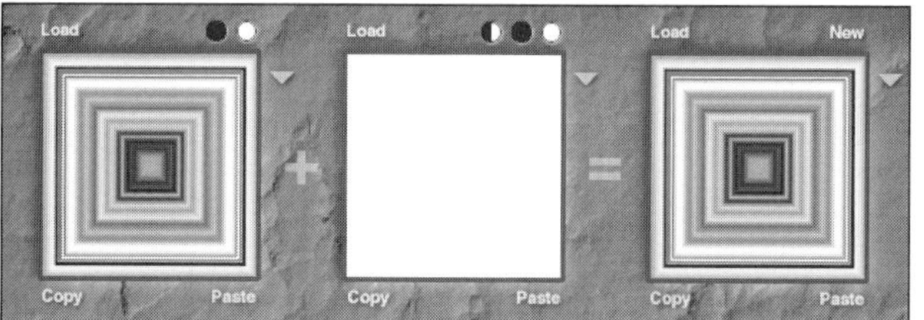

Figure 3.57a
The Picture Editor interface with the P_PCock texture in place.

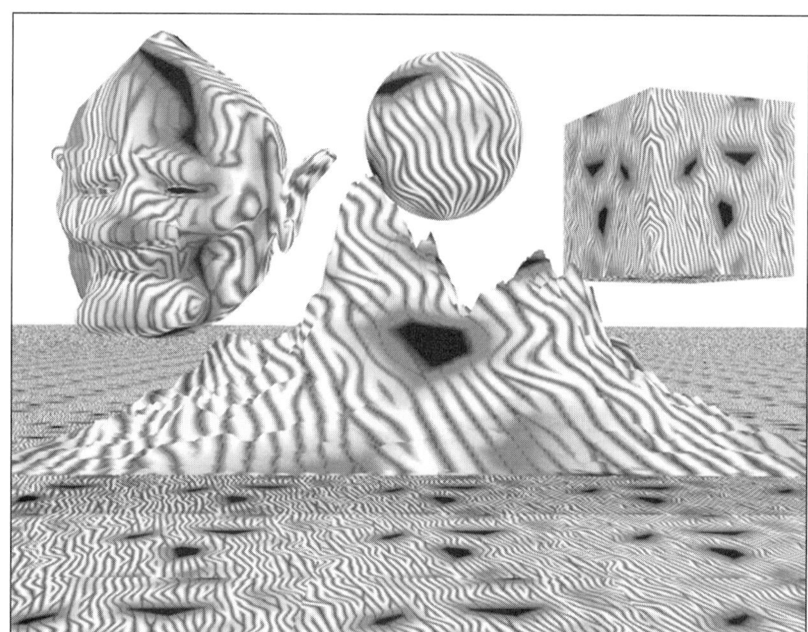

Figure 3.57b
The result of applying the P_PCock texture as a Bitmap Material.

P_Shaz

This material emulates patterned blocks. Use it to tile a wall or floor. See Figures 3.58a and 3.58b.

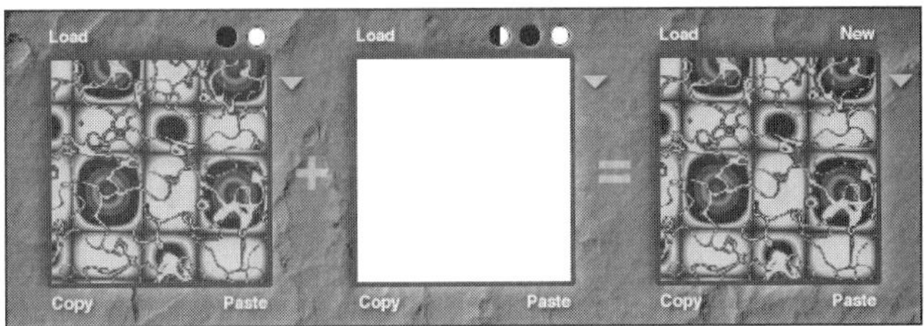

Figure 3.58a
The Picture Editor interface with the P_Shaz texture in place.

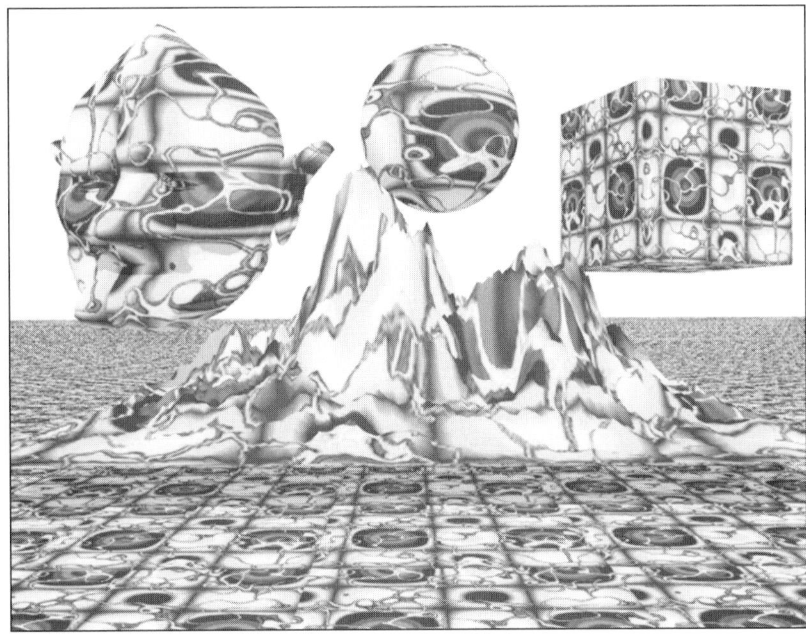

Figure 3.58b
The result of applying the P_Shaz texture as a Bitmap Material.

P_Sym

This is a strange material that looks a bit like how I imagine alien lettering would appear. See Figures 3.59a and 3.59b.

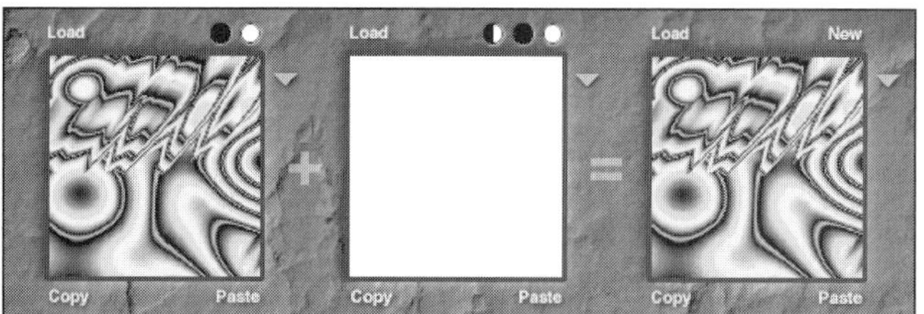

Figure 3.59a
The Picture Editor interface with the P_Sym texture in place.

Figure 3.59b
The result of applying the P_Sym texture as a Bitmap Material.

P_Veins

This Bitmap Image Texture based material has two grains moving against each other. You can use it as a unique wood material or to map the Ground Plane. See Figures 3.60a and 3.60b.

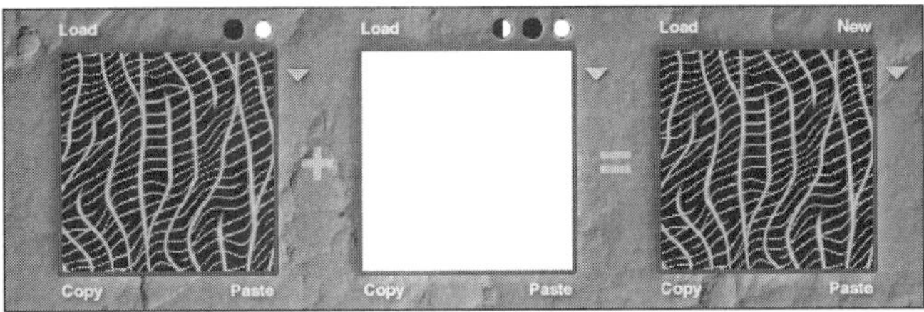

Figure 3.60a
The Picture Editor interface with the P_Veins texture in place.

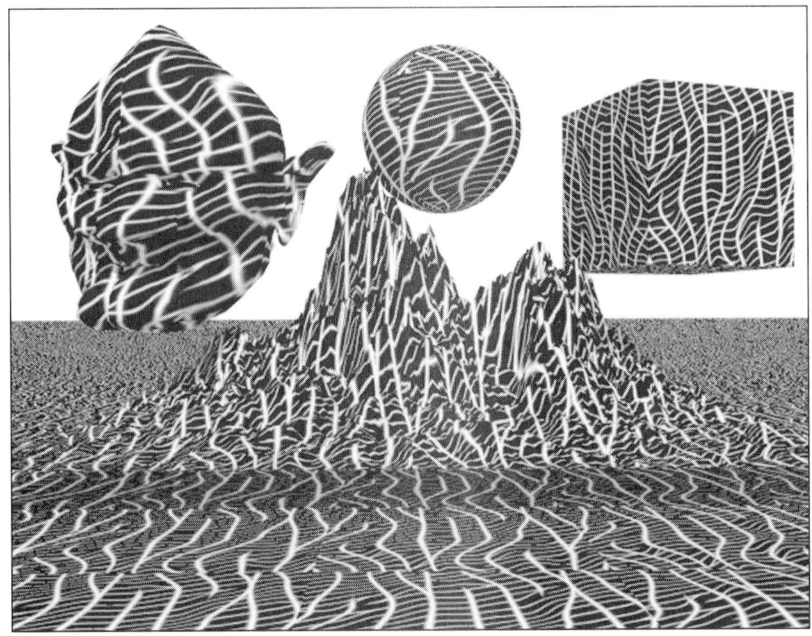

Figure 3.60b
The result of applying the P_Veins texture as a Bitmap Material.

P_Web

This Bitmap Texture-based material emulates molten gold, and it is particularly effective when mapped to either a Terrain object or a Ground Plane. See Figures 3.61a and 3.61b.

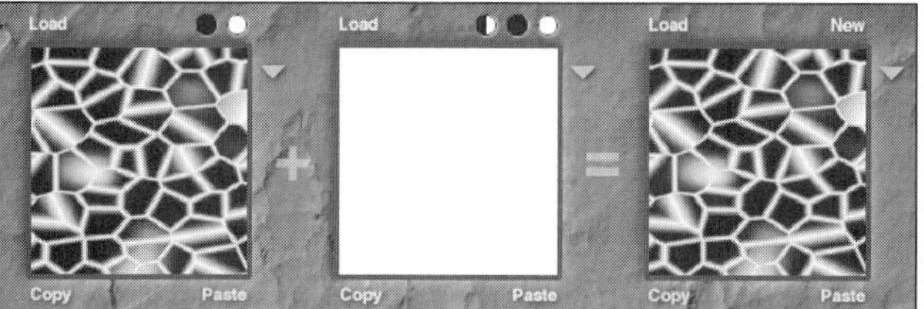

Figure 3.61a
The Picture Editor interface with the P_Web texture in place.

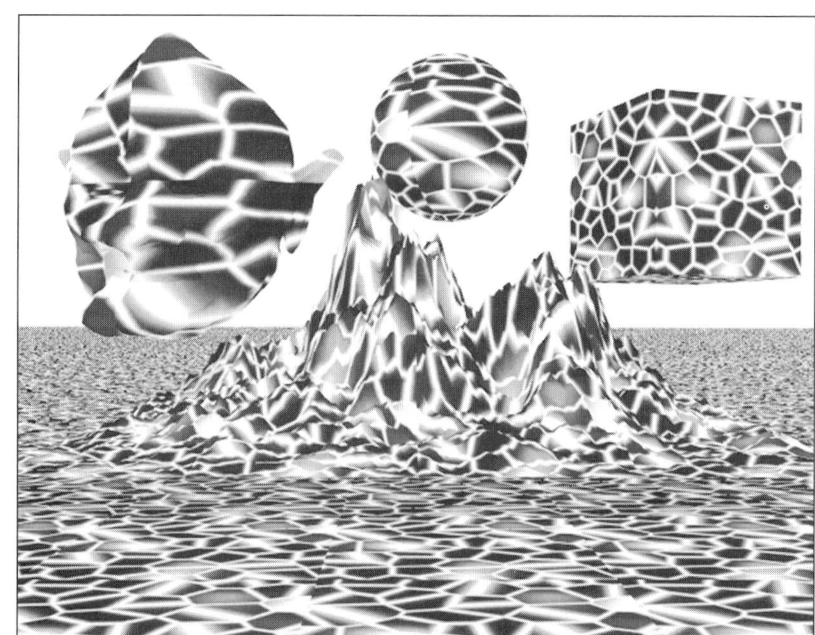

Figure 3.61b
The result of applying the P_Web texture as a Bitmap Material.

P_FibOptx

This material is based on a KPT 5 FiberOptix texture. Use FiberOptix to create strands or filaments. These materials are useful in Bryce for making excellent grass and other strand-based effects. You can create hair by mapping to a sphere, although this is tricky and takes a lot of experimentation. Without using transparency, map this material to a rock. It creates a series of parallel scratches across the rock's surface. See Figures 3.62a and 3.62b.

Note: *The next four texture-based materials were created using the filters in KPT 5.*

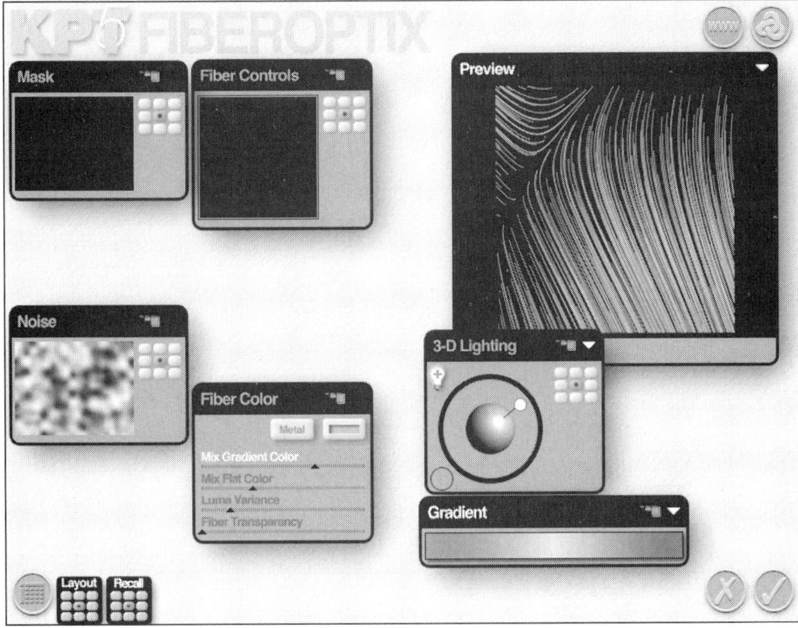

Figure 3.62a
The KPT 5 FiberOptix interface.

Figure 3.62b
KPT 5 P_FibOptx material applied to objects as a Bitmap Texture-based material.

P_FrExp1

Here's a material based on a KPT 5 FraxPlorer texture. Use this filter to create a wide range of fractal-based graphic textures for material components. See Figures 3.63a and 3.63b.

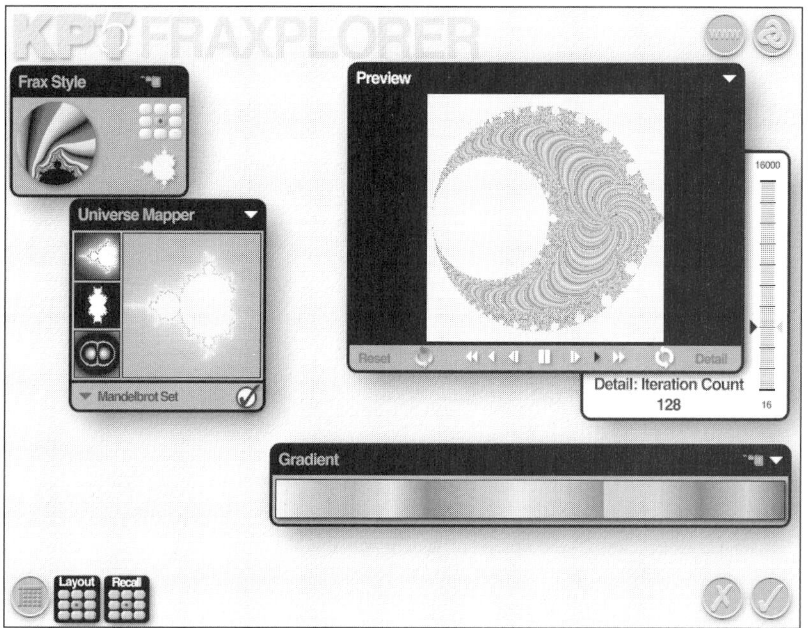

Figure 3.63a
The KPT 5 FraxPlorer interface.

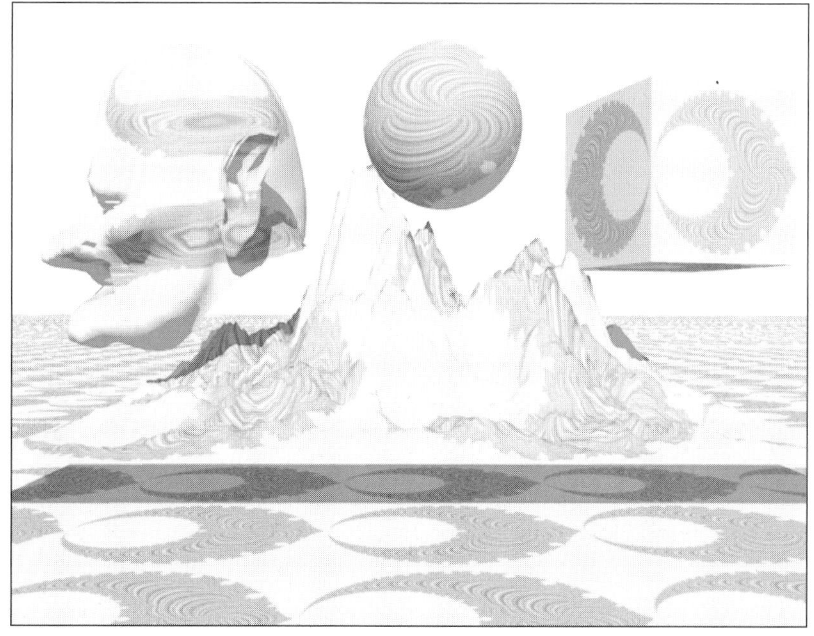

Figure 3.63b
KPT 5 P_FrExp1 material applied to objects as a Bitmap Texture-based material.

P_FrcFlm

I used the KPT 5 FraxFlame plug-in to create this Bitmap Texture-based material. Using a transparent background with FraxFlame textured materials allows you to generate delicate objects, such as the swirls of water spray that accompany a wave. See Figures 3.64a and 3.64b.

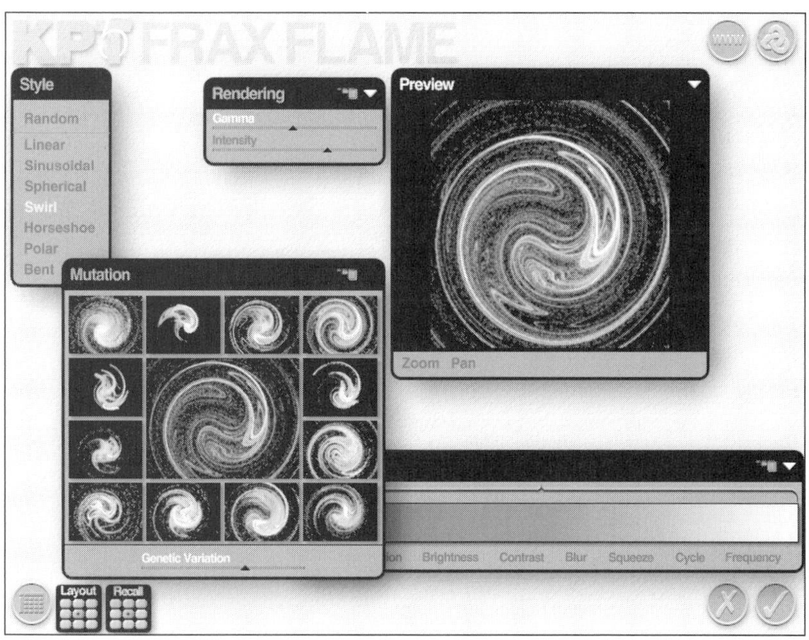

Figure 3.64a
The KPT 5 FraxFlame interface.

Figure 3.64b
KPT 5 P_FrcFlm material applied to objects as a Bitmap Texture-based material.

P_OrbIt

The KPT 5 Orb-It filter creates communities of bubbles. Using them as a texture in a material creates interesting images that you can tile to Infinite Planes or other surfaces. See Figures 3.65a and 3.65b.

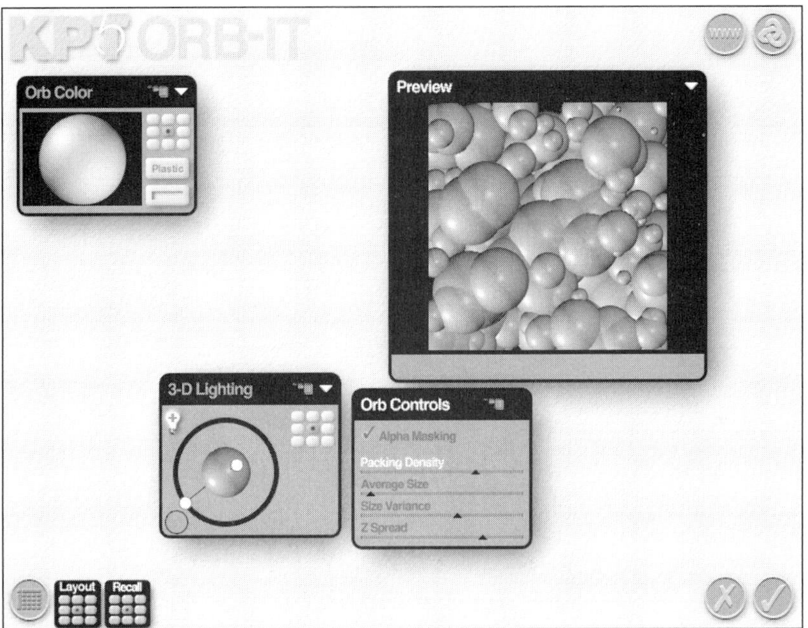

Figure 3.65a
The KPT 5 Orb-It interface.

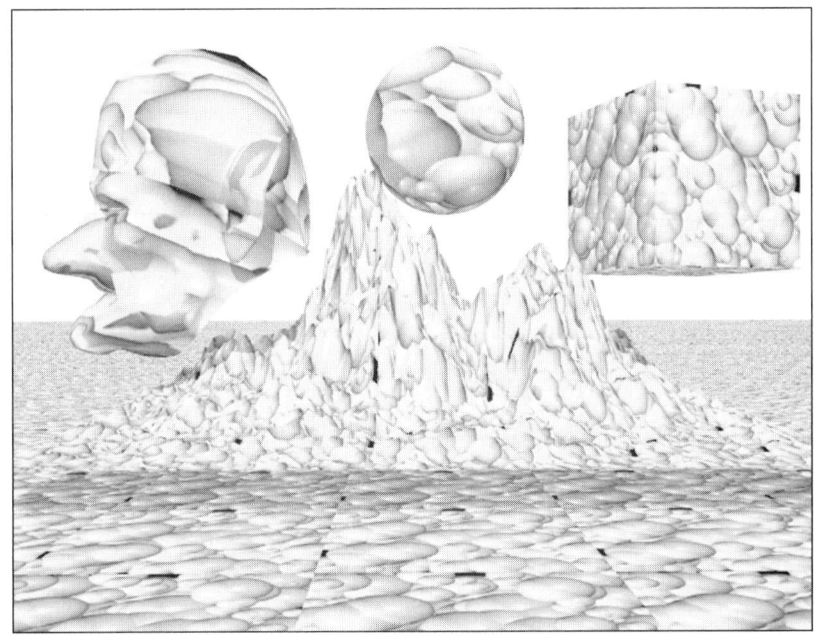

Figure 3.65b
KPT 5 P_OrbIt material applied to objects as a Bitmap Texture-based material.

Knoll Lens Flare Pro

The last material on this book's CD-ROM, P_Knoll, is a Bitmap Texture-based material that was created using the Knoll Lens Flare Pro plug-in from Puffin Designs. The lights in the scene were shut off, leaving the Ambient Channel of the image to light the scene on its own. See Figures 3.66a and 3.66b.

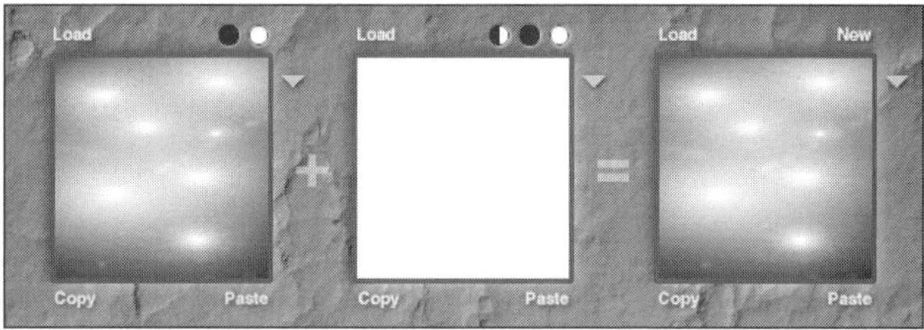

Figure 3.66a
The Picture Editor interface with the P_Knoll Pro texture in place.

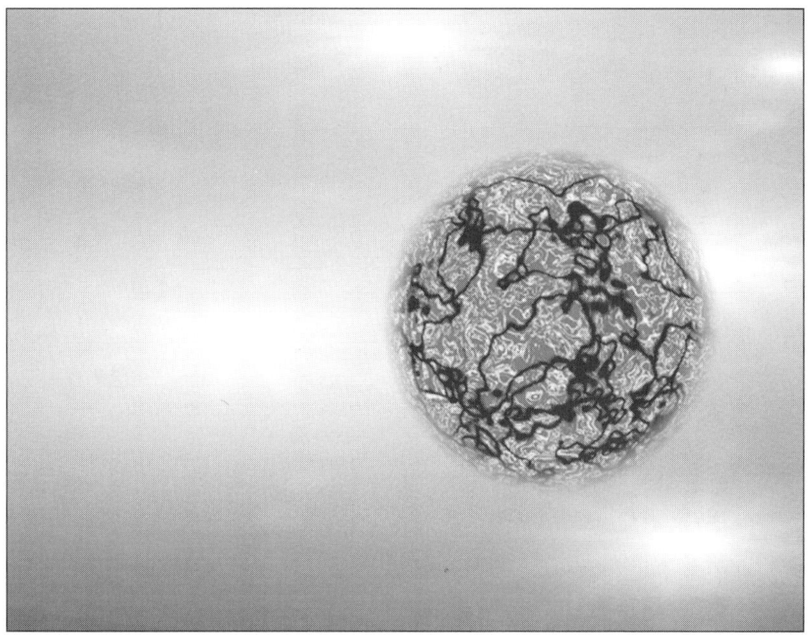

Figure 3.66b
The P_Knoll image is mapped to a vertical picture plane. The sphere was placed in front of it to give it more depth.

Creating Quick Spooky Eyes

You can use simple spheres and the Materials Lab to create eyes for your generated or imported creatures. Follow these steps:

1. Create a sphere and open its Materials Attribute (which opens the Materials Lab).
2. Set Diffuse and Ambient to the dark color that will serve as the dark part of the eyeball. (Remember that in Spooky Eyes, the "whites" are darker than the pupils.)
3. Set the Specular color to a bright hue. Set the Specular halo to whatever color you want the iris to be. (This has to be a light color.)

Note: *This method used to create Spooky Eyes produces a dark eyeball with a bright pupil. You cannot achieve a white eyeball using this method. The eye will seem to be looking in the direction the global light is coming from, so keep that in mind when you set the light's direction in the Sky & Fog mode.*

Note: *Use the Original Quick Spooky Eye for robots and animals. Use the Quick Spooky Eye grouped with a white eyeball for human and human-like creatures.*

4. Set Diffusion, Ambiance, and Specularity to 100 percent, and make sure Metalicity is set to zero. Preview the results. Changing the Specular halo color to another light hue creates pupils of different colors. See Figure 3.67.

The Quick Spooky Eye With A White Eyeball

If you want a more conventional eyeball, follow these steps:

1. Create the eye as detailed previously, only this time, the result will serve as the pupil only. The Specular Halo will become a highlight.
2. Group the eye inside a larger white sphere so that about one-fifth of it sticks out. This creates an excellent eye, although it is a little less spooky than the first example. See Figure 3.68.

Figure 3.67
(Left) Quick Spooky Eyes attached to a head.

Figure 3.68
(Right) A white eyeball is added to the eyes, toning down their spookiness.

Moving On

In this chapter, you learned about creating and customizing materials and textures. You explored the Materials Lab, the Deep Texture Editor, and the Picture Editor. A detailed look at the 50 materials provided on this book's CD-ROM also was provided. In the next chapter, I'll show you ways you can enhance your Bryce worlds even more by using lights, cameras, and environmental effects.

4 Scenic Wonders

This chapter describes a number of tools and techniques that help you create scenic wonders in Bryce. You'll learn how to use lights, cameras, and the Sky Lab to create stunning effects.

Light Up Your Worlds

Without light, you could not depend on your sense of vision to navigate in the world. Luckily, that isn't the case. Much of what you perceive as beautiful or inspiring comes directly or indirectly from your sense of sight. Even those without sight still dream in images. Light—its color, direction, and source—plays a large role in determining the emotional content of what you see. A scene bathed in harsh light looks less friendly than a scene with a subtle light source. The light's color is also important for setting a mood. Scenes lit with green light take on an eerie quality—great for impending mysteries and graveyard scenes. An environment awash in red light seems more alarming than the same scene cast in blue. A touch of yellow is soothing; too much yellow is disquieting.

The light's source also affects your mood. A candle illuminates only those elements in its proximity with a warm friendly glow, leaving more distant elements in moody shadows. A lamp gives the impression that a human element controls the scene, because lamps can be turned on and off at will. The sun and the moon have their own special mood-altering qualities, and the interaction of clouds, as they block these archetypal light sources, play a role as well.

In Bryce, you can add any or all of these light sources and many more, such as the light from a campfire or a volcano's cauldron. Illuminating the same scene with different lighting options alters the viewer's perception and the "intent" of the elements in that scene. Light has a major affect on the apparent 3D-nature of objects. Well-placed lights can add to depth perception; careless light placement can detract from an object's 3D believability.

Shadows

In Bryce, each object has three shadow attributes: Cast Shadows (the ability to cast a shadow on other objects), Receive Shadows (the ability to receive shadows from another object casting them), and Self Shadows (the ability of an object to cast shadows on itself). From the Materials Lab, you can easily toggle an object's shadow attributes on or off in the object's Materials Options list. The Sky Lab's Shadows option must be selected in order for shadows to be rendered. To see the variety of effects made possible by toggling these attributes on or off, see Figures 4.1 through 4.5.

Shadow Hints

Instead of leaving all the shadow attributes on by default, turn them on or off to create different effects in your renderings:

Figure 4.1
In the default scene, little light is coming from the environment, so all objects are in deep shadow.

Figure 4.2
This scene has a light source on the left, but all object shadow attributes (including those of the tabletop) have been turned off. Although the objects now have 3D definition, the scene remains flat and unconvincing.

- Turn an object's Cast Shadows attribute off to diminish the object's importance in a scene. Objects that cast shadows seem more substantial.
- Turn Receive Shadows off to increase an object's "ghastliness." This works especially well when the object is partially transparent.
- Objects that have shadow relationships with each other have a stronger perceived connection to each other. Use this to your best advantage.

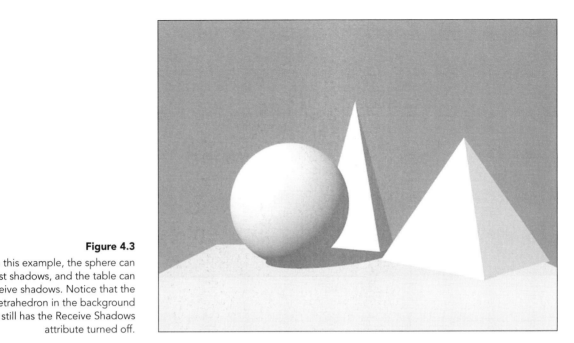

Figure 4.3
In this example, the sphere can cast shadows, and the table can receive shadows. Notice that the tetrahedron in the background still has the Receive Shadows attribute turned off.

Figure 4.4
In this scene, the sphere can still cast shadows, but the table cannot receive shadows. The sphere therefore has little relationship to the table and might as well be floating above it. The tetrahedron in the back has Receive Shadows turned on.

Global Shadow Settings

You can control the color and intensity of shadows by altering the components of the Shadow attributes in the Sky & Fog palette. If you set a high Shadow Intensity (by clicking on and dragging the controller toward the right), the shadows completely overwhelm the objects they fall on, as in Figure 4.6.

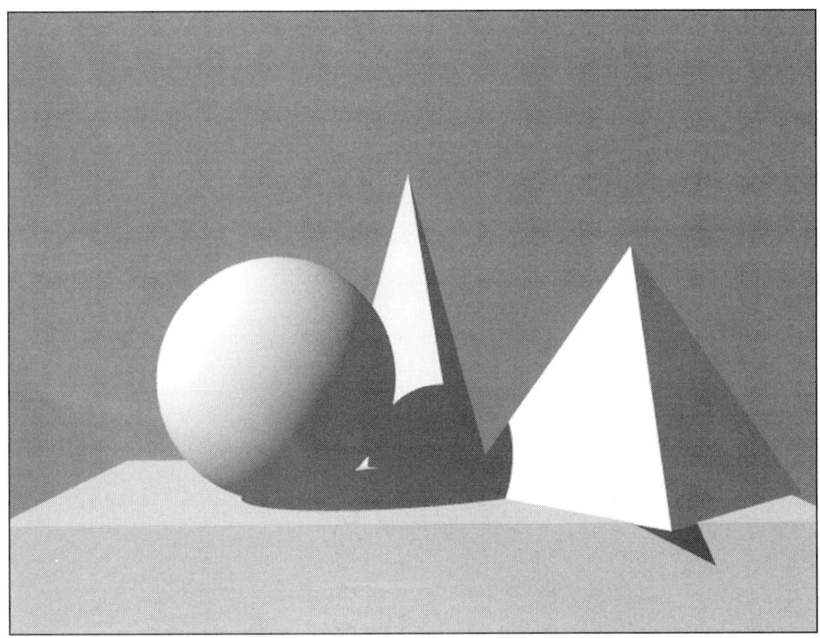

Figure 4.5
In this scene, all the elements can cast and receive shadows; this indicates that all the objects are related to each other.

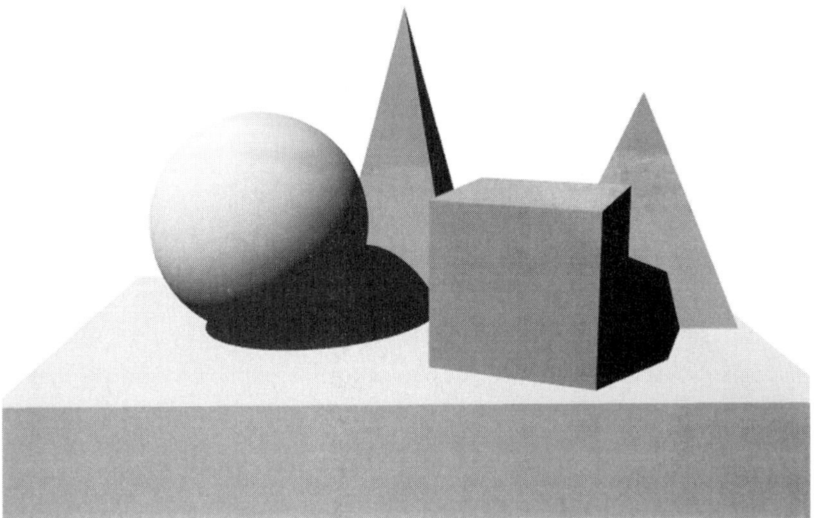

Figure 4.6
At full intensity (100 percent), shadows overwhelm the objects they fall on.

When you set the Shadow Intensity to a value between 20 and 45 percent, the shadows blend much more effectively in the scene, as in Figure 4.7.

A word about Shadow Color: If everything in your world is colorless and the Sun Color is set to white, the Shadow Color adds an even tint over the entire scene. This can be useful when you want to create a monochromatic picture or animation. Shadow Color and Sun Color combine to set the tint, with the Sun Color dominating. If you set the Sun Color to a light blue and the Shadow Color to yellow, for example, the result is white.

Figure 4.7
Shadows blend more effectively when their intensity is set to lower values (25 percent in this illustration).

Note: *Instead of thinking in terms of right and wrong when it comes to setting the intensity and color of your shadows, look for settings that enhance the scene's emotional content. Dark shows add mystery; light shadows create a hazy, vague feeling. Remember that you can keyframe animate Shadow Intensity and Color. (See Chapter 5 for more on Bryce animation techniques.)*

This is the result of the subtractive mixing of blue and yellow, not to be confused with the additive mixing often associated with combining lights.

The Lighting Categories: When And Where To Use Them

Bryce has three basic lighting categories: Sun Light, Placed Lights, and Pseudo-Lights. You can use them separately (to define a scene's components) or together in a number of combinations.

Here Comes The Sun

Because most users dwell on Bryce's capacity to create photorealistic natural scenes, setting the sun's direction and color is one of the first actions many users perform. You can set the sun's position by adjusting the virtual trackball in the Sky & Fog palette and watching the results in the shaded Nano Preview. See Figure 4.8.

Figure 4.8
Use the trackball to set the direction of sunlight and moonlight.

It is unwise to identify the positions on the trackball with the points on a compass: You can make the sun rise or set from any direction you want. Just choose a light direction that enhances the image content best. See Figures 4.9 through 4.11.

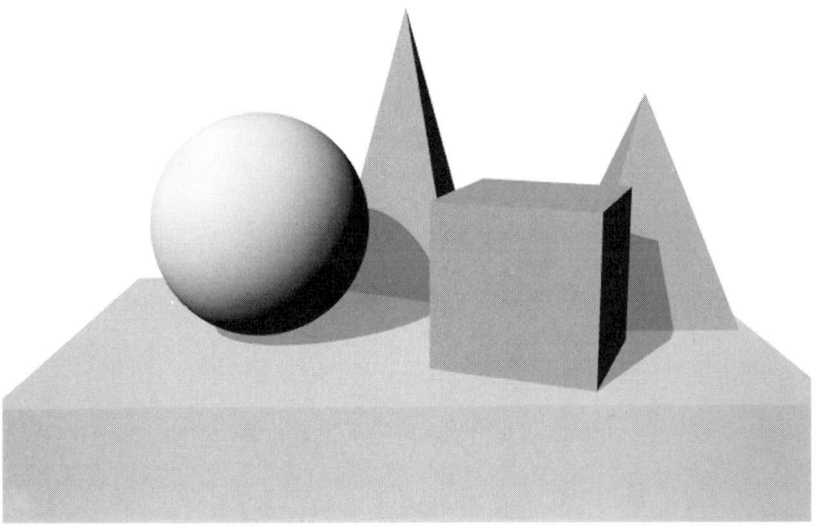

Figure 4.9
Placing the sun a little to the side adds good definition to all the elements.

Figure 4.10
Backlighting creates dramatic silhouettes.

Figure 4.11
Placing the sun more or less directly above the scene creates a partially silhouetted effect.

Sheer Lunacy

Later in this chapter, I'll explore Bryce's new Sky Lab, where you can accurately control sunlight and moonlight and generate a lot of atmospheric effects. You control lunar position by using the same trackball that controls the sun's position. The sun and the moon are placed directly opposite each other, so making the sun disappear by spinning the trackball makes the moon appear from the opposite direction. You can set the moon's color as well, but not by altering the sun's color. The moon's color (or more precisely, the color it casts) is determined by the selected Shadow Color. This makes it easy to add an eerie, greenish lunar glow to a scene, as shown in Figure 4.12.

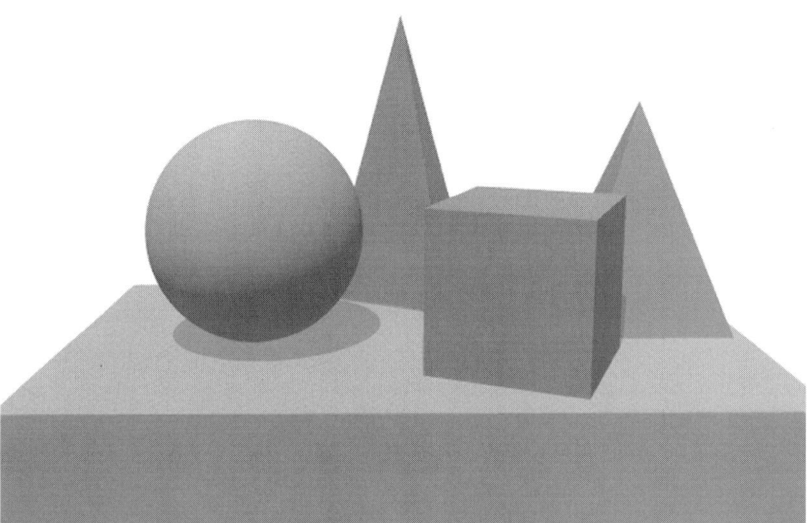

Figure 4.12
Moonlight is far more subtle than sunlight.

Placed Lights

To maximize the effects created with Placed Lights, turn the sun off. The best way to turn off the sun is to set its color to black. That way, no matter what direction it is set at, its light will not permeate the scene. You can also turn off the Sun Light by selecting the Disable Sun Light option on the Sky Lab's Sun & Moon tab.

Placed Lights come in four varieties: Radial Lights, Spotlights, Square Spotlights, and Parallel Lights. You can add them to your world by clicking on their icons (shown in Figure 4.13) in the Create palette.

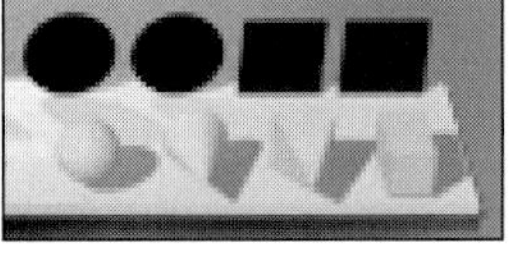

Figure 4.13
The Light icons in the Create palette represent (from left) Radial Lights, Spotlights, Square Spotlights, and Parallel Lights.

The Qualities Of Placed Lights

Each variety of Placed Light has a set of characteristics that alter the way objects are illuminated.

- *Radial Lights*—You will likely use this type of Placed Light most often. Radial Lights illuminate equally in all directions from a spherical source, much like a lightbulb. When placed in the center of an otherwise dark scene, Radial Lights cast light and shadows in all directions, as shown in Figure 4.14.

Figure 4.14
This scene is illuminated by a Radial Light placed at the center of the scene.

- *Spotlights*—Use Spotlights when you want to feature a particular area in the scene. You can use Spotlights as track lighting for indoor scenes. You can also use them in combination with other types of lights to enhance an object or group of objects. Spotlights maintain their character best when you keep the edge fuzziness to a minimum. They tend to behave more like Radial Lights when you set the edge fuzziness to 50 percent or more. See Figure 4.15.

Figure 4.15
In this example, a Spotlight shines down on the scene, producing a characteristic cone of light.

- *Square Spotlights*—Square Spotlights create a rectangular cone of light. Use them to call attention to specific rectangular components of your scenes. See Figure 4.16.

Figure 4.16
The Square Spotlight provides a more linear Spotlight.

- *Parallel Lights*—You can think of Parallel Lights as a form of Square Spotlight. The difference is that light from Parallel Lights does not spread. With Spotlights and Square Spotlights, the illuminated area gets smaller when you move the light closer to an object. But with Parallel Lights, the light source's distance from an object changes only the light's intensity: Closer lights are brighter, and distant lights are dimmer. However, the size of the lighted rectangular area does not change. As you will discover later in this chapter when I describe gels, Parallel Lights are the perfect choice for casting slide-show images in a scene. See Figure 4.17.

Figure 4.17
The Parallel Light casts a rectangular beam that doesn't vary in size as the light moves closer or farther away.

Faking It

A Pseudo-Light is an object that acts like a light but casts neither light beams nor shadows. You can create Pseudo-Lights in two ways. The first is to simply assign the GreenLit material from the Complex fx Materials presets and customize the color as needed. Or you can create a Pseudo-Light by selecting an object (usually a primitive cone) and altering its components in the Materials Lab as follows:

1. Select the Fuzzy option from the object's Material Options list.
2. Set the color of the Ambient component to the color you want the light to be.
3. Turn Ambiance up all the way.
4. Set the transparency to something between 50 and 80 percent.

You can also add to the effect by selecting Light from the Materials Options list. Pseudo-Lights rely on the Ambient component, and that component is seen best when all other light sources (especially the sun) are off or minimized. Both types of Pseudo-Lights are shown in Figure 4.18.

Figure 4.18
The ray of light running diagonally across this image is a cone mapped with the Pseudo-Light settings explained in the "Faking It" section. The objects below the ray of light are all mapped with the GreenLit material.

Use Pseudo-Lights for the following effects:

- Map Pseudo-Lights to a collection of small spheres to emulate fireflies on a dark night.
- Use Pseudo-Lights to give fish models the luminescence of deep-sea creatures.

- Map eyes with Pseudo-Lights to create eyes that glow in the dark.
- Use Pseudo-Lights to create sky objects: they make great stars and meteors.

Flames And Explosions

If you place a light in a volcano's vent, you create the appearance of glowing lava. The glow will be visible on low-lying clouds and on any ejecta. Placing a Radial Light in the middle of a virtual campfire lights all the beings sitting around the fire. You can create the flame emitted by a jet or rocket by elongating a sphere and mapping it with a Pseudo-Light. Or map a Pseudo-Light to a thin elongated cylinder to create a laser beam. Map a sphere with a rock material, duplicate the sphere, and then map the duplicate with Pseudo-Light to end up with a glowing a meteor. You can even wrap the textured sphere with a Radial Light to achieve the same effect.

Dark Lights

New to version 4 of Bryce is the ability to assign negative intensity values to any of the Placed Lights. The negative value can range from -1 to -999. Explore what happens when you add negative lights to your scene. If you use only negative lights, everything becomes invisible. If you use a negative light in combination with positive lights, the negative light moderates the illumination according to the negative light's intensity and placement. You can also explore negative illumination by setting the color of a Placed Light to solid black.

Using Gels

A gel is a partially transparent screen that is placed in front of or around a light. A gel has areas of transparency that allow the light to shine through and areas of opacity that block the light. Bryce supports two kinds of gels: Picture Gels and Texture Gels.

Picture Gels

You can use any image as a Picture Gel. However, if the image has an Alpha Channel, Bryce requires that the picture be a PICT (Mac) or BMP (Windows) file. You can use any Placed Light to project a Picture Gel, but different kinds of lights produce different results. For instance:

- A Radial Light casts the image in all directions from the center of the light, creating a circular pattern on objects. In the Materials Editor, you can set a higher frequency for the images that the light creates, which results in smaller images that spread out in a circle from the center. Use a Radial Light with a Picture Gel to cast image effects throughout your scene. The images will be most visible on the dark side of an object, away from any other light. It is best to disable the sun in the Sky Lab if you want the entire object to receive the image projected by the Picture Gel. When you set the Radial Light to a color other than white, the projected image is tinted. As the Radial Light that projects the Picture Gel moves closer to an object, the projection creates a smaller image. Leave the falloff set to Linear and use an intensity between 20 and 40 for the clearest results. Altering the size of the Radial Light makes no difference. However, changing the shape of the Radial Light in any direction does make a difference: The projected image stretches accordingly. Moving or rotating the Radial Light also causes the projection to shift. See Figure 4.19.

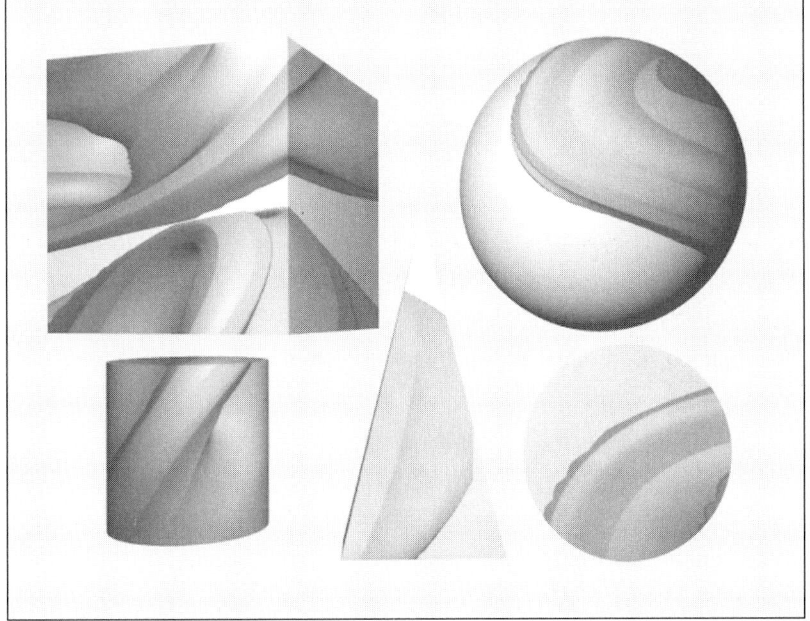

Figure 4.19
A single Radial Light using a Picture Gel casts images on all the objects in this scene. Notice that the projected image maps differently to each object.

- A Spotlight casts the image from a Picture Gel in an oval pattern. As the Spotlight projecting the Picture Gel moves closer to an object, the projection creates a smaller image cone, but the content being projected does not change. Parametric is the most common mapping type, but you can explore the others. The projected images are arranged in a circular or oval pattern within the light cone. Leave the falloff set to Linear and use an intensity between 20 and 40 for clearest results. Adjusting the size of the Spotlight alters the size of the projected cone. Changing the shape of the Radial Light in any direction stretches the projected image accordingly in the modified light cone. Moving or rotating the Radial Light also shifts the projection. Rotating the light so that the cone no longer falls on any objects makes the projection invisible. If you want the Spotlight to cast a projected picture on all objects, even those far away, set Falloff to None. Adding a fuzzy edge to the Spotlight cone diminishes the intensity of the entire projected image. See Figure 4.20.

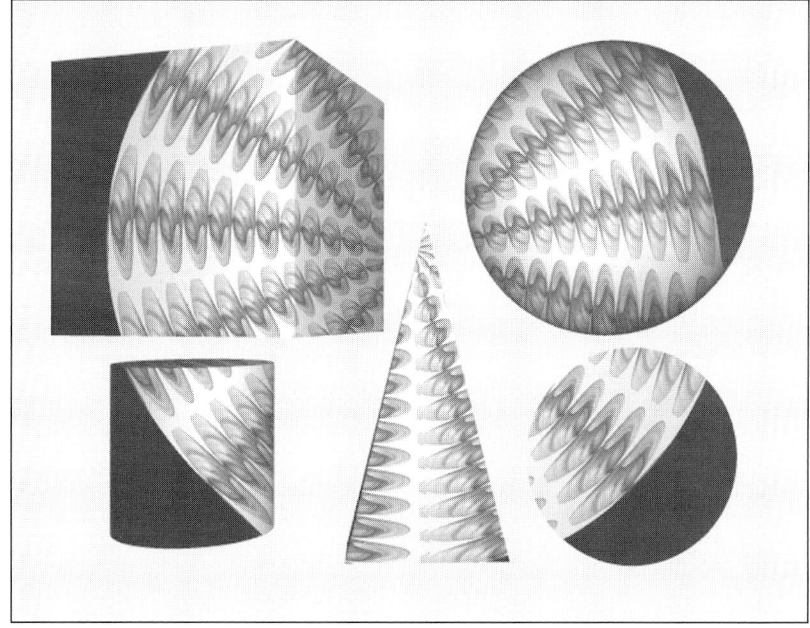

Figure 4.20
When you use a Picture Gel with a Spotlight, a circular pattern of projected images from the Picture Gel is cast on targeted objects.

- Everything I said about the Spotlight also applies to the Square Spotlight, with a minor set of differences. First, the Square Spotlight has a rectangular light projection, so the projected data (when the mapping is Parametric) appears as a series of columns and rows, matching the Frequency set in the Materials Lab. See Figure 4.21.
- The Parallel Light is very special when it comes to using gels of any type. When you adjust the light's size to match a targeted object and point the light directly at the object, the image is projected onto an object without polluting other objects in the vicinity. You could, for example, cast images onto a virtual movie screen in a virtual theater without having the image spill onto the virtual audience. As you move the Parallel Light farther from the targeted object (without altering its size or position) the projected image gets dimmer. See Figure 4.22.

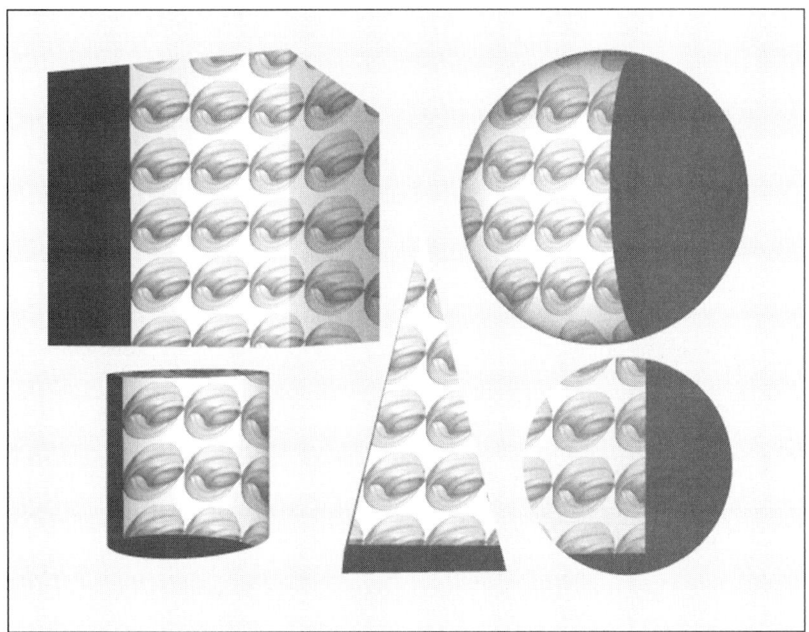

Figure 4.21
The Square Spotlight casts a rectangular light, displaying the Picture Gel data in columns and rows.

Figure 4.22
The Parallel Light is perfect for casting images onto a flat screen, simulating a projector in a movie theater. Two separate Parallel Lights are shown here, casting images on the cube and the sphere.

Two-Color Picture Gels

Two-color Picture Gels create a special gel effect. Two-color Picture Gels must have an Alpha Channel to work properly. There is a large collection of two-color gels on the Bryce CD-ROM. The Alpha Channel contains the reversed image shown in the Picture's Color component. See Figure 4.23.

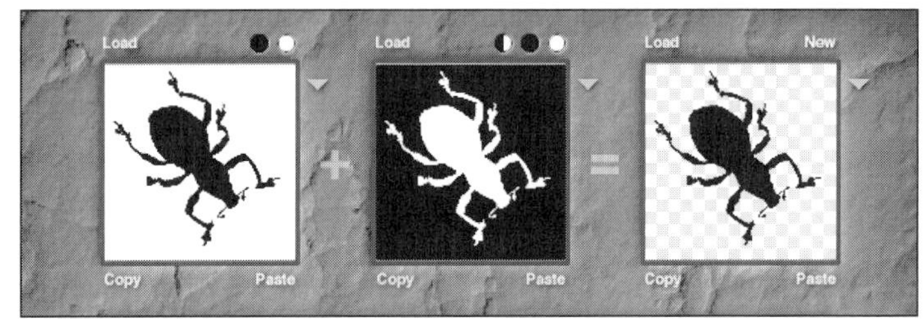

Figure 4.23
A two-color Picture Gel in the Picture Editor.

You can reverse both the color and Alpha Channel images to create a reverse projection with a two-color gel. Just copy the Alpha Channel data back to the Color Channel, and reverse the Alpha Channel again. You can use a two-color Picture Gel to simulate an object's shadow, even when the object itself doesn't appear in the scene. This is especially useful when creating a creature's shadow or light streaming through a window. To cast shadows of objects, use Parametric mapping with a Frequency of zero for best results. Of all the types of Placed Lights, Spotlights and Square Spotlights work best with two-color Picture Gels. See Figures 4.24 and 4.25.

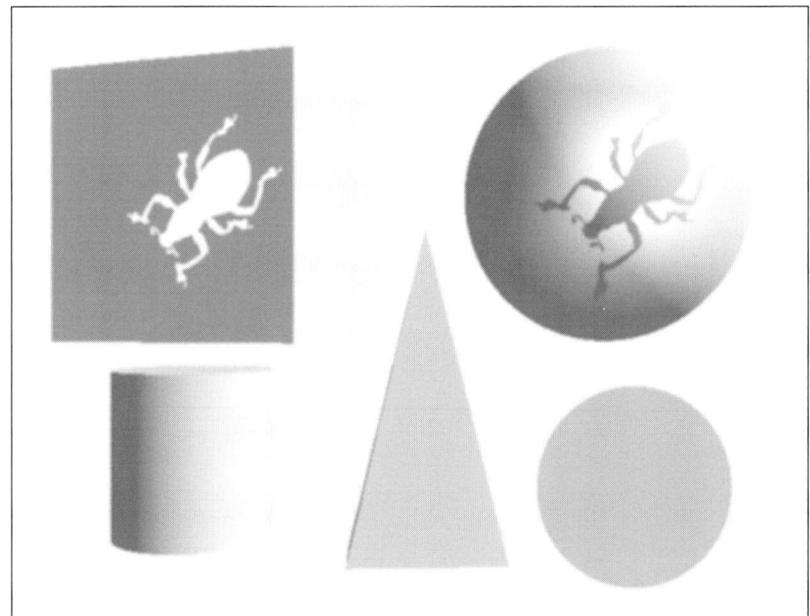

Figure 4.24
This scene features two Spotlights. The one on the left shows the cast image reversed and looks like light streaming through a bug-shaped window. The same projection appears cast on the sphere as a normal silhouette.

Texture Gels

You can apply a Texture Gel from a light's Edit dialog box or from the light's Materials Lab. If you use the Edit dialog box, you can select from any of the Materials Presets in your collections. When you apply a Texture Gel from the Materials Lab, you can create a multitextured material to use as the gel. Applying a Texture Gel is much the same as applying a Picture Gel; however, when you use a Texture Gel, you can use your expertise with Procedural Textures.

Figure 4.25
Here, the same two-color Picture Gel is used with a Radial Light at a Frequency of 75. Note the many ways the image is mapped to objects of different shapes.

Texture Gels interact with the varieties of Placed Lights in the same ways as Picture Gels. Working with both types of gels combines your lighting skills with your knowledge of textures and materials. But when you work with Texture Gels, you have more options for creating the effects you want—options you don't have when you work with Picture Gels. Here are some tips for using Texture Gels:

- In general, use textures that have an Alpha Channel. You can create a gel that allows the object's material to shine through the Alpha Channel. In the Materials Lab, set the texture to a picture texture using the small, lower button (second from the left), and then click on the small, upper button (second from the left). This takes users into the Picture Room where bitmaps and Alpha Channels can be loaded.
- Although Parametric mapping is usually the best choice for a gel, you should explore other mapping options to preview the effect.
- Explore reflection mapping to get an even application of the gel image across objects' surfaces (especially when using a Radial Light).
- Use random mapping to create *caustics* (the random patterns of light produced at the bottom of a pool of water).

Surface And Volumetric Lighting

When you make a light either a Surface Light or a Volumetric Light (from the light's Edit dialog box), the light source—in addition to its light cone—becomes visible. Radial Lights appear as disks (when set to Surface

Light) or spheres (when set to Volumetric Light). Other light sources (with either of these options applied) are visible only when they face the camera. Surface Lights are best mapped with Surface Picture or Texture Gels. Volumetric Lights are best mapped with Volumetric Texture Gels. When you make the light a Surface Light or a Volumetric Light, the light becomes a visible actor in the scene. Mapping the light with a Picture or Texture Gel emphasizes its participation as an object. See Figure 4.26.

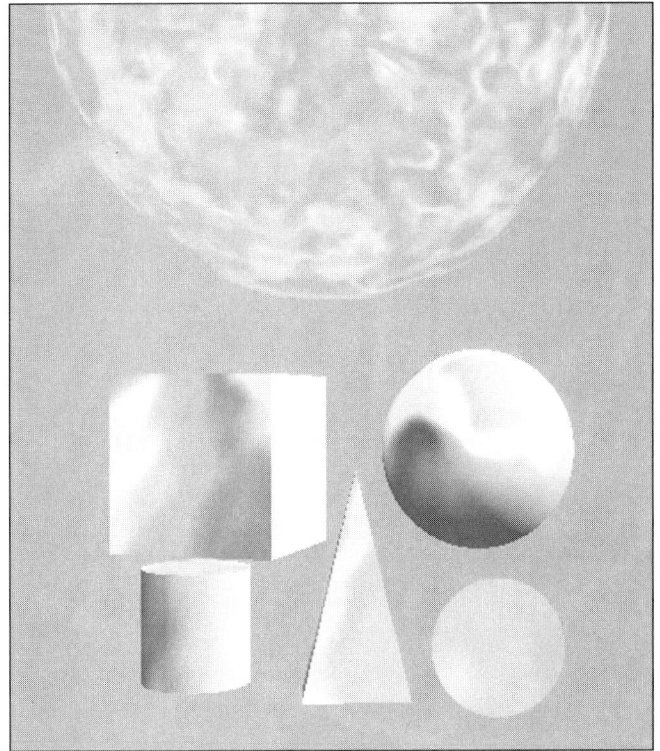

Figure 4.26
The Radial Light displayed here is shown as a Volumetric Light and mapped with the Nebula Volumetric Texture Gel. The light illuminates the scene, casts gel imagery, and can also be seen as an object itself.

Behind The Camera

Mastering the camera is vital to your Bryce work. After all, the camera is the portal through which the viewers see the world you create. Changing a camera angle calls attention to a different arrangement of elements. Whether you are creating keyframes for an animation (see Chapter 5) or developing single images, you must understand camera use thoroughly.

Repositioning The Camera

The position of the default camera is poor, to say the least. It faces in a direction that makes it awkward to orient yourself to the sun's movements and difficult to understand the location and rotation of objects. You should reposition the camera to remedy these problems. From the top view, orient the camera so that it points up from the bottom of the screen toward the top of your monitor, as shown in Figure 4.27. Select the camera's attributes and set the rotation to X=0, Y=0, and Z=0. (You can always adjust the camera's rotation later, if needed.) Save this new blank scene in the Bryce directory, and load it as your default camera view each time you use Bryce. Sadly, Bryce does not remember to use this new camera location and rotation, so you'll have to load it each time you open the software. See Figure 4.27.

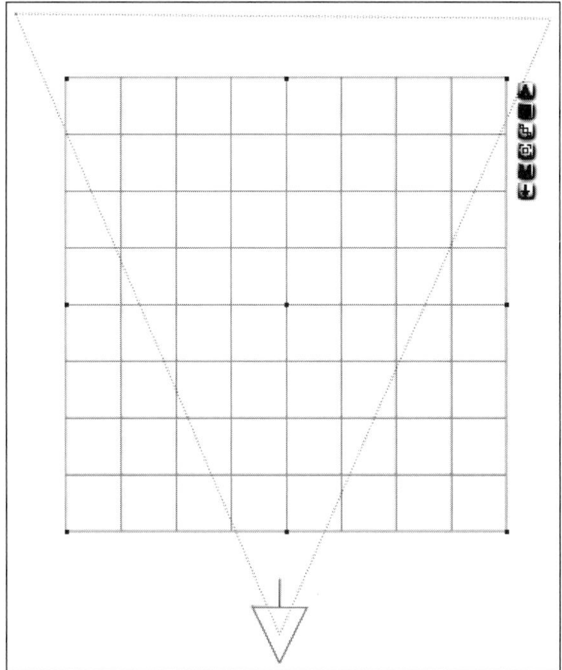

Figure 4.27
This top view shows the new camera position you should use as a default before you do anything else in Bryce.

Understanding Camera Attributes And How To Customize Them

In Bryce, the camera is an object like other objects, so you can manipulate it in space and time. Altering the items in the Camera's Attributes dialog box must become second nature to you if you are to master Bryce.

The General Tab

The General tab in the Camera & 2D Projection dialog box contains a series of customization options, shown in Figure 4.28.

This version of Bryce does not allow you to rename the camera. But a Bryce scene has only one camera, so there is really no need to rename it. The Free option (which allows you to move the camera anywhere) is selected by default. If you select the Locked option, you can't move the camera. This is this useful in certain views (most notably the front view) in which the camera can get in the way when you try to select another

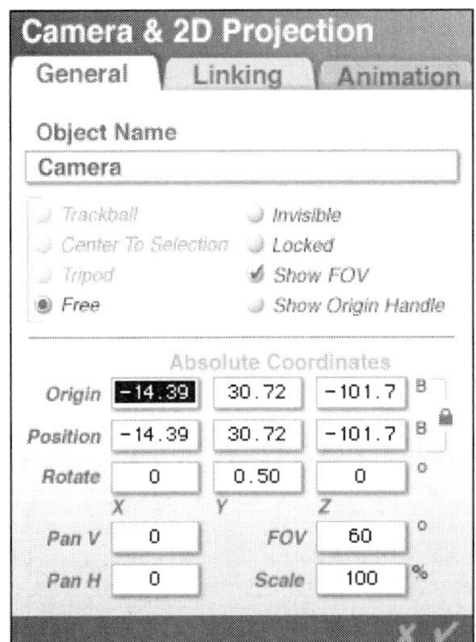

Figure 4.28
The General tab of the Camera & 2D Projection dialog box.

object. When you lock the camera, you can select it only from the selection list below the preview window.

When you select the Invisible option, the camera is not visible in the preview window. This is useful while initially configuring the scene's elements. The Show FOV option should always be turned on so you can see exactly how the cone of the camera's lens takes in parts of the scene. (FOV stands for Field Of Vision.) The Origin Handle option should always be turned on, too. This option allows you to place the camera's center anywhere within the scene to create animated rotations around selected objects. (See Chapter 5 for more on animation.)

The FOV and Size controls play a large role when you create camera-based animations. The FOV defaults to 60. Although decreasing FOV to 40 has the same initial affect on the image as increasing Camera Scale to 160, these actions are not the same. FOV sets the camera's Field of Vision (that is, how much of the scene the camera takes in). Taking in more of the scene widens the view and makes everything appear smaller at the same time. But Camera Scale is a zoom mechanism. Maximizing these settings results in some strange depth effects: Objects warp as they move closer to or farther away from the camera. Maximizing the Scale setting creates more exaggerated warping effects. Explore both of these controls at various settings to get a feel for exactly what they produce.

The Linking Tab

The Linking tab in the Camera & 2D Projection dialog box (shown in Figure 4.29) provides a list of the objects in the scene to which you can link the camera.

Bryce 4 Studio

The color images in this section highlight how computer graphics and animation professionals are putting Bryce 4 through its paces. All of the images in this section are discussed in Chapter 6.

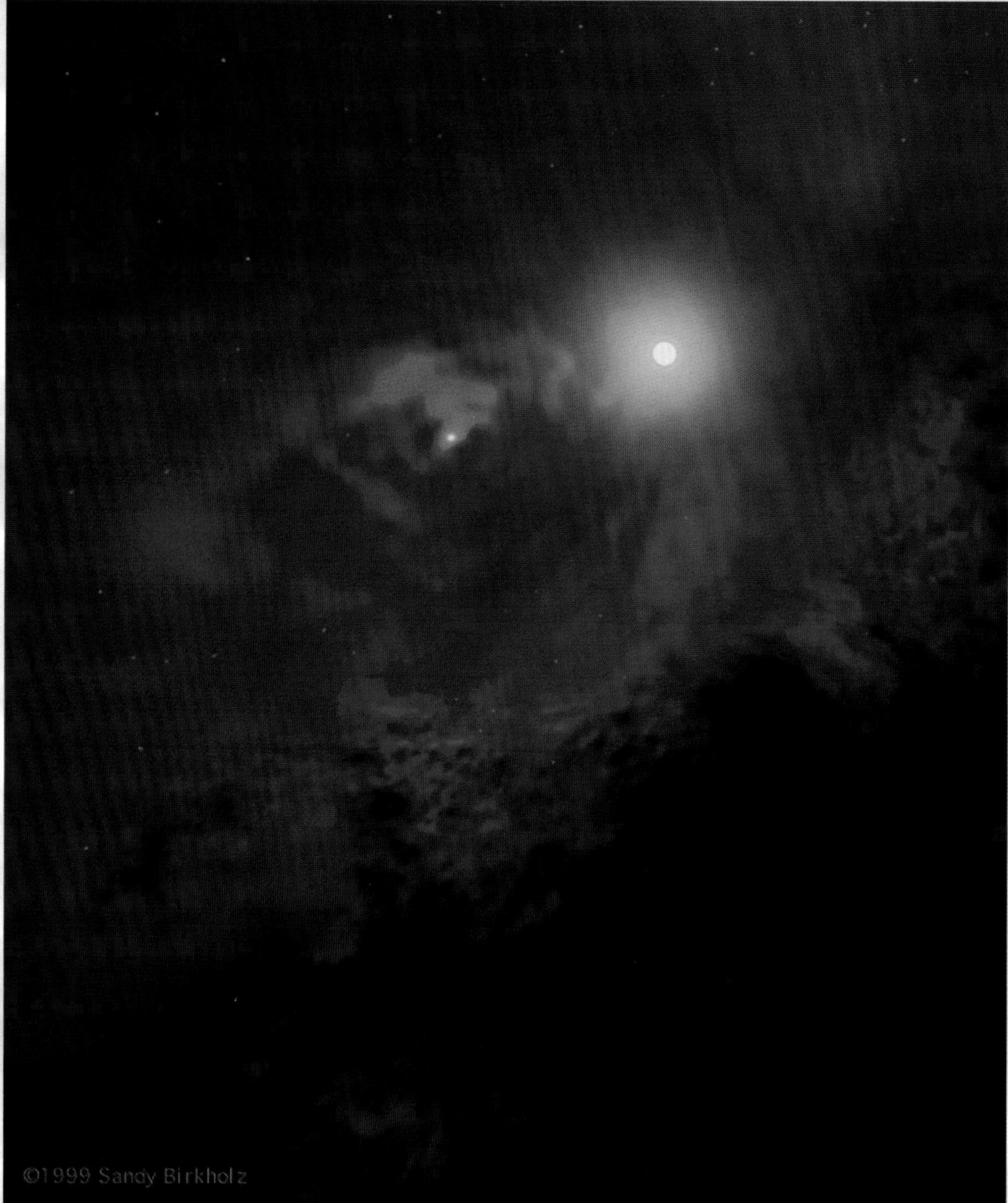

Dusty Nebula
Sandy Birkholz

This artwork displays Bryce's ability to create naturalistic cloud phenomena.

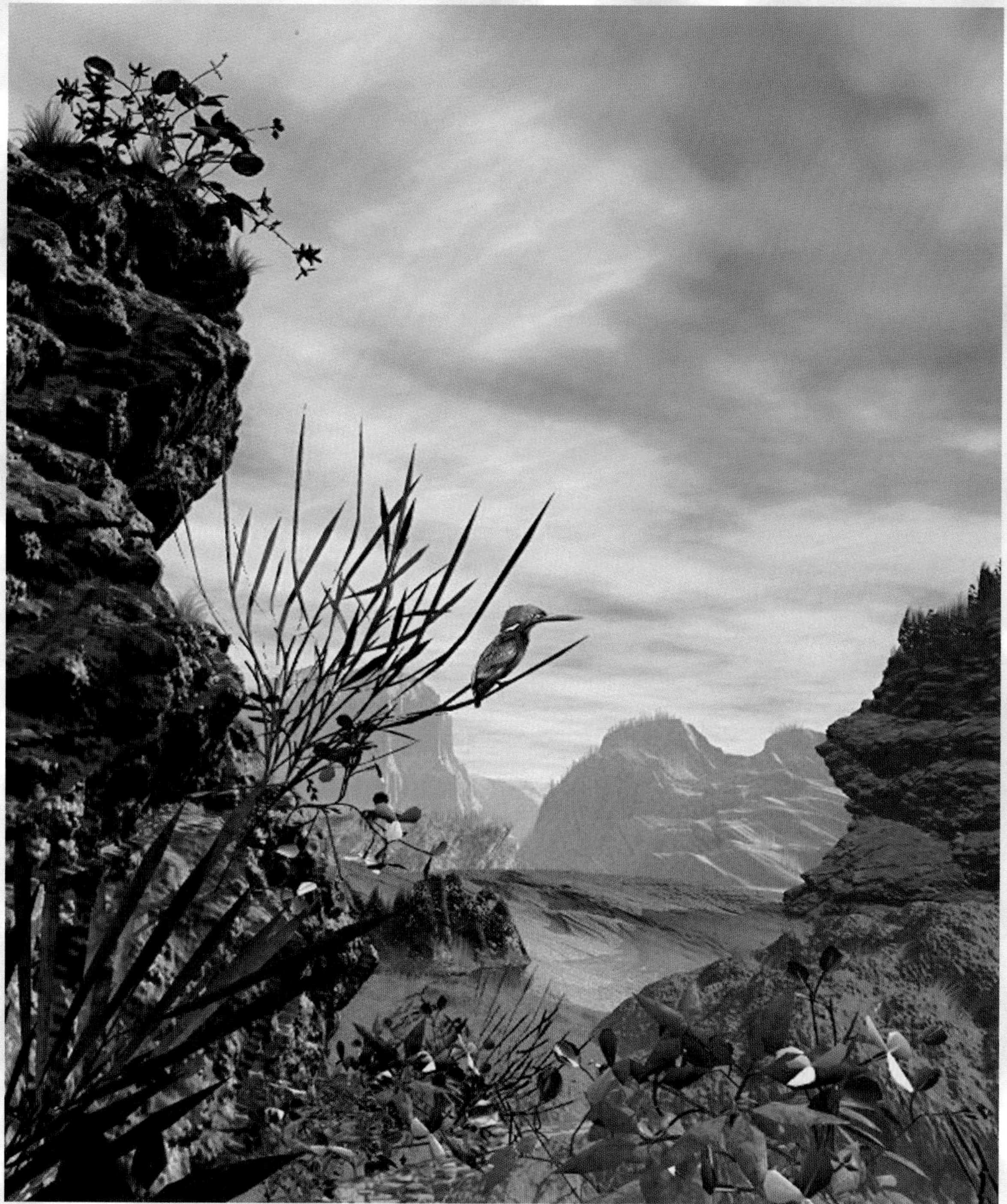

Almost Eden
Jeff Richardson

Bryce terrains and materials make photorealistic natural worlds possible.

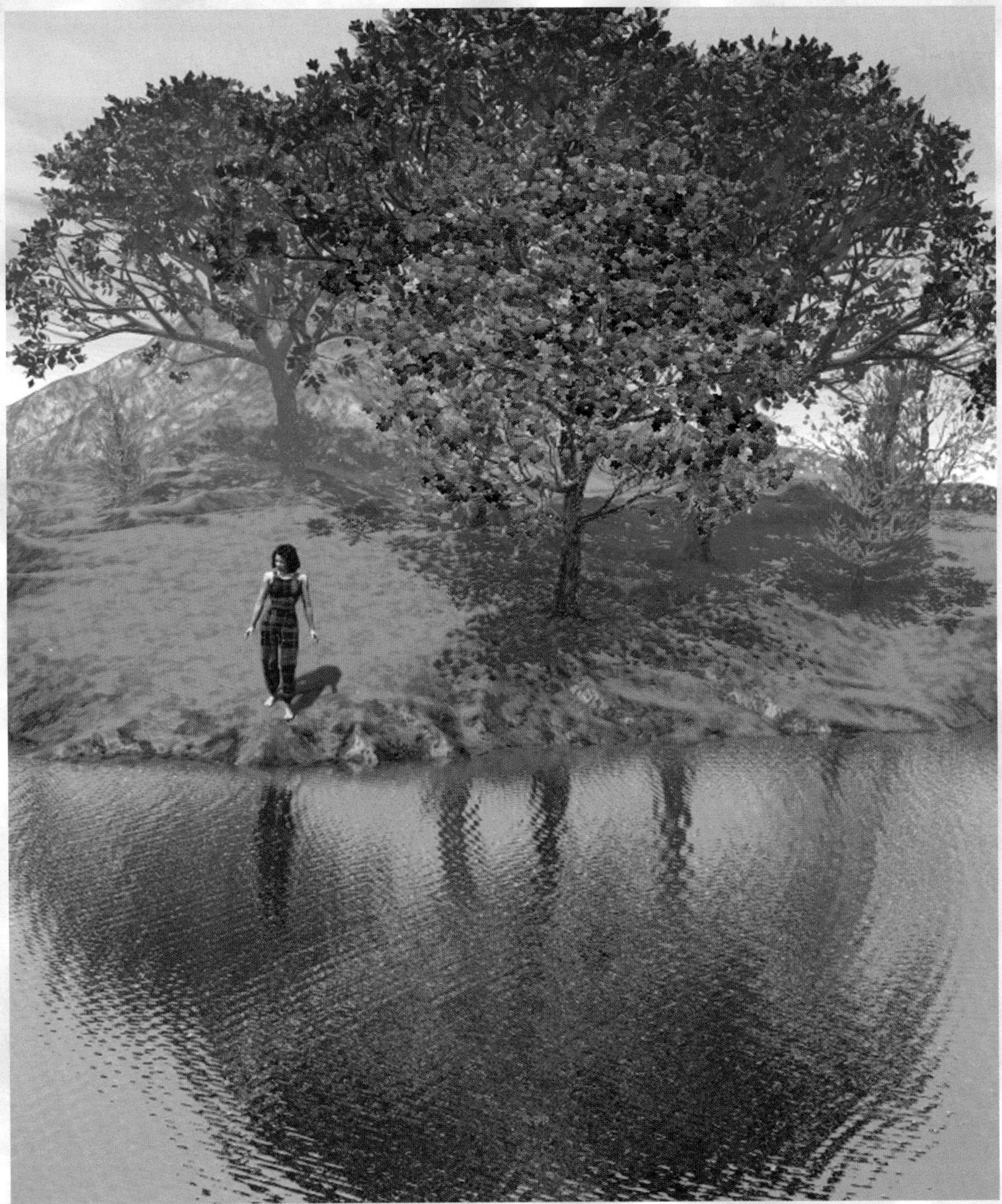

Promenade dans l'île
Martial Fauteux

In the right hands, Bryce is capable of creating muted paint effects.

Melbourne, Australia
Kuzey Atici

The city of Melbourne, Australia, was modeled faithfully in Bryce.

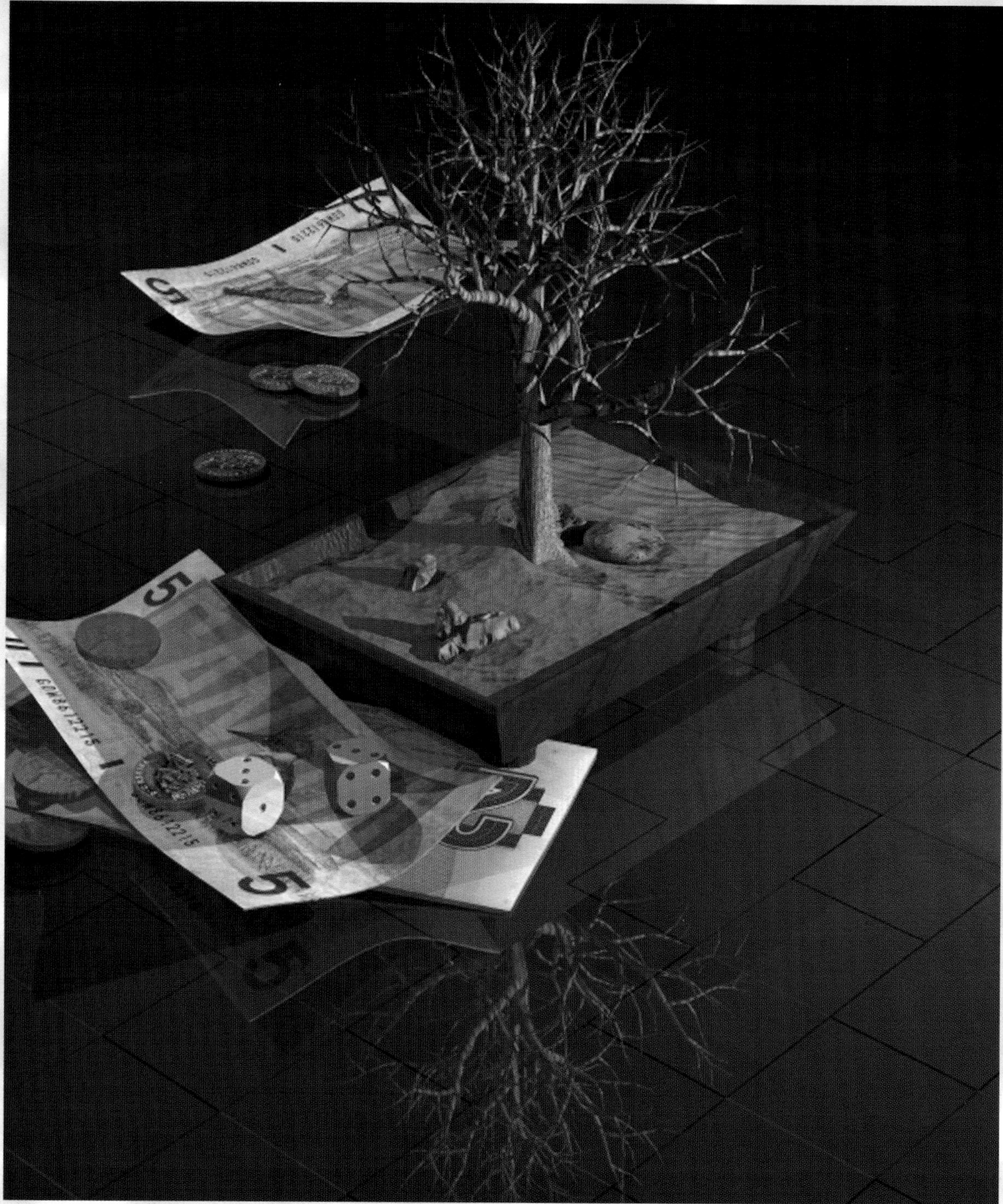

Bonsai
Andrew Paul

This complex still life owes its existence to a master Bryce artist.

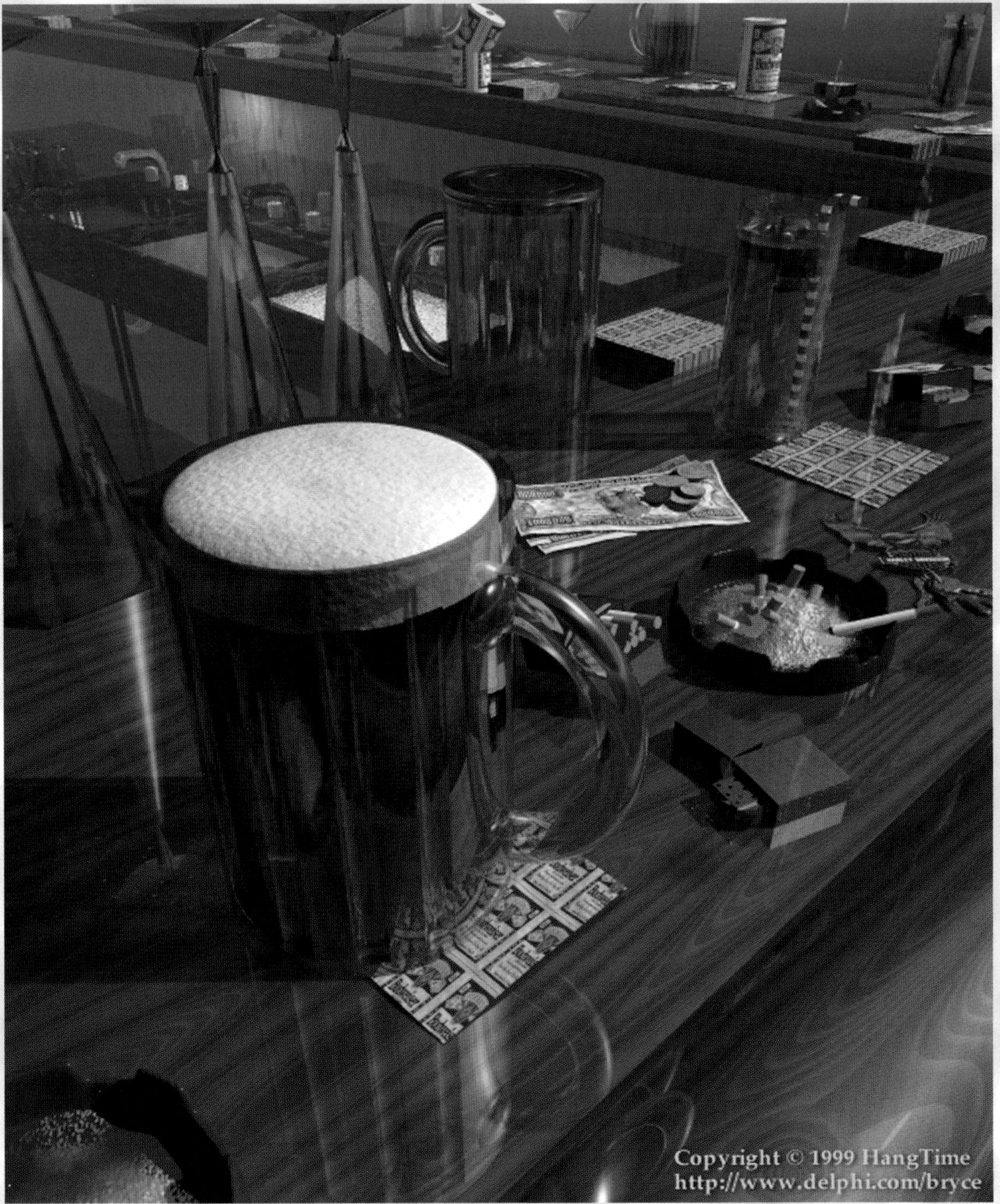

Digital Tavern
Bruce "HangTime" Caplin

Bryce can be used to create indoor masterpieces that contain complex transparent surfaces.

In Praise Of The Best Seller
Robert Cross

Bryce's picture mapping capabilities make creating a book cover a simple task.

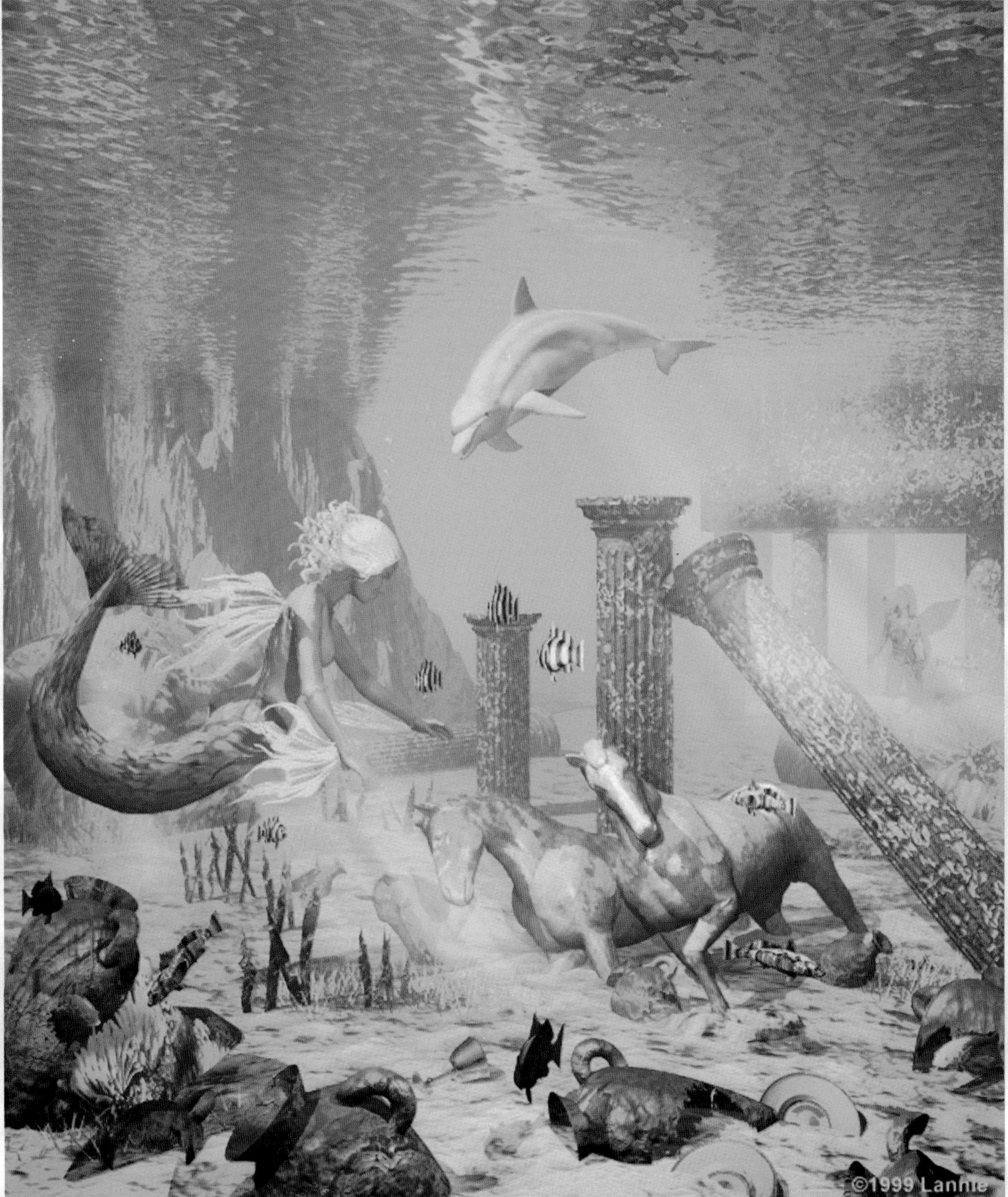

Treasures
Lannie Caranci

The tools that create atmospheric effects can also be used for underwater scenes.

A Friendly Card Game
Lee Chapel

MetaCreations' Poser figures can give a Bryce scene that extra touch of believability.

Creada
Mark J. Smith

Surrealistic worlds can be expressed effectively in Bryce art.

Thor
Mark J. Smith

Using a mix of realism and fantasy, Bryce artists can shape dreams.

Forbidding Hands
Celia Ziemer

This image mixes atmospheric effects with imported Poser figures.

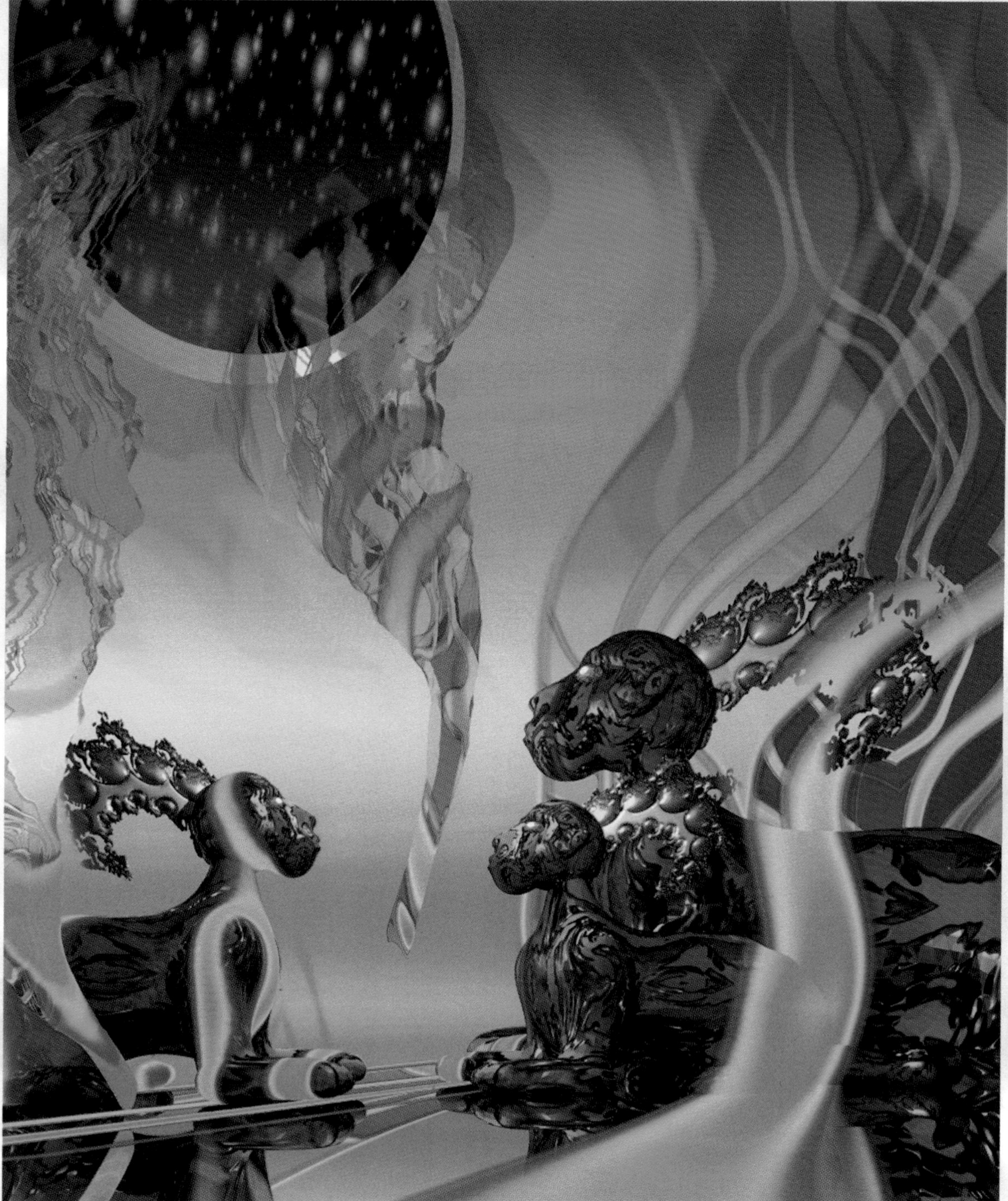

Environment
Celia Ziemer

The artist used a Photoshop filter to create a bitmap. Then, she wrapped the bitmap around a background object to produce an interesting atmospheric effect.

A City Somewhere Else
R. Shamms Mortier

Glowing effects created with ambient materials add lights in this image's shadows.

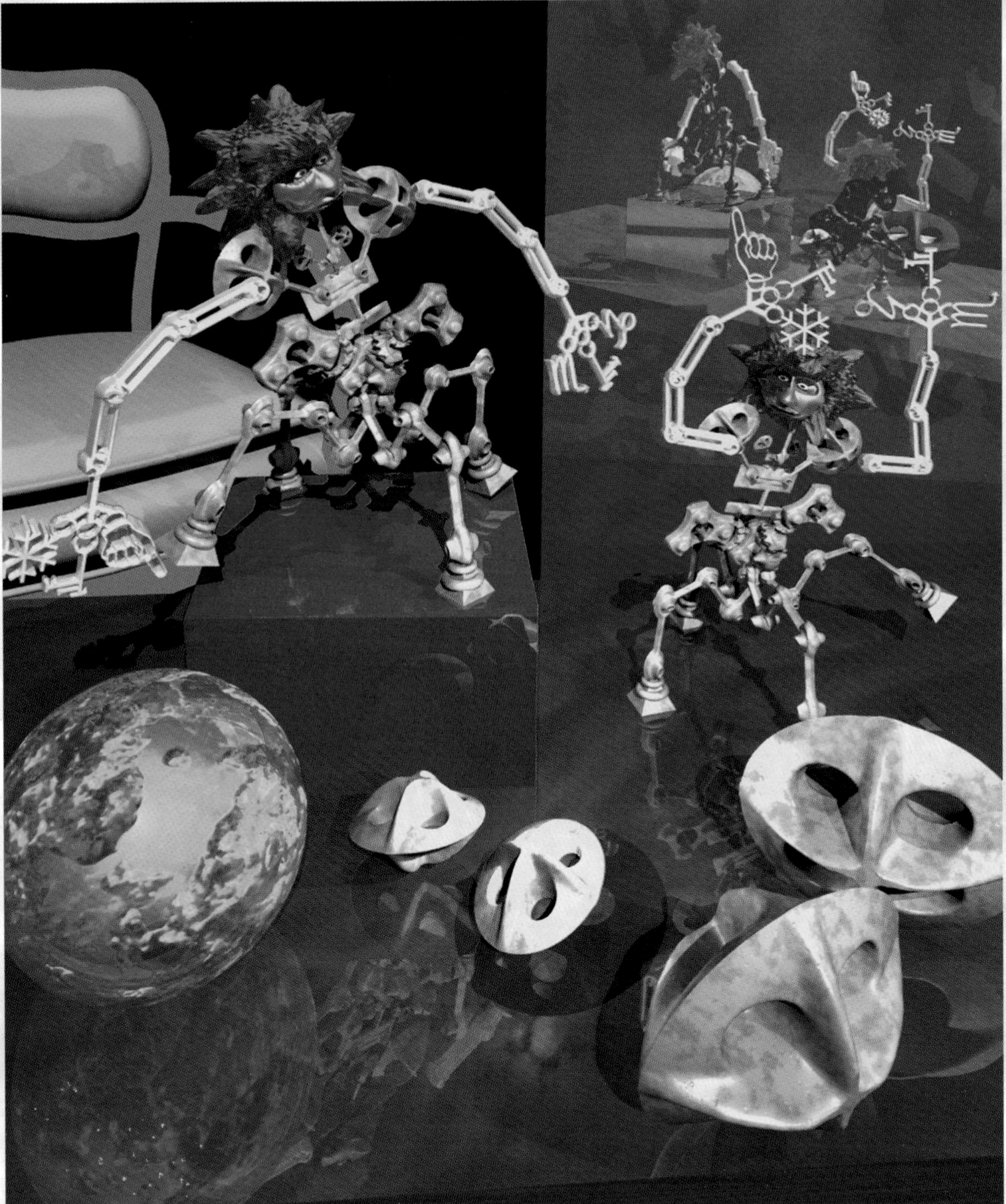

Tabletop Dance
R. Shamms Mortier

These figures were created entirely in Bryce's Terrain Editor using symmetrical lattice objects.

Watchers
R. Shamms Mortier

Layered fog and haze create mystery and enhance the depth of a 3D scene.

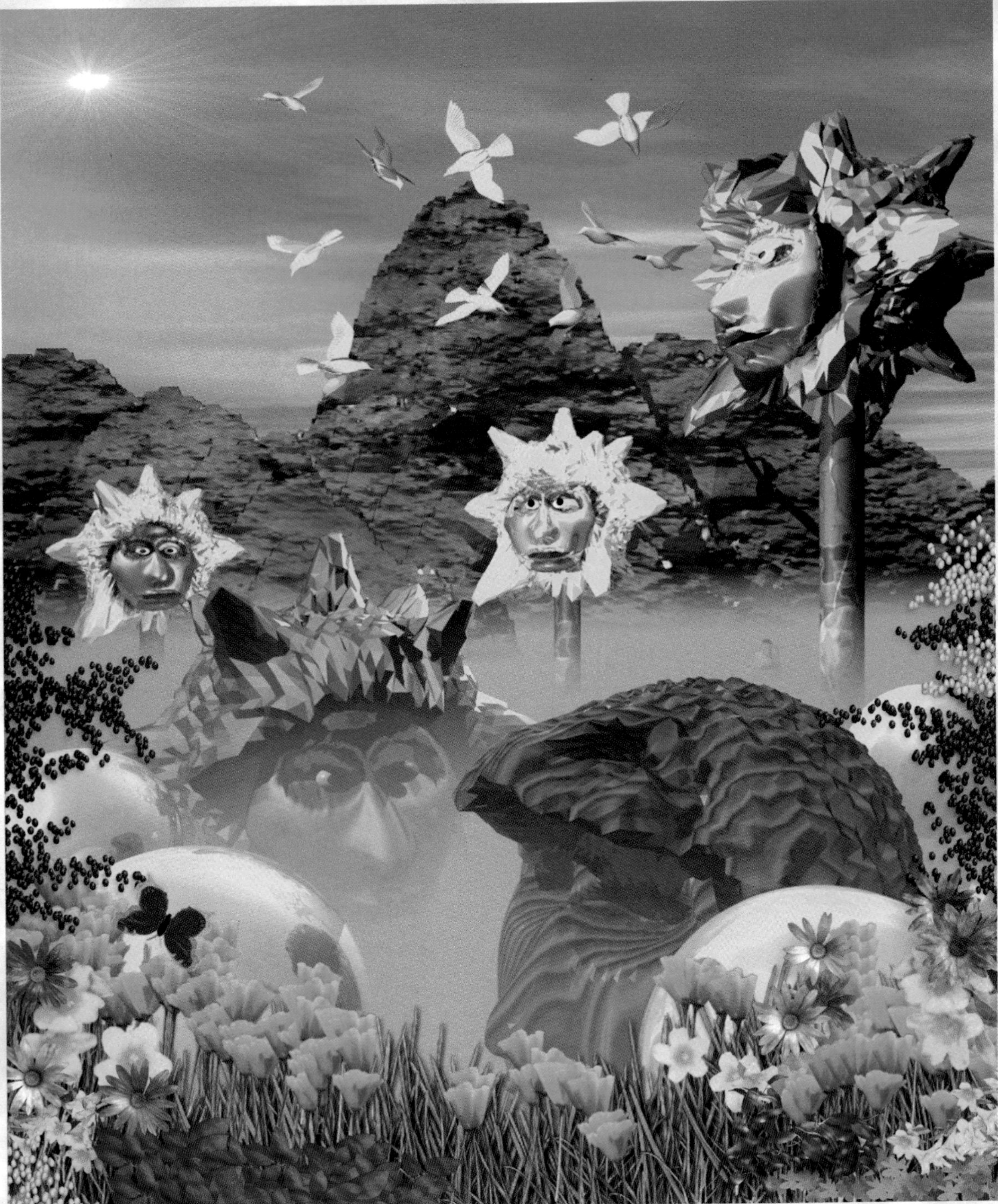

Springtime
R. Shamms Mortier

Mixing 3D objects and mapped 2D planes can foster the creation of complex scenes.

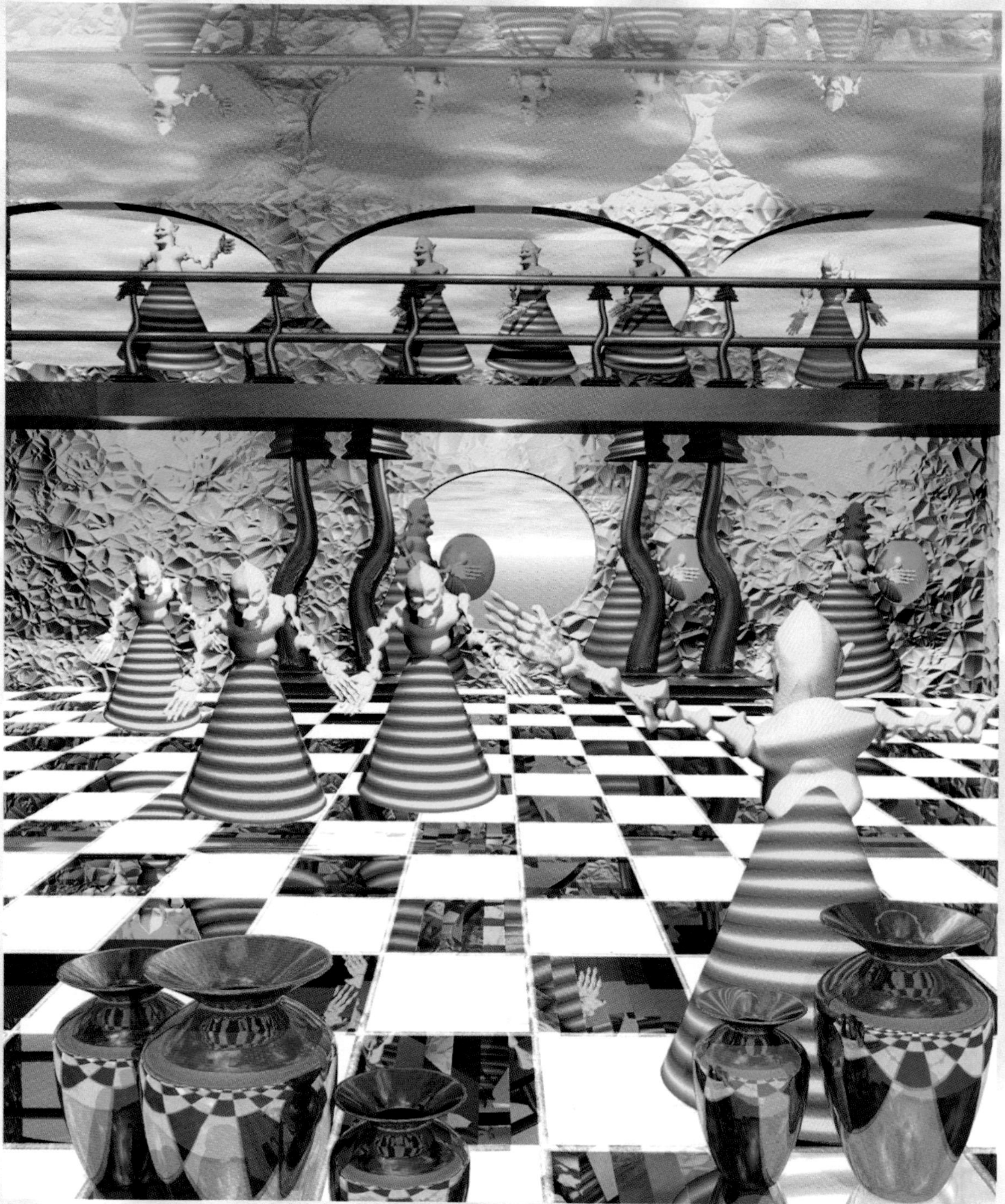

Fantasy Palace
R. Shamms Mortier

These figures are bitmaps created and rendered in Bryce. Then, they were mapped to 2D planes for compositing.

Altar
R. Shamms Mortier

Subtle fog and atmospheric effects help to create mesmerizing images in Bryce.

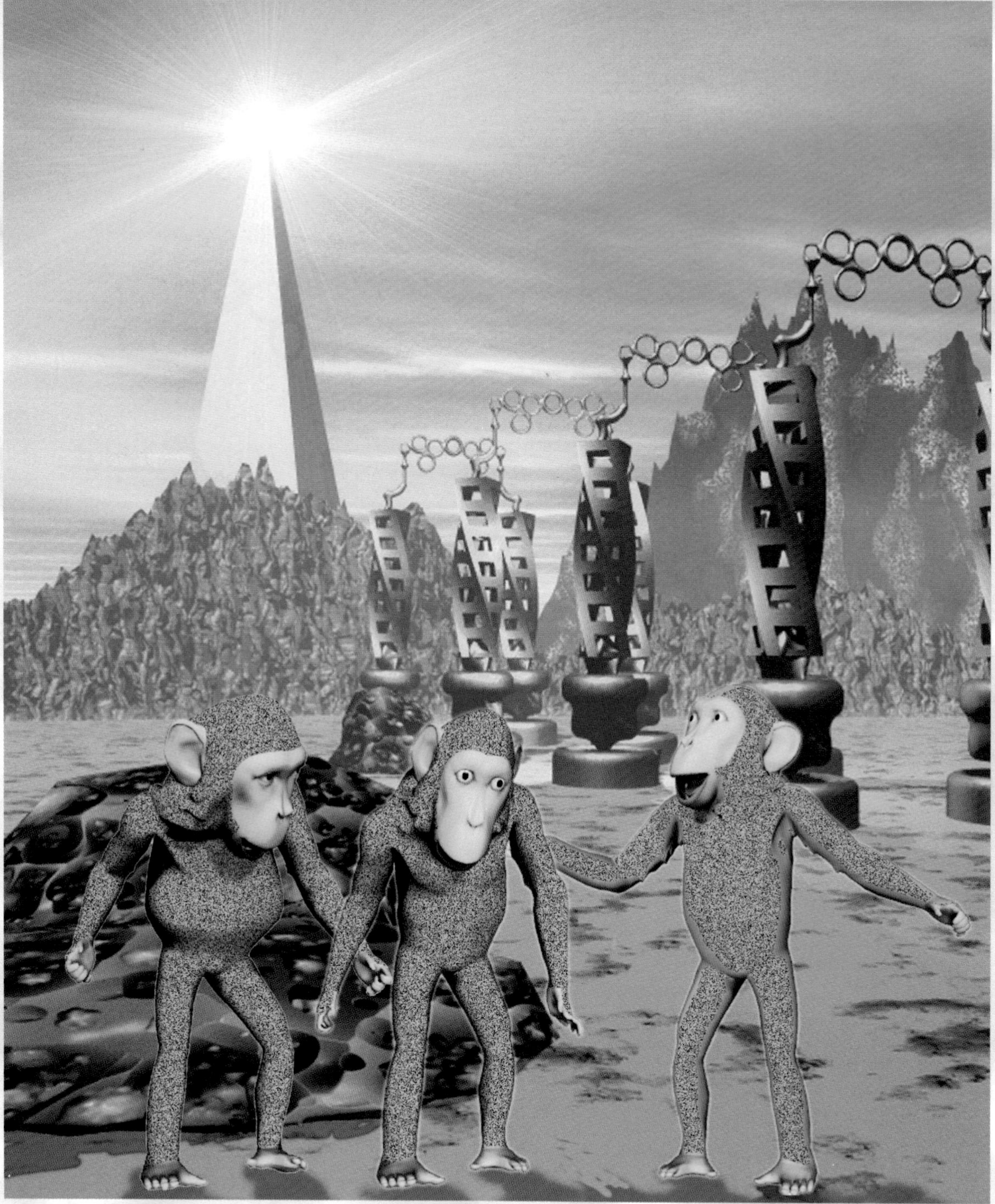

Three Comrades
R. Shamms Mortier

A customized chimp from Poser's Zygote collection adds creature content to this scene.

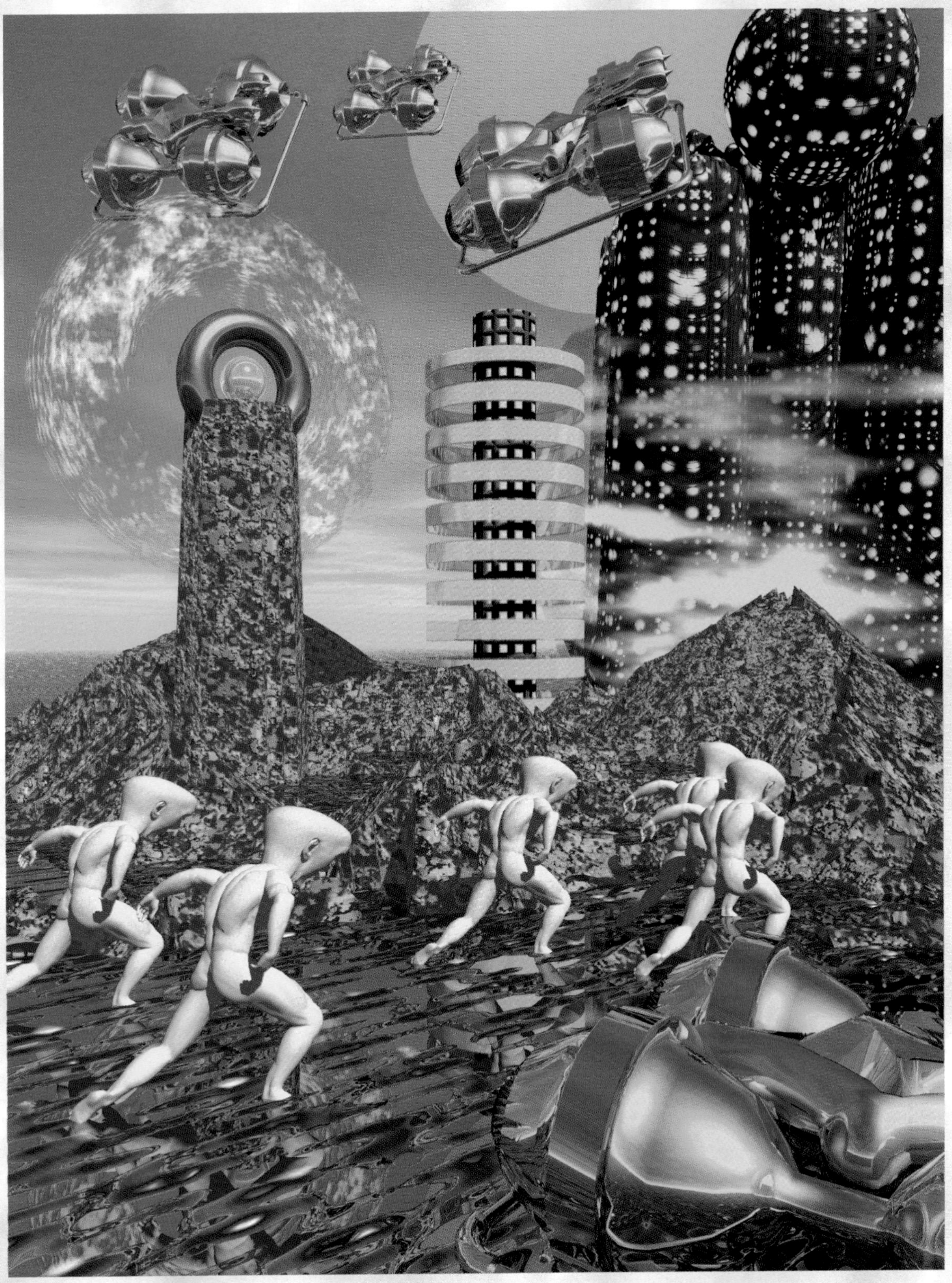

Off To The Mines
R. Shamms Mortier

Bryce can now import Lightwave models, such as the ships in the background of this image.

Frozen Outpost
R. Shamms Mortier

This artwork uses materials that simulate ice and a dark backdrop to give shape to an alien landscape.

Arrival
R. Shamms Mortier

Photoshop filters applied in Bryce add effects that would be otherwise impossible.

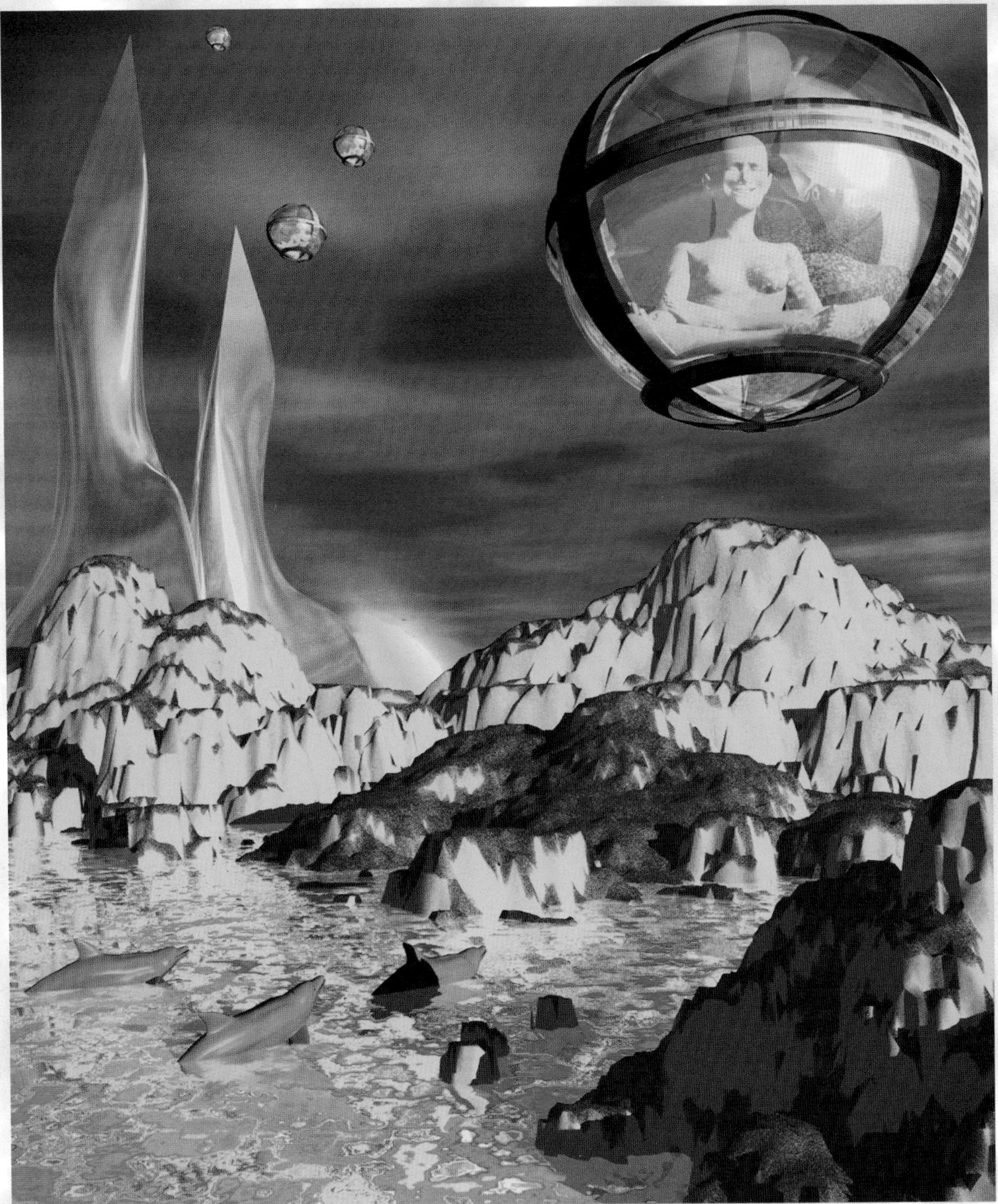

Air Bubble

R. Shamms Mortier

The globe floating above this scene was created by using a Bryce material with an active transparent channel.

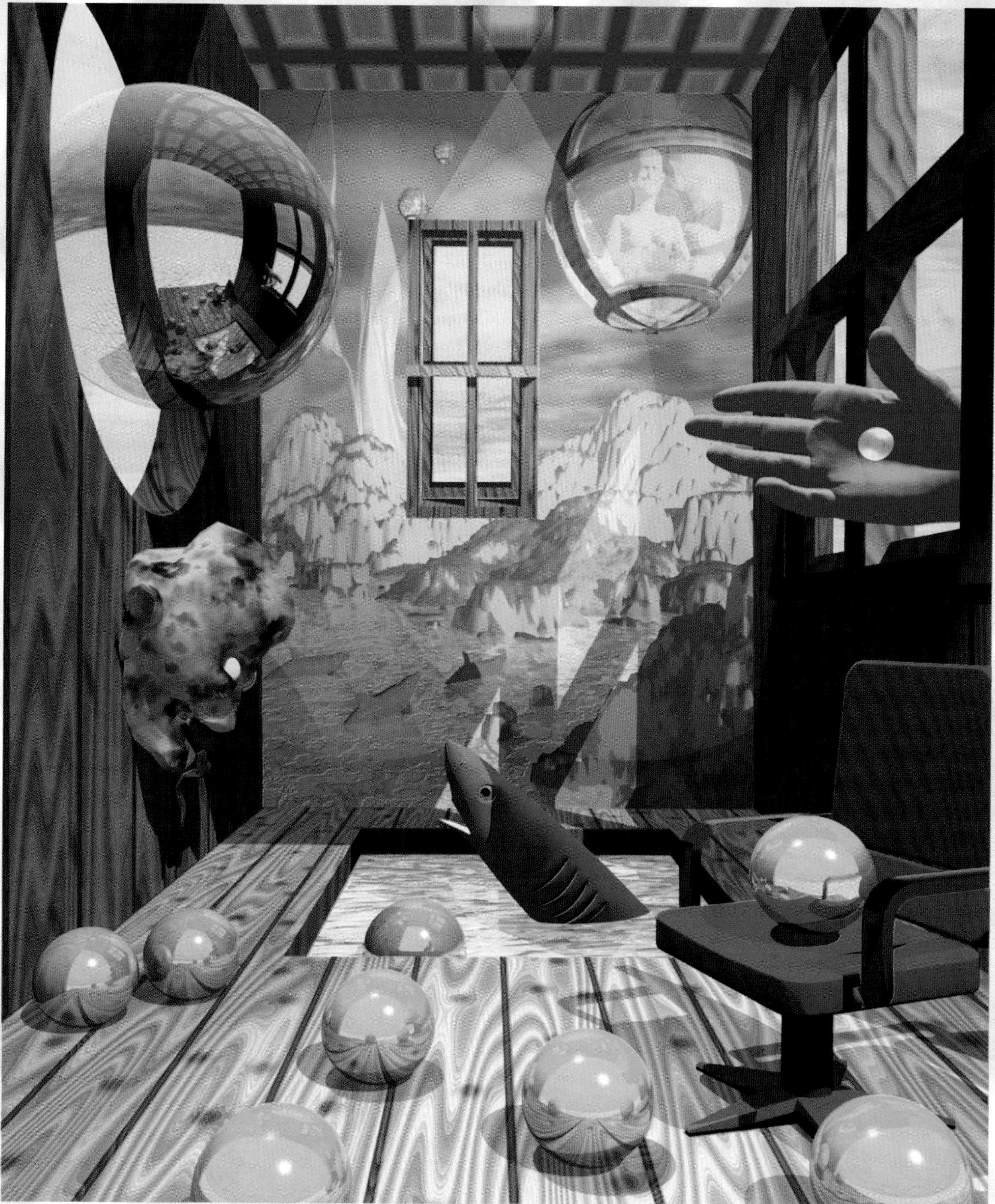

Extreme Surrealism

R. Shamms Mortier

The image on the previous page was used to map the back wall in this scene.

Insectium

R. Shamms Mortier

The background flowers were created by mapping a photograph taken outside of Westminster Abbey in London.

Mystery Island
R. Shamms Mortier

This image shows how Bryce allows you to develop extreme perspective views.

Transcending
R. Shamms Mortier

Designing customized skies is one of the strongest features in Bryce.

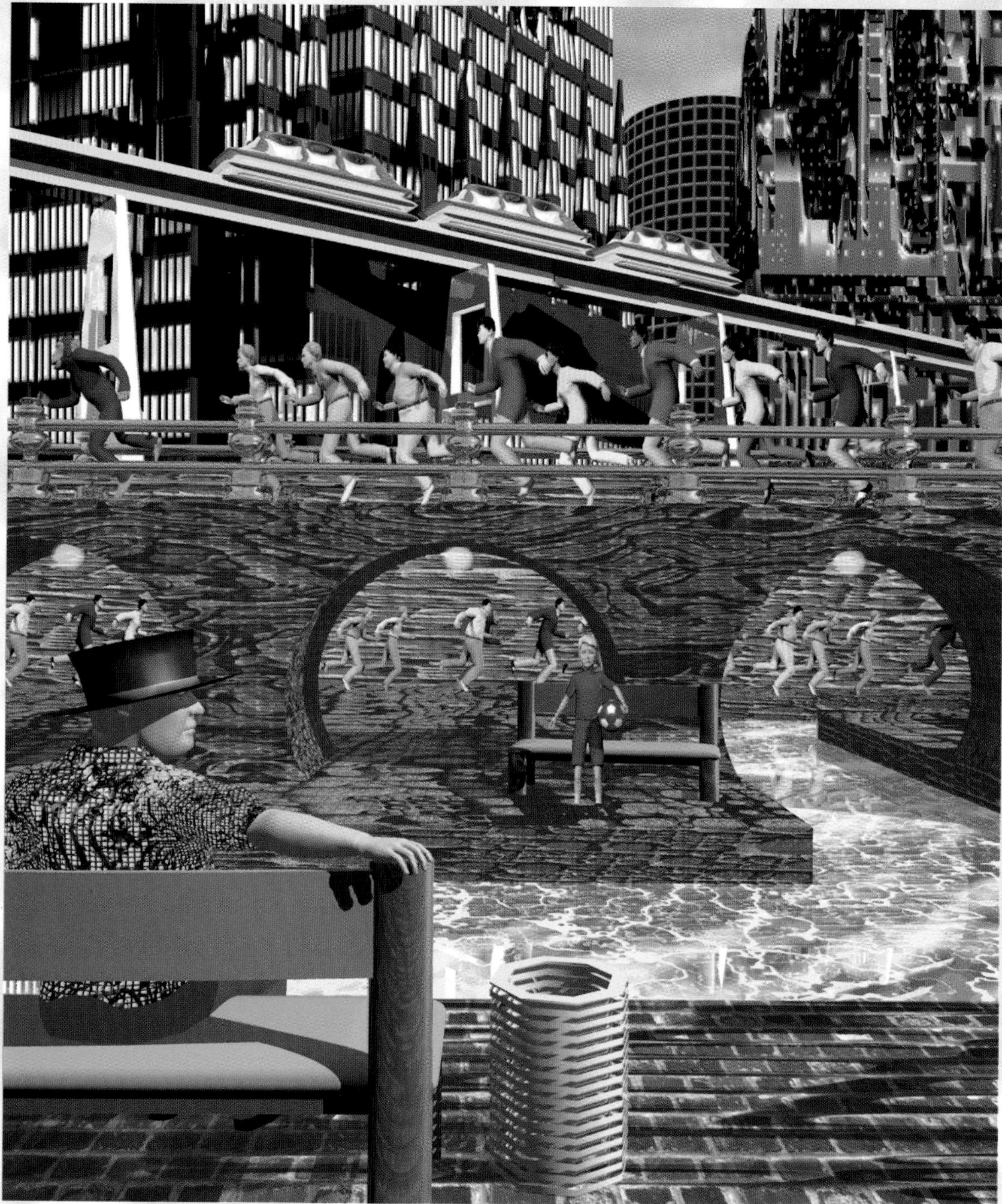

Rush Hour
R. Shamms Mortier

Although the man sitting on the bench is a 3D model, the other human figures are 2D image maps.

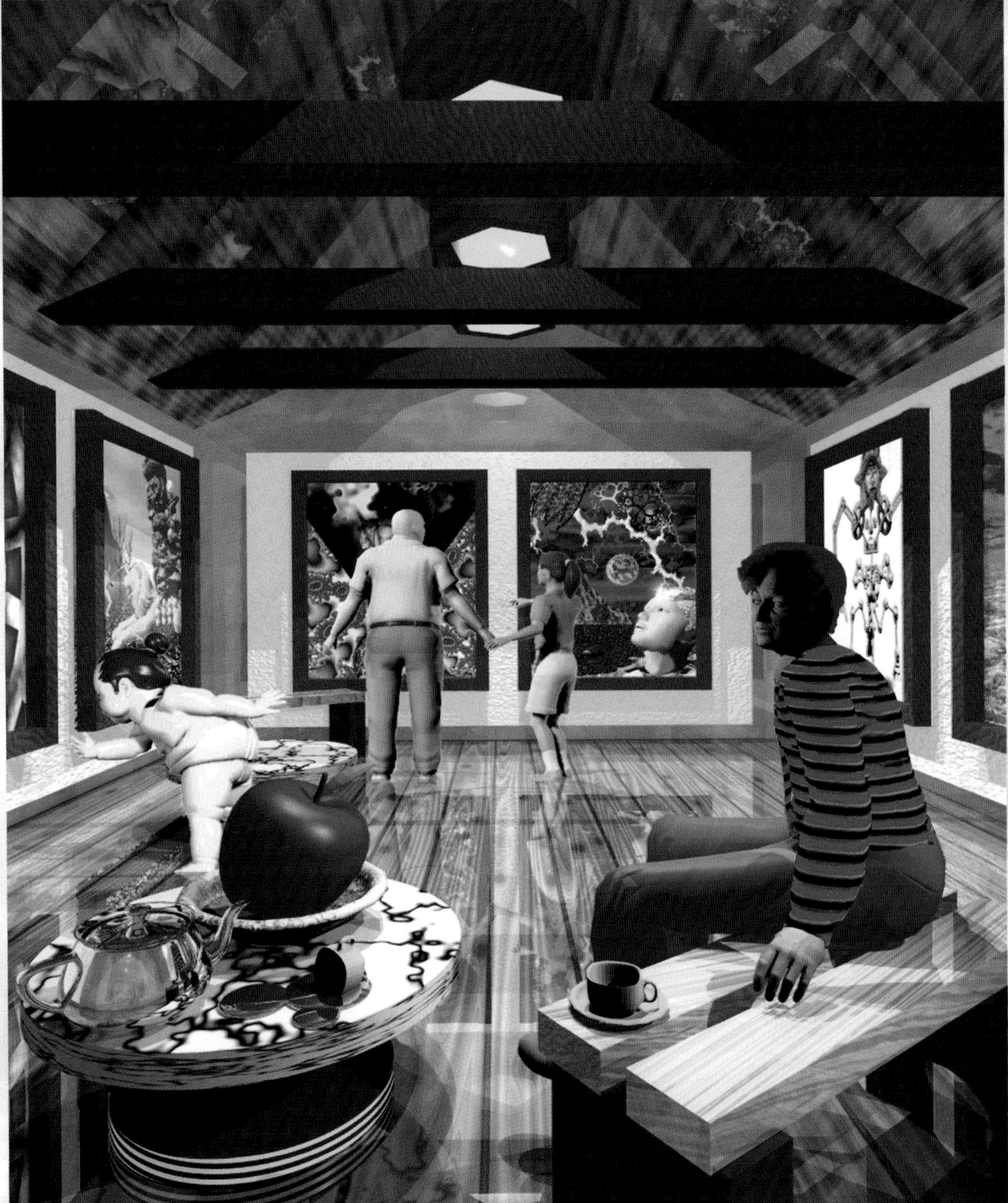

Art Gallery
R. Shamms Mortier

The author used large picture files of his work to create the paintings on the walls.

Tea And A Good Book

R. Shamms Mortier

The Bryce documentation rests on the table, ready for you to study.

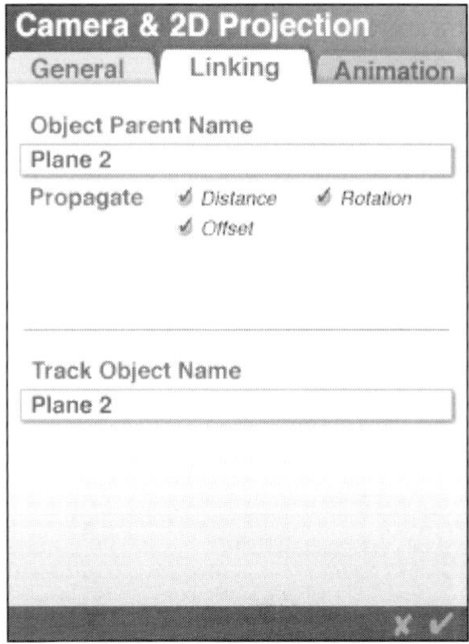

Figure 4.29
The Linking tab in the Camera & 2D Projection dialog box.

You can link the camera to any targeted object you want the camera to stay focused on. But when you do this, the contortions the targeted object goes through (such as changes in position, bouncing, and so on) cause the camera to repeat. Use the Linking function only when the camera is close to the object. Using the Tracking function (from the Linking tab in the Camera & 2D Projection dialog box) is a lot safer. Tracking is an important Bryce skill to master: You can cross-track a scene's items with each other, and this leads to complex animations. When tracking objects with the camera, keep the following points in mind:

- Track from moving camera positions to prevent intervening objects from popping into view.
- Make sure to move the object's origin point to a central location.
- Allow the camera to have its own path as it tracks an object. (See Chapter 5 for animation procedures.)

The Animation Tab

Camera animation processes are described in Chapter 5.

Family (The Color Box Icon)

The color you choose here becomes the color used to indicate where the camera is when it's not selected. Be sure to give the camera a color that stands out. The default color, blue, often gets lost among other scene components. Do not use the camera color for any other objects. See Figure 4.30.

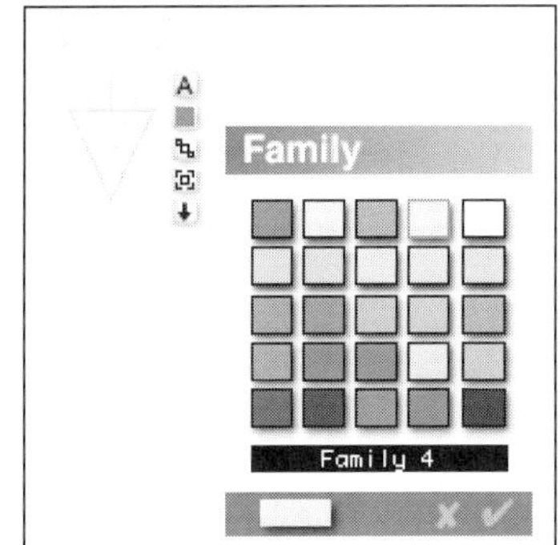

Figure 4.30
Select the camera's color in the Family dialog box.

Adjusting Camera Gravity

The camera's Gravity Arrow is useful for moving the camera to the Ground Plane or to the next item below it. Click on the Gravity Arrow icon and the camera drops to the next item below it. (The camera must be over the Infinite Plane's grid in order for this to work.)

Creating Your Own Camera Lens Effects

You can create some amazing distortion effects in Bryce by using camera lenses. Yes, that's right. In many ways, the Bryce camera acts like a real camera. And just as you can with a real camera, you can fit the Bryce camera with a variety of effects lenses. All you have to do is to create the lenses and position them. See Figure 4.31 for an example of an image created without a special lens. I'll use that image to demonstrate how lenses deform what the camera sees.

Figure 4.31
Here is a scene as it appears without special lenses.

Spherical Lens

The spherical lens is the simplest type of lens. Just map a sphere with a Glass Material preset (Light Glass works well), and place the sphere in front of the camera. A spherical lens acts like a magnifying glass when placed in front of the camera. See Figures 4.32 and 4.33.

Figure 4.32
The scene as it appears with a spherical lens in front of the camera.

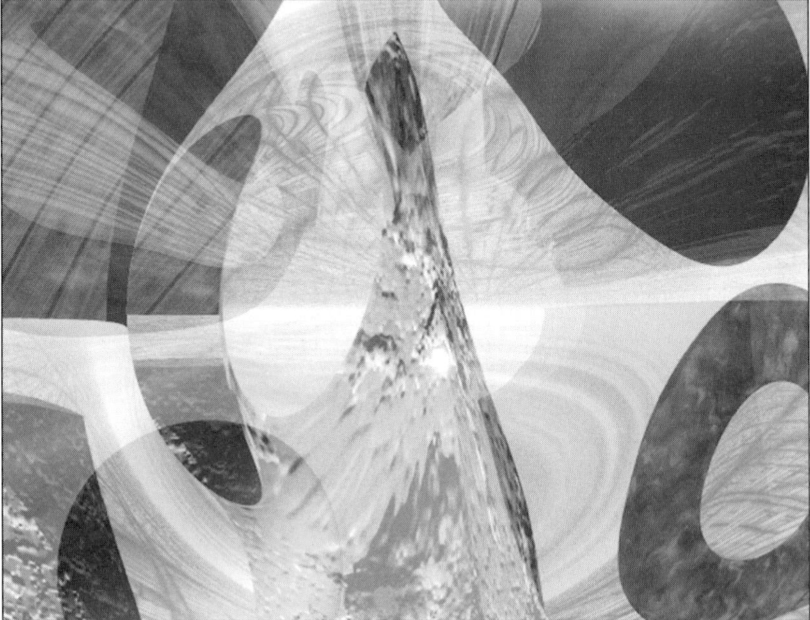

Figure 4.33
Elongating the glass sphere on its Z axis and placing the camera inside the sphere creates a severely warped image.

Conic Lens

You can use Bryce to create lenses that have yet to appear in the real world. You can use a cone as a lens, for example, and warp the resulting image in a number of ways depending on the cone's orientation, as shown in Figure 4.34.

Figure 4.34
In this example, the camera looks through a conic lens. The cone's base is toward the camera; the apex is pointed away from the camera.

Boolean Lens Effects

By using Boolean operations to combine objects, you can create lenses that exist nowhere in the real world. Each has its own way of warping images. You can create endless variations on this theme. Figure 4.35, for example, shows a lens constructed from three Boolean spheres (two negative spheres placed on opposite sides of a positive sphere). This results in a spherical lens that is concave facing the camera and convex at the other end. Explore the construction of your own Boolean lens objects.

Cubic Lens

At first, the thought of a cubic lens seems silly. After all, such a lens would cause little distortion. But remember that you don't have to place a cubic lens parallel to the camera. You can place the lens so that the camera looks at an edge of the cube. When you do this, the resulting image shows multiple, overlapping images of the scene. See Figure 4.36.

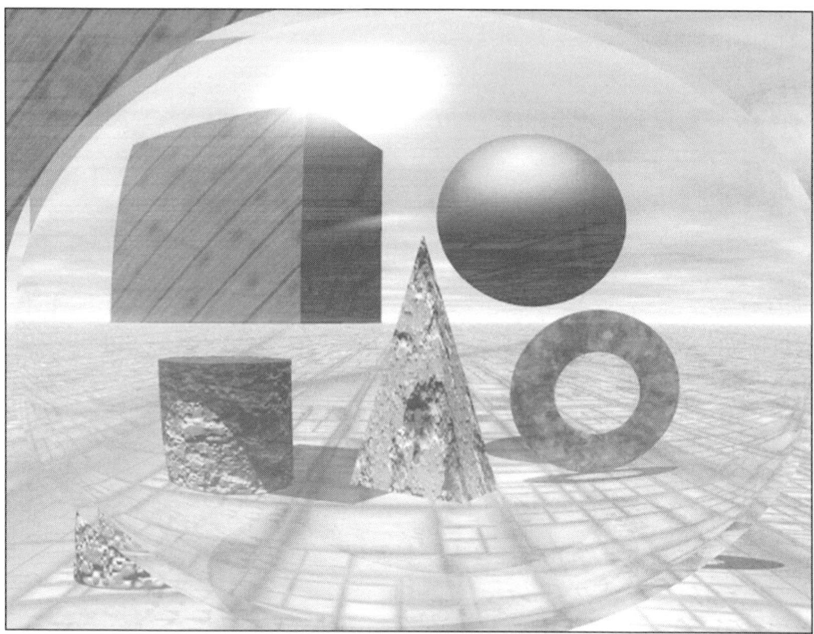

Figure 4.35
Here is what a Bryce world looks like through a Boolean lens created from three intersecting spheres.

Figure 4.36
This lens is a glass cube turned so that the camera looks at one of the cube's edges. The image is split and overlapped in several places.

The Bump Mapped Lens

The more curves on a lens, the more distorted the resulting image. You can create unusual, curvy lenses by sculpting them in another 3D application and importing them into Bryce, by using Boolean operators to create convoluted shapes, or simply by applying Bump Maps to the lens. The Bump Map's pattern determines the extent and shape of the distortion. Because you can create an infinite number of patterns to act as

Figure 4.37
In this example, the camera is inside a spherical lens. The lens is Bump Mapped with Beveled Tiles at -100 with Parametric mapping and a Frequency of 111.

Bump Maps for any object, it follows that a potentially infinite number of Bump Mapped lenses wait for you to discover them. See Figure 4.37.

Sky Lab Magic

The Sky Lab (completely reworked for Bryce 4) is the core engine devoted to the creation of atmospheric effects. The Sky Lab features three tabbed pages, each with its own controls for creating and modifying the atmosphere of your Bryce world. I'll show you each one and point out ways you can use the Sky Lab to create startling effects. Because you have already read and worked through the Bryce documentation, I won't explain the location and purpose of each control.

Sun & Moon

This is the first tabbed page in the Sky Lab. It has controls (shown in Figure 4.38) for a number of sky effects.

The following describes each element that is labeled in Figure 4.38:

A. *Starfield*—Here you can turn the stars on or off and set their intensity and density. If you plan to use stars, I suggest that you push the intensity and amount all the way up. Also, make sure that you work on a night sky that is fairly cloudless. You will often want to add your own sky objects; even at full intensity, these stars are rather dim.

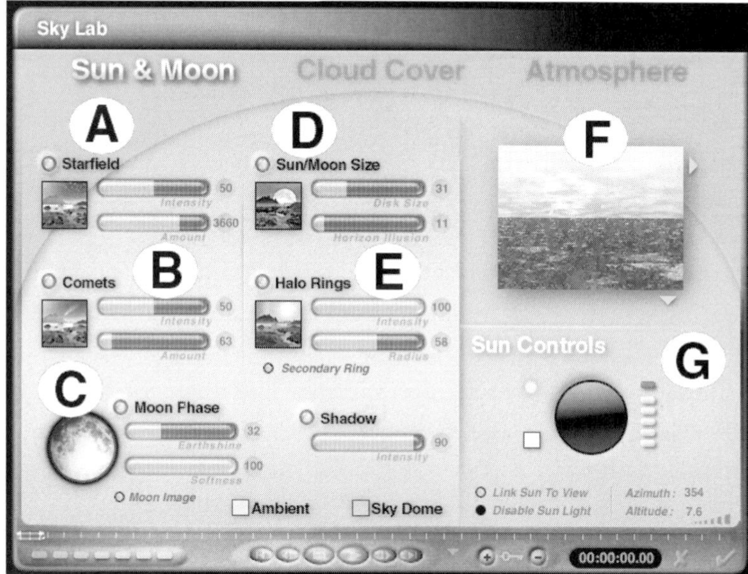

Figure 4.38

The Sky Lab's Sun & Moon page. (See the following text for an explanation for each of the elements.)

B. *Comets*—In Bryce, comets are smears of light, rather like a dim comet. Don't count on creating any Armageddon comets with this feature. Generally, it's best to keep the intensity of comets maximized and to set their amount to no higher than 25 percent.

C. *Moon Phase*—When you turn the moon on, it is rendered in the night sky. Click on Moon Image to include a bitmap of the moon's surface. Earthlight creates a more realistic image, and you can set the phase interactively. But all is not perfect. Bryce is far too realistic in depicting the moon. The bitmap of the surface is too vague, and there are no options for creating alien moons. I prefer other alternatives, such as placing my own textured moons in a sky. But be sure to explore this option anyway; it may work well in your designs.

D. *Sun/Moon Size*—You really should explore these options each time you want the sun or the moon visible in the sky. Both Disk Size and Horizon Illusion affect the size of the sun or the moon, so play until you have what you want.

E. *Halo Rings*—I love halo rings. I use them by default, especially around the sun, because they interact well with most cloud renders.

F. *Nano Preview*—Keep your eye on the Nano Preview to keep track of all the alterations you make. I prefer to see the preview of the sky against the scene rather than as a stand-alone effect. This allows me to judge whether I will like the rendering or not, and if the sky will fit what I had in mind. It is also wise to leave Fine Rendering off; fine renders take a long time, and the Nano Preview is too small to provide any useful insight anyway. The arrow twirl on the right launches the Sky presets, so you can always drop in another preset sky from the Sky Lab. This control appears in all three tabs, so I won't mention it in the next two. Use the memory dots to save your favorite sky and fog settings while you experiment.

G. *Sun Controls*—This is just like the trackball control found on the Sky & Fog palette. The most important addition here is the Disable Sun Light button. The neat thing here is that you can still render an image of the sun on the horizon while disabling its light. Always disable Sun Light when you want to use Placed lights as the source of illumination in your scene. Leave the Link Sun To View option on by default.

Cloud Cover

This is the most important tabbed page in the Sky Lab. Here you can create a variety of extraordinary skies. See Figure 4.39.

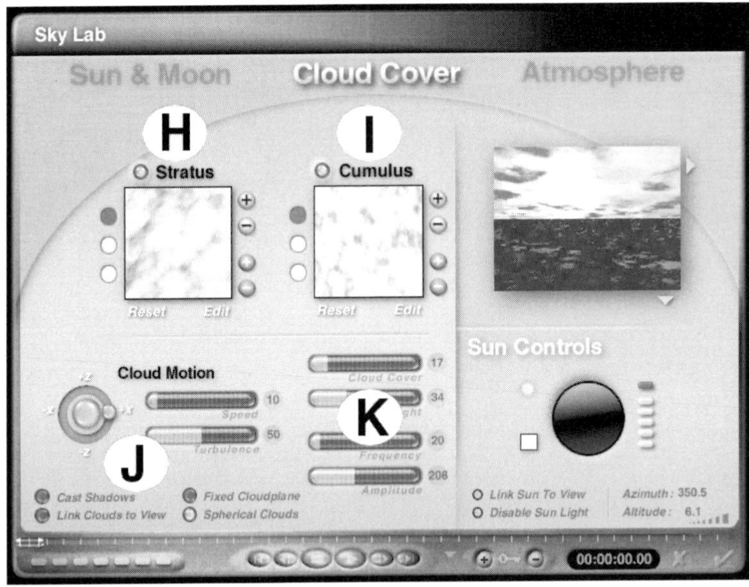

Figure 4.39
The Sky Lab's Cloud Cover page. (See the following text for an explanation for each of the elements.)

Picking up where the previous lettered list left off, the following describes each element that is labeled in Figure 4.39:

H. *Stratus*—Here you can create or customize the Stratus cloud layer. You'll find this tab's most important feature—the Edit button—beneath the preview to the right. The Edit button launches our old friend, the Deep Texture Editor (described in Chapter 3). From the Deep Texture Editor, you have access to the unlimited Procedural Texture variations that you can apply to stratus clouds.

I. *Cumulus*—Create or customize cumulus clouds here. Again, you can access the Deep Texture Editor by clicking on the Edit button.

J. *Cloud Motion*—These basic animation controls determine the clouds' direction and motion. (See Chapter 5 for information about Bryce animation.)

K. *Cloud Settings*—Although these controls are technically part of the Cloud Motion controls, I have separated these four controllers because you can keyframe animate these settings. These controls allow you to adjust the clouds' Cover, Height, Frequency, and Amplitude. Play with these sliders until the Nano Preview displays something you like.

Follow this procedure to create a new Sky preset:

1. Open the Sky Lab.
2. On the Cloud Cover page, click on the Edit window of either the Stratus or Cumulus layers. (You can modify the Stratus and Cumulus layers in turn, so it doesn't matter which you select first.)
3. After the Deep Texture Editor launches, use your skills to create a new texture. If you really like it, save the texture as a preset. (Refer to Chapter 3 if your skills with the Deep Texture Editor are a bit rusty.)
4. Accept the new texture. Back in the Sky Lab's Cloud Cover page, preview your creation. Use the Cover, Height, Frequency, and Amplitude sliders to customize your sky. Save it as a preset, and jump back to your Bryce world for a test render.

The Skyz folder on this book's companion CD-ROM contains a collection of new Sky presets. All were designed using the Deep Texture Editors from the Stratus and Cumulus cloud layers on the Cloud Cover page. See Figure 4.40.

Atmosphere

This tab includes more Sky Lab utilities for altering the coloration, animation speed, and frequency of the sky elements. See Figure 4.41.

Picking up where the previous lettered lists left off, the following describes each element that is labeled in Figure 4.41:

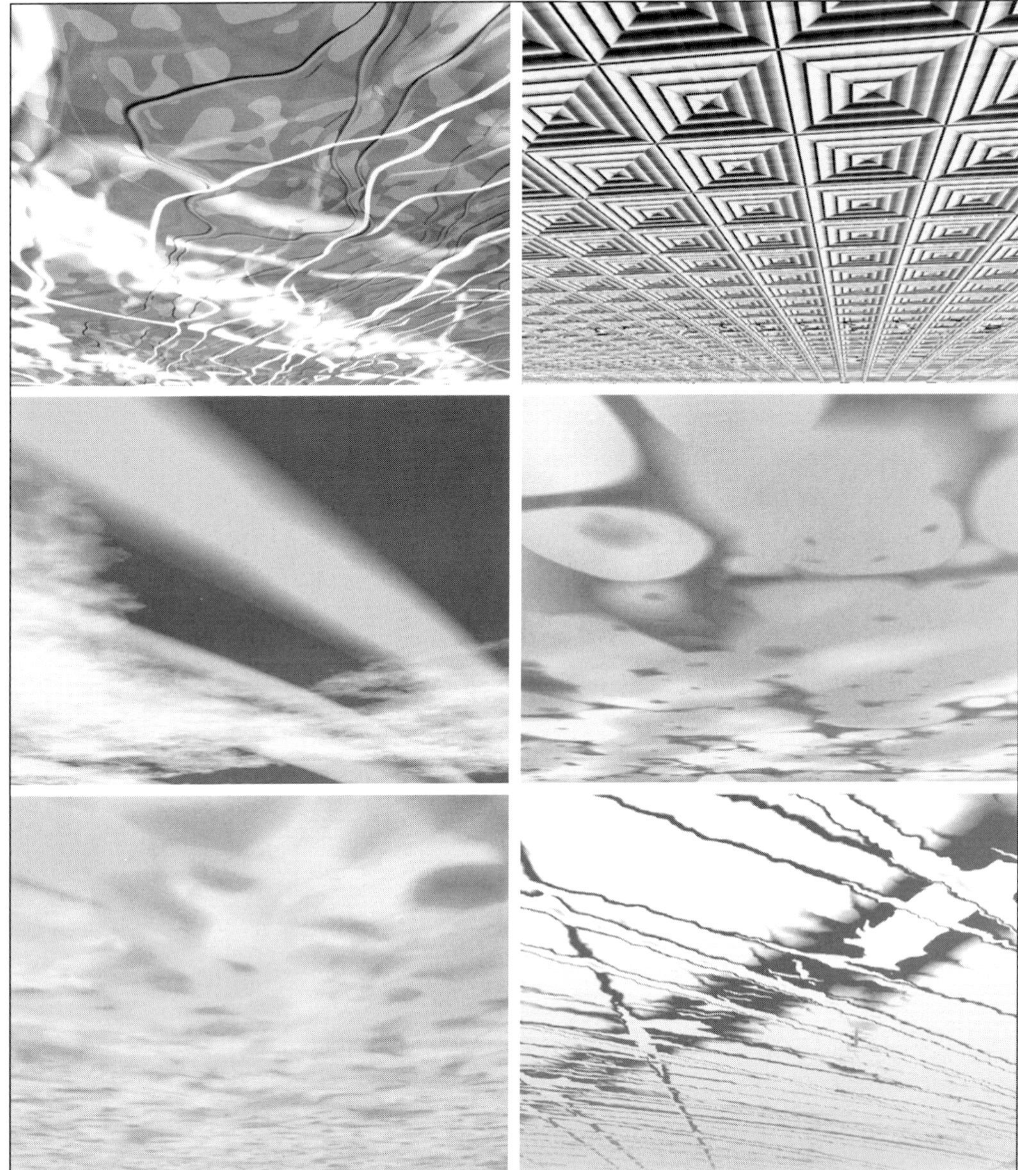

Figure 4.40

Here is a selection of renderings that use the Sky presets contained in the Skyz folder on this book's CD-ROM (upper-left to bottom-right: Brancher, Ceiling 1, Fire Ring, Planet X1, Unreal, and Wild Streak).

L. *Fog*—It's much easier to use these sliders to develop Fog parameters than it is to use the click-and-drag method in the Sky & Fog palette.

M. *Haze*—As with Fog settings, it's much easier to use these sliders to develop Haze parameters than it is to use the click-and-drag method in the Sky & Fog palette.

N. *Rainbow*—You have to play with Rainbow controls as you tweak various cloud parameters. You can make rainbows stand out or become subtle additions to a sky, based on your skill with the Sky Lab. Just keep an eye on the Nano Preview to see what your alterations

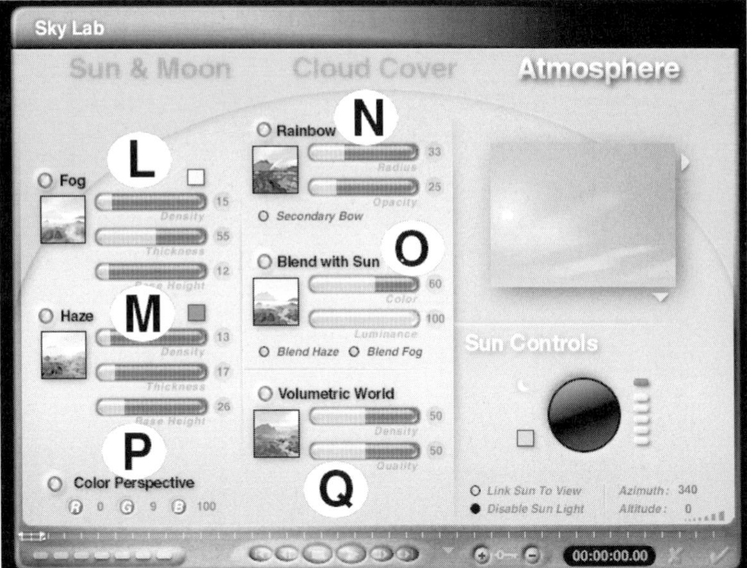

Figure 4.41
The Sky Lab's Atmosphere page. (See the following text for an explanation for each of the elements.)

do. If you plan to use cumulus clouds, make them high enough to prevent them from interfering with the rainbow. See Figure 4.42.

O. *Blend With Sun*—Selecting this option allows you to blend the atmosphere with the sun's settings. This makes for more realistic renderings.

P. *Color Perspective*—Controls the red, green, and blue components of the atmosphere.

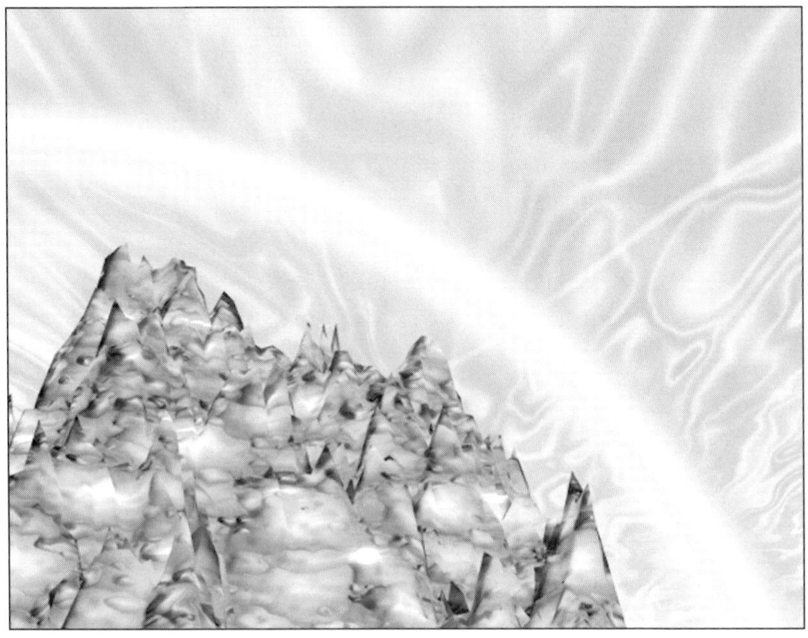

Figure 4.42
A vision of the Bryce rainbow.

Q. *Volumetric World*—When you select this option, the entire atmosphere becomes a volumetric object. Although this leads to realistic renderings, you'll pay the price in increased rendering times. Do not use this option unless you're using a fast machine. See Figure 4.43.

Figure 4.43
When you select the Volumetric World option, the atmosphere becomes more muted and responsive to density settings. On a 350MHz system, this image took five times longer to render than its non-Volumetric World counterpart shown in Figure 4.42.

ReelFire

There are times when you need fire: not for warmth, but for effect. When these necessities arise, be sure to check out the ReelFire and ReelExplosions collections from Artbeats (**www.artbeats.com**). The ReelFire and ReelExplosions CD-ROM volumes offer a selection of fire in all of its guises—from flames to plasma explosions. They come as QuickTime movies in a variety of resolutions. When used as Picture Textures, they are perfect for use in Bryce. Use them in the sky as fireworks, explosions, and meteors. Use them on the ground for weapons fire, explosions, and subtle campfire effects. See Figure 4.44.

Sandstorm

You can generate atmosphere effects with methods other than those available in the Sky Lab. Here's a special project idea that creates a sandstorm effect. You will need the Kai's Power Tools 5 filters installed in Photoshop in order to create this effect. Follow these steps:

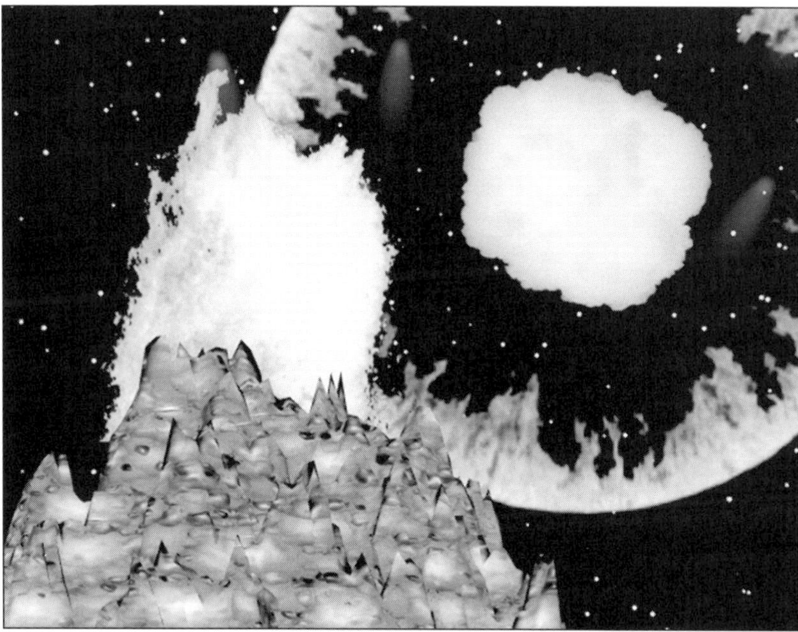

Figure 4.44
This scene uses images from the ReelFire and ReelExplosions collections. (Sky Lab stars are turned on in the background.)

1. Create a blank 600-by-600-pixel image in Photoshop. Open the KPT5 FraxFlame filter. Accept any one of the presets that catches your eye, and render it to the blank image space. Save the image as a TIFF file (for example, Myfraxfl_1.TIF).
2. Select the background and invert the selection. Clear the image area with a black hue. Now you have a silhouette of the image to use as an Alpha Channel in Bryce. Save the image as a PICT file on a Mac or as a BMP file on Windows. Use the same file name, but add a *g* and the appropriate file extension (for example, Myfraxfl_1g.BMP).
3. In Bryce, create a sphere that is large enough to cover your scene and include the camera. Go to the Materials Lab, and map the sphere with the bitmap you just created (including its Alpha Channel). Map the bitmap to the Diffuse Color Channel. Make the material Volumetric, and set the Volume Channel as follows (although you can explore other settings here): Base Density, 22; Edge Softness, 44; Fuzzy Factor, 160; and Quality/Speed, 25. Use Cylindrical mapping and a Size of 1 percent.
4. Render a preview after accepting the material. You can keyframe animate the sphere by rotating it on its Y axis. (See Chapter 5 for animation information.) The results are pretty startling, as shown in Figure 4.45.

Figure 4.45
The completed KPT5 Sandstorm effect.

Moving On

In this chapter, I've shown you a number of ways you can use lights, cameras, and the controls in the Sky Lab to create astounding effects in your Bryce worlds. The next chapter is devoted to creating animations, using everything you have learned so far.

5 Animation On Demand

Objects, terrains, Infinite Planes, cameras, lights, skies, and materials—you can animate them all. Specific animation techniques are associated with each of these components, and all the techniques are covered in this chapter.

Standard Animation Controls

Before you can create animations, you must be familiar with the Animation Controls palette and the Animation Settings dialog box.

Animation Controls Palette

The Animation Controls palette appears at the bottom of every Bryce module. Learning to use it in one place gives you mastery over its uses throughout the program. See Figure 5.1.

The Animation Controls palette hasn't changed in this version of Bryce. Because the documentation covers its uses, I'll just present an overview here. You can leave this book open to Figure 5.1 and use the figure as a reference when you begin to animate your Bryce worlds. The following describes each element that is labeled in Figure 5.1:

A. This symbol toggles between the Animation Controls and Selection palettes. You usually need to switch between the two palettes as you choreograph an animation.

B. Clicking on and dragging this lozenge along the Timeline takes you to a specific frame for viewing or keyframing. The display on the left indicates the exact frame number and time.

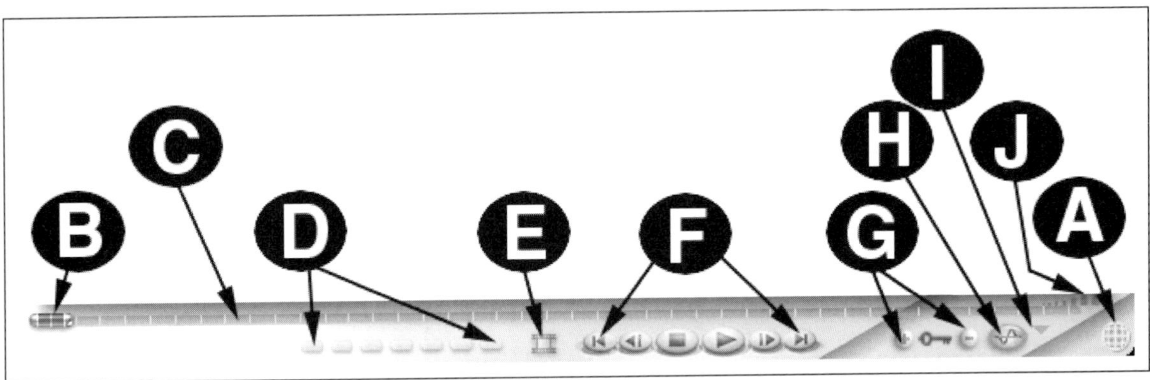

Figure 5.1
The Animation Controls palette. (See the following text for an explanation for each of the elements.)

C. The Timeline includes ticks that indicate the separate frames in the animation. Stop on any frame to add a keyframe or to edit any of the selected objects in the scene.

D. The memory dots store frame numbers from the Timeline. Use them to snap to a particular frame instantly.

E. The Preview Animation button is a new feature of version 4. Clicking and holding on this button presents a drop-down list of options; the most important one is the Storyboard option. This option renders

Nano frames of the animation to your workspace and plays the animation in the Nano Preview.

F. The VCR controller includes buttons for Start Frame, Previous Keyframe, Stop, Play, Next Keyframe, and Last Frame. You can play the animation as wireframes or as boxed elements. When the scene gets complex, it's best to use boxes unless you have to see the outline of specific objects.

G. Click on the plus to add keyframes and the minus to delete keyframes. When you hold down the Add or Delete Keyframes buttons, you can access specific parameters for the camera, sky, sun, or selected object. These options allow you to control the parameters of the selected item (as opposed to the global controls that come into play when you simply click on the Add Keyframes button). These advanced controls (covered later in this chapter) are important as you fine-tune your animation.

H. Click on this button to access the Advanced Motion Lab (which will be described later in this chapter).

I. From this Timeline Options menu, you can turn Auto-Key on or off and define what the tick marks on the Timeline indicate. Leave Auto-Key on until you start to fine-tune your animation. Tick marks can indicate either frames or time. The Time option allows a choice of SMPTE (Society of Motion Picture and Television Engineers) or Frames mode for the time display. The Ticker Mark option allows the option of 1, 2, and 5 seconds or every frame, every 2 frames, and every 5 frames. Later, as the animation grows more complex, use the option that allows you to see all of the ticks on the Timeline at once.

J. When you click on and drag this Scale Timeline controller, you can zoom in or out of the Timeline. This is another method of scaling the Timeline in whatever mode it is set to, frames or seconds, so that all of the Timeline can be seen at once.

Note: *When you select OpenGL or Sree 3D as the render mode, animations play fully rendered. However, they will probably not play at the frame rate you have set.*

Using The Advanced Animation Controls

As you begin work on your animation, use global controls for animating the items listed in the advanced options and enable Auto-Key. Move or manipulate the camera or any other component in its present keyframe. Then, use the advanced controls to delete or modify specific actions in the selected keyframe. You can add or delete a specific actions in advanced controls, which are accessed by holding down the Add Keyframe or Delete

Note: *You should select the Auto-Key option (the small triangle to the right of the animation controls) when you use the advanced controls. Within a single keyframe, try to use as few advanced controls as possible. It's easy to forget where you are and which actions you have taken.*

Keyframe button. However, actions can only be modified in the Advanced Motion Lab, by clicking on Expand All Timelines. For example, by holding down the Delete Keyframe button and accessing the advanced controls, you can selectively delete the rotation for the camera (or for any other item) in that specific keyframe without tampering with the repositioning activated for the camera at that keyframe. You can also use the advanced controls available from the Add Keyframes button.

Advanced Camera Controls

In the Advanced Camera Controls, you can select the following options for the camera: Position, Origin, Banking, Rotation, Field Of Vision (FOV), Focal Length, Pan X or Y, and Zoom X or Y. You don't need to select the camera in order to use the advanced controls to delete a specific camera function in the current keyframe. For example:

1. Make frame 1 a keyframe for the camera.
2. Move the Lozenge to frame 30, and then rotate and reposition the camera.
3. Using the advanced controls available from the Delete Keyframe button, select the camera to access the Rotation option. Holding on the Rotation option deletes the camera function from the keyframed elements.

Now, in frame 30, you have removed the new rotation while leaving the new camera position in place. If you had done this globally by selecting the Delete Keyframe button, you would have removed the new camera rotation and position from frame 30.

Advanced Sky Controls

The Advanced Sky Controls work just like the Advanced Camera Controls, except you have 35 items to chose from. You can select every sky parameter individually, or you can access them through the Sky & Fog palette or the associated Sky & Fog Edit dialog box. It depends on what makes you feel most comfortable when setting the animation parameters for the sky.

Advanced Sun Controls

All these controls are offered in a more interactive manner in the Sky & Fog palette.

Advanced Selected Object Controls

These options work on the selected object or object group. When an object is selected, its name appears on the advanced controls drop-down list.

The Advanced Selected Object Controls include Position, Rotation, Scale, Shear, and Origin. If the selected object is a terrain or a Symmetrical Lattice, additional controls are listed.

The Animation Setup Dialog Box

Access the Animation Setup dialog box (shown in Figure 5.2) from the File menu to begin to design your animation. The items listed in this dialog box affect all the following parameters of the animation:

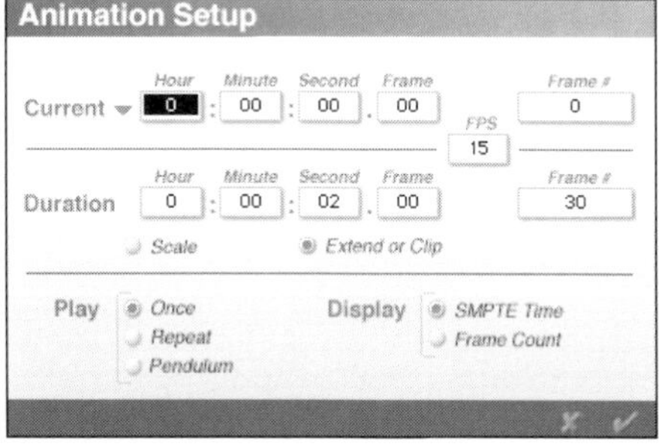

Figure 5.2
The Animation Setup dialog box.

- *FPS*—FPS stands for frames per second. The most common FPS rates are 15, 24, 29.97 (and other SMPTE rates), and 30. Bryce does not offer the interleaved 60 FPS field rendering commonly used in broadcast video productions. With the exception of SMPTE work, 30 FPS is the best video choice for NTSC; a rate of 25 FPS is the best choice for PAL. SMPTE work (also called *drop frame*) involves the use of specific hardware to add and edit synchronized audio. If you are a professional video editor, select the appropriate SMPTE setting. Otherwise, select a non-SMPTE setting.
- *Once, Repeat, and Pendulum*—These options affect how the animated objects are displayed during a preview and how they act in a rendered animation if the sequence is long enough. Play Once is the default: The animation plays from start to finish as expected. Repeat loops the animation continually until you hit the stop button. Pendulum (also known as *ping-pong*) plays the animation from start to finish and then from finish to start until you hit the stop button.
- *Make Circular*—This option creates a closed loop in which the object's position in the first frame is the same as its position in the last frame. Every time you move the object, it expands the circle (which is really a warped oval). Making the animation longer would show the object racing around madly, over and over again. Use this technique to create an object that orbits another.

ASSIGNING REPEATS AND PENDULUMS TO A RENDERED ANIMATION

If you want an object to either repeat its actions or to act as a pendulum in an animation, follow these steps:

1. Set up an object movement over 10 frames. The object movement should have keyframes at frames 1 and 10.
2. While the object is selected, click on the Animation tab in the object's Attributes dialog box. Then, select Repeat or Pendulum as desired.
3. Go back to the Timeline, deselect the object, and move the lozenge to frame 30. When you preview the animation, you see the object either repeating its 10-frame action or moving back and forth, depending on your selection of either Repeat or Pendulum in the Animation Setup dialog box.

The Advanced Motion Lab

The Advanced Motion Lab (shown in Figure 5.3) features animation controls for every aspect of your Bryce 3D world. Everything is at your fingertips in the Advanced Motion Lab, and you have an instant preview of any alterations you make. The Advanced Motion Lab features animation tools that can be found nowhere else within Bryce. The Advanced Motion Lab is activated when you click on its icon in the Animation palette.

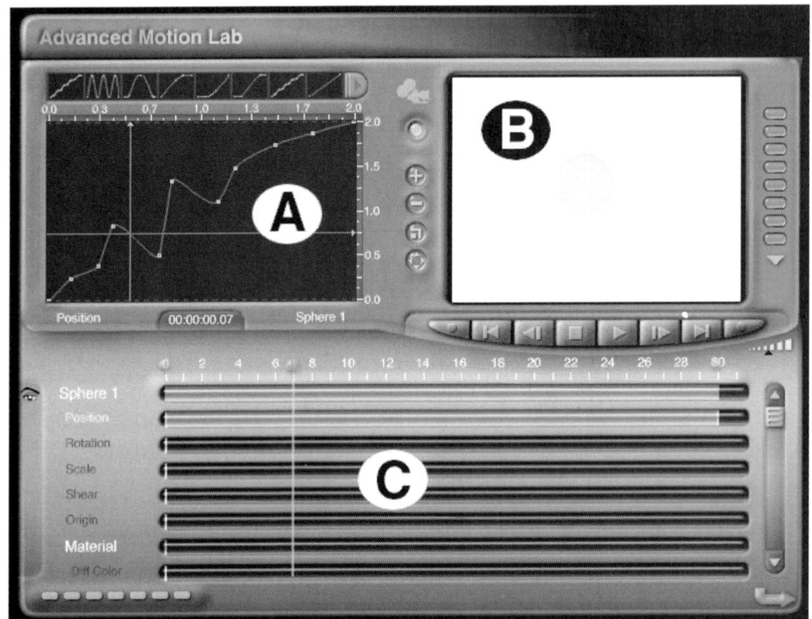

Figure 5.3
The Advanced Motion Lab includes (A) Motion Wave assignments, (B) Preview/Playback screen, and (C) Object/Item selection.

Motion Wave Assignments

By clicking on any of the waveforms, you can create choreographed animations. You can reshape the wave by moving the wave's control points, or you can use the Pencil tool (which appears when you move the mouse over a blank section of the curve) to draw a waveform. You can save all customized waveforms to an empty slot in the waveform thumbnail section simply by clicking on that empty slot.

Each waveform determines the movement of the selected object during the time allotted. The bottom of the waveform shows the selected item's attribute at the start of the animation, while the top of the waveform represents the animation's last frame. The left-right axis shows the time from the first to last frame. A noncustomized waveform would appear as a straight diagonal line that extends from the bottom left to the upper right. Such a waveform causes the selected object or item attribute to move smoothly in a continuous movement. For instance, if an object's color is set to red at the beginning of the animation and to blue at the end, the default diagonal waveform creates a steady movement from red to blue as the animation progresses.

What if you wanted an object's color to move evenly from red to green and back, but you assigned it red at the start and green at the end when you designed it initially? You could apply the appropriate waveform in the object's color attribute channel (in this case, a smooth curve that starts at the lower left, climbs to the top at the middle of the animation, and then finishes at the lower right). You can manipulate all the other attributes of the selected object the same way.

Understanding Motion Wave Shapes

Motion Waves can customize only those attributes that have at least two previously configured keyframes. The Advanced Motion Lab is a post-editing module. For example:

- Vertical parts of the waveform force the object to move very quickly between the beginning and ending attributes. In the case of colors, vertical lines in a waveform cause the colors to flash between the beginning and ending colors.
- Horizontal parts of the waveform cause the selected attribute to remain stable at the state indicated at that time in the animation.
- The points between the beginning and end of a waveform indicate a blend of the starting and ending attributes.
- Tiny fluctuations in a waveform cause the selected object attribute to fluctuate between the lower and upper points of the smaller curve. For example, when such a waveform is assigned to a brightness attribute, the light dims and brightens just slightly.

- If you move beyond the vertical as you move control points, the curve becomes a smooth curve that contains the points of the vertical line (time reversal is not allowed).

Preview/Playback Screen

The Preview/Playback screen allows you use the VCR controls to see the result of the customizations you've made.

Object/Item Selection Options

You can expand the Timeline to show all of the object's attributes by simply clicking on their names. You must first keyframe animate a selected item before you can alter its parameters. For example, if an object's position is not animated but its rotation is, you can customize only its rotation in the Advanced Motion Lab. Use the Advanced Motion Lab to customize the following attributes:

- *Object Attribute Options*—Alter the selected object's Position, Rotation, Scale, Shear, Origin, or Material attributes by selecting the attribute in the Object/Item list. This also works for some objects' (terrains, for example) Gradient Shift, Geometry, Gradient, Low Clip, and High Clip.
- *Material Attribute Options*—Alter every item in the Material's color, value, and optics channel attributes. (This works with both Surface and Volumetric Materials.)
- *Camera Attribute Options*—You can alter a camera's Position, Origin, Rotation, Banking, Focal Length, FOV, Pan XY, and Zoom XY attributes.
- *Light Attribute Options*—The light attributes you can alter include Position, Rotation, Scale, Shear, Origin, Color, Falloff, Range, and Intensity.
- *Sky Attribute Options*—You can customize the 34 Sky attributes in the Advanced Motion Lab by applying Motion Graph Waveform to them (provided the selected attribute already has an assigned beginning and ending keyframe).
- *Sun Options*—You can alter the sun's Color, Intensity, Disc and Halo Colors, and Directional Movement. A pulsar, for example, is a star that pulses in brightness and sometimes in color as well. To create an animated pulsar, alter the sun's color and brightness attributes by using appropriate waveforms in the Advanced Motion Lab.

Paths

An object, camera, or light that changes its position over time defines a *path*. You can create a path by moving an element to a new position and adding a keyframe by using the Add Keyframe button. You can also create the path first, making it ready for the objects that follow it.

Standard Paths

The paths created by the movement of an object, camera, or light cannot be modified unless you reposition the element that created them. Such paths are not objects: They are the result of the defined actions of objects. For example, if you set a keyframe for a sphere in the first frame of an animation and then, after moving the sphere, set another keyframe at frame 30, you will see a blue line that indicates its path of motion. When you preview the animation, you'll see the object moving from its position at frame 1 to its new position at frame 30. The time it takes the object to travel the entire distance depends on the FPS setting. At 15 FPS, the object travels from frame 1 to frame 30 in two seconds (30÷15=2). At 30 FPS, the journey takes only one second (30÷30=1). If you want a curved path instead of a straight one, you can't change the path by clicking on it. At this point, the path does not exist as an element that you can edit. To customize the path, you must follow these steps:

1. Go to the frame where the maximum value on the needed curve should exist (perhaps frame 15).
2. Select the object, move it to its new position for that frame, and keyframe it.

The path now has a new shape. When you select the object that created the path, the path is visible, but it cannot be selected separately.

Ribbon Paths

Bryce uses the terms *ribbon path* and *motion path* interchangeably. First introduced in Bryce 3D, ribbon paths are a new way to edit paths. Unlike standard paths, ribbon paths are actual objects that you can select and edit directly, without selecting an object assigned to it. You can create ribbon paths by loading them from the Create Objects library or by transforming a standard path into a ribbon path.

Creating A Ribbon Path Separate From An Object

1. Access the Create Objects library.

2. Select a ribbon path from one of the presets found in the Paths directory. (See Figure 5.4.) Then, click on the check mark to place the ribbon path on the screen.

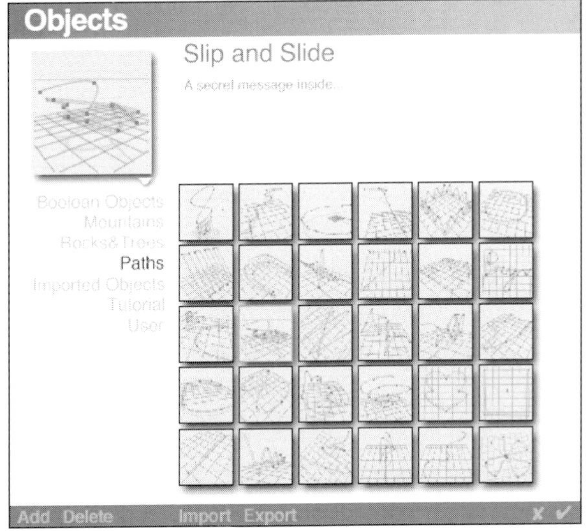

Figure 5.4
Ribbon paths can be selected and added from the presets in the Paths folder in the Create/Objects library.

Creating A Ribbon Path From A Standard Object Path

1. Select the object whose path you want to convert to a ribbon path.
2. From the Objects menu, select Create Path. The object's path has now become a ribbon path.

Customizing Ribbon Paths

Because ribbon paths are objects, you can resize, rotate, or reposition them just as you would any other object. Until an object, camera, or light is linked to them, ribbon paths exist on their own. When you move a ribbon path you created by transforming a standard path, the object whose path was transformed does not move. However, deleting the original object also deletes the new ribbon path. To delete the original object from the new ribbon path, select the object in the Selection palette and use the Edit|Clear command.

Editing A Ribbon Path

Ribbon paths have visible nodes that you can push and pull just like those of a Bezier curve. A ribbon path has two kinds of nodes: Resize nodes and Reshape nodes. A Resize node allows you to resize the ribbon path along an axis indicated by the node, just as you can resize any object. To resize the ribbon path along all axes simultaneously, use the Edit palette's Resize tool.

Reshape nodes are placed at selected keyframe intervals on the ribbon path. Using these Nodes, you can squash the ribbon path or stretch it at that point. Add or delete keyframes to add or delete Reshape nodes.

The Attributes dialog box of a selected object contains the Show As Ribbon Path command. This command allows you to see the standard path as if it were a ribbon path, although you cannot interact with the path until it is transformed into a ribbon path. Use the top view to initially resize and reshape the ribbon path.

Making Sharp Corners On A Standard Animation Path

The shape of a path from one keyframe to the next is usually a straight line or a smooth curve. To create a sharp corner on a path, set two keyframes (one frame apart) for the object while it is in the same place. With a bit of tweaking, this produces a square corner.

Animating Ribbon Paths

You can also animate a ribbon path:

- Resize the path over time. Objects linked to the path are also resized accordingly.
- Rotate the path over time.
- Reposition the path over time.
- Apply Repeat, Pendulum, and Make Circular in the Attributes dialog box of a selected ribbon path to create repetitive patterns over time.

Links

You can establish a link between two objects by clicking on the small chain-shaped icon in a selected object's Attributes list and dragging the mouse to another object (the target object turns blue). You can also link objects by using the Linking tab in the object's Attributes dialog box. Under Parent Object, find the name of the object to which you want to link the selected object. When the parent object is resized, rotated, or moved, the child object is affected in the same way. However, you can resize, rotate, and reposition child objects without affecting the parent object.

Linking Options

An object can be linked to any other object. Objects can also be multilinked: A parent object can have multiple children (a child object can have only one parent). You could, for example, have a figure with two hands linked to one parent arm, but you could not have one hand

Note: *DX models often import with their groups severely mixed up, and ungrouping the object to get to the parts can be a nightmare. Import Wavefront OBJ objects instead whenever possible.*

linked to two parent arms. However, if you group the two arms, linking one hand to them would really be linking to one parent.

Multilink Options

In order to animate an object that has multiple moveable parts (mechanical or organic), all the parts must be linked in a hierarchy. One core element is the topmost parent. On a human or human-like figure, this element is usually the abdomen, but it can be any central part on other objects. The separate elements of the linked figure can be keyframe animated one at a time, creating complex animations.

Linking Is Not Grouping

A number of issues are important when you decide whether to link or group objects:

- After selecting a group, use the Ctrl or Command key to select an individual member of the group. If you link the member to one of the other elements in the group, the member is no longer part of the group. Linking supersedes grouping.
- Grouped objects can accept a material as a single object. This usually results in a look that is quite different from the look you get after applying the same texture map to each object in the group individually. To get the same result in a linked hierarchy, multiselect each object and then apply the material. The linked objects retain their individuality.
- Boolean objects that are assigned Negative, Positive, or Intersect qualities must be grouped and not linked in order to create the expected composite object.

Targets And Links

You cannot link a targeted object to the object that tracks it. This would lead to an infinite loop. If you did this, your system might crash.

You can generate complex orbits by making a child object target the parent object. As the child object orbits the linked parent, the child object also rotates. This is a useful technique when the child object emulates a moon that always turns the same face towards the planet, as does our Moon.

Animating Singular Objects

The animation techniques you use will depend on the type of object you are working with. A singular object is one that cannot be ungrouped to form more than one object. Whether primitive-based or imported, singular objects are the most common type of objects. When animated, primitive objects tend to warp and skew more than imported ones. Use basic primitive objects for the most basic animation projects.

The Bryce 3D Primitives

All the Bryce primitives are singular objects, even the Symmetrical Lattice. When used as singular objects in an animation, Terrain and Symmetrical Lattice objects are usually reshaped in the Terrain Editor first (unless you have some reason to show hills moving on a path).

Singular Object Linking and Grouping

When you link or group singular objects, bear a few things in mind:

- Remember that when you move, resize, or rotate a parent, the changes are applied to all of the children and other offspring in the hierarchical chain.
- Even if the parent element is hidden, you can always link a singular or composite object to a stable element in the scene.
- Always link a light to an object if you want the object lit in the same manner regardless of its position and the global lighting settings (as shown in Figure 5.5).

Figure 5.5
This object is illuminated by four lights, all linked to the object. The sun is turned off. The lights illuminate the object in the same manner, no matter where the object is placed within the environment.

Ribbon Path Animations And Singular Objects

To assign a singular object to a ribbon path, link the object to the path. The object snaps to a position on the path. If you move the object, it moves only to another position on the path while it is linked. The object will not automatically use the path as an animation path until you set specific keyframes on the path. Set the object's beginning keyframe at the start of the path, and add a second keyframe at the path's end. In the resulting animation, the object follows the path from beginning to end.

When you move animated elements a large distance apart in the scene between any two keyframes, the object must go faster in order to make its targeted destination at that keyframed moment. If you want the object to move smoothly, move it only a small amount at a time; widely separated keyframes produce quicker movements. Any object on a ribbon path can reverse or bounce back and forth between any two keyframes without effecting the path.

Singular Object Origin Handles

You can view an object's Origin Handle by turning it on in the Object Attributes dialog box. When the Origin Handle is on, it turns green, and you can reposition it. Any child object linked to a parent object is also linked to the parent's Origin Handle. Moving the parent's Origin Handle moves the child object.

An object's Origin Handle is its center of rotation, so moving its Origin Point allows it to revolve and be resized from the new position. Place the Origin Point inside another object, and the initial object orbits the second object like a planet around a star. Move the Origin Handle again to give the object a new center of rotation and resizing. If you set a satellite's Origin Handle at the center of one object and then move the Origin Handle to the center of another object, the satellite orbits the first object and then the other.

A linked child points to a parent object's Origin Handle, so the parent's Origin Handle also controls the placement of the child object. Although the parent object might not move at all, it can still control child objects through the mere displacement of its Origin Handle over time.

Singular Object Animation Tips

When you animate singular objects, consider these tips:

- Create your initial animation path by first keyframing only the beginning and ending frames. Then, go back and create keyframes at points where the path has to move around objects and move the resulting control points of the path into place. This is a quicker way to work.

- Remember that you can link ribbon paths to other ribbon paths or objects.
- Select Constrain To Path in the Object Attributes dialog box if you want the linked object to exist on the assigned path. Otherwise, it will relate to the path from whatever distance it is at when linked.
- To create a smoother animation, use as few keyframes as possible.
- If you want the object to make a sudden or angular move, place two keyframes one frame apart on the Timeline.
- Except when animating the camera, work with Auto-Key off.

Composite Objects

A composite object is made up of any number of grouped or linked elements. In addition to their path assignments, composite objects have their own movements. Most organic forms are composite objects. The most common composite objects are those that have been imported from other programs, such as 3D Studio, Wavefront, and LightWave. Bryce has problems delineating the correct groups in DXF composites. It's wise to import the DXF into an application that can export it as one of the formats that Bryce can import.

Symmetrical Lattice Composites

Because Bryce 4 can now export Symmetrical Lattice objects in any of a number of 3D formats, Symmetrical Lattice objects may be the most sought-after composite objects around. Symmetrical Lattice objects have no base plane to erase. By using Elevation and Effects Brushes in the Terrain Editor, you can create extremely convoluted shapes for compositing into larger objects (as described in Chapter 2). When you require animated elements made from Symmetrical Lattice objects (such as flapping wings or moving appendages), link these elements to the parent object.

Composite Linking And Grouping

You can group all the non-moving parts of a composite object. In many cases, grouped objects behave with greater stability than linked objects, though each composite object has to be judged on its own. The placement of the Origin Handle always determines the fulcrum point that the moving element relates to.

Paths And Composite Objects

Create the animated composite object first, and save it as a project file. When you load the object and alter its rotation, size, or position (in the standard path creation manner), you can increase the animation's duration You can also use the Repeat or Pendulum functions to make the animated object repeat its movement as it also moves on a path. This is the way to create walking and other complex motions.

Boolean Object Animations

In a Boolean animation, objects seem to magically disappear and reappear. Bryce supports two types of Boolean animations: Negative/Positive and Intersecting. Create all the separate elements first, and tag them as Booleans in the Object Attributes dialog box. Finally, group all the items that will form the Boolean composite.

Negative/Positive Boolean Animations

A Negative Boolean object can drill a hole in a Positive Boolean object. The negative object is not seen, so the hole appears to be drilled by an invisible force. When you want this type of Boolean animated effect, observe the following:

- When you use a text block or a 3D logo as a Negative Boolean, the positive object looks like it is being branded. Eventually, a hole cut in the shape of the text or logo appears in the positive object.
- Use a variety of forms as negative objects. Cubes, cones, spheres, and pyramids add interest because the holes they drill change size and shape as the animation progresses.
- Stagger a group of Negative Booleans so that as one hole is partially complete, another is just beginning. This is a way to create machine-gun bullet holes.
- Choreograph multiple Negative and Positive Booleans so that unexpected interactions take place.
- Don't forget that you can use imported objects as either Negative or Positive Booleans.
- Rotate the Positive Boolean object so that the viewer sees a hole starting on one end of an object and then exiting at the other end.

Animating Intersecting Booleans

Intersecting Booleans create visible objects from the intersecting parts of a negative and positive object, leading to abstract results. To explore their use, follow these steps:

1. Create a sphere, and make it a Intersecting Boolean.
2. Create a cube, and make it a Positive Boolean.
3. Group the sphere and the cube and move them so they intersect. Notice that the portion of the cube covered by a section of the sphere is the only part visible. Using a text block or a logo instead of a cube, you can generate interesting titling effects.

***Note:** Do not link elements in a Boolean group to each other; this ungroups the objects, removing their Boolean properties. You can link a complete Boolean group to another object.*

The Boolean Camera Drill

Here is an interesting project idea for a Negative/Positive Boolean animation. Follow these steps:

1. Place a cube in the workspace so that it blocks the camera's view, and reduce its Z dimension to 75 percent. Make the cube a Positive Boolean.
2. Now place a sphere primitive in the scene, and elongate it on its Z axis by three times. Move the sphere in front of the camera with its far end just touching the cube. Make the sphere a Negative Boolean, and group it with the cube.
3. Working from the top view, place the camera just inside the elongated sphere. Place a Spotlight in front of the camera (100 percent intensity and fade, linear drop-off, and any color you like). Link the Spotlight to the camera, and then link the camera to the sphere.
4. Use the Ctrl or Command key to select only the elongated Sphere. Create an animation that uses the scene as it exists now as the first keyframe. Move the elongated sphere all the way through the cube, and make that the last keyframe of the animation.

Animating Terrains

Why animate terrains? After all, terrains don't normally get up and walk around. But terrains do change over time as they react to wind, rain, and more severe geological forces. Bryce allows you to create a mountain that changes over time, growing from a gentle hill to a volcanic peak. Here's what to do:

***Note:** To preview the results of this project, take a look at the CanDrill.mov QuickTime animation in the Anims folder on this book's companion CD-ROM.*

Note: *To see the results of this technique, look at the VolGrow.mov QuickTime animation in the Anims folder on the book's CD-ROM.*

1. Place a Terrain object in your workspace, and go to the Terrain Editor.
2. Using the Blobmaker and the Lower and Smooth functions, reduce the terrain until it is a low, rounded hill. Keyframe this new terrain at the first frame.
3. While still in the Terrain Editor, move the Timeline lozenge to 4:00. Use the Raise control to increase the terrain's height, and add erosion with the Erode brush. Smooth the terrain a bit, and use the Elevation brush (with the lowest gray level) to drill a volcanic hole in the top. Keyframe this new terrain at time 4:00.
4. Accept these modifications, and jump back to the workspace. Preview the animated terrain and render it as an animation to disk.

Animating Infinite Planes

You can create unusual and unexpected effects by making Infinite Planes pass through each other at various angles. Depending where you place the camera, you see a number of optical illusions unfolding as the Infinite Planes pass and intersect. This is an area for your diligent exploration, but to get started, try this:

1. Place four Infinite Planes in your Bryce world, and map each with a different material. Use a rough rock surface for one, water for the next, a sandy surface for the third, and a cloud surface for the last. Stack them one below the other with a space in between.
2. Place the camera so that it looks down at a 45-degree angle (as seen from the right view). This allows the rendering to show some sky as well as the surface of the upper plane.
3. Keyframe animate a four-second sequence in which each of the Infinite Planes rises in turn to become the top plane. This results in an animation that shows different surfaces becoming visible as the Ground Plane.

Camera Animations

To create animations that keep the viewer's attention, you have to know what the camera can do and how to control it. You can control the camera by adjusting paths, links, and targets.

Note: *See the InfPlanez.mov QuickTime movie in the Anims folder on this book's CD-ROM.*

Here are a few things that are important to remember when creating camera animations:

- If you want the animation to loop, set the first and last keyframes of a camera animation exactly the same way. This is especially important when the camera looks at objects from a circular path.
- If the camera moves when you don't want it to, use the Undo command immediately. Never try to reset the camera manually: You will never get back to exactly the same place, and the animation will jump at that point.
- Lock the camera in invisible mode when working on a complex scene from the front view. This keeps you from constantly selecting the camera by mistake. When you need to reposition the camera, select it from the Selection palette and unlock it.

Camera Animation Options

There are infinite ways to create animations based upon camera movements alone. Some important examples are provided in the following sections.

Orbiting A Selected Object

To make the camera orbit a selected object, follow these steps:

1. Select the camera, and then click on and drag the Target icon in the camera's Attributes dialog box until the icon is over the target object and the target object's display box turns blue.
2. Go to the camera's Attributes dialog box, and select Make Circular on the Animation tab. Set the camera's first frame position as a keyframe.
3. From the top view, move the camera to create a circular path of keyframes.

Tracking

Whether it creates an arrow that tracks a moving target or a figure's eyes that track a falling leaf, tracking is a valuable animation tool. Bryce features two camera tracking modes:

- *Stand And Track*—In this mode, the camera is placed in an optimal position from which it can see most of the actions of the targeted object. The camera never moves from this position.
- *Follow And Track*—Follow And Track is best used when the camera is close to the object. The camera shadows the object through all of its movements. Use this mode when you want the camera to ride along with the object.

Note: *See the CamOrb.mov QuickTime movie in the Anims folder on this book's CD-ROM.*

Camera Linking

When you link the camera to an object, the camera duplicates every motion the object makes. This works best when the camera is close to the object and the object doesn't bounce or wiggle too much.

Linking To The Camera

Linking to the camera creates an effect similar to the Hollywood effect in which the camera tracks two people dancing and the room seems to twirl around them. The child object defines no path: It just follows the camera's moves. Linking a light to the camera is a good use of this option because it allows you to light the scene from the direction the camera is looking.

Linking The Camera To A Ribbon Path

Use this capability for Follow And Track animations. Both an object and the camera can be linked to the same ribbon path. You may select the same path. Duplicate the path first, setting the object to one path and the camera to the other. The camera path can then follow the same general curve as the object path, but it can do so from the side, top, bottom, or even from changing angles. Sometimes the camera outruns the object and looks at it from ahead, and sometimes the camera lags behind. This method is useful for tracking vehicles in motion.

Field Of View

If you use the camera's Attributes dialog box to alter the Field of View (FOV) over time, radical distortions occur near the edge of the visual plane. The larger the camera's FOV setting, the smaller all of objects in the scene become. FOV animations emulate hallucinogenic zooms. Use the maximum FOV settings with the camera pointed at the sky to create expansive vistas.

Camera Scale Factor

Setting the camera's Scale Factor to 100 percent provides a normal, undistorted view of the scene. A setting of 1 percent creates the maximum zoom out. Alter the camera's Scale Factor setting when you need a zoom that has an undistorted view as the first or last frame. When you require severe distortions on either or both ends of a zoom, alter the FOV setting.

Camera Pans

Altering the Camera Pan settings in the camera's Attributes dialog box allows you to create an animated pan—horizontal or vertical—of the scene. Bryce features two types of pans: General and Targeted. General Pans present panoramic vistas. Targeted Pans move from one object to another, just as a camera moves between actors engaged in a discussion.

Animating Lights

By animating lights in your Bryce world, you can create a number of interesting effects, including the following:

- Create an animated flashlight that pans across the darkened scene. Just link a Spotlight to a flashlight object and adjust the beam as needed. Be sure to look at the Flite project in Chapter 7 and the Flite.mov QuickTime animation in the Anims folder on this book's CD-ROM.
- Create a pulsating flame for use as a welding torch or as the exhaust from a spaceship. Use an elongated sphere, and select Light as a material option from its Materials Lab. Use any color you like for the flame.
- To create a marquee of moving lights, follow these steps:
    1. Place a cube in your workspace. The cube will serve as the structure.
    2. Place a series of Radial Lights around the bottom edge.
    3. (This is the time-consuming part.) Using the Lights Editor for each light or the controls in the Advanced Motion Lab for each Radial Light, toggle the lights on and off in succession. Each one should remain on for no longer than two frames. The result is a moving line of lights, perfect for a movie marquee or a detour sign.
- Make a swarm of fireflies by creating a bunch of yellow Radial Lights with Visible Volume turned on. Make sure you are working in a nonsunlit environment. Animate the lights so that they swarm in a realistic manner (be sure to build some randomness into the movement so that they don't all move the same way). At random times in the animation, change the hue of one of the lights to red for a few frames. Your lightning bugs will sparkle and flash in the dark.

Animating Skies

Bryce supports the animation of two sky types: the default sky and Infinite Sky Planes. Use the Sky Lab to animate the default sky, and use the Materials Lab for animating the Infinite Sky Plane.

Note: *The Animation palette is included at the bottom of the Sky Lab, so you can create keyframes and preview them without jumping back to the main interface. You can keyframe animate the sun and moon position and the sun color from all three tabbed windows.*

Sky Lab Animations

The Sky Lab is the place from which to control the animation parameters for the default sky. Let's look in greater detail at what you can do in the Sky Lab.

The Sun & Moon Tab

Use the control sliders on the Sun & Moon tab (shown in Figure 5.6) to animate Stars, Comets, Sun/Moon Size, Halo Rings, Moon Phase, Shadows, and Ambient and Sky Dome color. Here's more information on each of the sliders:

Figure 5.6
The control sliders in the Sky Lab's Sun & Moon tab.

- *Stars*—Use these sliders to control the stars' Amount and Intensity parameters. Make sure the sky is dark before you apply stars. Animating Intensity in a cyclical fashion makes the stars sparkle. Animating the Amount parameter can be interesting if you want the scene to move from day to night. Use fewer stars at twilight and more stars as the sky darkens. I always use the maximum number of stars for a deep space scene.
- *Comets*—Comets show up as small blurred streaks in a Bryce night sky, and it's always good to add a few (say between 30 and 50) to break up the Sky Plane. You can control the Intensity and Amount of the comets, just as you can with stars. Leave Intensity at 100 percent most of the time because the comets are rather weak to begin with.
- *Sun/Moon Size*—You can control the Disk Size and Horizon Distortion of both the sun and the moon. You can think of Horizon Distortion as a control that enlarges Disk Size even more. Maximizing the Horizon Distortion makes the sun look like the explosion of an atomic bomb.

This might be an interesting effect to explore in an animation by changing the Disk Size from 0 to 100. To enhance the naturalism of a scene, the apparent size of the sun is larger at sunrise and sunset and smaller as it rises to midday. Use the Disk Size and Horizon Distortion sliders to reinforce this effect.

- *Halo Rings*—Halo Rings produce interesting anomalies when combined with haze. Make sure you don't have too many clouds in the sky, or the Halo won't be visible. You can keyframe animate both the Intensity and Radius of the Halo. Animate the Radius from 0 to 100 to make the Sun seem to cast out the Halo over time. Selecting the Secondary Rings option adds a second Halo Ring beyond the first one.
- *Moon Phase*—As I discussed in Chapter 4, I prefer other methods for creating moons in the Bryce sky. The Bryce moon is too weak for my tastes, but it may be just right for your purposes. I would like to see far more moon controls, including multiple moons and the ability to apply your own textures to them. I would also like to be able to divorce the moon from the sun; this would make it possible to place moons in the day sky. If you use the Bryce moon, keep the Moon Image option selected if the moon is large enough to make the craters visible. You might want to explore animating the moon's phases. As in the real world, a clear, dark sky is best for moon gazing. See Figure 5.7.
- *Shadows*—There isn't that much call for animating Shadow density, but you can do it if needed.
- *Ambient and Sky Dome color*—Animating these colors alters the coloration of the sky. You can use such animations for special effects or in more subtle ways to indicate sunrise or sunset variations.

Animating Infinite Sky Planes

Using the Infinite Sky Plane's Materials Lab, you can create a wide array of animated skies. All you need is a material for the Sky Plane, usually selected from either the Sky presets or from your own bitmap texture.

Procedural Texture Options

You will use Procedural Textures to map a Cloud Plane 99 percent of the time, because Procedural Textures look more natural, and they don't suffer from the repetitive tiling you get with a bitmap. When you use one of the Procedural presets as the texture for your Cloud Plane, you have a number of possible animation options:

Figure 5.7
This image features stars and a moon that were created with the Sky Lab. You can also see a few comets. In case you're curious, the material used on the mountains and the ground is the Dried Mud preset, World Mapped. Because the sun is turned off, a Radial Light was added in the foreground to illuminate some of the terrain's features.

- To add animated turbulence to the Cloud Plane, alter the frequency setting. The greater the variance in frequency from keyframe to keyframe, the more turbulent the clouds will be. Randomly alter the frequency by 10 or so over the length of the animation for a natural look. You can also spin the cloud plane on its Y axis over time, creating a spinning vortex effect. Alter the X and/or Y positions over time, and the clouds appear to move with the wind.
- To add a more chaotic look to the clouds, use Random Mapping.

Picture Texture Options

Bitmapped Cloud Planes work better as effects than as naturalistic clouds. Because bitmaps tile when you map them to an Infinite Plane, they look manufactured instead of naturalistic. When you select a bitmap as the texture for your Cloud Plane, you have a number of possible animation options:

- Use Random Mapping to create a more natural look when you use a bitmap. This creates interesting chaotic cloud-patterns, but the bitmap's image content is no longer recognizable. If you use a bitmap with Random Mapping on a Cloud Plane, use a bitmap with interesting colors (the image content will be sacrificed anyway). Animate the frequency of the Random Mapped bitmap.

- Mapping a Cloud Plane with a tiled bitmap can serve as an infinite "ceiling" or "floor" for a room, or as an infinite wall if the plane is rotated. The only caveat is that cast shadows no longer operate as they would with standard 3D objects used as room elements. You can achieve bizarre and unexpected movements by animating the frequency or rotation of bitmaps used as parts of a room. These effects are more useful for dream sequences than for displaying an artifact of the real world.

Animating Materials

Why animate materials? After all, once something is created from a substance, doesn't it remain the same under most conditions? Well, yes and no. Yes, as long as you are referring to something in the real world, and as long as the thing is not subjected to fire, water, or another deforming condition. But a Bryce world is not the real world: It is a world you create. In essence, you can alter all the physical laws that constrain material behaviors in the real world. You can do this to create more realism or more fantasy, all depending on the looks you try to achieve. Here are just a small number of project ideas that involve animated materials:

- Map a Liquid preset to a Infinite Water Plane, and keyframe it for the first frame. Map a second Liquid preset to the plane in the middle frame of the animation and a third in the final frame. The result is a body of liquid that changes its substance over the length of the animation. If you placed this liquid in a container and placed a fire under the container, it would look like the heat was altering the liquid's composition.
- Apply a Volumetric Texture preset to a cube. Keyframe animate the Base Density attribute in the Materials Lab: Make the Base Density 100 percent in the first frame and 0 percent in the last. What do you think will happen? The cube dissolves into 3D fragments before your eyes, and each of the fragments uses the same Volumetric Material. The Red Corpuscles texture is a great Volumetric to try this effect with. If the same cube is struck by another animated object or a laser beam, that interaction appears to result in the dissolution of the targeted cube. This opens the door to myriad similar effects.
- This effect appears to be an animated material effect, but it really isn't. Map any primitive or imported object with any material, making sure the material is World Mapped. Keyframe animate the object's position. The result is an object whose material seems to be sliding on its surface.

Why? Because when you use World Mapping on an object and then move the object, the object moves through the projected material.

- Create a sphere, and map it with any material you like. Make sure the sun is off, and place no other lights in the scene. Use the Atmosphere Off option and a solid black background color. In an animation, set the Ambience of the sphere's material to 0 percent in the first frame, 100 percent in the center frame, and back to 0 percent in the last frame. At the beginning of the animation, the object is invisible. The sphere gradually becomes a bright glow that peaks at the middle of the animation. As the animation progresses, the sphere fades again.
- Place a large sphere on a table in a room, surrounded by other objects of your choice. Create a six-second animation in which the sphere has a 0 percent reflectivity at the beginning and 100 percent reflectivity at the end (that is, it becomes a mirror). Use the Materials Lab to set these values. What happens when the animation is rendered? The sphere's surface is initially flat, gradually becoming more reflective as the animation progresses until it becomes a full mirror at the end of the animation. You can achieve an even more fantastic effect by applying a bitmap to the sphere in the Diffusion and Ambience channels. Set Diffuse and Ambient color to 0 percent at the beginning and to 100 percent at the end. The image gradually appears on the sphere. This is an interesting way to use material effects to create a mystical crystal ball.

More Animation Tips And Tricks

There are a number of techniques that you can employ to stretch the potential of your Bryce animations.

Arms, Legs, And Other Appendages

If you want to animate creature parts, you must link the parts so you can create articulated movements. Strange warping of the animated appendages occurs if you don't link the parts of an animated figure correctly.

The Appendage Control

An Appendage Control is an intervening sphere inserted between the moving child object and its linked parent. Using Appendage Controls allows you to animate the child objects in a linked chain without distorting any of the objects. See Figures 5.8 and 5.9.

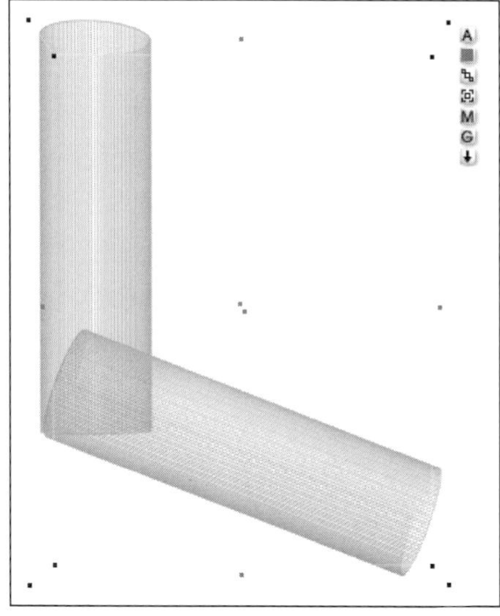

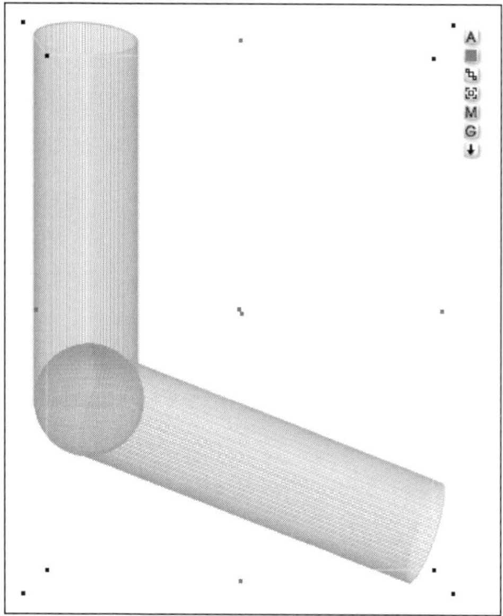

Figure 5.8

(Left) These two cylinders are part of a mechanical arm that rotates at the place where the cylinders meet.

Figure 5.9

(Right) A spherical Appendage Control is inserted in between the two components to act as a more stable mechanism for rotation. The sphere makes the joint between the two arm elements look smoother.

Linking The Appendage Control

When you link the parts of a model and embed Appendage Controls, do not link the Appendage Controls to objects in the hierarchy (for example, a hand/lower arm/upper arm hierarchy). Link the hand to the Appendage Control between the hand and the lower arm. Link the Appendage Control between the hand and lower arm to the Appendage Control between the lower and upper arm. Link the lower arm to the Appendage Control between the lower and upper arm. Link the Appendage Control between the lower and upper arm to the Appendage Control between the upper arm and the body. Finally, link the upper arm to the Appendage Control between the upper arm and the body. When you are ready to create keyframes based on the rotation of the parts, rotate the Appendage Controls, not the body parts. This creates smooth animated movement with no warping or skewing of the elements. Add a *C* to the names of all the Appendage Controls (for example, "LHandC", "LowerLArmC", and so on.)

Visibility

Appendage Controls are invisible most of the time. However, there may be times when you want them to be visible because they can smooth out an otherwise blocky joint. The shape of the object that acts as an Appendage Control doesn't need to have anything to do with the animated objects you want the viewer to notice. Any object in your scene can serve as an Appendage Control.

Note: *If the Appendage Control sphere is to remain visible, you should resize it so it is embedded inside the rendered figure.*

Propagation

The Animation tab in the Attributes dialog box includes a number of propagation toggles: Distance, Offset, Rotation, and Size. These toggles control which actions the child object inherits from the parent object. When you activate Rotation for the parent object in a linked chain, the linked child also rotates when the parent is rotated. When Size is activated, resizing the parent also resizes the child. Select the propagation features you want to use before moving an object into place in a linked hierarchical chain.

Animating Conglomerate Objects

A conglomerate object is made up of a mixture of different components (for example, an animated object that includes some imported elements, a few primitives, and some Terrain Edited parts). Here are some tips you can use when creating a conglomerate object whose elements are to be keyframe animated:

- Consider using Appendage Controls between animated parts if either of the parts is a grouped object.
- Move the Origin Point of selected elements so that rotation takes place around the correct axis fulcrum.
- Use the Advanced Motion Lab to apply repetitive Motion Curves to the selected elements.

Body Part Collections

No, this section is not about grave robbing to create Frankenstein monsters. In order to create composite animated models, you should build a library of individual parts. Keep similar parts in separate subfolders.

Linked Shells

Any object can have an outer shell created from a clone of that object. You can use shells to map clothing on a human figure or for more exotic uses. For instance, you might wrap a shell on a human figure and give the shell a fuzzy light material. This results in a figure that has a glow. Keyframe animating the parameters of the shell's material can result in countless spectacular effects. The shell is commonly linked to the element from which it was cloned. Organic shells (smoke, fire, water) are animated separately from the object to which they are linked, usually by altering the frequency and rotational components of their material.

Nulls

A Null object is any object that has power over other objects (or over facets of an animation) but which is not rendered itself. Null objects are usually invisible. Appendage Controls are one type of Null object, but there are others: Gravity Wells, Negative and Intersecting Booleans, Camera Targets, and Propagation Engines.

Appendage Controls

Appendage Controls (which I have already described) are Null objects. They control every aspect of an animated figure, yet they do not appear in the rendering.

Gravity Wells

A Gravity Well Null object controls a number of moving objects in a scene by simulating the effect of a super-magnet. A Gravity Well influences all the objects that are linked to it. When used as a core parent object with a multitude of children, a Gravity Well's effects can be stunning. To create a Gravity Well, simply link a diverse group of objects to the parent Null. As the Null moves, the children obediently follow. Note that each of the children can have their own movements while the Null drags them. This is one way to create a flock of diverse birds, all flapping their wings in their own rhythm while being dragged in unison by a Gravity Well Null object.

Negative And Intersecting Booleans

Boolean Negative and Intersecting objects are Null objects. They are invisible, but their influence on the positive objects grouped with them is readily apparent in a rendering. When you animate the position of a Negative or Intersecting Boolean object so that it collides with and passes through a Positive Boolean object, it creates an invisible force that magically eats away at the Positive Boolean. There is no limit to the amount or structure of Negative or Intersecting Booleans that you can group with one or more Positive Boolean objects. When everything starts to move at once, the potential for creating bizarre effects increases.

Camera Targets

You can control the movement, rotation, and other animation parameters of any object by linking it to a Null object. A Null object works very well as a target for a tracking camera. This is much easier than moving the actual camera, especially in complex scenes. By having the camera track an invisible Null object, you can pause the camera wherever the Null pauses.

Propagation Engines (Dispersions)

By using the Dispersion techniques (with the Dispersion options listed in the Edit palette), you can move multiple selected objects in unison on one or more axis. When you select a number of ungrouped objects and disperse them, they remain single objects. Using rotation on single objects rotates them in place around their own singular Origin Handles. But grouping the objects and using the Rotation tool makes them rotate around a common Origin Handle. When you link every member of a collection of ungrouped objects to a Null parent object, all the linked children objects rotate around the Null's Origin Handle (provided rotation is used with only the Null object selected). Because the objects remain ungrouped, marquee-selecting all the objects also allows you to rotate the objects individually around their own Origin Points. This allows you to maintain both options.

Visibility Revisited

When you need to, you can render Null objects along with the other objects in a scene. Turn off the Hidden option in the Null object's Attributes dialog box, and then you can treat them the way you would treat any other object. You can use a group of Null objects to simulate an ocean wave to control the rotation and movements of a school of fish. When you create a Null object that is visible in the rendering, make sure the object won't be suspected as the controlling influence. Place it, for example, in an inconspicuous part of the scene.

Moving On

If you have worked through this chapter (and have also read Bryce's documentation describing paths, links, targets, animation controls, and camera animation), you have all of the basic knowledge you need in order to start creating astounding animated sequences. The next chapter deals with this book's Bryce Studio by detailing how Bryce effects and tools were used in to create the color images.

6 The Color Plates

The best way to master Bryce is to study the work of others who use it and read their explanations of what they did. This chapter looks at each plate in the Bryce Studio and presents them not just as alluring eye candy, but as learning resources as well.

How To Use This Chapter

As soon as you picked up this book, you probably turned to the color plates first to see the images that depict the magic of Bryce. Most computer graphics and animation books use color illustrations only to "wow" you. But the images in the color section of this book are more than just beautiful: They are carefully crafted to exemplify specific techniques and tools and to present a wide range of effects and designs.

With that in mind, this chapter might be the most valuable learning resource this book has to offer: It dissects each of the color images, showing you the details of the image's components and how they were produced. This chapter presents some of my work and the work of 11 other Bryce professionals. The artists themselves explain the images in their own words, so you can gain insight into their creative processes and the techniques they use. Look at each color plate in turn, and then read the section of this chapter devoted to that image. You can find biographies of each contributing artist in Appendix B.

"Dusty Nebula" By Sandy Birkholz

When I compose a scene like this one, I try to remain less controlling in my approach and allow Bryce to surprise me. Refer to the numbers in Figure 6.1 as you read the following explanations:

1. Begin by selecting Camera view and removing the Ground Plane from the scene. In the Advanced Display palette to the right of the working window, turn off the Wireframe Underground option. This allows you to place objects anywhere in your 3D scene without losing them below the ground level. Choose False Dawn for the sky and place the sun slightly to the upper right. The sun position might change depending on how the scene develops, although I kept it toward the upper right of the frame for this picture. Change the sun color to a deep red-gold, and set the solar halo color in the Sky & Fog palette to a deep indigo. Select the Stars and Comets options in the Sky & Fog Options dialog box. A test render shows a deep golden sun in a sky that fades from indigo to black.

2. Create a sphere, and from the top view, use the Resize tool to enlarge the sphere until it overtakes the camera. The space environment's appearance depends on how large you make this sphere. Making the sphere too large might cause the loss of some interesting effects, depending on the type of material you assign to it. However, you *will* need to make the sphere large enough to accommodate a scene. Now,

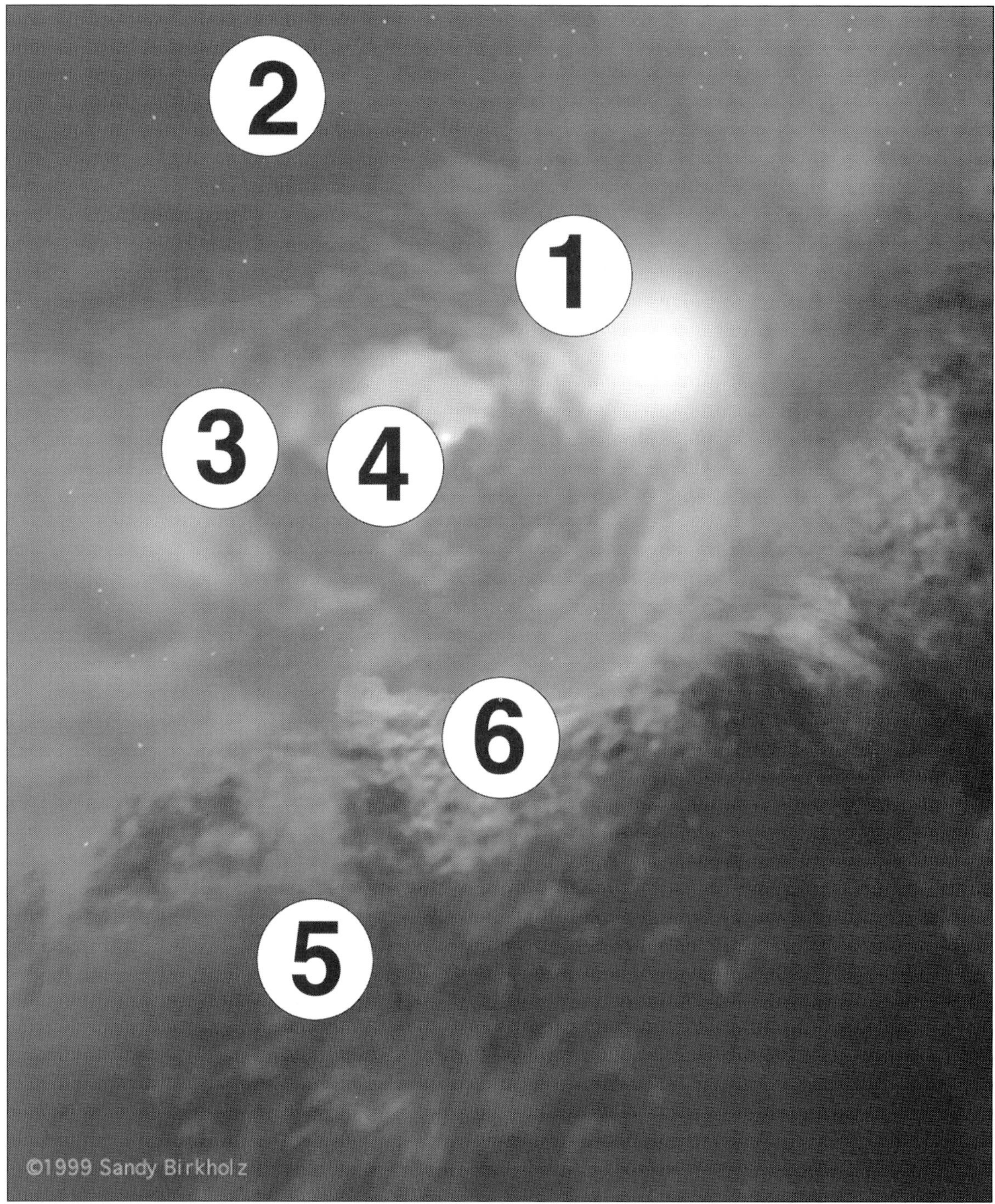

Figure 6.1

Dusty Nebula. (Refer to the color version in this book's Bryce Studio.) The chapter text details each labeled element.

while still in top view, move the camera to the approximate center of the sphere. Assign the sphere to a family color by clicking the gray family button located under the Objects Attributes button. Also, assign a material from the Materials library. I chose Romantic Sunset from the Clouds presets and increased the bump height to 100.

3. Return to Camera view and give your scene a vast, "spacey" appearance by clicking on the Zoom Out icon in the Advanced Display palette a time or two. Repeated clicks on this icon can produce some amazing results, but be aware that as you zoom out, the process distorts the Field Of View (FOV) as well as the appearance of objects placed within the field. A test render reveals subtle clouds floating around in space. Rotate the main sphere until you are happy with the clouds' appearance.

4. To begin to light the environment a bit more (and give it an extra star or two), create a Radial Light and place it just within the inner surface of the sphere. Use the various views to move the light to just the right position. The light reflects off the cloud material on the main sphere, creating a large star. I colored this Radial Light a deep red-gold (by clicking on the *E* for edit and clicking on the color chip to the right of the selected light) and set the intensity set to about 75. This not only produced the star effect, it also gave a vibrant red-gold glow to the clouds on the main sphere and to objects placed within the sphere. Now is a good time to reposition the sun if you need to. Because of the distortion produced by zooming out, numerical sun values become relatively unimportant. At this point, all that is important is that you are pleased with your developing composition.

5. Now build the dust and gas clouds. Build a cluster of spheres (my scene is composed of six of these spheres) and give them different sizes. Make them about one-third the size of the main sphere (or smaller). Assign the spheres a family color and a cloud material. I used Cotton Ball Storm from the Clouds & Fogs presets. Using the various views, arrange the cloud spheres so that they overlap and occupy a variety of levels and areas within and around the main sphere. It's fine if portions of these cloud spheres go outside the boundaries of the main sphere. Arrange the spheres until you are happy with the way they look from the Camera view when rendered. The number, size, and arrangement of the cloud spheres gives the effect of large clouds of gas and dust within a growing universe. In this picture, most of the cloud spheres are situated slightly below and

immediately in front of the camera. The spheres' wireframes appear stretched because of the wide angle of the Camera view.

6. In order to create the illusion that the dust and gas clouds are backlighted by the brilliant light behind them, create another Radial Light. You might want to assign a different family color to the new Radial Light in case you need to make some adjustments without ruining the settings for the first light. Again using the various views, place this light so that it illuminates the edges of the clouds and also produces some illumination within them. To add drama to your scene, give the new light a contrasting or complimentary color. Keep in mind that any lights placed in this environment can greatly change the mood and character of your scene. In my picture, the Radial Light that backlights the clouds is a white light set to 23 in the Light Editor. Placing Radial Lights in your scene can be one of the most effective ways to introduce variety and interest to your images. I try to maintain a spirit of playfulness as I work (which often ensures that it doesn't become "work"). Allowing Bryce to make some decisions for me almost always results in delightful surprises and, ultimately, better images.

"Almost Eden" By Jeff Richardson

This image takes advantage of Bryce's capability to generate naturalistic phenomena. Refer to the numbers in Figure 6.2 as you read the following explanations:

1. This sky is one of the most complex I've ever created. It took about two hours of experimentation in the Deep Texture Editor to get the cumulus and stratus clouds to do what I wanted them to do. Some of the color is present in the clouds themselves, and some comes from the sunlight. The shadows are set to very dark red. The Haze value is set to 24 and to a very pale yellow color, and the Sky Dome Height is set to 42 with a gray-yellow color. The cloud coverage is set to 26; the sun is also set to a gray-yellow color. The cloud materials are available for download from the Bryce Forum at Delphi (**www.delphi.com/bryce/**). Many other excellent Bryce presets are also available from the forum's file database. If you'd rather dive into the Deep Texture Editor yourself, use these settings:

    - *Cumulus clouds*—A single channel 2D texture. No Filter and no Phase are used. The Noise is set to Type: Time Random, Mode: Standard, Octaves: 4, Direction: XY 62, YZ 312. The Frequency of X is set to 143, Y to 166, Z to 302.

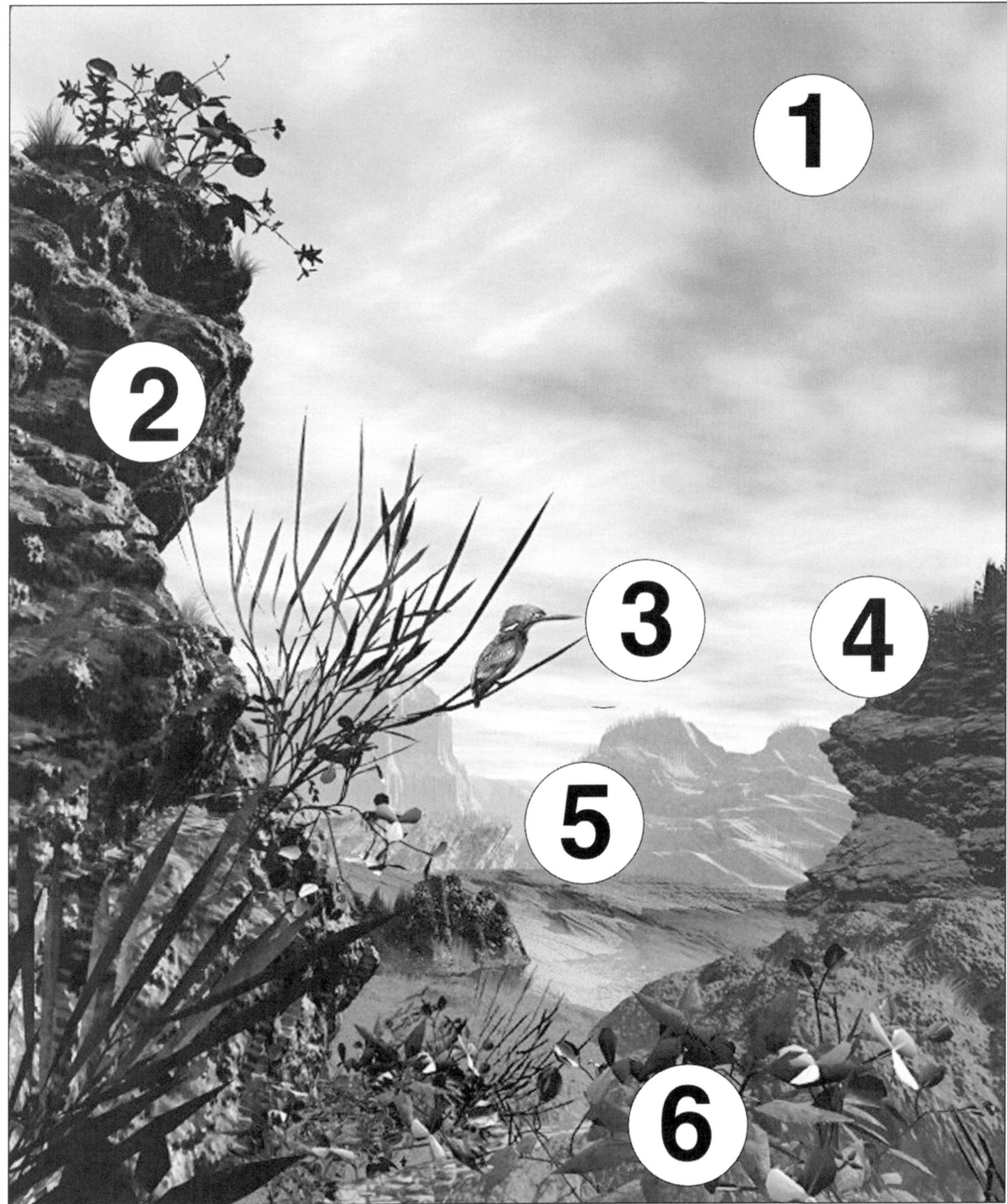

Figure 6.2

Almost Eden. (Refer to the color version in this book's Bryce Studio.) The chapter text details each labeled element.

- *Stratus clouds*—A single channel texture 2D texture. Noise is set to Type: Waves, Mode: Standard, Octaves: 2, Direction: XY is 10, YZ is 0. The Frequency of X is set to 202, Y to 438, Z to 269.

2. The cliffs are made from terrains that have been flipped on their sides so they face the camera. I used the Terrain Editor's Fractal Terrain option, and when I got a terrain I liked, I hit the Invert button. This provides an excellent and detailed appearance of a rock outcropping. When you use the Fractal Terrain option, make sure you set the Terrain Editor's Terrain Grid to 512 or higher: The terrain will have greater detail.
3. The bird is a picture object taken from a clip-art CD-ROM. I altered its color to make it more three-dimensional and to fit the overall color scheme of the scene. I positioned the bird carefully to look like it's sitting at the end of the wireframe leaves.
4. The trees atop the second cliff are actually Symmetrical Lattice objects. I set a terrain to a resolution of 256 and used a soft brush to draw random blobs of white. Then I clicked on and dragged the Spikes control to the right to add finer elements to the grayscale. I placed the Symmetrical Lattice object slightly behind the cliff face and applied one of the two Forest Material presets (in the Miscellaneous presets) with a bump height reduced to zero.
5. The terrains in the distance are made of many overlapping terrains. Most are low resolution (the grid is set to 256), and there are at least two terrains for each distant hill. The terrains are also set back into the scene and enlarged to enormous proportions to create a sense of scale. I made the trees by duplicating a terrain, and, in the Terrain Editor, hitting the Sharpen button. I used the Unpaint Effect brush to paint out random areas of the newly sharpened bits. Then, I left the Terrain Editor and lowered the terrain slightly. Finally, I applied the Distant Forest material from the Miscellaneous presets.
6. I created the foreground foliage with a fantastic shareware application for Windows: PlantStudio by Kurtz-Fernhout Software (**www.kurtz-fernhout.com**). PlantStudio creates wireframes of just about any plant or shrub you care to imagine, all of which can be ungrouped in Bryce and textured to suit your scene. There are only six different plants in the scene, but they've been duplicated, scaled, and distorted to create more variety.

***Note:** A demo version of PlantStudio for Windows is included on this book's companion CD-ROM.*

"Promenade dans l'île" By Martial Fauteux

This image resembles a muted impressionistic painting. Refer to the numbers in Figure 6.3 as you read the following explanations:

1. The reflections help this image's composition by creating an oval form that draws the eyes to the woman (the most important element).
2. The atmosphere and sky use a surrealist blue mood that I explored by trial and error. I ended up using soft sky mode with Shadow Intensity set to 90, Fog Height to zero, Haze Intensity to 74, Cloud Altitude to 3, and Cloud Coverage to 9.
3. For the terrain, I selected Deep Mossy Grass and modified the colors in the Deep Texture Editor. I used the Narcissus Pool preset for the water.
4. Bryce does not have tree-creation tools, so I used a Ray Dream Studio 5.02 plug-in called Tree Druid (from the BioGraphics Research Group of Hutchison Avenue Software Corporation, **http://bgr.hasc.com**). Tree Druid helped me generate the maple trees in this project.
5. I created the foliage separately in Painter, using the Jungle 3D plug-in from DigArts (**www.gardenhose.com**). A foliage texture mapping nozzle was made inside Painter by using a transparent layer and tonal controls. One tree uses autumn colors with a touch of blue. I used a different Painter Image Hose nozzle for adjusting the shadows.
6. To create the woman, I used Poser 3 and files from the Poser Forum (**poser@lists.metacreations.com**) to customize a character called Baggy Pants Woman (originally a soldier carrying a large gun). The Poser morph was created by Roy B. on the Poser Forum. I created a new texture for her clothing by using Painter's Scottish Baird 4 weave. I customized her hair with Female Hair 03, created by E. Ewestay from the Poser Forum. (Thanks to all contributors on the Poser Forum.)

"Melbourne, Australia" By Kuzey Atici

An unbelievably realistic city is the subject of this image. Refer to the numbers in Figure 6.4 as you read the following explanations:

1. I began by importing a simple overhead map of Melbourne as a Picture object. I enlarged the map and rotated it into a horizontal position. Once I placed the map on the Ground Plane, I had a template that indicated where everything should go. After the city was completed, I deleted the map.

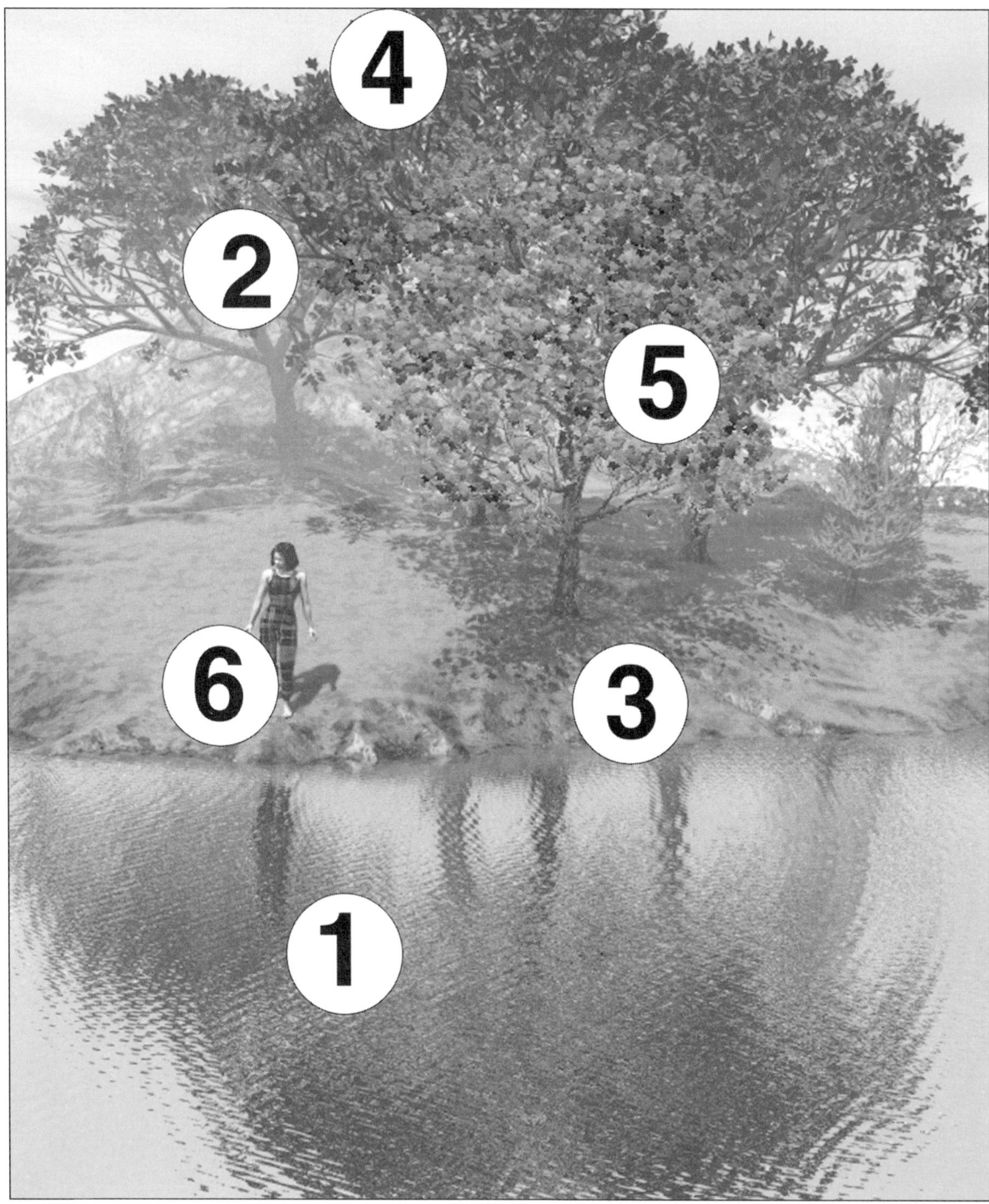

Figure 6.3

Promenade dans l'île. (Refer to the color version in this book's Bryce Studio.) The chapter text details each labeled element.

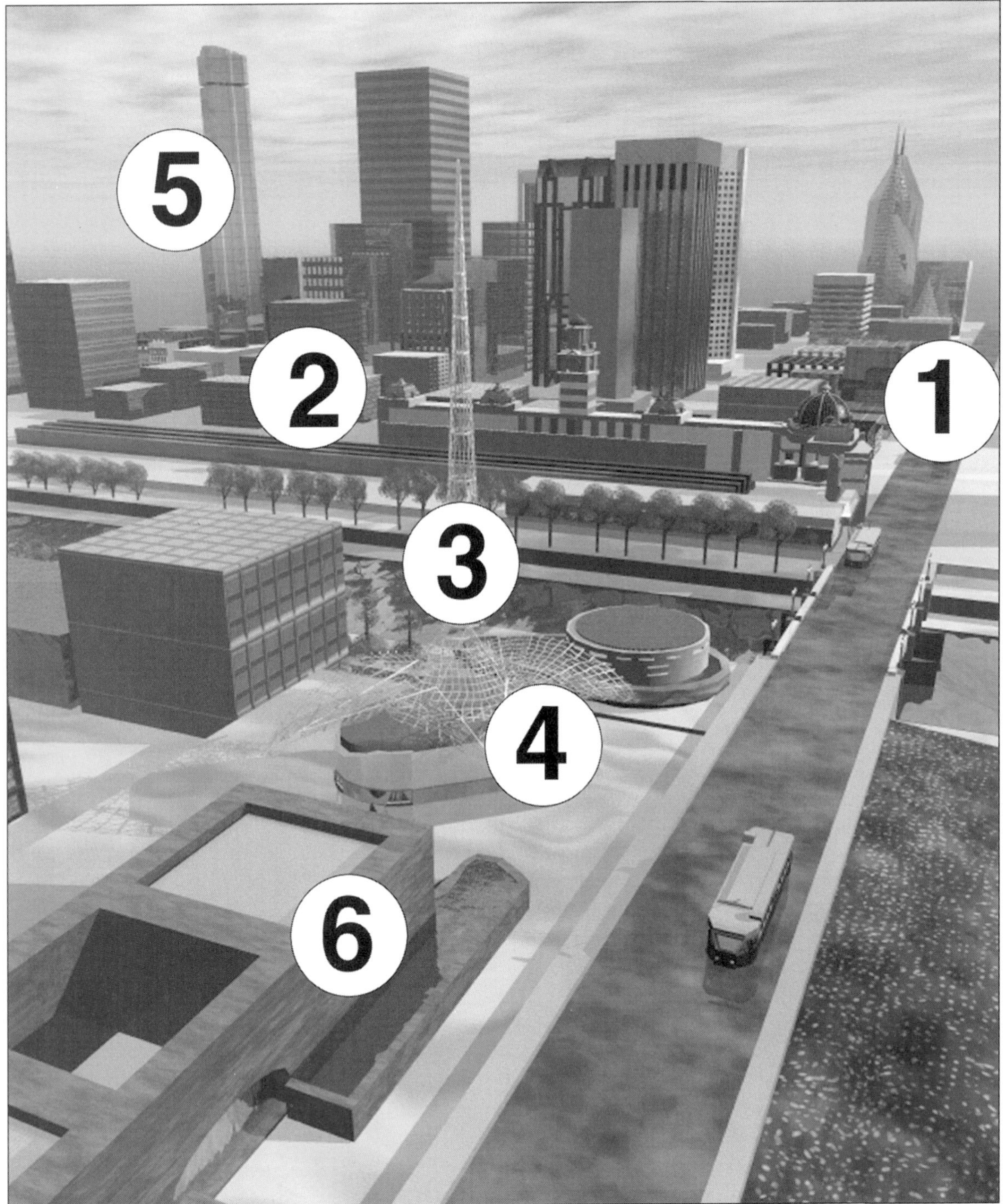

Figure 6.4
Melbourne, Australia. (Refer to the color version in this book's Bryce Studio.) The chapter text details each labeled element.

2. To keep the size of the Bryce project file down to a workable level, I used primitive cubes in place of large, detailed models. I created a single cube and positioned it on the map, but I didn't add textures until all the buildings were in place. Working from the top view, I duplicated the cube and moved it into the next location (resizing it as required). Soon the city began to take shape. I did the same for the streets by using stretched Horizontal 2D Face objects.

3. My first attempt at building the spire in Ray Dream Studio 5 was a failure. I wasn't able to get the fine detail I needed in order to make it look realistic. I ended up using 256 cylinders in Bryce to complete the model and then applied the white metal texture.

4. Here's how you can create these textures in the Materials Lab: Ctrl/Command and click on the Diffuse channel's B column. Replace the current texture in Texture A with Basic Sin 24 and set Texture B to basic grid. Click on the A column of both Ambient and Bump Height channels. Now click on the B column of the Transparency channel and set Diffusion to 22.3, Ambience to 25.4, Bump Height to 4.3, and Reflectivity to 37.6. Change the component frequency of both textures to suit your needs.

5. Bryce may not be a true 3D modeler, because it lacks most of the standard modeling tools, but it can come close depending on how you approach it. Building highly complex models can be rewarding. It took 416 Bryce primitive objects to complete this Melbourne landmark.

6. I modeled complex buildings in Ray Dream Studio 5 using photographs as a guide. I modeled the major buildings and landmarks only—just enough to add needed realism. I imported each model into an empty scene to apply the textures and then saved the models to the Object library. You can use the same process to complete your own 3D city.

"Bonsai" By Andrew Paul

This still life image was created with Bryce and other 3D applications. Refer to the numbers in Figure 6.5 as you read the following explanations:

1. The Bonsai Bowl was a simple object created in trueSpace. It is basically a shaped cube with legs. After importing the DXF into Bryce, I applied Old Metal from the Metals presets (what a great material!). It was too light for the cast-iron appearance I was aiming for, so I turned down the Diffusion setting to darken it, boosted Specularity to

Figure 6.5
Bonsai. (Refer to the color version in this book's Bryce Studio.) The chapter text details each labeled element.

42, adjusted Metallicity to 33, and increased the Bump Height to 16. Metal has a reflective sheen that suggests its density, so I wanted to give it a reflective quality while maintaining darkness and depth. Scaling the material from 50 percent to 125 percent made it look finer and denser. I also found that changing the texture mapping mode to Object Space made it look a bit more like metal. The Bryce materials are fantastic building blocks, but I think they all have to be adjusted and tuned to create unique images. Scaling materials is one way to make them your own.

2. I began making the dice in Caligari's trueSpace, but later I realized this would be a great opportunity to try Bryce's Boolean functions. Bryce doesn't have a modeler, but you can do a lot with Booleans. I created a positive cube and added small negative spheres that removed portions of the cube's surface. Correct placement is important, and I found it necessary to change views from the side to the top. I made a larger sphere that just encompasses the cube, grouped it with the existing cube and spheres, and chose Intersect. This Boolean function leaves whatever is common to the two forms, and this sheared off the corners of the cube that were outside the large globe, leaving a cube with rounded corners. I used a flat white material on the dice and then gave it some reflective qualities because it was too bland. I pushed Metallicity up to 169, Reflection to 35, and used a very mild Bump pattern (Marble sand is great for a fine effect) with a Height of 3. To keep the dice from looking too white, I added a touch of yellow to the Ambient component color.

3. The coins are squashed cylinders with scanned bitmaps applied to them. Applying bitmaps to objects is a great way to introduce effects to an image, but it has limitations, and it can cause problems. The scanned bitmap was applied to the coins with Object Top selected as the texture mapping mode. This places the image on top of the cylinder, but it leaves the sides bare. By setting the Scale to -1, you can extend the image from the top to cover the sides. If you want more accurate coverage in a detailed image, you could add a texture to the outside of the image. The coin would then stretch properly. The coins are not actually touching the table—they are placed just above it so a reflection is created that would not normally exist if the coins touched the table. This enhances the glassy surface of the table.

4. The table is an elongated cube. I used the Diffuse color component to make the surface dark gray, set the Ambient color to very dark, and

performed some other fine-tuning in the Materials Lab. I pushed Specularity up to 40, Metallicity to 80, and Reflection to 72. As I played with these settings, I realized how powerful the Materials Lab can be (not to mention the Deep Texture Editor). I ended up with the effect of a glass or metal table with a highly polished surface. To keep the table from looking too much like a distant background, I applied a basic texture, CheckBlue. I scaled the texture to 14 and applied it in World Space mode. There is no reflection from the sky because all the Atmosphere controls are set to black (with the exception of Shadows, which are dark gray). This allows only the light from my three Radial Lights to enter things. This is an odd Bryce picture in that has none of the things that Bryce is known best for: skies, mountains, and water. The Materials Nano Preview window is invaluable for creating your own materials. Try moving around in it with your left mouse button held down while you hold down the Control (Mac) or spacebar (Windows) to zoom in or move up and down.

5. The paper money, like the coins, uses a scanned bitmap image; this scanned image was a 45MB file. I applied it to a form I created in trueSpace. Instead of just using a Bryce primitive, I created a rectangle and warped it to give it an organic, flowing feeling, and then I imported the DXF into Bryce for mapping. I used Parametric Mapping mode as I placed the image on the object. Combining images and textures is a favorite technique of mine, and it adds interesting possibilities. Although Photoshop and trueSpace created elements used in this image, the final image is still all Bryce. The final image included no post-production work: no layers, masks, transparency, or anything else.

6. Regarding the tree, it's a good thing software makers are out there creating programs like Tree Druid and PlantStudio. I imported this tree into Bryce from Tree Druid, scaled it to fit the pot, and textured it. For the texture, I used a scanned piece of bark from a tree my daughter plays in; fitting, because this image is dedicated to her. Altering Ambience to about 20 was all the tinkering I did. This tree actually gave me a lot of problems, for a stock object. I tried many perspectives—looking up, from the sides, from above—and nothing seemed to work. Finally, I happened upon just the right angle: one that framed both the tree and its reflection. Experimentation is the best way to find what works and what doesn't.

"Digital Tavern" By Bruce "HangTime" Caplin

Step up to this bar for a long, tall cool one at the end of a hectic week. Refer to the numbers in Figure 6.6 as you read the following explanations:

1. The beer mug, although fairly simple to build, turned into a huge file, and it required a very long rendering time. The mug is made up of a negative cylinder that carves out another cylinder, along with a series of cylinders that carve the dents around the outside of the glass. I used a torus for the base and another for the handle. The bubbles are made of a couple hundred spheres with a glass texture applied in order to get some different refraction. It is these spheres that make the file size so large, and the transparency, reflection, and refraction are what slow down the raytracing. The beer itself is just a cylinder inside the glass, and the foam is yet another cylinder topped with a flattened sphere. Although the mug was built in a very short time, the foam texture was not. This texture is available for free download from the Bryce Forum's textures database (**www.delphi.com/bryceObjects**).
2. The money is made from Terrain Objects and cylinders, both covered with 2D pictures. For the paper money, I used a feature of Bryce 3.1 to make smooth fractal hills (Shift+Command and the Fractal button in the Terrain Editor on a Macintosh). I made a subtle set of fractal hills, stretched the terrain into a long rectangle, and applied the 2D picture of a one-million dollar bill. I made the coins much the same way by using some pictures of coins and applying them to flattened cylinders.
3. The keys turned out to be extremely simple to make. I found a black and white drawing of a few keys, used a photo-retouching program to separate the individual keys, and then used the keys as a height map in the Terrain Editor. Each key is actually a terrain shaped like a key. The Grayscale to Height maps for these keys are available for free download from the Bryce Forum's objects database. The keychain is even simpler; it is a 2D picture placed on a cube, using the Alpha channel for transparency.
4. The coasters, like the paper money, are gentle fractal hills covered with a 2D tiled picture. The stacks of coasters in the bar gutter are cubes with the same texture applied.

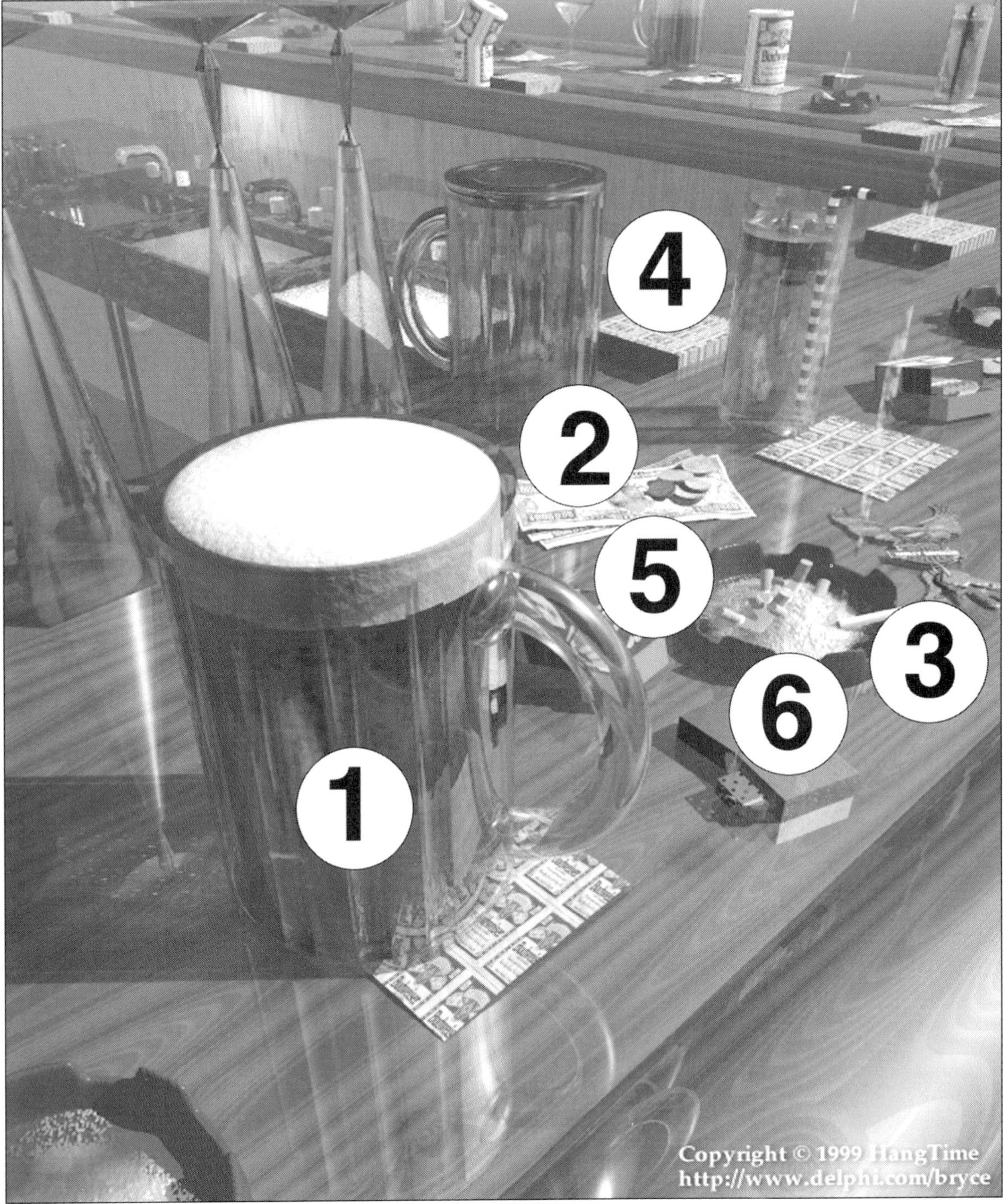

Figure 6.6

Digital Tavern. (Refer to the color version in this book's Bryce Studio.) The chapter text details each labeled element.

5. The cigarette packs are made up of a couple of cubes, hollowed out with negative cubes and covered with a 2D picture texture. The cigarettes are individually made using two cylinders. The tip of the lit cigarette uses a sphere with a modified Hot Lava texture applied. The entire cigarette pack—with cigarettes—is available for free download from the Bryce Forum's objects library (**www.delphi.com/bryceObjects**).

6. The ashtray is a terrain. First, I drew a large gray circle in the Terrain Editor. Next, using a slightly darker shade of gray, I painted dips at the edge of the first circle to create the cigarette holders. Finally, I drew a circle that was slightly darker than the first two and somewhat smaller than the original circle. The ashtray is available for free download from the Bryce Forum's objects library (**www.delphi.com/bryceObjects**). The ash pile is just a randomly generated terrain, and the cigarettes are the same as those used in the cigarette packs. (However, these cigarettes actually stick through the bottom of the ashtray. But I followed the Hollywood model of picture making and worried about only what shows on camera).

"In Praise Of The Best Seller" By Robert Cross

I created this piece for the cover of a daily broadsheet newspaper section devoted to summer reading. The final image was 10.5 by 22 inches at 200 dpi. The top 10 inches or so of the final piece (not shown here) consisted of the rippling sand texture fading into the distance. This is the area in which the layout artist placed the newspaper logo, headlines, and other introductory text for the section. I feel that the greatest accomplishment of this piece is that it was conceived, created, rendered, and on the press in three days. Refer to the numbers in Figure 6.7 as you read the following explanations:

1. Each book consists of two grouped shapes created in another 3D modeling program (3D Studio MAX) and imported into Bryce as DXF files. This allowed for easy mapping of both a cover and inside pages. I knew the red book would have a cutout on the cover that allowed the first page of the book to show through, so in the 3D program, I nestled the second book shape within the first book shape and exported them both as a DXF. In separate layers of an Adobe Illustrator file, I created color, bump, and transparency maps. This guaranteed that the different maps aligned perfectly. The hole in the cover is the result of the

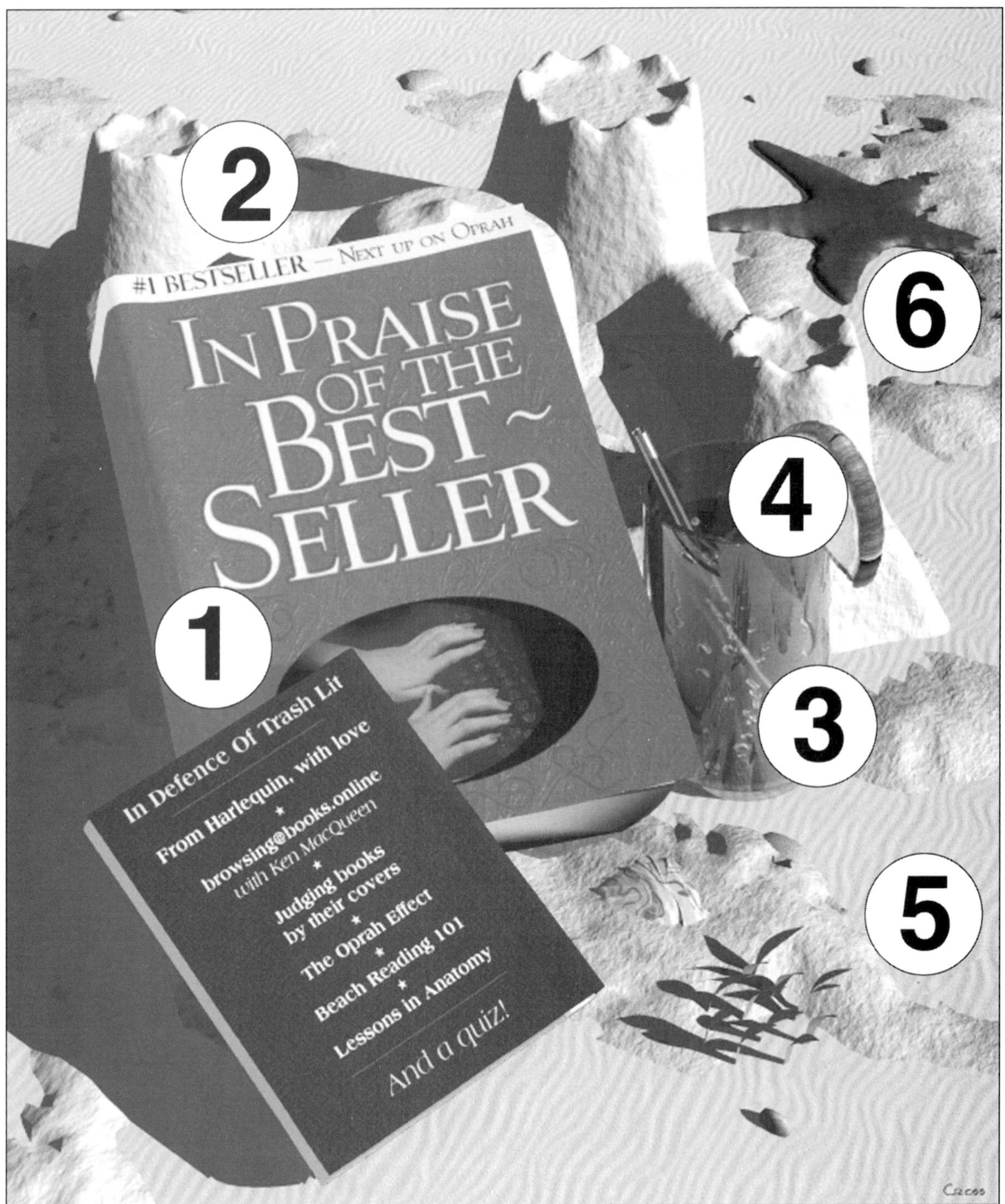

Figure 6.7

In Praise Of The Best Seller. (Refer to the color version in this book's Bryce Studio.) The chapter text details each labeled element.

transparency map. In order to make the text completely legible, I added glow maps and increased the textures' Ambient settings in Bryce. It might have deleted the shadows, but I knew that the text would be completely legible once published on newsprint.

2. The sand castle also began in Illustrator as a basic top view drawing in shades of gray. I opened this file in Photoshop and applied a few blur effects. In Bryce, I created a new terrain and applied the sand castle map. Then, I opened the terrain in the Terrain Editor and edited the map further with Bryce's Terrain Editor tools. This involved many back-and-forth jumps between Bryce and Photoshop before I was satisfied.

3. I used Boolean operations to create the glass, drink, and straw. The glass consists of two cylinders and a cone for the base. I used a negative Boolean cube to cut off the pointed end of the cone. The drink is a slightly reduced duplicate of the smallest glass cylinder. Both the glass and drink use negative Boolean cubes to define the top edges. There are several spheres replicated inside the glass to create bubbles. The condensation is a detailed Bump Map created in Illustrator and Photoshop.

4. I created the wedge of lime by first finding a good photo. I converted the photo to grayscale, adjusted the contrast, and then used the photo to define a new terrain. Then I used the original color photo as a picture texture map.

5. For the beach, I created a seamless ripple texture and mapped it to a new terrain. I chose one of the default sand-like textures and slightly adjusted its color. Then I duplicated the terrain several times and aligned them all in a grid. My theory was that if the terrain texture was based on a seamless tile, and if I could get all the edges lined up perfectly, it would produce an endless beach. And it did work except for a few rough edges. I used Photoshop to fix any hard edges I noticed after rendering. This was the only post-rendering work I had to do on this piece.

6. As the deadline loomed ever closer, I dared not invest time in modeling the starfish in order to import it as another DXF object (not to mention what this would have done to memory requirements, render times, and so on). Instead, I created the starfish as a Symmetrical Lattice. I applied a color and Bump Map based on the map I used to create the terrain, and I was very satisfied with the final appearance.

"Treasures" By Lannie Caranci

Bryce is not limited to scenes on or above the ground. As this image displays, Bryce can also create underwater compositions. Refer to the numbers in Figure 6.8 as you read the following explanations:

1. Light rays are always an interesting effect, whether they come from the sun streaming through a window, from a flashlight, or (as in this image) from the sun's rays penetrating the ocean depths. Begin by creating a cone (not a light cone, just a regular cone). Stretch the Y axis as needed. I pulled the cones way up so they extended beyond the surface of the water. Go to the Materials preset library and use the Texture Lit Rays in the Complex fx presets. Set the Transparency to 50 or whatever looks best in your picture.

2. The creation of the broken pots is a good example of how using Boolean objects can create great effects. (Thanks to Dany Eilat for the use of his pot.) Make or find a model of a pot or a vase and import it into Bryce. On the Object Attribute buttons, click on *A* to bring up the Object Attributes dialog box. Select Positive. Select a rock from one of the rock presets in the Object library. Make the rock Negative. Move the rock into the vase so that they intersect. (This is the tricky part.) The more the rock and vase intersect, the more of the vase is missing when you render. Size the rock accordingly. You may have to experiment a little to get this right. Highlight both the rock and vase and group them. Add the texture of your choice.

3. The white fins on the mermaid are an interesting use of a Symmetrical Lattice in Bryce. (I would like to thank Phil Hokusai, who modeled the mermaid, and Eric Westray, who modeled her hair.) The fins provided an opportunity to experiment with Symmetrical Lattices and the Terrain Editor. I created the initial drawing of the fins in Jasc Software's Paint Shop Pro, but you can use any drawing program for this. In your favorite drawing program, create a 512-by-512 image with a black background. Draw the fins using a medium light-gray color. Save the image as a TIFF or BMP file (for Windows) or as a TIFF or PICT (on the Mac).

   Open Bryce and click on the Symmetrical Lattice. Click on the *E* to go to the Terrain Editor. In the Terrain Editor, clear the work area by clicking on New. Click on the grid box and select 512-Superfine. Import the image of the fin you created in the drawing program. Select the Raise & Lower button and flatten the fin to be as thin as you want it. Click on the check mark to go back to the main screen.

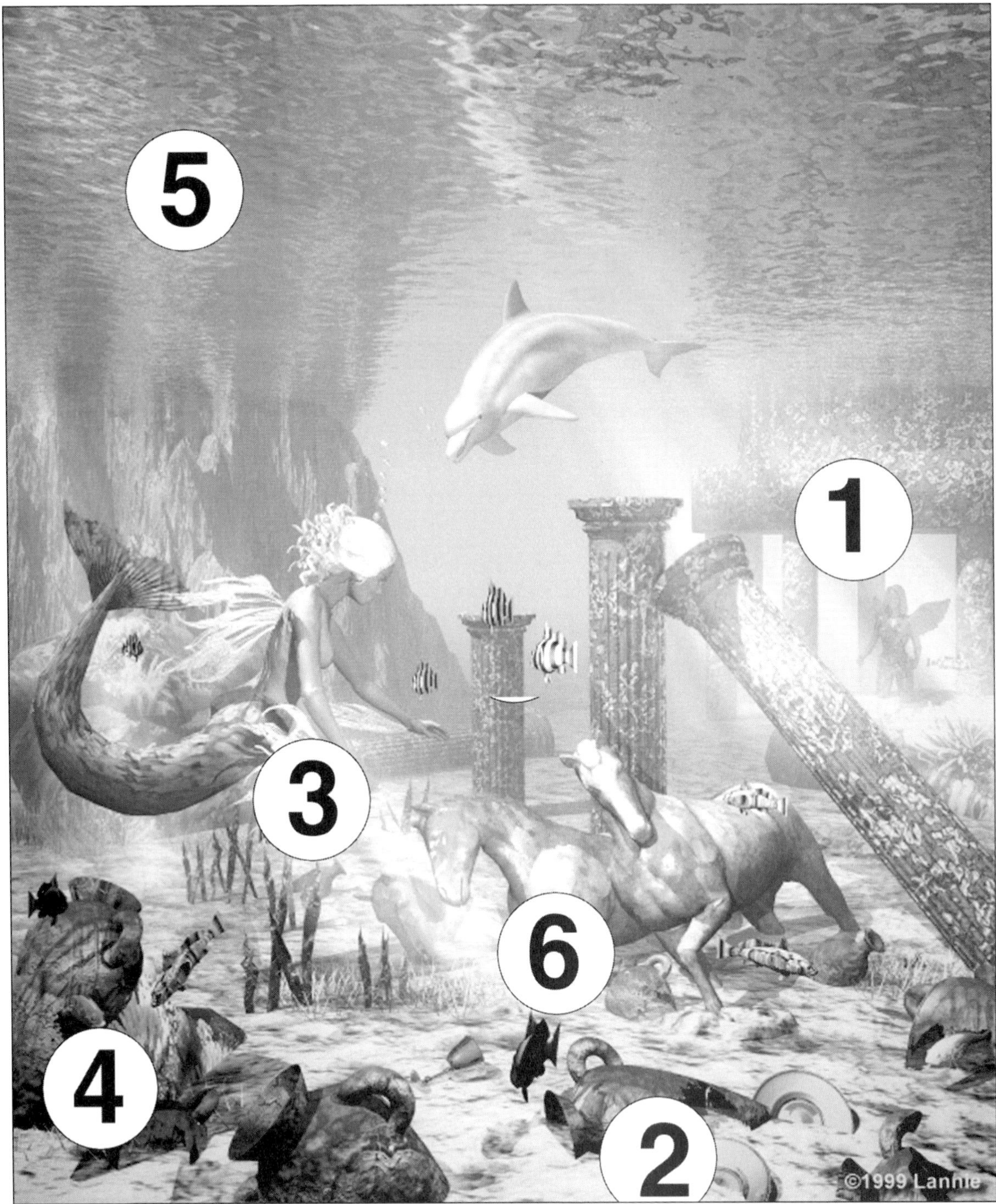

Figure 6.8

Treasures. (Refer to the color version in this book's Bryce Studio.) The chapter text details each labeled element.

Rotate the image 90 degrees on its X axis and place it where you want. Use any preset texture. I used the White Metal texture found in the Simple & Fast presets. Set the Diffusion attribute to 77.9, Ambience to 23.5, Reflection to 52.9, and Refraction to 100.

4. I created the yellow clumps of algae on rocks by using a picture of multicolored coral and algae. (You can map any image directly to an object.) Begin by choosing a picture you want to map. Get a rock from the Objects library. On the Create bar, click on the gold guy with his arms outstretched (Leo). This takes you to the 2D Picture Objects screen. Click on Load and import the picture you want to use. Click on the check mark. Now you are in the Materials Lab, where you can make whatever adjustments you want. Then, click on the check mark to return to the main screen. Position the rock anywhere you'd like.

5. Creating an underwater scene can be challenging at first, but after a few tries, the relationships become understandable. Remember that even though the scene is underwater, the Sky and Cloud settings are extremely important. Highlight the Ground Plane and go to the Materials library. From the Planes & Terrains presets, choose the new Mexico Cliffs texture and apply it to the terrain.

   Create a Water Plane and apply the Deep Blue preset located in the Waters & Liquids presets. Raise the Water Plane almost to top of the screen—you'll need to experiment with its size and height.

   Regarding the Sky & Fog settings, your choice of colors is subjective, and you must experiment to get the desired effect. Some of the Sky & Fog icons have a color bar below them: click on it and a color chart appears. Select colors from there.

   To create the Darker Sky, set Shadows to 98 (Ambient color is medium blue), Fog to 7 99 (color is dark green), Haze to 90 (color is aqua with greenish blue tint), Cloud Height to 4 (color is aqua with light blue tint), Cloud Cover to 9 (color is aqua with light blue tint), Frequency and Amplitude of Clouds to 200 68, Sun Color to aqua blue, and Sun Direction to 8 o'clock.

   At the far right of the toolbar (just past the Sun control) is a column of buttons. At the bottom of this column is an arrow. Click on the arrow and a pull-down menu appears. Select Link To Sun View, Stratus Clouds, and Cumulous Clouds.

6. In addition to the horses, this scene features several Poser 3 models: the mermaid, the statue, and the dolphin. Using Poser 3 models adds a great deal of variety to a Bryce scene. To create the horses in Poser 3, go to Figures|Animals and select the horse. Pose the horse as you like. Go to File|Export As and export the model as a Wavefront object file. In the Export Range Box, click on single frame. Name the file and save it wherever you want. Remember to click on Export Object Groups for each body part.

   In Bryce, go to File|Import Object. Select the Poser 3 horse you just saved. Apply a material to the horse (I used Tarnished Copper found in the Metals presets) and place the horse anywhere you'd like. I used three horses in different poses and grouped them before I positioned them.

"A Friendly Card Game" By Lee Chapel

Here, two unlikely card players—Bigfoot and an alien—engage in a game of chance. Refer to the numbers in Figure 6.9 as you read the following explanations:

1. I used Bryce to create the painting of the wolf-riding gremlins as a separate file. I rendered the image at a resolution of 400 by 300 pixels using Fine Art Antialiasing. After the painting had been rendered, I wanted to make it look more like a painting, so I loaded the painting in MetaCreations' Painter Classic and used the Autoclone feature with the Watercolor Cloner brush to give the picture a more painted look.

   After saving the painting, I went to Bryce and created the picture frame. I created a cube, and then I duplicated the cube and resized the duplicate to the size and dimensions of the area I wanted to cut out of the first cube (this is where the picture would go). Making sure the fronts of both cubes were aligned, I set the first cube's Boolean attribute to positive and the second cube's Boolean attribute to negative. Upon grouping the cubes, I had the picture frame, its middle hollowed out and ready for the picture.

   Then, I created a thin cube that fit inside the picture frame I had created. In the Materials Lab, I clicked on the Diffuse and Ambient buttons in column A. I clicked on *P* to switch to a picture source, and then I loaded the picture I had created in Painter Classic. I left the other settings at their defaults. Upon leaving the Materials Lab, I had a picture in a frame.

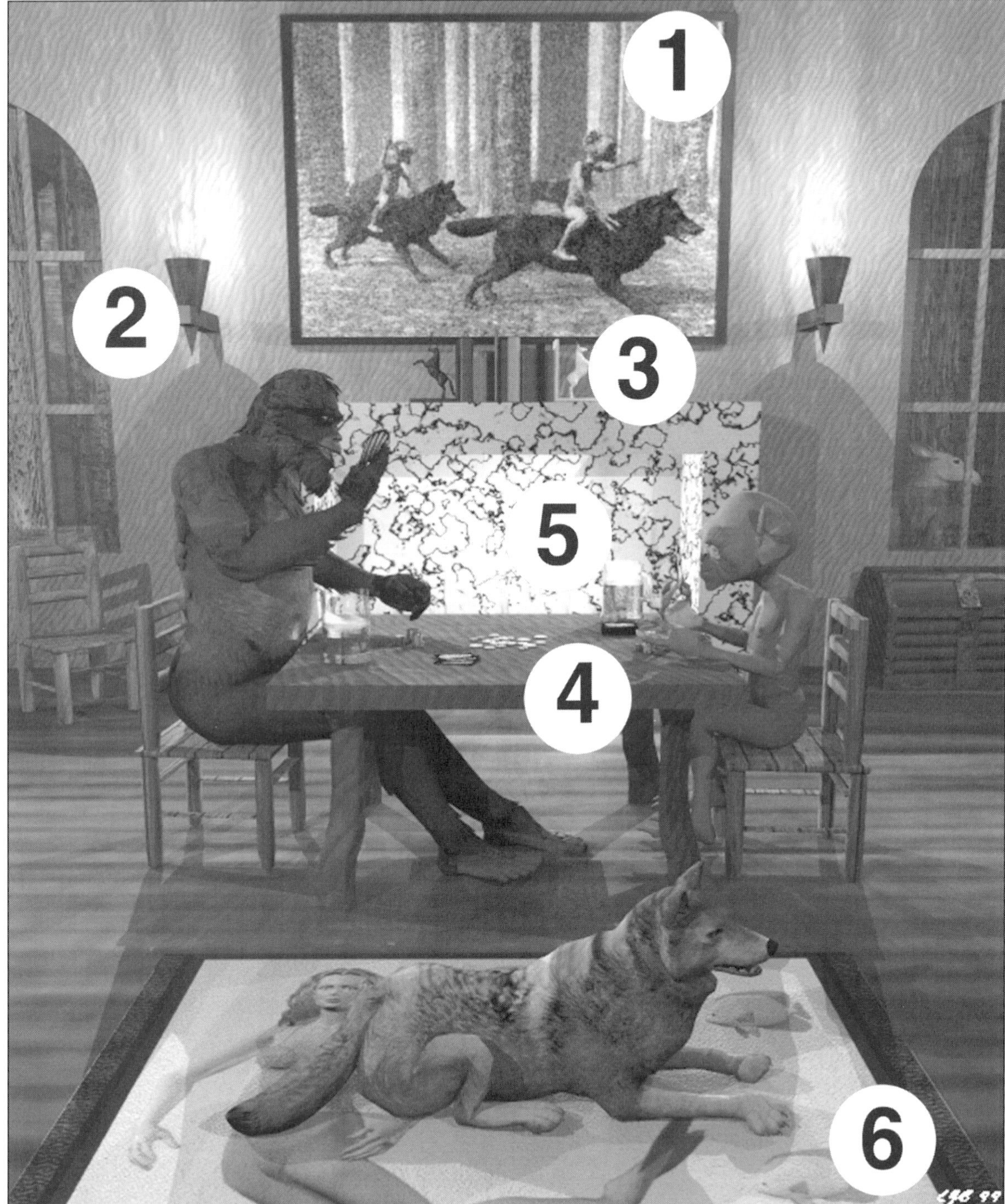

Figure 6.9

A Friendly Card Game. (Refer to the color version in this book's Bryce Studio.) The chapter text details each labeled element.

2. For the torches, I first created a sphere stretched along the Y axis and narrowed the X and Z axis. Then, I duplicated the sphere and converted the duplicate to a Radial Light. I decreased the light's X and Z dimensions by 0.5 and the Y dimension by 1 so that it was slightly smaller than the original sphere. Then I went into the Lights Editor, set the brightness to 75, and made sure Linear Falloff was selected. I applied one of the flame textures from the Tutorial presets to the original sphere.

   For the torch's bracket, I created a rectangular cube, which I then positioned so it stretched from the wall. I placed a cone at the end of the cube, with its narrow end pointing down. I applied a dingy metal from the Metals presets to the cube and the cone. Then, I placed the sphere and Radial Light on top of the cone, allowing a small portion of their bottoms to overlap the top of the cone. Finally, I selected all these pieces, grouped them, and called the group Torch 1.

   I made five duplicates of Torch 1. The first two torches—the ones visible in the picture—were placed on the south wall. I placed two torches opposite them on the north wall and two torches each on the east and west walls. These six torches and the fire in the fireplace are the only light sources for the scene.

3. I initially created the books and bookends as a separate Bryce file. This made it easier to work with them. In complex scenes, I often make a section of the scene as a separate Bryce file and then merge it with the main file.

   The unicorn used in the bookends was created in Poser 3. I created it from the horse in Poser and gave it a horn I created with MetaCreations' Ray Dream Studio 5. After I posed the figure, I exported it as an OBJ file and imported it into Bryce. In the Materials Lab, I set the Diffuse, Ambient, and Specularity colors to solid white. Then I set Diffusion to 100, Ambience to 19.6, Specularity to 100, and Reflection to 10.1.

   I used two cubes to create the remainder of the bookends; one behind the unicorn, another underneath it. I adjusted the cubes' sizes to work relative to the unicorn. Once the cubes were properly sized and positioned, I went to the Materials Lab for the unicorn, copied its material, and pasted it to the two cubes.

   Once the first bookend was done, I grouped all the pieces and duplicated the group. I went into the Materials Lab of the second unicorn and changed the Diffuse and Ambient colors to solid black, leaving everything else the same.

Each book is formed from a cube and a squashed sphere (the sphere acts as the book's spine). Once the first book was created, I duplicated it eight times. Then, I changed the size and color of each book, lined up the books between the bookends, and grouped the books and bookends. Once the books were done, I saved the file and loaded the main project file. Then, I performed a File Merge with the books file. I adjusted the size of the books and bookends (they were initially much too large relative to the other objects in the scene) and then placed the entire group on top of the fireplace.

4. I also created the coins in a separate Bryce file. I created a cylinder, made it very thin, and applied the Brushed Silver material from the Metals presets. Then, I duplicated the coin nineteen times. I moved the coins around so that they were in a scattered group, placing a couple of coins on top of the others. I selected several coins, resized them, and changed their material to achieve a mixture of gold, silver, and copper coins. Finally, I grouped the coins.

   To create the piles of coins in front of each player, I made two duplicates of each of the three kinds of coins: copper, gold, and silver. Then, I multireplicated each of those coins, specifying the number of coins I wanted in the pile and a change in Y that equaled the thickness of the coin. Next, I selected several coins in each pile, adding or subtracting 0.1 or 0.2 to or from the X or Z coordinates. This made the coins in the piles just slightly out of line with each other. To make it easier to move the piles around, I grouped the coins in each pile.

   After saving the coins file, I loaded the main file and merged the coins. Because the coins were all in a group, I could move them onto the table and then resize them to a suitable size. I placed the group of scattered coins in the center of the table and moved each coin pile to its final location in front of one of the players.

5. To create the drink glasses, I used a positive Boolean cylinder. Then, I duplicated the cylinder, made the duplicate a little smaller, and set its attribute to Negative. I grouped the two cylinders, making sure the tops of the cylinders were aligned. This created the basic drink glass. Then I created a torus (to use for the handle) and set its attribute to Positive. Next, I created a cube that was half the size of the torus, set its attribute to Negative, and grouped it with the torus, resulting in the handle. I created another torus and adjusted its size so it fit around

the bottom of the glass, giving it a sloping bottom. I applied Heavy Glass from the Glass materials presets to all these objects.

To create the drink inside the glass, I duplicated the smaller, inner cylinder of the glass and lowered its top to below the rim of the glass. The texture for the liquid was a modified variation of Santraginus V from the Water & Liquids materials presets. After setting the texture to Santraginus V, I went to the Materials Lab and used the Deep Texture Editor to change any colors that were a shade of green to a brownish-orange. I also changed the Specular and Transparent colors to a brownish-orange.

Once I had the first glass made, I duplicated it to create the second glass. I adjusted the height of the liquid in the second glass so that the two glasses contained different amounts of liquid.

6. The mermaid and fishes were created using Poser 3. Once the figures were posed, I switched the display style to Texture Shaded and antialiased the document. I exported the resulting image as a 400-by-300 TIFF. I loaded the image into Paint Shop Pro, enlarged the canvas by nine pixels on all four sides, and added a blue border around the picture. Then, I increased the left and right sides of the picture by 20 pixels and filled those areas with a darker blue color.

   After saving this image as Mercarp.tif, I made the mask for the rug's transparency. I created a new grayscale image—the same size as Mercarp.tif—with a black background. Then, I placed a 16-pixel-wide white border on the left and right of the new image. I selected the paintbrush and chose a special brush I had created previously for making carpet tassels. The brush is 20 by 20 pixels and has a series of jagged lines that run left and right to create the carpet's tassels. I set the foreground color to black and the background color to white, and then I painted the border on each side of the carpet using the special brush. Because the brush was wider than the border, I could move the brush left and right a few pixels from the center of the border in order to create a more random pattern. After touching up areas that appeared to have too much black, I saved the picture as Mercarptrn.tif.

   To create the carpet's Bump Map, I used Painter Classic to generate a grayscale image with Painter's Silk texture. I saved as this image as Mercarpbmp.tif. Now that all my images were ready, I loaded Bryce and created a thin cube to use as the rug, making sure its proportions were the same as the bitmaps I had created. I went to the Materials Lab and clicked on the Diffuse, Ambient, and Bump Height buttons in column A and the Transparency button in column B. I made Texture A a picture and loaded Mercarp.tif as the image and Mercarpbmp.tif as the Alpha channel. Then, I made Texture B a picture also and loaded Mercarptrn.tif as both the images and the Alpha channel. Then, I set Diffusion to 100, Ambience to 25.4, Bump to 22.4, and Transparency to 10.1 (leaving all other values at their defaults).

"Creada" By Mark J. Smith

Bryce is an excellent venue for creating surrealistic imagery, as the work of Mark Smith displays. Refer to the numbers in Figure 6.10 as you read the following explanations:

1. Bryce does not offer as much control over lights as I would like. I often use lights as fillers for shading. In concert with the characteristics of a surface (that is, Diffusion, Metallicity, Specularity), light can enhance the appearance of a surface. Here I have used the surface Specularity to take remnants of the orange light from behind the Creada object. This makes the open space at the bottom of the image more interesting visually. It also helps accentuate the bumpy sheen of the mud and provides a surface with greater contrast for the chain's shadow.

2. The title object in the scene is the *Creada,* a shape born from experimentation with my newest object-creation tool, Amorphium from Play, Inc. Amorphium has been an excellent source of inspiration for Bryce imagery. I can create many shapes that I had otherwise failed to create in the past. The texture on the Creada is the same texture that appears in the sky (with the exception of the metallic quality). I often use Bryce to generate textures. I use a standard scene file with a textured plane which encompasses the entire screen. This was the case for the sky. This sky is actually a texture mapped to a plane, not a real Bryce-generated sky. I was trying to experiment with pseudo-environment mapping. Although the experiment failed, I like the image.

3. The orange glow comes from a light between the object and the rock. This is an example of using light to enhance a shader. The bulk of the image is dark and dreary, so I needed spots of contrast to help the viewer distinguish between objects more effectively. This light also has a fractal gel on it to break up the light just a little. I use gels in Bryce often: They are another tool for using light effectively. When my work is more geometric than organic, I love to use a series of grid-like gels of varying intensities and falloffs.

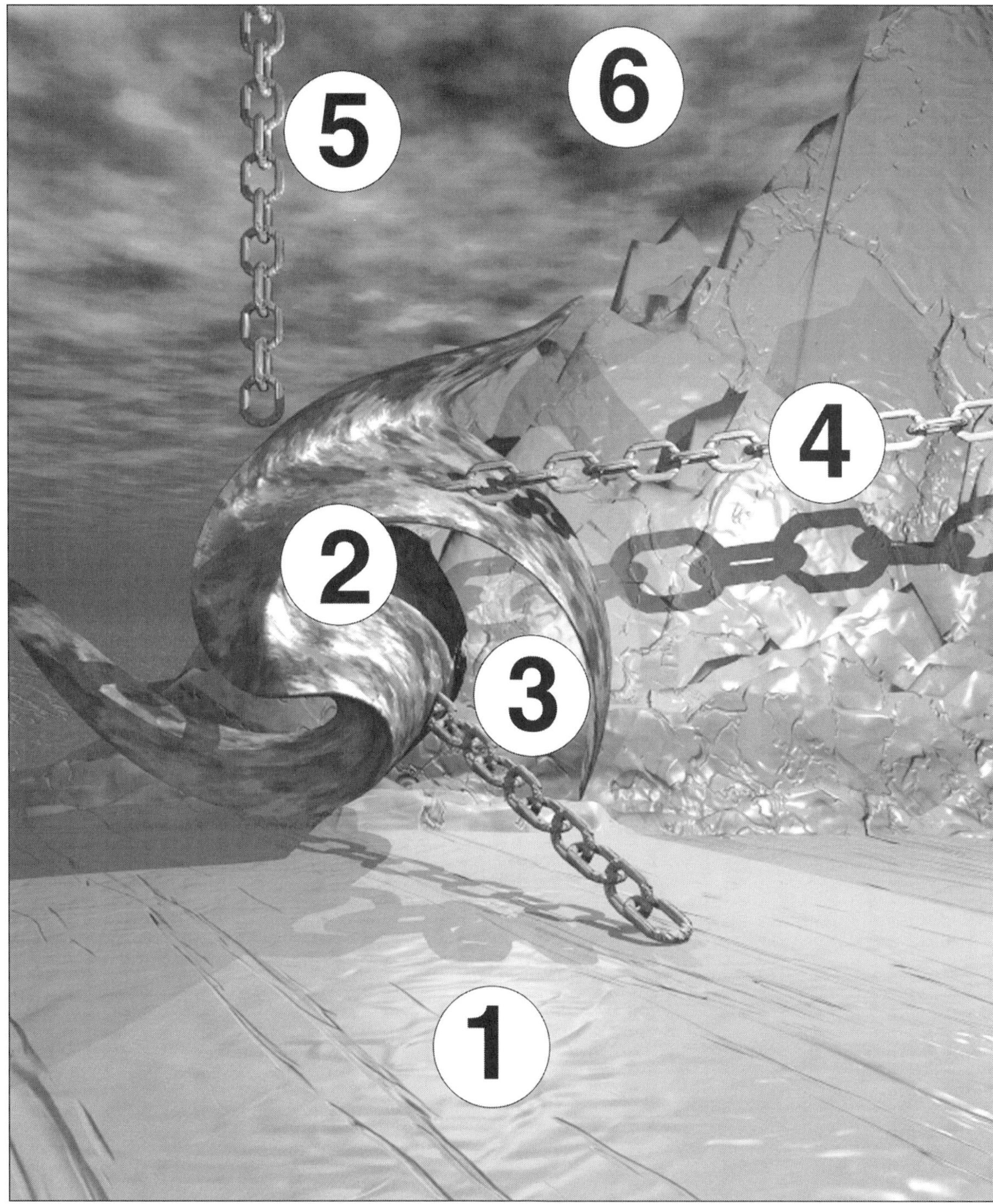

Figure 6.10

Creada. (Refer to the color version in this book's Bryce Studio.) The chapter text details each labeled element.

4. I added this taut chain because I felt I needed to segment the picture a bit. I actually created two interlocking link objects in LightWave 3D. I created only two links. As I needed more chain, I multireplicated the object to create more length. The chain is not the only element that segments this image: Its shadow does as well. The shadow is cast by a second light designed specifically to cast the shadow.

5. I placed this chain here to segment the false sky a bit. I had originally sketched a very "Gieger-esque" object partially visible in the upper left portion of the picture. Initially, I wanted to hang several chains from the other chain. But I decided that this would make a good segment for an animation project I am working on, so I kept it off camera. In the animation, it will be revealed. I like the fact that it may invite the user to ask about its origin. Of the three chains in the image, this is the only one that does not attach to the Creada.

6. As I've mentioned, the sky is an object texture and not a Bryce Sky texture. I created this texture within Bryce as a separately rendered image. I manipulated the image in Photoshop 4 to give it perspective and to build up the haze. I was experimenting with reflecting environments in other objects. It was actually a poor attempt at environment mapping, a way of making an object reflect it's environment without true reflection. Ultimately, I want to animate this piece. However, the methods I used to created this image are not consistent with animation. As I move a camera around the image, my solution will reveal itself as a poor substitute for the real thing.

"Thor" By Mark J. Smith

In this image, Mark Smith explores Bryce's water texturing capabilities. Refer to the numbers in Figure 6.11 as you read the following explanations:

1. I have always liked the way Bryce handles water. Just as with real water, there is a point or angle at which you can see through the water to what is below it. At higher angles, the water becomes reflective to the point that the objects beneath its surface are lost. Small portions of this object are submerged and can be seen through a watery surface. Interestingly, I have never seen real water have a shadow cast upon it.

2. This object was modeled in my new favorite toy, Amorphium. I had a great deal of fun experimenting on paper and then translating drawings into models. Once I created my object in Amorphium and

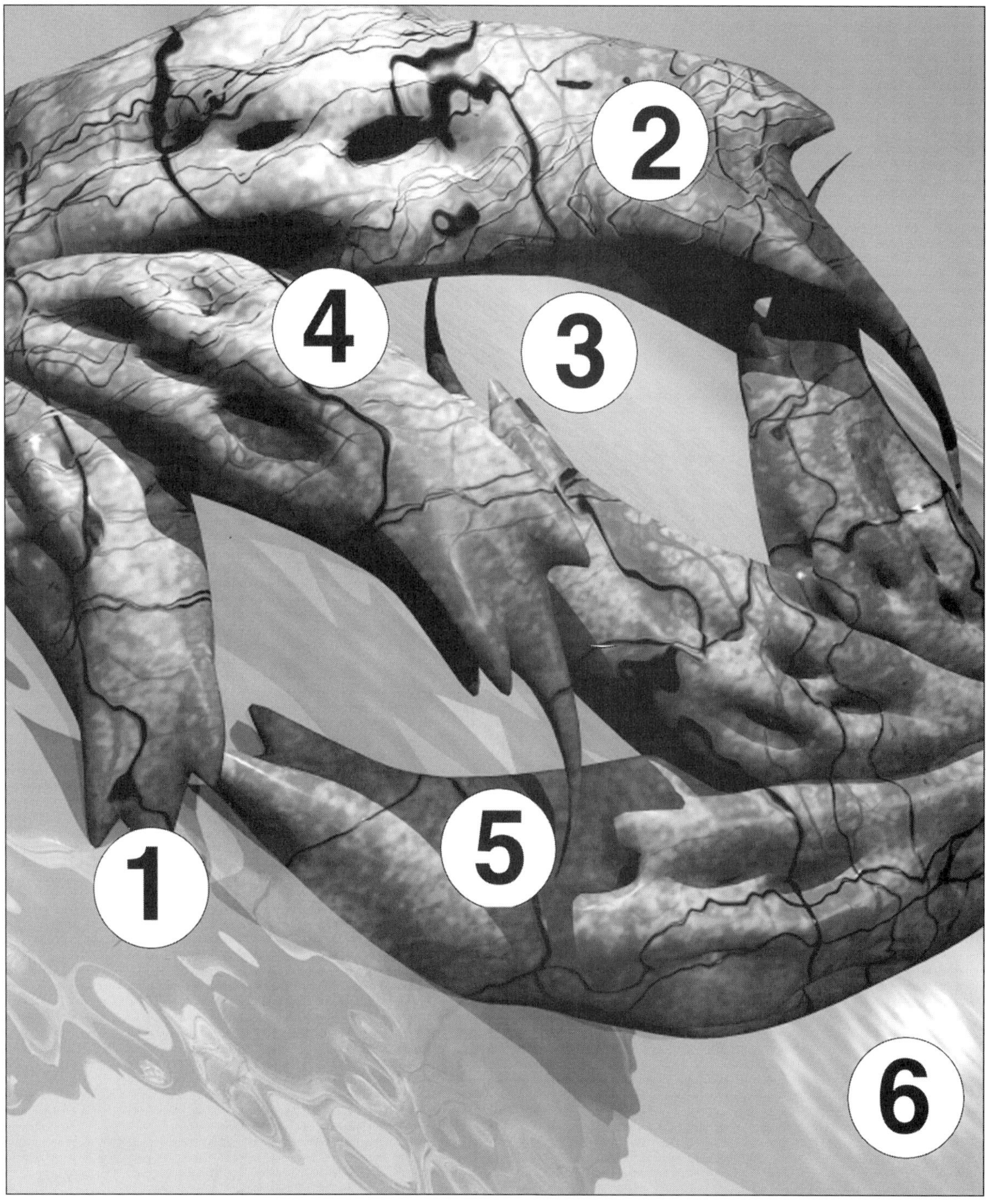

Figure 6.11

Thor. (Refer to the color version in this book's Bryce Studio.) The chapter text details each labeled element.

saved it in 3DS format, I imported it into Bryce. (Don't forget to smooth out faceted objects that have been imported into Bryce.)

3. Although two of these objects exist in the foreground, the scene actually contains many more. This scene was designed for animation. The animation reveals other objects as the camera passes across the water and through the haze. Bryce's Haze and Fog settings add to the sense of realism that some images require. The haze and fog in this image conceal the other objects located somewhere beyond the visual range.
4. This object has an amazingly cool texture on it. The texture is a stock texture found on the Bryce CD-ROM (Black Veined Marble). I fancied it because the black veins were just right for the object. I wanted to accentuate the fact that the veins were a raised surface, so I added a strategically placed light to catch the specular highlights of the raised veins and other bumps and indentations.
5. I try to use light in interesting ways within Bryce. I used a small green light to bring out some highlights across the object. I chose a green light to contrast with the object's color. The green specular hot spots help accentuate the 3D nature of the foreground objects.
6. I tilted the camera slightly in this image. I often skew the viewing angle of the whole image. It adds a certain appeal to the result and helps to maintain the fact that this is a frame from an animation.

"Forbidding Hands" By Celia Ziemer

Here Bryce creates an experimental world. Refer to the numbers in Figure 6.12 as you read the following explanations:

1. I modeled one hand in Impluse's Organica, and then I exported it to Ray Dream (as 3DMF) for selective mesh decimation, shape tweaking, and resizing to 50 percent. I exported the model as a Wavefront OBJ file, and then imported it into Bryce 4. I smoothed the model, and then textured, duplicated, and mirrored it. Finally, I attached the model to the gate.
2. The material on the hands and Ground Plane is a combination of Wavey (which I filter-edited in the Deep Texture Editor for more bump and rotation then applied to Object Space), Wave2 (applied to Object Space), and Sandy (applied with Parametric Scale). In the Deep Texture Editor, I scaled Wavey to 31.7, Wave2 to 12.8, and Sandy to 128.7. I saved the basic material to the User Presets. The

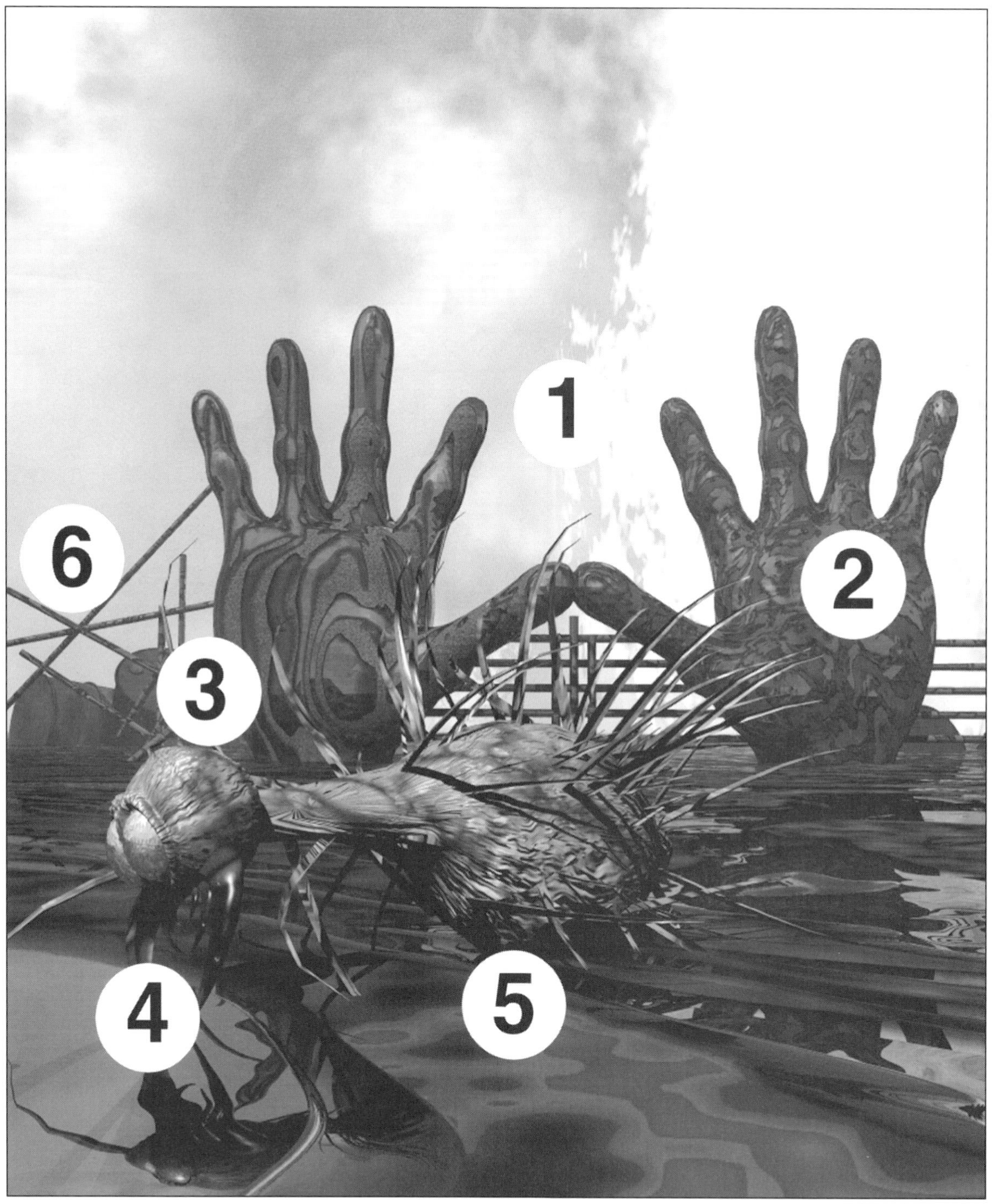

Figure 6.12

Forbidding Hands. (Refer to the color version in this book's Bryce Studio.) The chapter text details each labeled element.

scale is different for each hand and for the Ground Plane. I used the following settings:

- *Color*—Diffuse: Channel C; Ambient: orange; Specular: Channel B; Specular Halo: light yellow.
- *Value*—Diffusion: Channel C, 49.1 percent; Ambience: 0; Specularity: Channels A and B, 72.8 percent; Metallicity: Channel B, 100 percent; Bump Height: Channels A, B, C, -100 percent.
- *Optics*—Transparency: 0; Reflection: Channel A, 31.3 percent.

3. I used a sphere created in CyberMesh (a Photoshop plug-in from Puffin Designs) to create a height map in Photoshop, which I exported as a DXF. The map is a fractal created in Kai's Power Tools 5 (KPT 5), converted to grayscale and rescaled to 1 inch by 3 inches, Photoshop spherized -100 (horizontal only), and motion blurred toward the edges. I smoothed the head in Bryce to eliminate the DXF artifacts. The eyes are four distorted Bryce spheres. The larger lenses are transparent with high Bump, Specularity, and Refraction settings; the smaller spheres within them are opaque red with a high Ambience setting.
4. I created the triple Mandibles in Ray Dream Studio 5.0.2. I used a freeform model with a scaling envelope to create a single mandible, which I then replicated, scaled in Bryce 4, grouped, duplicated, and flipped.
5. The body began as a Ray Dream Studio 5.0.2 object. I modeled and twisted the irregular bottle shape (a line of vertices at a time) in the Mesh Form modeler, and then I subdivided the model. Next I spiked the model (maximum length, close to minimum radius), and grouped it for additional Bend and Twist with Deformers in the perspective window. I exported the model as a Wavefront OBJ file. The material used for the body and head is an edited version of the Wave material.
6. The oil drums consist of Bryce cylinders and tori with flattened cylinder caps. The material is just a dull brown with Waves in Specular Color Channel A and Specularity Channel A set to about 20 percent. The gate and fence consist of stretched cylinders.

"Environment" By Celia Ziemer

Refer to the numbers in Figure 6.13 as you read the following explanations:

1. This is a 900-by-900 sphere, textured with a Volumetric that drapes over the objects inside (including the camera, in certain instances).

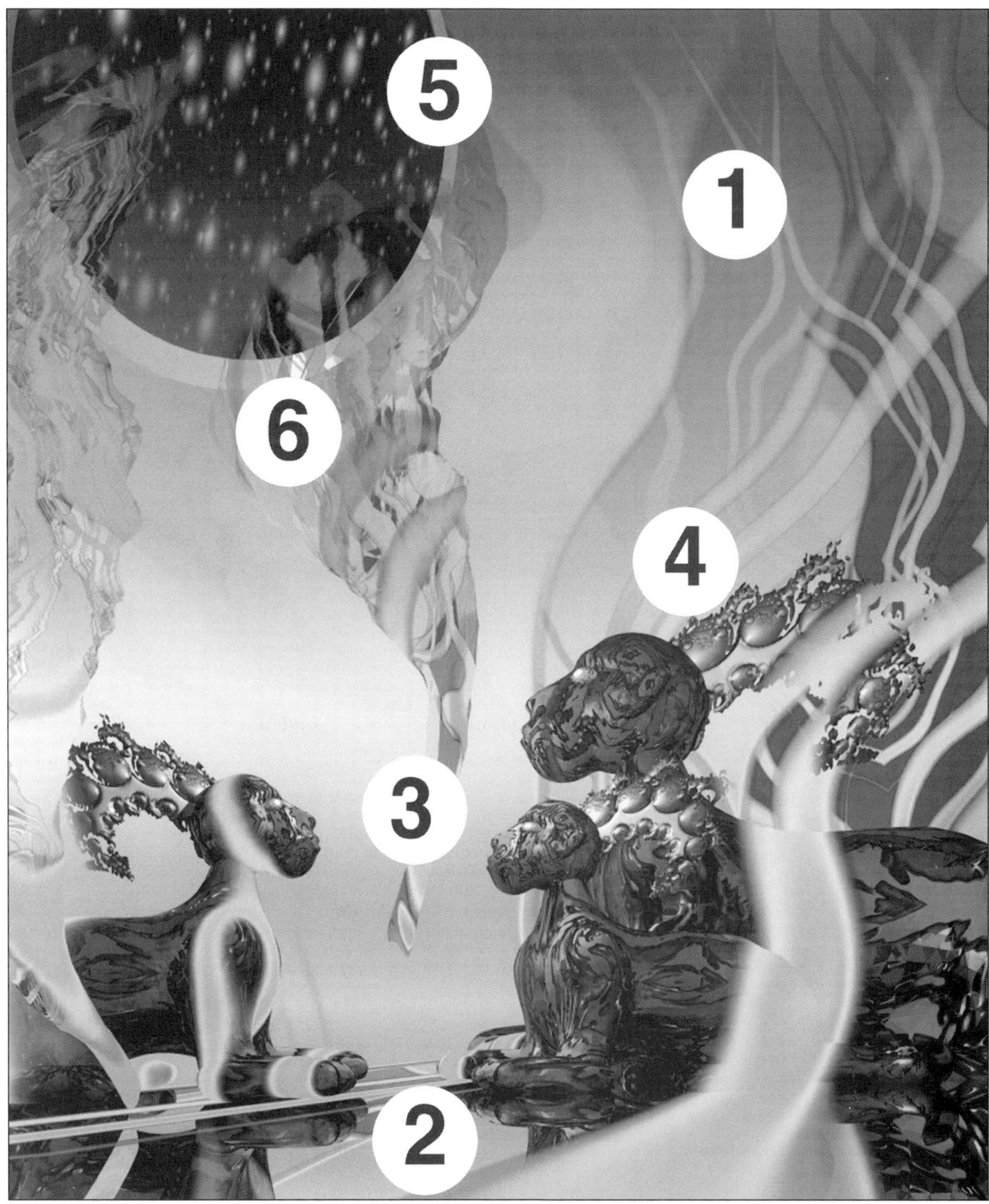

Figure 6.13

Environment. (Refer to the color version in this book's Bryce Studio.) The chapter text details each labeled element.

The material is a combination of an orange-red Distance Origin Noise in Channel A and an edited Gradient Vein (filtered for contrast in the Alpha channel, 90-degree rotation on the Z axis, and made less green) applied in Object Space with Symmetric Tiling enabled. The settings are:

- *Color*—Diffuse: A, B; Ambient: A, B; Specular: white; Specular Halo: deep blue; Transparent and Volume colors are both set to white.
- *Value*—Diffusion: A, 100 percent; Ambience: B, 5 percent; Specularity: A, 5 percent.
- *Volume*—Base Density: B, 66.1; Edge Softness: 0; Fuzzy Factor: 100; Quality/Speed 25 percent. The low setting for Quality/Speed keeps the edges fairly sharp; increasing this setting produces a softer, blurrier material. The scale setting of Base Density (B) depends in this example on the scale and rotation, relative to the rendering camera, of the sphere on which the material is placed, and here it's 51.1.

2. The rotation of the environmental sphere is set to X 0.0, Y 155.37, and Z -0.46. The Ground Plane is 100 percent Reflective with no other settings.

3. To create the Sphynges, I used a head that was sculpted from an Amorphium sphere (it was intended as a cat head, but it had plans of its own). I used BioSpheres to create one Sphinx-like body with a neck, a tail, and one front and one back leg. I duplicated the legs in the Compose window, and then I mirrored and scaled them. Then, I attached the four legs, the tail, and the head to the body. I smoothed the whole works one last time, and then I exported it to Bryce. The eyes are Bryce spheres. The kittens are scaled duplicates of the large figure.

4. The head crests consist of symmetrical lattices—two per kitty—height mapped with a grayscale Bubble-rendered KPT 5 fractal. Metallicity is set to 100 percent.

5. The portal consists of two concentric cylinders. The outside texture is a default metallic gold; the inside texture is hyped-up Starflowers.

6. The vortices began as Amorphium donut objects, scaled 300 percent along the Y axis and spiraled on the Potters wheel. They were then rotated 180 degrees on the X axis and Bottled for taper. The vortices use the same texture as the environmental sphere.

Bryce Images By R. Shamms Mortier

This chapter continues by presenting some of my work. I'll explain my creative processes and the techniques. Look at each color plate as you read the section of this chapter devoted to that image.

"A City Somewhere Else"

This image shows how a Bryce composition that looks complex can actually be simple to create. This project file occupies 324K. It is included in the Projects Folder on the CD-ROM. Refer to the numbers in Figure 6.14 as you read the following explanations:

1. The sky is always extremely important because it adds to the narrative content of any image in which it appears. The settings for this sky are Darker Sky, Red Shadows (with an Intensity of 72), no Fog, Haze set to 10 (with an orange hue), Cloud height set to 42 (with a black Sky Dome hue), and Cumulous Color set to white (with a frequency of 3). Both Stratus and Cumulous clouds are activated. The result is an orange sky that looks brooding and dark.

2. A look at this project's size (only 324K) tells you something immediately. Although the image looks very dense, it is quite small. That must mean that the objects contain very few polygons. One of the best ways to create objects with very few polygons is to construct them in the Terrain Editor, which is exactly where this cityscape was created. You can use one of the Cityscape Terrain presets from the Bryce CD-ROM or create your own height map in the Terrain Editor. I used both methods for this object, overlaying an imported Cityscape 2 map with my own cylindrical buildings (just draw white circles on the map in the Terrain Editor). If you want to see the height map, load this project. It is included free on this book's CD-ROM.

3. My favorite material preset for mapping urban objects is definitely Tyrell Building from the Wild & Fun presets. The material used to map this cityscape is related to Tyrell Building in the way the textures light up in the shadows. In the Materials Lab, I created this material by using the CityLitsC22 texture for both Diffuse and Ambient colors. A Diffusion value of 78 draws its content from the color, while a Ambient value of 30 draws its content from the texture. A Bump Height of 17.6 also draws its value from the texture.

4. The shadows of this material are worth special attention. As the shadows deepen toward the city streets below, the lights get very red.

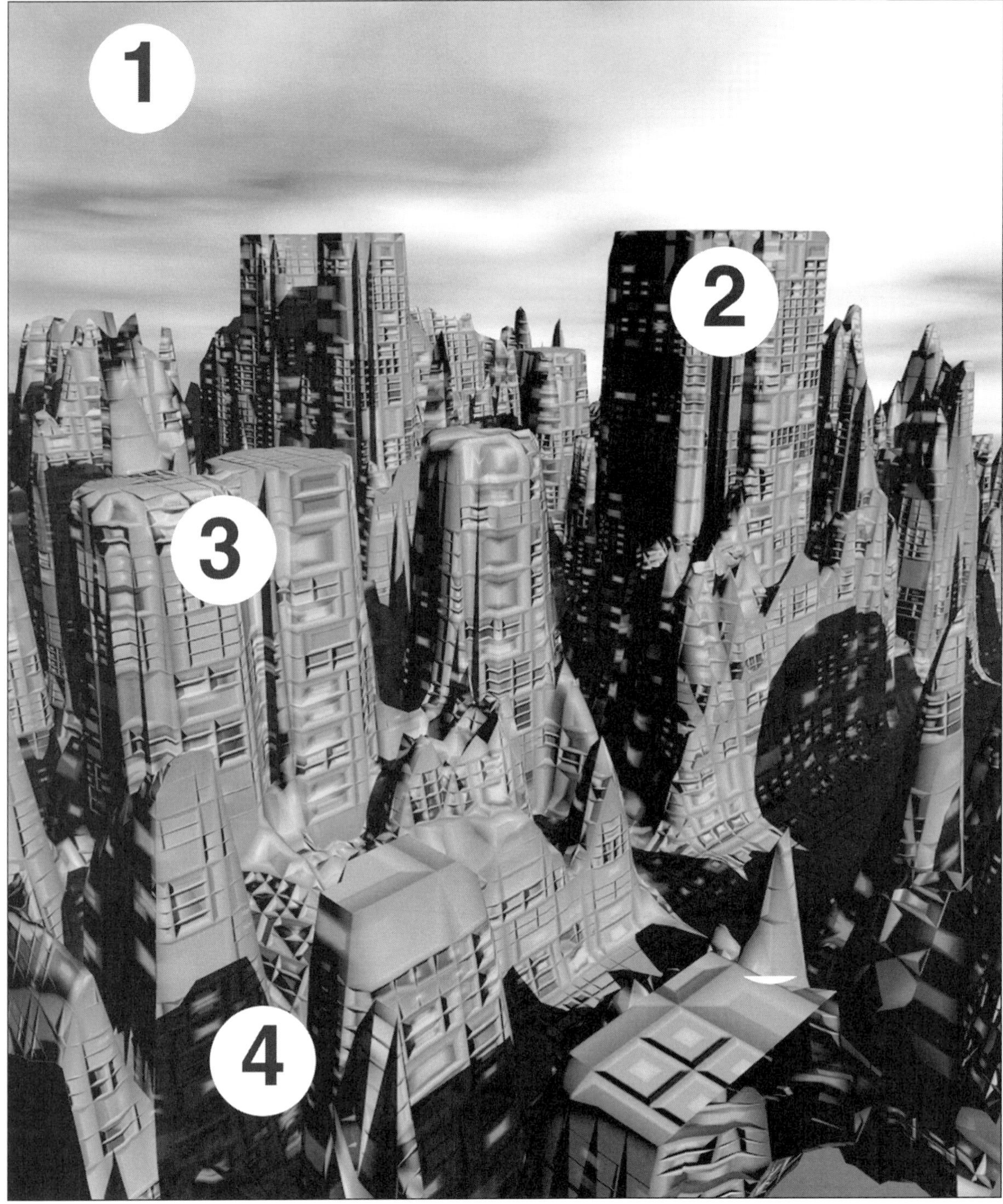

Figure 6.14
A City Somewhere Else. (Refer to the color version in this book's Bryce Studio.) The chapter text details each labeled element.

The Ambience value makes the lights pop out in the shadows (also because the Shadowing is set to red).

"Tabletop Dance"

The focus of this image is the mechanical toy created entirely in the Terrain Editor. This project file occupies 15MB, and you'll find it in the Projects Folder on this book's companion CD-ROM. Refer to the numbers in Figure 6.15 as you read the following explanations:

1. The Robo Toy is the star of this composition. The Robo Toy is important because it was created entirely in the Terrain Editor, using a combination of Painting and Elevation Brushes. This project is included on this book's companion CD-ROM, so you can open it and click on each of the components of this robotic object to see its height map in the Terrain Editor.

   Take a close look at the components that make up the fingers. I created them in Photoshop from characters from the Zapf Dingbats font. I used white characters on a black background and exported them to the Bryce Terrain Editor, where I used them as a height map to structure the 3D objects. This is one of my favorite uses for dingbat fonts because the font family contains so many symbolic characters.

   The entire figure is articulated: That is, I moved all the Origin handles moved so that you can click on and rotate the parts. This allows you to animate the entire figure. The second figure is a duplicate of the first with some variations applied to the rotation of its elements. To map this figure, I used the Martian Sand texture (with Object Space mapping) with a Frequency of 20 percent on all axis. The Diffuse and Ambient color are set to the texture, but Diffusion and Ambient values are not. Diffusion is set to 100; Ambience to 22. A Bump Height of -1 is set to the texture. A Reflection of 55 completes the settings. All in all, this makes a scratched metal material that is richer than any of the metal presets.

2. This mirrored surface is a simple cube primitive mapped with a blue-green Diffuse and an orange Ambient hue. Diffusion is set to 29, Ambient to 5, and Specularity to 58. Reflection Optics are pushed to the max: 100. The result is a surface that reflects the entire scene while tinting the reflection at the same time.

3. This chair is a QuickDraw 3D object from the Macintosh's Apple folder.

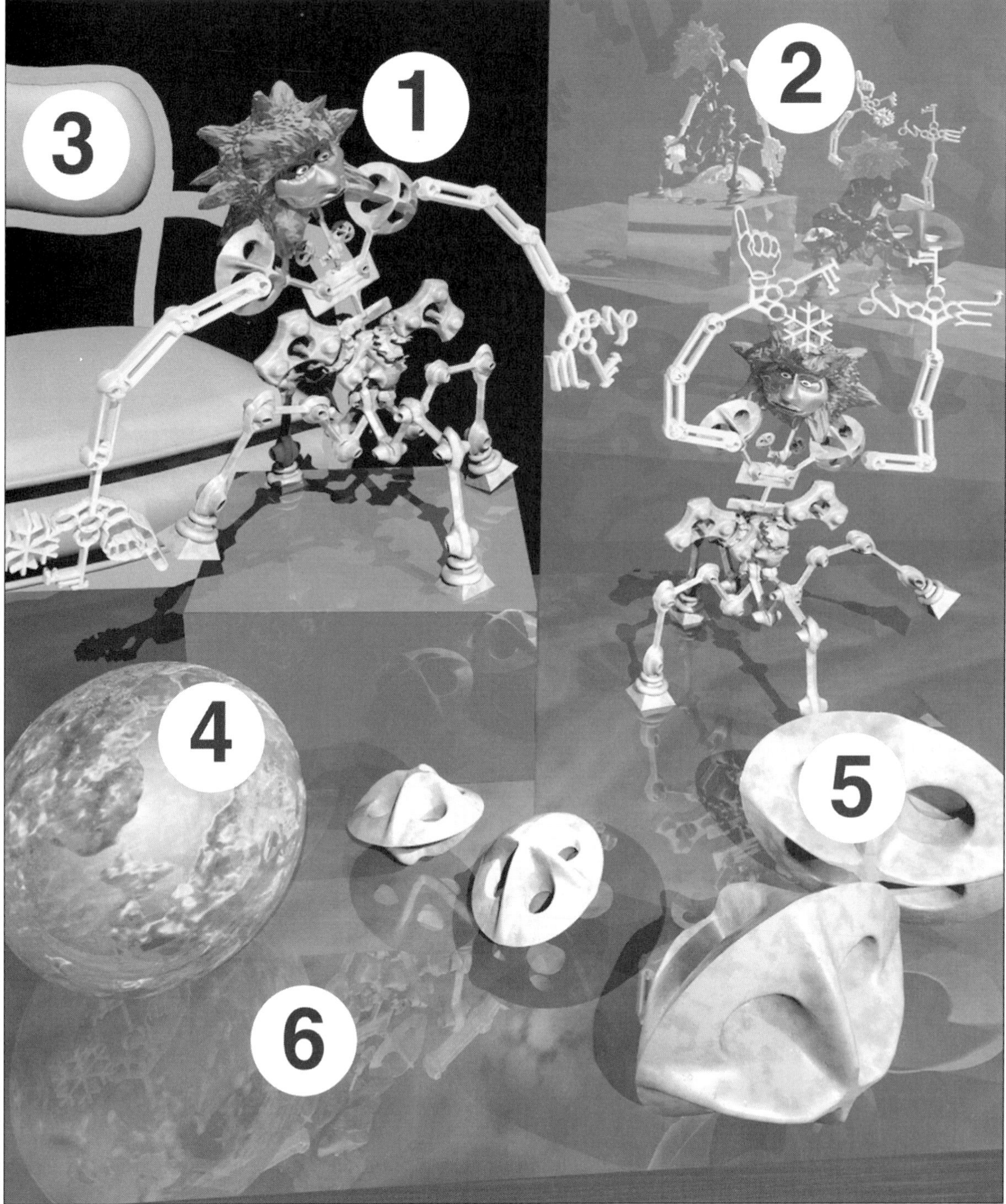

Figure 6.15

Tabletop Dance. (Refer to the color version in this book's Bryce Studio.) The chapter text details each labeled element.

4. What makes this sphere special is the material that defines it. It is mapped with the Geographic texture, but only in the Bump Channel. I used a Frequency of 8 percent and Object Space mapping. Diffuse color is dark green; Ambient color is orange. Diffusion is set to 86.4, Ambience to 0, Specularity to 100, Bump Height to 57.6, Transparency to 47.4, and Reflection to 71.1. Combined, these settings create a material that is both metallic and glass-like.

5. The pieces of metallic errata that populate the tabletop are duplicated elements from the character in the background. I like to use pieces of a project for different applications—something you might call a Dadaist motivation.

6. The table's reflective material gives it a character of its own. The texture is WoodA24, mapped in Object Space with a Frequency of 114 percent. Both Diffuse and Ambient color relate to the texture. Diffusion and Ambient values do not relate to the texture and are set at 37 and 8.6, respectively. Specularity is set to 27, and Reflection to 20. The table has a slight reflective quality, but the grain of the wood is also apparent.

"Watchers"

This image demonstrates Bryce's atmospheric effects and how you can use them to augment perspective within a scene. This project file occupies 56MB. Refer to the numbers in Figure 6.16 as you read the following explanations:

1. In the distance is a terrain with X, Y, and Z dimensions of 12,000, 8,000, and 8,000, respectively. This is a huge object. I pushed the terrain to a maximum distance in the background, so it looks like a large terrain very far away. I duplicated and rotated the terrain to add variety. The terrain is mapped with the SnowyCanyon8 texture from the Planes & Terrains materials presets with Parametric mapping. The snow looks like fog or mist from a distance.

2. I used Amorphium to create the globular objects that populate the entire scene. Amorphium is a must-have if you want to create organic-looking components for your Bryce worlds.

3. Fog increases the believability of the scene even more because it adds Level of Detail (LOD) to an image or animation. A LOD means that objects farther from the camera have less detail than those that are closer. There is a light gray Fog in this image with a setting of 10 and a white Haze setting of 3.

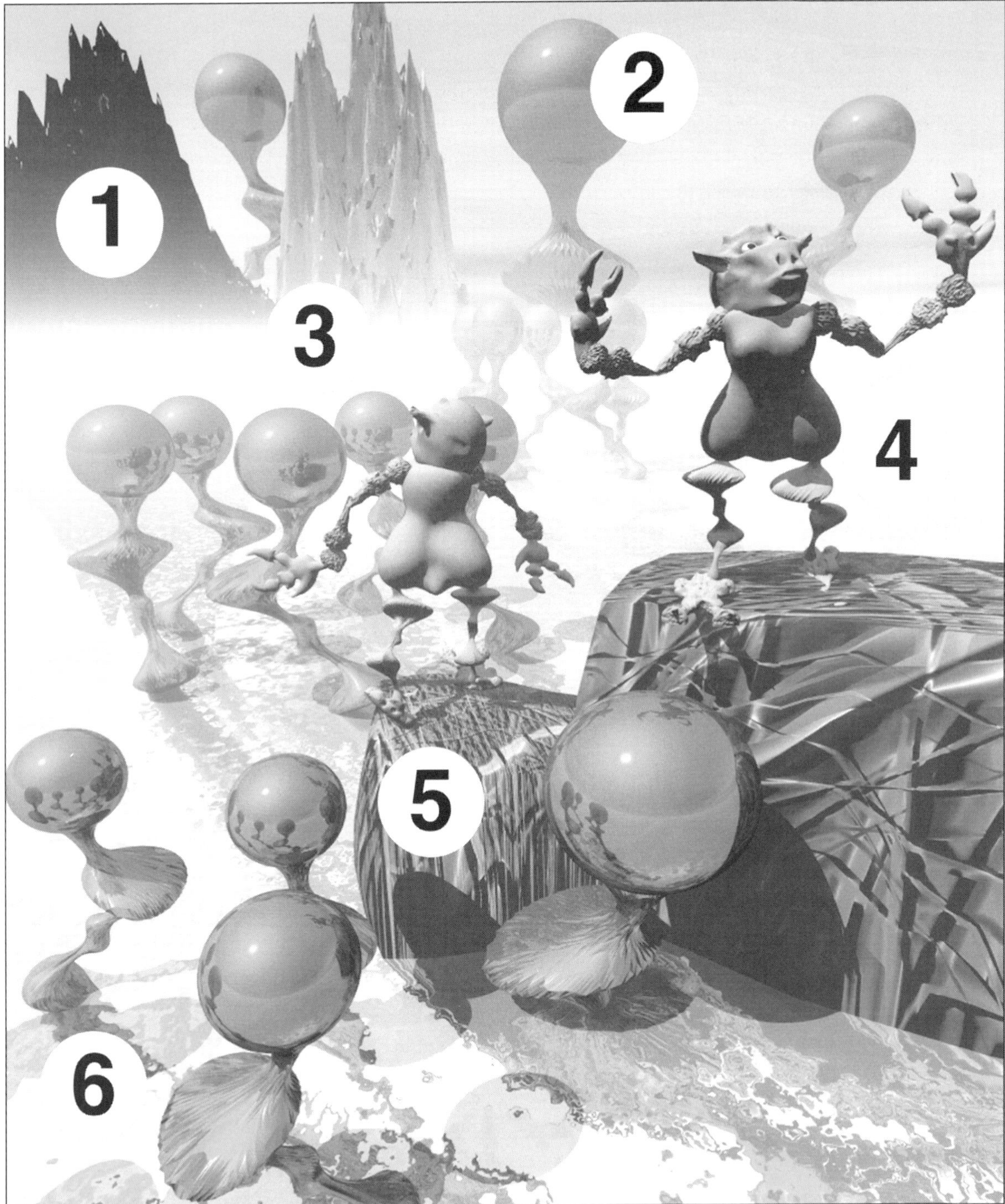

Figure 6.16

Watchers. (Refer to the color version in this book's Bryce Studio.) The chapter text details each labeled element.

4. This creature is the reason this project weighs in at a whopping 56MB. I used Amorphium to create all the parts that can be animated, and then I saved them as a dense mesh. When you export object elements from Amorphium, it's best to simplify the mesh in order to reduce the polygon count in Bryce. If you look carefully at the lower part of the globular objects, you'll see it is a duplicate of the creature's arm and leg elements.

5. These rocks are closer to the camera, so adding textural detail creates a scene with a more realistic perspective. For the rocks, I used the White Vein material with a Frequency of 6.7 and Parametric mapping. Bump Height is set to 27.

6. The material used on the water plane was created from the Wave5 texture with random mapping and a Frequency of 2.7. Using random mapping on water textures creates interesting swirls close to the camera. I set Bump to -57 with a Reflection value of 82.

"Springtime"

This image captures the magic of a newborn vernal world. This project file occupies 22MB, and it is included in the Projects Folder on this book's companion CD-ROM. Refer to the numbers in Figure 6.17 as you read the following explanations:

1. This sky is an adaptation of the Wenger's Sunset preset created by Eric Wenger, the original developer of Bryce. To create the sun, I created a bitmap lens flare painting with the Knoll Lens Flare Pro plug-in (from Puffin Designs) and mapped it to a plane.

2. I imported these birds from the Accu-worlds CD-ROM, created for Bryce 2 by Accuris. Unfortunately, this CD-ROM is no longer on the market, but if you search on the Web you may still be able to purchase a copy somewhere.

3. I modeled this flower in Amorphium and imported it into Bryce as a 3DS object. I attached the model to an elongated cylinder to create the flower's stem.

4. The head is a duplicate of the Amorphium object I used for the flower.

5. This foreground object is another duplicate of the Amorphium object, rotated to be less recognizable. A ground pink-gray Fog (with a Density of 5, a Thickness of 27, and a Height of 11) adds a spring morning mist to the image. To simulate a humid environment, I added a pink-orange Haze with a Density of 35 and a Thickness of 50.

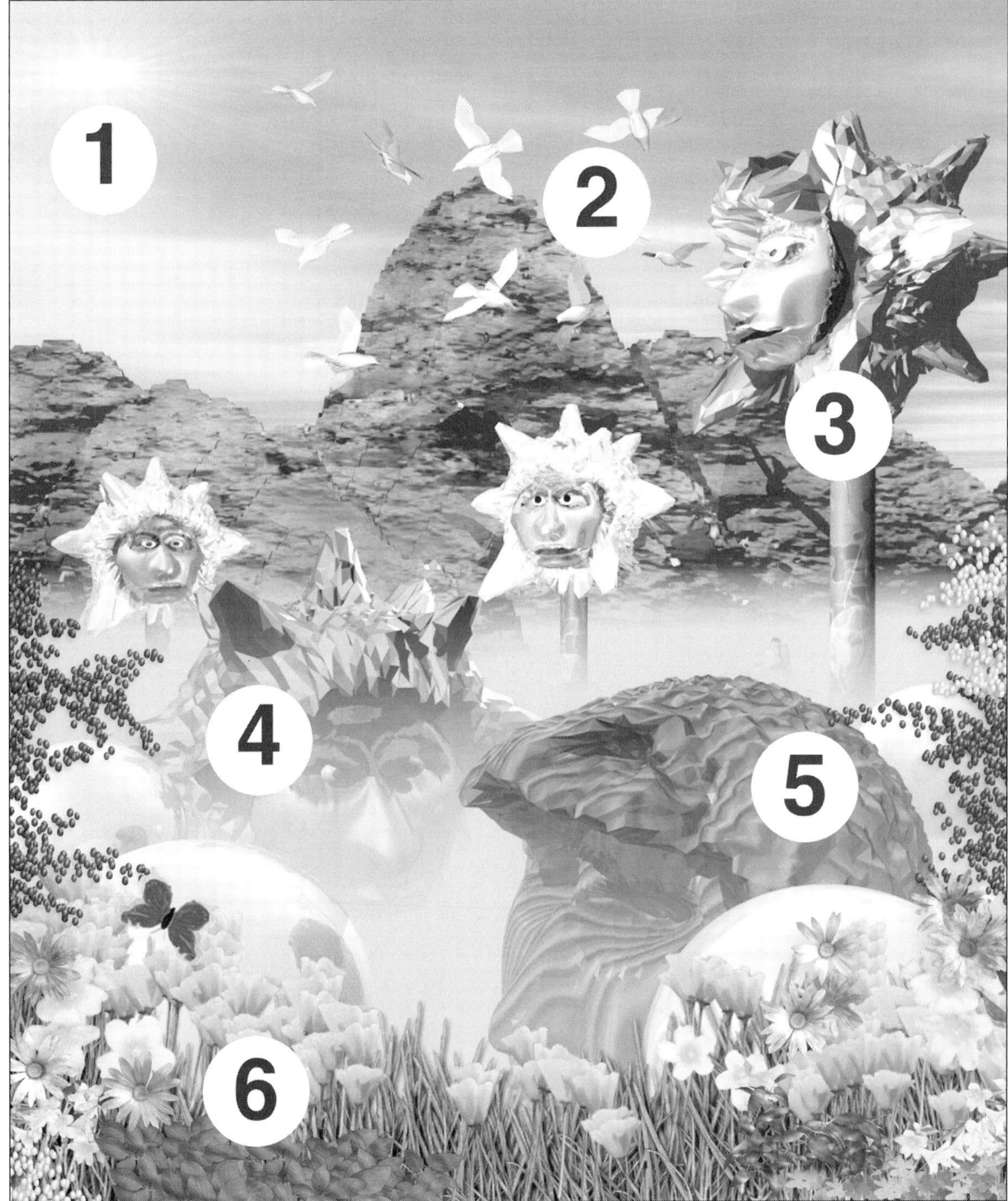

Figure 6.17

Springtime. (Refer to the color version in this book's Bryce Studio.) The chapter text details each labeled element.

6. The foliage border defines the entire image. Bryce has no adequate tools for creating flowers or other foliage, so I had to turn elsewhere. In Painter, I used a series of Image Nozzles with the Image Hose tool to create these flowers as a 2D painting. I left the background black. Within Bryce, I imported the bitmap into the Picture Editor. I created a separate Alpha channel image from the painting and used it to define the dropout areas of the image. The result, when mapped to a vertical plane, was a perfect blend of 2D and 3D elements in one image.

"Fantasy Palace"

Bitmap mapping is the central feature of this dream-like composition. This project file occupies 15MB. Refer to the numbers in Figure 6.18 as you read the following explanations:

1. I created the ceiling from a flattened cylinder, and it has some interesting material properties. The ceiling is partially transparent, so you can see the cloudy sky through it. It is also reflective, so the whole scene below is mirrored. The ceiling uses the RedFractal texture with Object Space mapped at a Frequency of 18.5 on all axes. The texture is mapped to the Transparent Color only (which is black). Diffusion is set to 32, Specularity to 100, and Ambience to 0. Transparency is set to 90 with a Refraction of 152. Although there is a zero Reflectivity, the reflection comes from the Refraction setting. This strange material has many glass-like properties.

2. The windows are cut out of a positive cube with negative cylinders, creating smooth arches. The back wall from which the windows are cut (the cube) is mapped with a Waves2 texture using World Space mapping at a Frequency of 17. The texture is created by the Diffuse and Ambient color channels and by the Bump value 22. Diffusion is set to 96, with a zero Ambient value. All of this creates an interesting rocky material.

3. I created the vertical portions of the balcony railing in Amorphium. If you look closely, you will see that I duplicated them to create the columns below that hold up the balcony. It is often a good idea to use design elements for more than one purpose when possible: It ties a composition together. The horizontal bars of the balcony are just elongated cylinders. The balcony and columns were mapped with the Yellow Gold material in the Simple & Fast presets. Diffuse color was changed to bright yellow and Ambient color to dark brown.

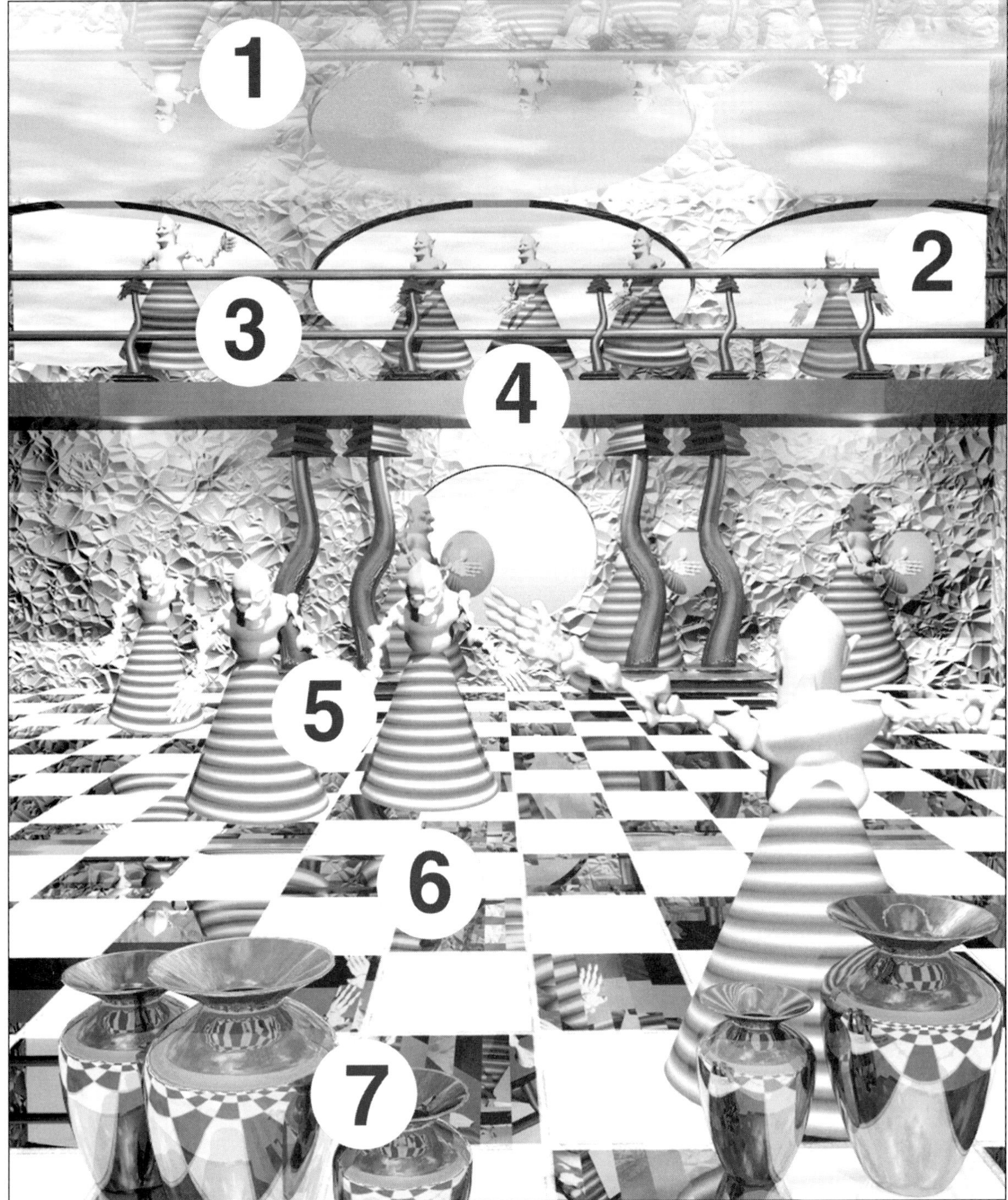

Figure 6.18

Fantasy Palace. (Refer to the color version in this book's Bryce Studio.) The chapter text details each labeled element.

4. If you look closely, you can see that lights are attached to the bottom of the balcony so that the area beneath is illuminated. There are five Radial Lights, randomly colored with blues, reds, and yellows. All their Intensities are set to 15 with zero fuzziness. All are set to Surface Visible with a Linear Falloff. This casts a multicolored hue on the figures walking under the balcony.
5. All the creatures in the image are mapped to 2D planes after having been composited and rendered in Bryce. Their top parts are from Amorphium, while their skirts are simple cone primitives mapped with the Dali Bee material preset, customized with red and yellow hues.
6. The tiled floor is interesting because only alternate tiles are reflective. For the material I used a composite of two textures: B&WTilePict (Frequency set to 52) and Pic2 (Frequency set to 0). Both bitmaps are from the Texture folder on the Bryce CD-ROM. Both use Parametric mapping. The first texture addresses both Diffuse (100) and Ambient (18) color, and the second addresses the Bump Height (-18). General Reflectivity is set to 60.
7. Although the urns could be imported objects from any compatible 3D object library, they were in fact imported as LightWave objects. All are mapped with a Yellow Gold from the Simple & Fast Material preset. The Diffuse color is set to red and the Ambient color to orange. Specular Color is light green; the Specular Halo is medium green with a Diffusion set to 35.5, Ambience to 0, Specularity to 100, and Reflectivity Optics to 50. This created objects that have a purple-tinted patina while reflecting the elements of the scene on their surface.

"Altar"

In this image, I sought to create a secret altar on a high hill. This project file occupies 25MB. Refer to the numbers in Figure 6.19 as you read the following explanations:

1. The Sky settings use Darker Sky with dark red shadows set to 90. Fog is light blue at 52, 100. You would expect a Fog height of 100 to obliterate the scene, but the scene (including the camera) is raised so that the Fog remains below the higher elements. Haze is white at a value of 2. Cloud Height is a light purple at 56, and Density is 12 with a deep red hue. Cumulus is switched on; Stratus is off. By accident, this created a beautiful pink and blue sky, which I saved as a Sky preset.

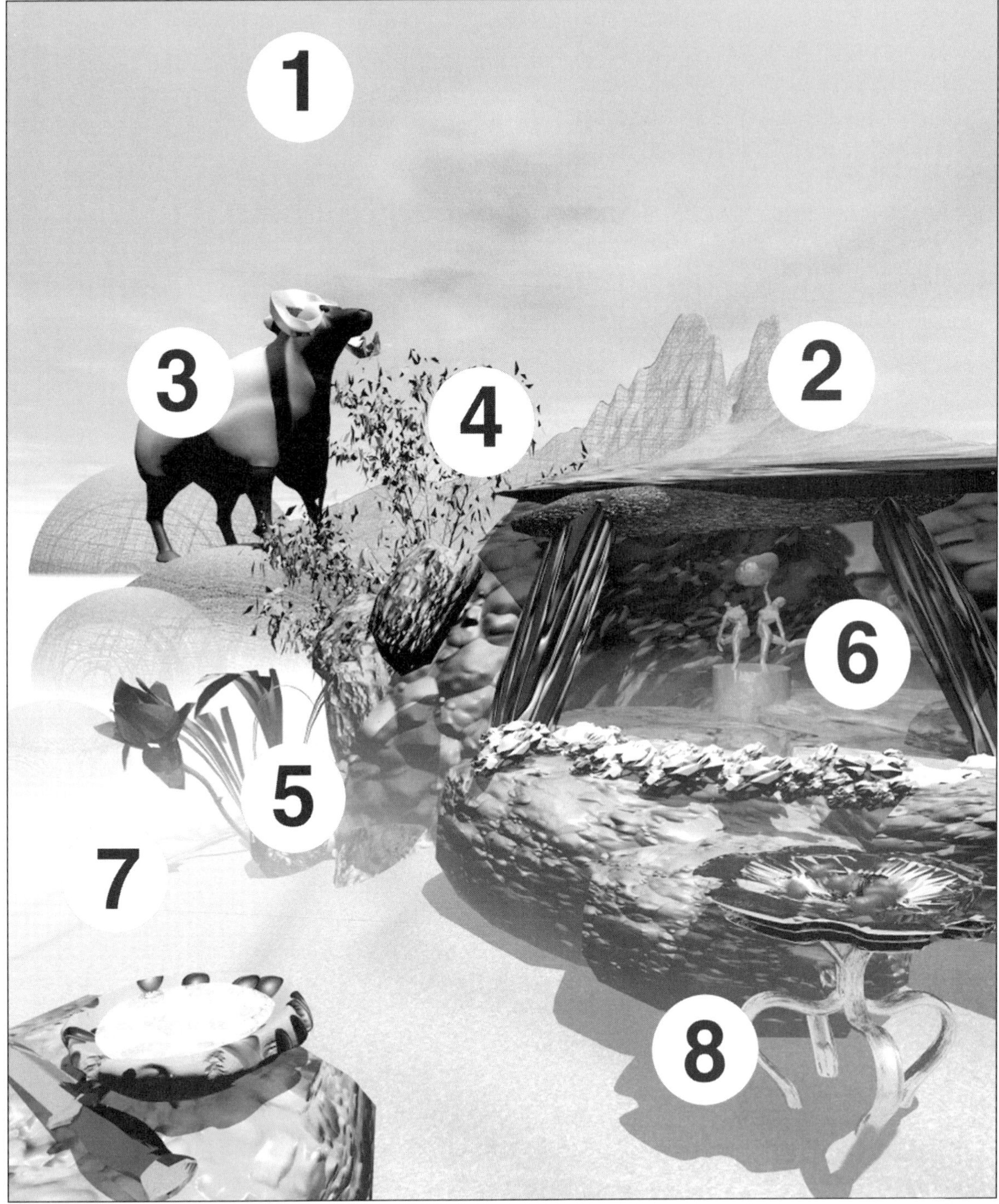

Figure 6.19

Altar. (Refer to the color version in this book's Bryce Studio.) The chapter text details each labeled element.

2. This terrain is special in that it was not created in Bryce. I created it using Natural Graphics' Natural Scene Designer. Natural Scene Designer allows you to export a wide selection of terrains as Digital Elevation Model (DEM) formats that Bryce can import.

3. This 3D Ram object was imported from the Volume 2 Fantasy Figures of the Epic Model Library, a collection of objects for LightWave. This CD-ROM was developed by the Epic Software Group.

4. I created the bush with Onyx Software's Tree Professional, exported it as a DXF, and imported it into Bryce.

5. These flowers were imported from the Apple QuickDraw 3D objects folder that comes standard on a Mac.

6. The cave of the altar was created as a Boolean construct, with a negative stone cutting away a positive stone primitive. I placed the sun in such a position that although you can see inside, the Sun still casts some very dark shadows. If you look closely, you can see a small figurine crafted with Poser figures and exported to Bryce as a Wavefront OBJ model. I mapped the figurine with Yellow Gold from the Simple & Fast materials presets.

7. Although I already described the exact Fog settings in the first item in this list, it is worth noting here that this represents the maximum height of the Fog, as if hiding a valley below. I created this effect by raising everything to over 90 percent of the Fog's height.

8. Two object vignettes appear in the foreground. On the left, resting on a rock, is a bowl of water and a knife. The knife and bowl are both imported LightWave objects. On the right is a brazier with hot coals. I created the brazier in Amorphium. The coals are Bryce Stone presets mapped with a texture that has a bright red Ambient color and an Ambience value of 100.

"Three Comrades"

Here the three "see-no-evil" monkeys are depicted in an otherworldly setting. This project file occupies 38MB. Refer to the numbers in Figure 6.20 as you read the following explanations:

1. I added this light after the Bryce image had finished rendering. I imported the image into Photoshop and used the Knoll Lens Flare Professional plug-in. I could just as well have done this in Bryce by accessing the plug-in from the Picture Editor and applying it to a 2D plane that covered the background. I used Wenger's Sunset Sky preset for the sky.

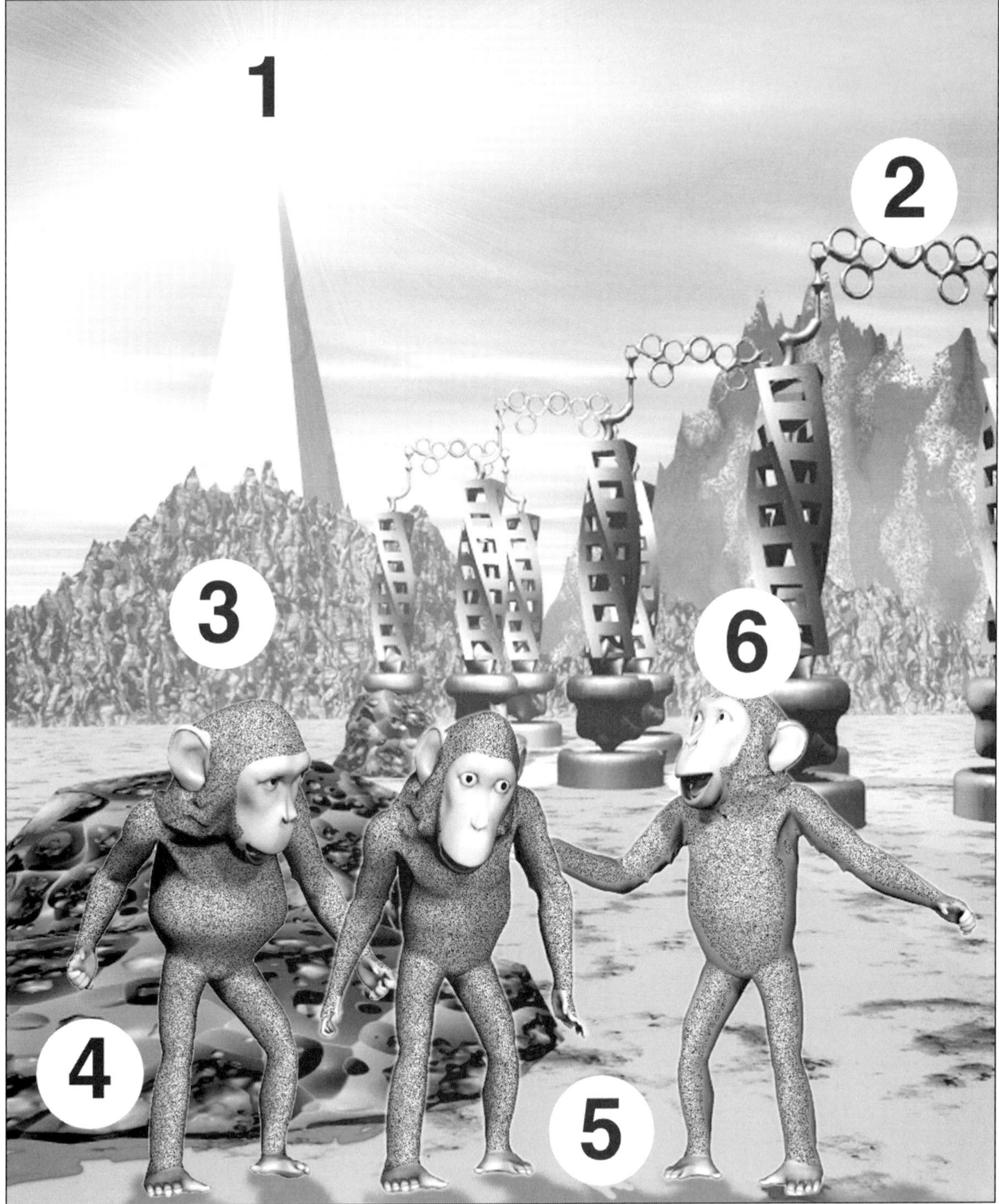

Figure 6.20

Three Comrades. (Refer to the color version in this book's Bryce Studio.) The chapter text details each labeled element.

2. These structures, duplicated from a single source, owe their existence to Impulse's Organica software. Organica allows you to create models for export by using Meta Block objects that stick together to form organic shapes. Organica is a wonderful addition to your utilities for Bryce.
3. This small mountain with the pyramid embedded in it uses the CountryRock5 texture, World Space mapped with a Frequency of 14.5. Texture is set to the Diffuse and Ambient color channels and to the Bump channel. Diffusion, Ambient, and Bump values are set to 87, 30, and 68, respectively.
4. Every single element within a composition is not necessarily planned. For this rock, I just used the Stone preset and let the random texture stand.
5. The material mapped to the Ground Plane is Desert Rock from the Rocks materials presets. The material is World Space mapped at a Frequency of 30.5, and Bump is set to -100.
6. All these creatures were created and posed in Poser, exported as Wavefront objects, and imported into this Bryce composition. I enlarged their heads in Poser to give them a more cartoony look. Their lively conversation sets the narrative tone of the image.

"Off To The Mines"

This image was inspired by the seven dwarves marching off to the mines in Disney's *Sleeping Beauty*, but it's a bit more sinister. This project file occupies 20MB. It is included in the Projects Folder on this book's companion CD-ROM. Refer to the numbers in Figure 6.21 as you read the following explanations:

1. All these ships are imported objects from the Space folder of the LightWave Objects library. I duplicated them within Bryce and textured them with the Yellow Gold material in the Simple & Fast presets.
2. This sky has no Stratus Clouds. For the other Sky settings, I used Soft Sky with white Shadows at 90 percent intensity, light blue Fog at a setting of 16 11, light green Haze at 8, black sky dome color with a Height of 26, and a deep red Cumulous color with a Cloud Cover of 85.
3. This large building is a Terrain Object created in the Terrain Editor with overlapping circular brushes set at maximum height. I placed a sphere on top for effect and grouped it with the terrain. Then, I

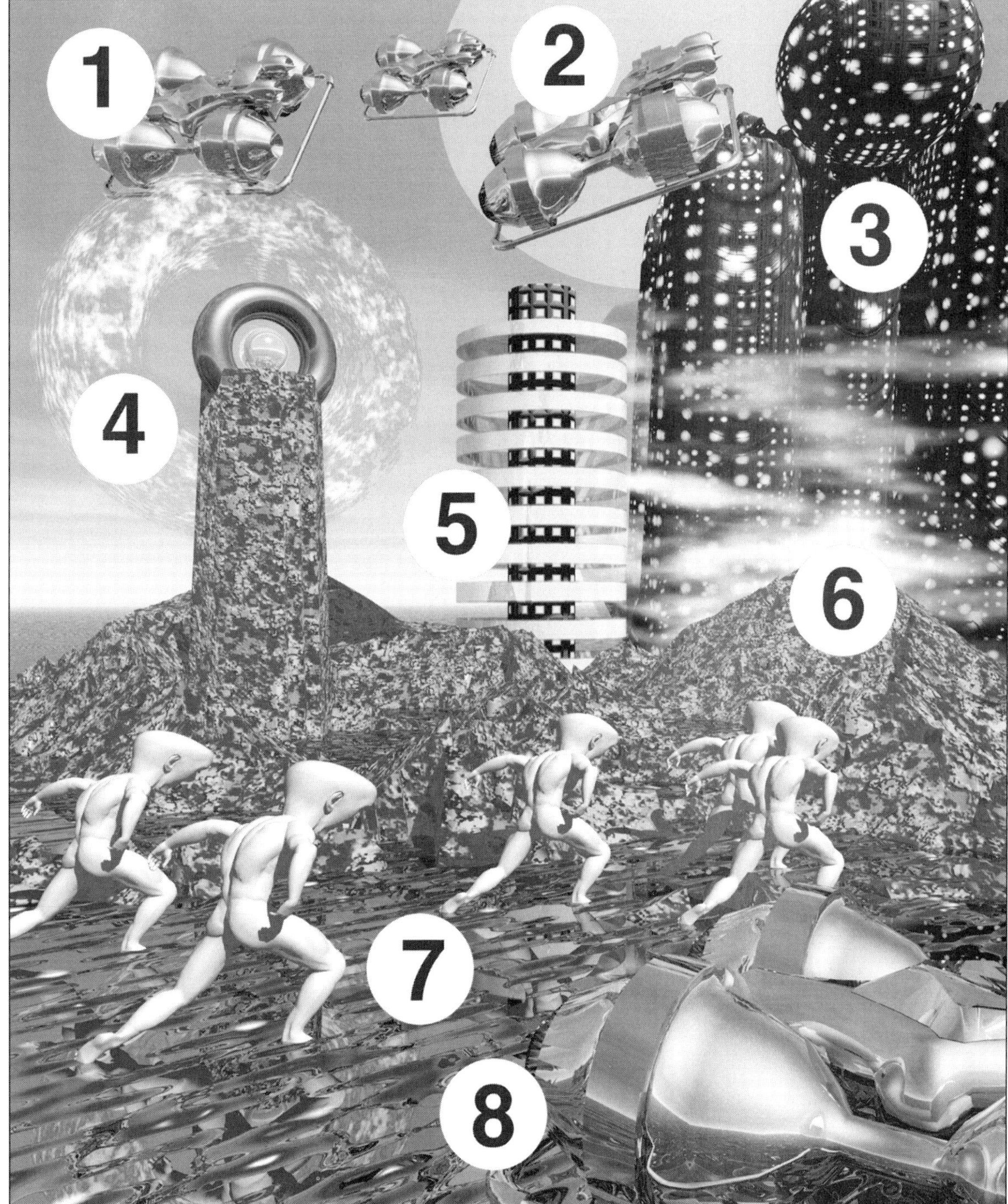

Figure 6.21

Off To The Mines. (Refer to the color version in this book's Bryce Studio.) The chapter text details each labeled element.

mapped the entire group with a CityLitsC10 Procedural Texture at an Object Space Frequency of 80.5.

4. This smoke ring is one of the neatest effects in the composition. I created it by using a Volumetric Greystone material on a vertical torus. The Base Density is set to 22, Edge Softness to 71, Fuzzy factor to 112, and Quality/Speed to 42.3. This provided just enough transparency to turn the torus into smoke.

5. The small structure is actually a combination of two cylinders, one inside and one outside. I mapped the internal cylinder with an Office Building At Night texture (from the Wild & Fun presets) with a Frequency of 25 in World Space. The outer cylinder uses the Dali Bee Stripes texture from the same library, with the yellow stripes changed to light blue-green in the Deep Texture Editor.

6. If you look closely at the terrain, you see that the tower rising from it into the torus smoke ring is part of the same Terrain Object. I mapped the terrain with a material composed of a Rocky Planet texture with a Bump height of 222. Bump heights over 100 or under -100 make objects look extremely broken up. This makes the whole stretch of terrain look like a slag heap, which is exactly what I wanted.

7. All the creatures are Poser creatures duplicated to create the group. Just to make them look less human, I flattened their heads in Poser before exporting them to Bryce as Wavefront OBJ objects.

8. I wanted the ground to have a rough feel, like the ground at an industrial site or a dump. I settled on modified version of the Wave4 texture preset, with a Bump Height of -100 and a Reflection component of 62 (Object Space mapped with a Frequency of 126.5). This broke up the ground into what looks like dirty reflective puddles, an unexpected but fortunate discovery.

"Frozen Outpost"

In this image, I tried to create a sense of cold and desolation. This project file occupies 9MB. It is included in the Projects Folder on this book's companion CD-ROM. Refer to the numbers in Figure 6.22 as you read the following explanations:

1. The Moon is a sphere mapped with the RockyPlanet texture, with Diffusion, Ambience, and Bump all set to 100. The texture is mapped in Object Space with a Frequency of 62. I would much rather design my own moons with real 3D objects than rely on the Moon settings in Bryce's Sky Lab.

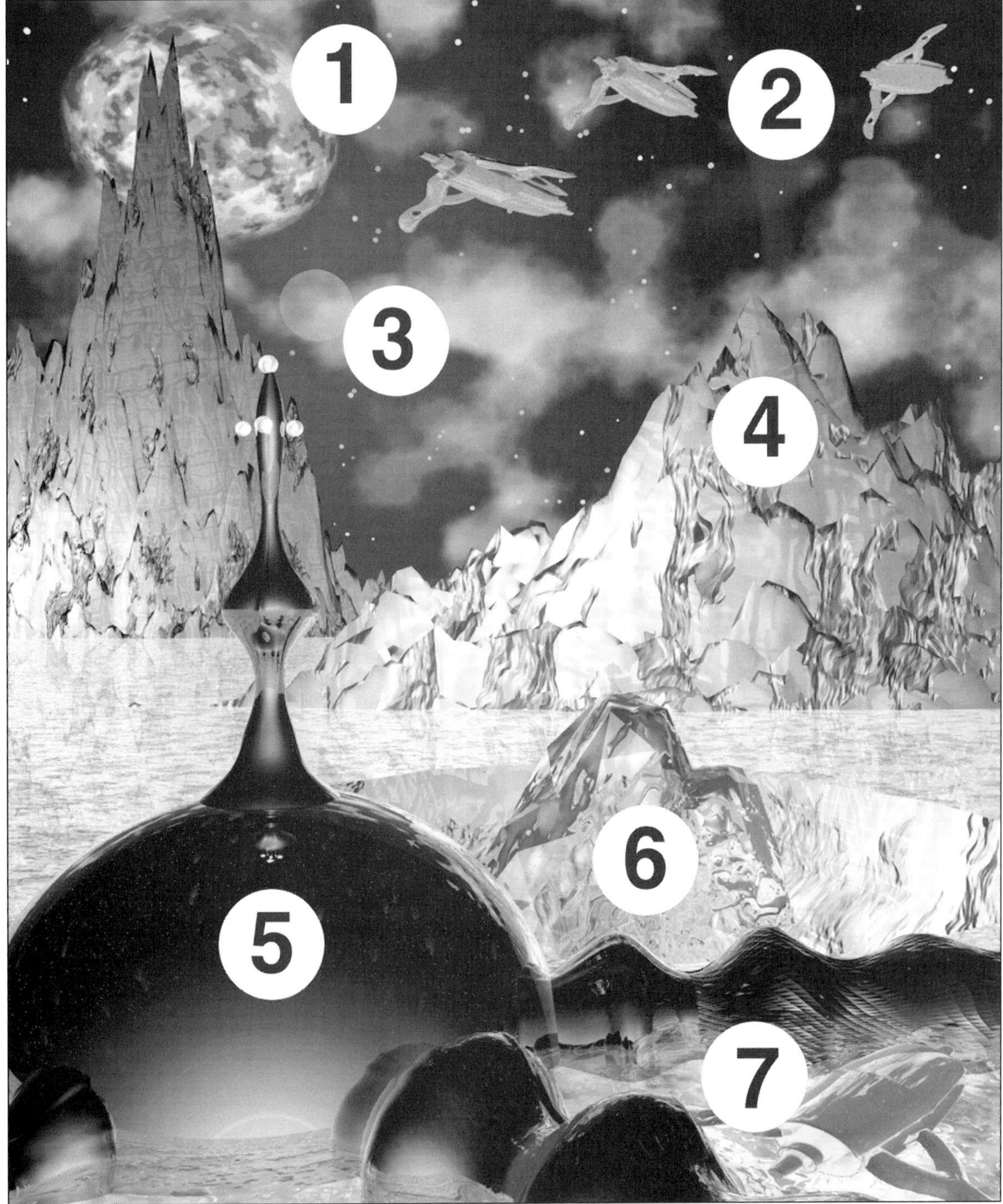

Figure 6.22

Frozen Outpost. (Refer to the color version in this book's Bryce Studio.) The chapter text details each labeled element.

2. LightWave has some of the best spaceship objects out there, and these spaceships are an example. I duplicated the additional ships after importing the first and then rotated them for variety.

3. The most interesting part of this image's atmosphere is that Volumetric Heavy Pollution Clouds were used to map a cubic primitive in the background. The texture was mapped with a Frequency of 4 in World Space and a 90 degree rotation applied on the X axis. This created a wall of vapor that seems to sit between the mountains and the sky. For the sky, Stars and Comets are turned on, and because I disabled Sunlight in the Sky Lab, the sky is solid black.

4. All the Terrain is mapped with a material that references the Iceberg texture in the Plains & Terrains folder. I added a Bump of 86 to create more-visible cracks, and the World Space mapped material uses a Frequency of 86.

5. The Dome has three parts: the spherical base, the light tower, and the extended arms. The sphere is a Bryce primitive. I created the tower and sculpted arms in Amorphium and exported them to Bryce. I grouped every part of the structure and mapped the parts with a customized version of the Yellow Gold material from the Simple & Fast presets. I changed the Diffuse color to orange, and I used no Diffusion or Ambience values. I set Specularity, Metallicity, and Reflection to 100. This created an object that draws its personality more from the surrounding landscape than from its own materials.

   The five lights on the tower are all created from the same specs. They are not really lights at all: They shine because of their Ambience value, which is 100. Diffusion and Specularity are also set to 100.

6. I used Boolean interactions to create the crater. The ground is a volumetric positive cube, and the hole creator is a large negative Boolean rock grouped with the ground.

7. The ground is mapped with the same Iceberg material as the terrain. To create terrain that looks as if it really belongs on the ground it is sitting on, use the same material for both (although you might want to alter the Frequency components).

"Arrival"

This image resembles the cover of a 1950s science fiction magazine. This project file occupies 15MB. It is included in the Projects Folder on this book's companion CD-ROM. Refer to the numbers in Figure 6.23 as you read the following explanations:

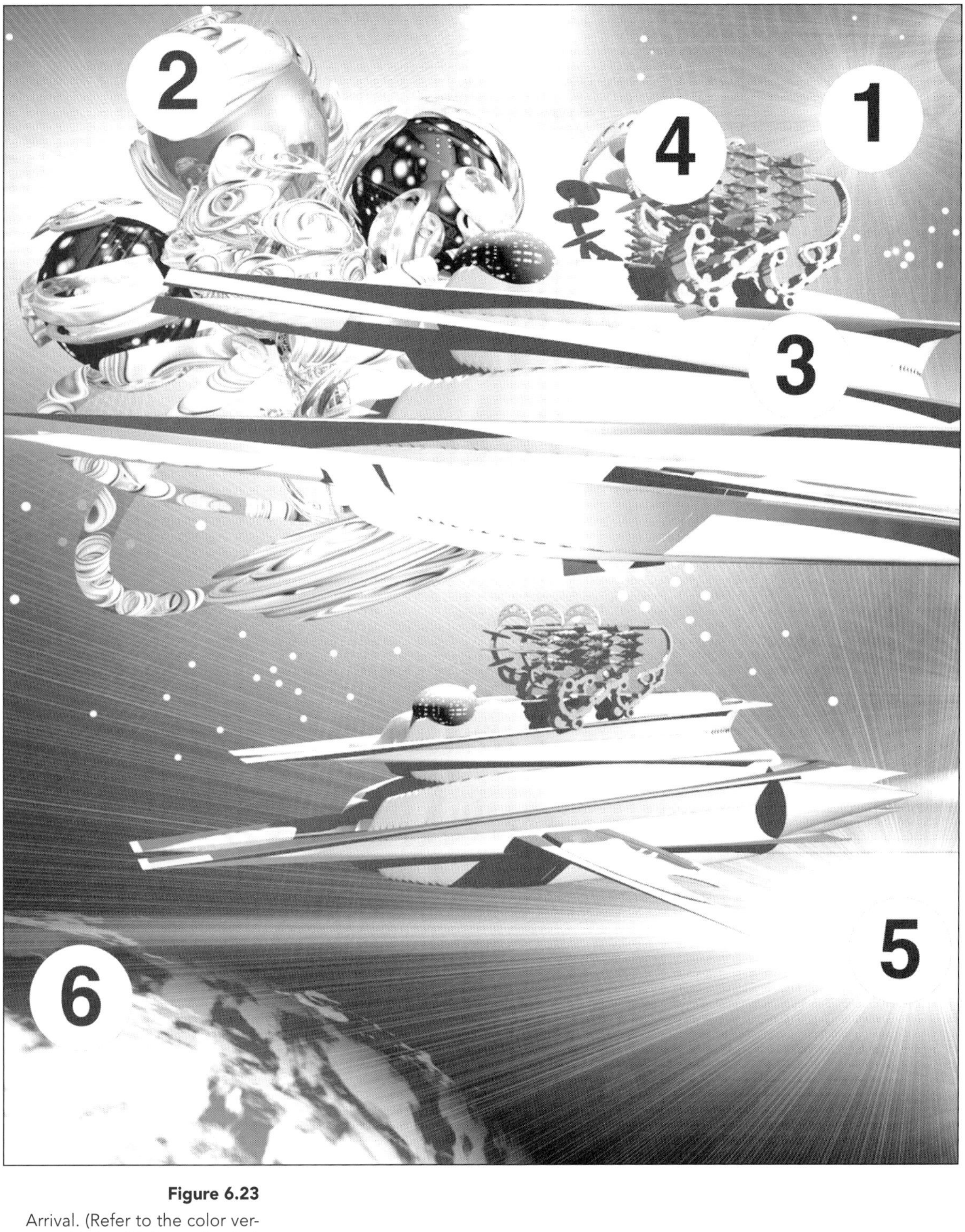

Figure 6.23

Arrival. (Refer to the color version in this book's Bryce Studio.) The chapter text details each labeled element.

1. I created this starfield as a separate painting in Photoshop, and then 2D Parametric mapped it to a vertical plane that covers the background. I used the Knoll Lens Flare Pro plug-in to create the starbursts. I gave the image a 40 percent Transparency, causing the background starfield (created in the Sky Lab) to peek through at certain points.

2. I didn't want to create the usual spinning torus space station for this composition. I wanted the station to be more organic—something that added a strange, almost living personality to the scene. I used the Picture Editor to import a Photoshop bitmap I'd created with the KPT 5 Frax4D plug-in. This plug-in creates shapes that are a cross between metallic and organic blobs. Then, I made an Alpha painting of the same graphic, white against a black backdrop. I imported both images into the Picture Editor and mapped them with Object Space to a series of spheres and cylinders. The result is an object that displays unexpected transparent areas when it rotates, which fits my design needs perfectly.

3. The ships have a protruding element at the back. Perhaps its a warp-drive processor or some other necessary part—I don't know. All that I do know is that the part *looks* intriguing. I created it entirely from Symmetrical Lattice objects in the Terrain Editor. Once the parts were finished, I grouped them.

4. I also used the Terrain Editor and Symmetrical Lattice objects to create the layered ship body. I drew the parts using the Elevation Brush with straight lines. (Hold down Shift to draw straight lines in the height map area of the Terrain Editor.) The result was a craft that looked very sleek except for the almost gothic protuberance on its back—just right for 1950s sci-fi.

5. The large flare is also part of the background painting. Like the other flares in the background painting, it was created in Photoshop using the Knoll Lens Flare Pro plug-in.

6. The planet has some interesting properties that create one of the most spectacular effects in the image. I used two grouped spheres for the planet. The inner sphere uses the Atomsphere6 texture with a Fuzzy Edge and a Frequency of 29 in Object Space mapping. The outer sphere, the planet's atmosphere, uses a Sunset Clouds preset with Parametric Scaled mapping and a Frequency of 237. The outer sphere is also 20 percent transparent. The Textures' transparency and fuzziness created a planet that allows the rays emanating from

the large flare to penetrate deep into the atmosphere. This is extremely beautiful when you zoom in on it. So there it is, the secret of designing in Bryce: Play and explore, and invite fortuitous accidents.

"Air Bubble"

I wanted to create an otherworldly vehicle for this image. This project file occupies 20MB. It is included in the Projects Folder on this book's companion CD-ROM. Refer to the numbers in Figure 6.24 as you read the following explanations:

1. This sky is the result of explorations in the Sky Lab. The sun has a yellow hue to add a warm tint to the entire scene. The Sky Lab's Blend With Sun option is selected, as are Blend Fog and Blend Haze. This creates a very wispy atmosphere. I used both Cumulous and Stratus clouds. Cloud height is 17, and Cloud Cover is 11. I used a dark-red hue for Cumulous color. All this creates a very cloudy atmosphere in which reds and purples dominate.

2. The spires in the background were created in Amorphium and exported to Bryce for texturing. I used a variation on the Yellow Gold preset on them, switching the Diffuse color to a light brown and the Ambient color to green. This gives the objects subtle green highlights.

3. This bubble is the star of the scene. A Poser figure meditates within the bubble. The bubble itself is created from two grouped spheres. The inner sphere is mapped with the Light Glass 2 material from the Glasses presets. The bubble has a Transparency setting of 66, making it a bit cloudy and partially opaque. The outer sphere is a bit more complex. It is wrapped with a customized version of the Steel Cage material from the Miscellaneous presets. This material is a composite of two textures: A and B. Texture A is Parametric mapped with a Frequency of 13, and I used it with Bump (set to 100) and Transparency (set to 0). Texture B is Parametric mapped at a Frequency of 200, and it is used for Diffuse and Ambient color (set to 100 and 12, respectively). This creates a steel cage with large metallic bands encircling the sphere.

4. The character of this terrain comes from the material I used to map it. I used the Storybook Grass material from the Miscellaneous presets. I set a Frequency of -2 with a Random mapping. Diffusion is set to 87, Ambience to 42, and Bump to 100.

5. I used the Sky Lab's Rainbow option to create the rainbow. The rainbow has a radius of 79 and an Opacity of 100, and I had to tweak the

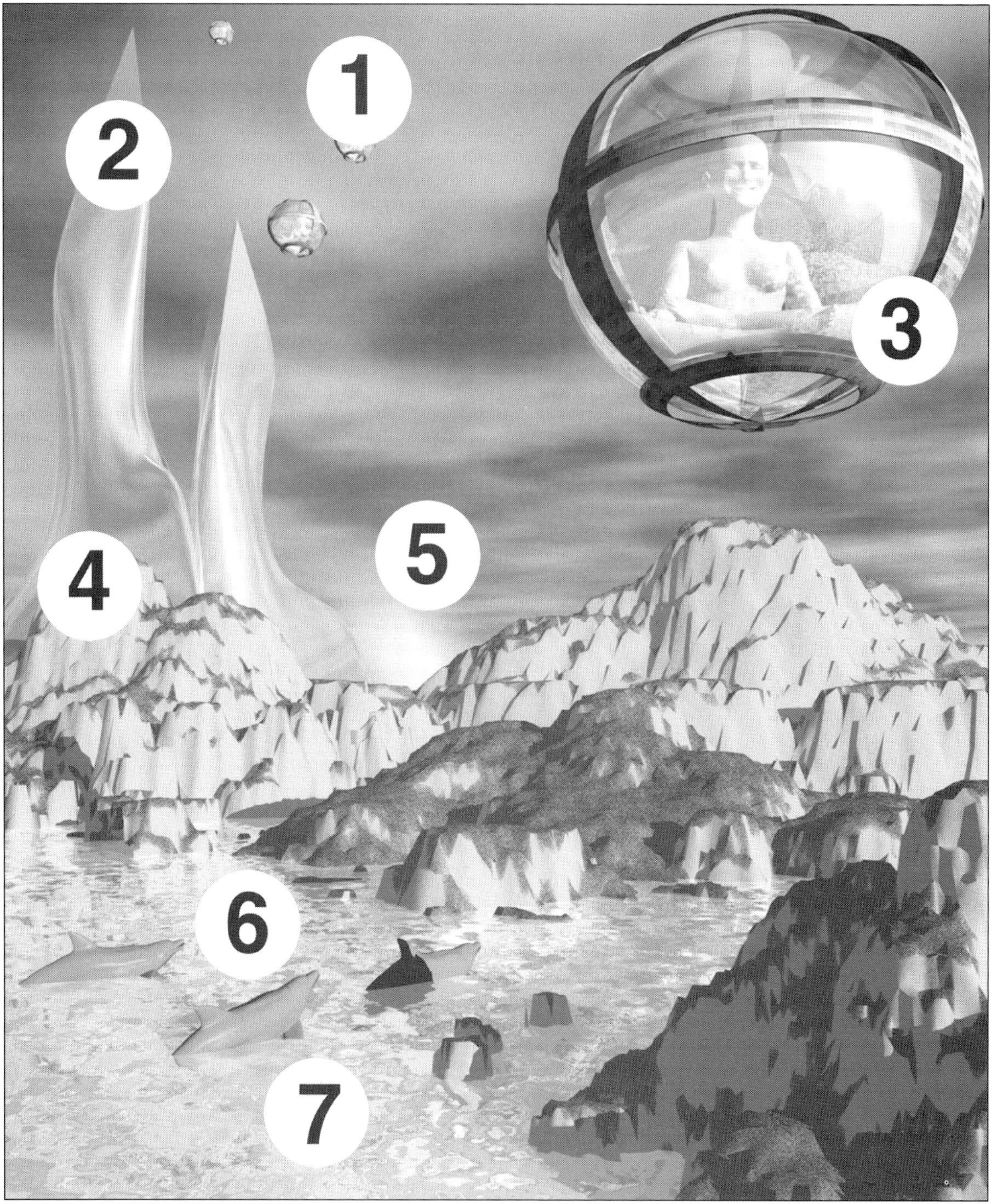

Figure 6.24

Air Bubble. (Refer to the color version in this book's Bryce Studio.) The chapter text details each labeled element.

sun's direction just right in order to make it appear. Because of the cloud covering, the rainbow appears in only a small section of the sky. This was *another* fortunate accident born of a lot of exploration.

6. Swimming in the water is a pod of dolphins. These are LightWave models imported from Replica Technology's (**www.replica3d.com**) Dolphin and Shark volumes.

7. I used the Backyard Pool material from the Waters & Liquids presets as the basis for the Water Plane. Bump height, Transparency, and Reflection are set to 61, 20, and 61, respectively.

"Extreme Surrealism"

Computer graphics are the perfect medium for developing surrealistic scenes. This project file occupies 11MB. It is included in the Projects Folder on this book's companion CD-ROM. Refer to the numbers in Figure 6.25 as you read the following explanations:

1. I created the tiled ceiling by mapping a resized cube with the Beveled Tiles Procedural Basic texture, with Object Space mapping and a Frequency of 49. Bump height is set to 100, and Ambience is set to 66 (with a Diffusion setting of 100). The high Ambience setting makes the tiles glow even when there is no light. There is a complete ceiling over the room, so I had to add a series of lights to the scene. Three Surface Visible Spotlights—each with a light violet hue and an Intensity of 25—do the trick.

2. You should recognize the back wall. It is the image shown in Figure 6.24, mapped to a resized cube primitive. I created the window by making the wall positive and adding a series of negative cutter cubes. Then, I grouped the ensemble to activate the Boolean operations.

3. The globe is a simple sphere mapped with a Blue Metal texture from the Simple & Fast material presets. Reflectivity is set to 56, so the globe mirrors the surrounding scene. The globe sits in a hole in the wall cut by a negative sphere grouped with the positive wall.

4. I'd already created the window frame on the back wall from resized cubic primitives, so it was easy to duplicate the window frame and place it on the side wall. I used a negative cube grouped with the positive wall to create the hole.

5. This hand comes from Poser, imported into Bryce and mapped with a basic flesh color. I placed a small reflective sphere against it to create a feeling of mystery. If you look at the hand closely, you

Figure 6.25

Extreme Surrealism. (Refer to the color version in this book's Bryce Studio.) The chapter text details each labeled element.

might suspect that it is connected to an entire body on the other side of the window. But if you look at its reflection in the large sphere on the left, you'll see that it is only a disconnected hand.

6. I created this head in Amorphium and set in the wall. Its glowing eyes are spheres with a high Ambience value.
7. The shark is a LightWave object from Replica Technology's Dolphin and Shark CD-ROM volumes. I posed it by ungrouping the model so that I could open the mouth, and then I resized it to fit the scene.
8. The chair in the foreground is a QuickDraw 3D object from the Macintosh's Apple folder. The spheres are scattered on the floor for effect; they have a Reflectivity value of 50.

"Insectium"

Life hidden in the grass is the subject of this image. This project file occupies 77MB. Refer to the numbers in Figure 6.26 as you read the following explanations:

1. I explored several backgrounds until I got one I liked. This background is a bitmap image mapped to a vertical 2D plane. The image itself is a digital photo I took in London: a shot of the garden outside Westminster Cathedral. I tweaked the image a bit in Painter by adding sprigs and twigs with the Image Hose, and then exported the image for use in Bryce.
2. You can barely make out the twig that runs diagonally from left to right against the backdrop. This twig is a 3D object created in Amorphium. Amorphium was the perfect choice because it allowed me to apply Noise to a 3D object in order to make it appear rough—the perfect effect for a twig.
3. This 3D plant with leaves encircling it is another Amorphium import. I saved this to my Bryce User Objects library in case I need it for other compositions. This plant occupies about 8MB when put together, and I duplicated it to create another plant in the background (I also rotated and resized it for variety). So all by itself, the plant adds more than 15MB to the composition.
4. Are you getting tired of me mentioning Amorphium yet? I hope not. Amorphium is the perfect utility for Bryce because it allows you to create organic objects that work perfectly in a Bryce world. All the insect's parts were assembled in Bryce, and the whole insect can be animated, if needed. Most of this insect's parts are mapped as single

Figure 6.26

Insectium. (Refer to the color version in this book's Bryce Studio.) The chapter text details each labeled element.

colors, but the main body is treated specially. I mapped it with a bitmap (created in Painter) that has a green backdrop with red spots. I used Parametric mapping with a Frequency of 19. This gives the bug a beetle-like appearance.

5. I created the big leaf on which the bug sits in Painter with a single blast of the Image Hose and a leaf nozzle. I set the nozzle to maximum, creating a very large image of the leaf. Then, I created an Alpha image of the leaf by making the same leaf pure white against a black backdrop. I saved both the color and Alpha images and imported them into Bryce's Picture Editor. I mapped the image, with its Alpha dropout data, to a 2D plane to create the leaf. Note that there are some water droplets on the leaf. I created these from flattened spheres mapped with a mirror texture.
6. There's nothing too special about the group of rocks in the scene, except that they all are mapped with the same texture. This is sometimes wise because using too many textures in a Bryce scene can be visually confusing.
7. The two insects on the ground are duplicates of the insect on the leaf, reposed and resized for variety. There are also two insects on the branch in the background, but I just used bitmaps on 2D planes in order to conserve a little storage space.
8. I used a Boolean operation to cut the pool into the Volumetric Ground Plane. The Ground is positive, and I used a negative rock to create some jagged edges. The water is mapped with the Backyard Pool material from the Waters & Liquids presets. Reflection is set to 70.

"Mystery Island"

This image begins with the theme of treasure island. The biggest design problem I faced here was the creation of an impossible perspective—a distance render that depicts objects both close and far with balanced clarity. This project file occupies 21MB. It is included in the Projects Folder on this book's companion CD-ROM. Refer to the numbers in Figure 6.27 as you read the following explanations:

1. The Terrain Objects in the distance are huge, but I moved them so far from the camera that they would still be too small had I left them at a standard size. The terrain is mapped with a Waves2 texture with World Space mapping and a Frequency of 25. I set

Figure 6.27

Mystery Island. (Refer to the color version in this book's Bryce Studio.) The chapter text details each labeled element.

Diffusion and Ambience values to 73 and 29, respectively. This creates a nice rock appearance without the detail—the terrain is supposed to be in the distance.

2. The Haze plays a major role in solving the perspective problem. If everything depicted was in clear view, the image would be flat and unconvincing. The Haze is light blue with a value of 2.
3. The ship is a LightWave object imported from the Objects folder included with NewTek's Inspire 3D. I placed it in the distance and enlarged it considerably so that it shows up. I also gave it a Transparency of 65 so that it seems to fade into the mist. In many ways, the ship is the central character of the composition.
4. I created the castle from Bryce primitives and mapped it with a stone texture. It was going to be the central focus of the composition, but Bryce dreams took over and relegated it to the background. Because this project is on the CD-ROM, you can save the castle to your User Objects library and use it wherever you'd like. You can animate the gate fully, and you can place the camera in one of the turrets for interesting renderings.
5. The terrain upon which the castle sits is more complex than it looks at first glance. The terrain is mapped with the Grassy Peaks 2 material from the Planes & Terrains presets, using Object Space mapping at a Frequency of 200 and a Bump height of 444. Although this created very realistic peaks, the excessive detail made the perspective seem very wrong. So I added a series of two cubic cloud planes over the terrain; this created a ground fog look on the top. I used the Patchy Cloud Layers in the Volumetrics folder as the material (with an X, Y, and Z frequency of 3, 23, and 3, mapped in World Space). For the Volumetric settings, I used a base Density of 47.4, an Edge Softness of 100, a Fuzzy factor of 239, and a Quality/Speed of 38.9.
6. The mask that hangs on the gate is an Amorphium object imported into Bryce and textured. I used an old favorite—Yellow Gold—from the Simple & Fast presets, but with yellow Diffuse and bright green Ambient colors.
7. The sticks that make up the fence are all duplicates of one object created in Amorphium. After duplicating the objects in Bryce, I grouped the sticks to form the fence, the gate, and the pier.

8. The boats are LightWave objects imported from the Objects folder in LightWave. The Water Plane that they float on is mapped with the Backyard Pool material from the Waters & Liquids presets (used only for Ambient color and Bump Height). I used a World Space mapping with a Frequency of 2.5 and set Diffusion to 57.6, Ambience to 80.3, Specularity to 100, Bump Height to 80, Transparency to 35.5, and Reflectivity to 24. The low Frequency creates a surface texture that has more discernible waves and eddies.

"Transcending"

I created this image as the design for a meditation poster. This project file occupies 9MB. It is included in the Projects Folder on the this book's companion CD-ROM. Refer to the numbers in Figure 6.28 as you read the following explanations:

1. For the sky, I used Bow_1, a Sky preset included on this book's CD-ROM for your use and enjoyment. You can find this preset in the CD-ROM's Skyz folder.
2. What appear to be sparkles are actually three cones. The apexes of the cones meet at the head of the seated figure, and the cones are mapped with bitmaps that look like silhouetted birds. This is another instance in which Bryce created a look that I didn't expect, but which was nonetheless a pleasant surprise. The bitmaps are World Space mapped on the cones with a Frequency of 22.
3. This rainbow crosses the entire breadth of the sky. Using the Sky Lab controls to set the parameters, I used a Radius setting of 41 and a Density of 100 (with Secondary Bow turned on).
4. The bitmap I used to generate the halo effect is a circular fiery disk. But when I mapped it to a 2D circular plane, it created this heart shape. Bryce never ceases to amaze.
5. The mountain tops that poke through the clouds use the Mossy Rock material, from the Plains & Terrains presets, with a Frequency of 139 and Object Space mapping. I set the Bump height to 100 to give the mountains a craggy look.
6. If you look closely at the seated Poser figure, you notice she is covered with electrified arcs of energy. I created this "Energy Matrix" by duplicating the figure, enlarging it to form a shell around her body, and mapping the new, enlarged elements with a texture that is mostly transparent (Atmosphere Basic with a Frequency of 139 and Random mapping).

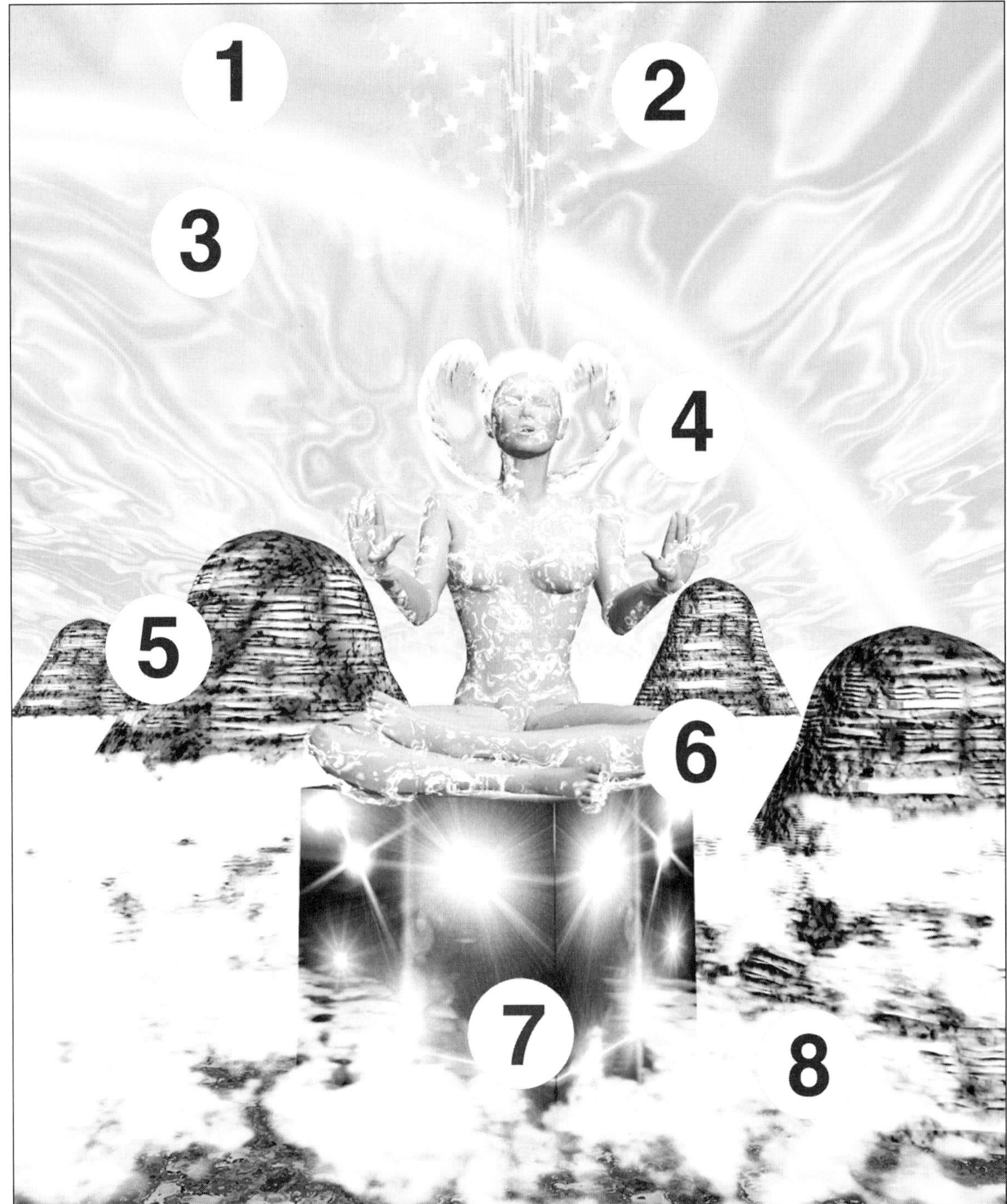

Figure 6.28

Transcending. (Refer to the color version in this book's Bryce Studio.) The chapter text details each labeled element.

7. The seat is a cube mapped with a bitmap created in Photoshop with the Knoll Lens Flare Pro plug-in. I painted a matrix of colorful star objects and mapped it to the cube with Parametric mapping and a Frequency of 0.

8. The clouds that cover the ground plane and the base of the mountains are mapped on a Volumetric Cloud Slab Plane. I used the Cotton Ball material from the Volumetrics folder with a Frequency of 15.1 with World Space mapping. For the Volumetric parameters, I set Base Density to 32, Edge Softness to 100, Fuzzy Factor to 188, and Quality/Speed to 12.

"Rush Hour"

This image tells the story of loneliness in the city. This project file occupies 54MB. It is included in the Projects Folder on this book's companion CD-ROM. Refer to the numbers in Figure 6.29 as you read the following explanations:

1. The buildings in the background are created from two Symmetrical Lattice objects, each mapped with the Office Building material from the Wild & Fun presets. I used a Frequency of 144 with Object Space mapping. The building in the center is an exception: It uses the same material mapped to a cylinder.

2. The train cars are all 3D objects that can be animated to move through the scene. I created the train and train tracks in Amorphium and imported them into Bryce.

3. The footbridge was created as a Boolean construct, using a positive cube cut by a series of negative cylinders. The result is a beautiful arched bridge. I used the StoneWall material from the Rocks & Stones presets to map the bridge, and I used a brick bitmap (in the Textures folder on the Bryce CD-ROM) for Ambience and Diffusion. I used a Frequency of 56 and Random mapping for the StoneWall component and a Frequency of 53 and Parametric mapping for the Brick.

4. All the runners on the bridge were rendered in Poser. Then, I imported the saved bitmaps into Bryce for picture mapping to a vertical 2D plane. Notice that another series of mapped runners can be seen running the other way behind the bridge in the background.

5. The boy with the soccer ball is also a bitmap mapped to a 2D plane.

6. The water uses one of my all-time favorite Bryce materials: Foamy Seawater. You'll find the material in the Waters & Liquids presets. I used it pretty much right out of the can.

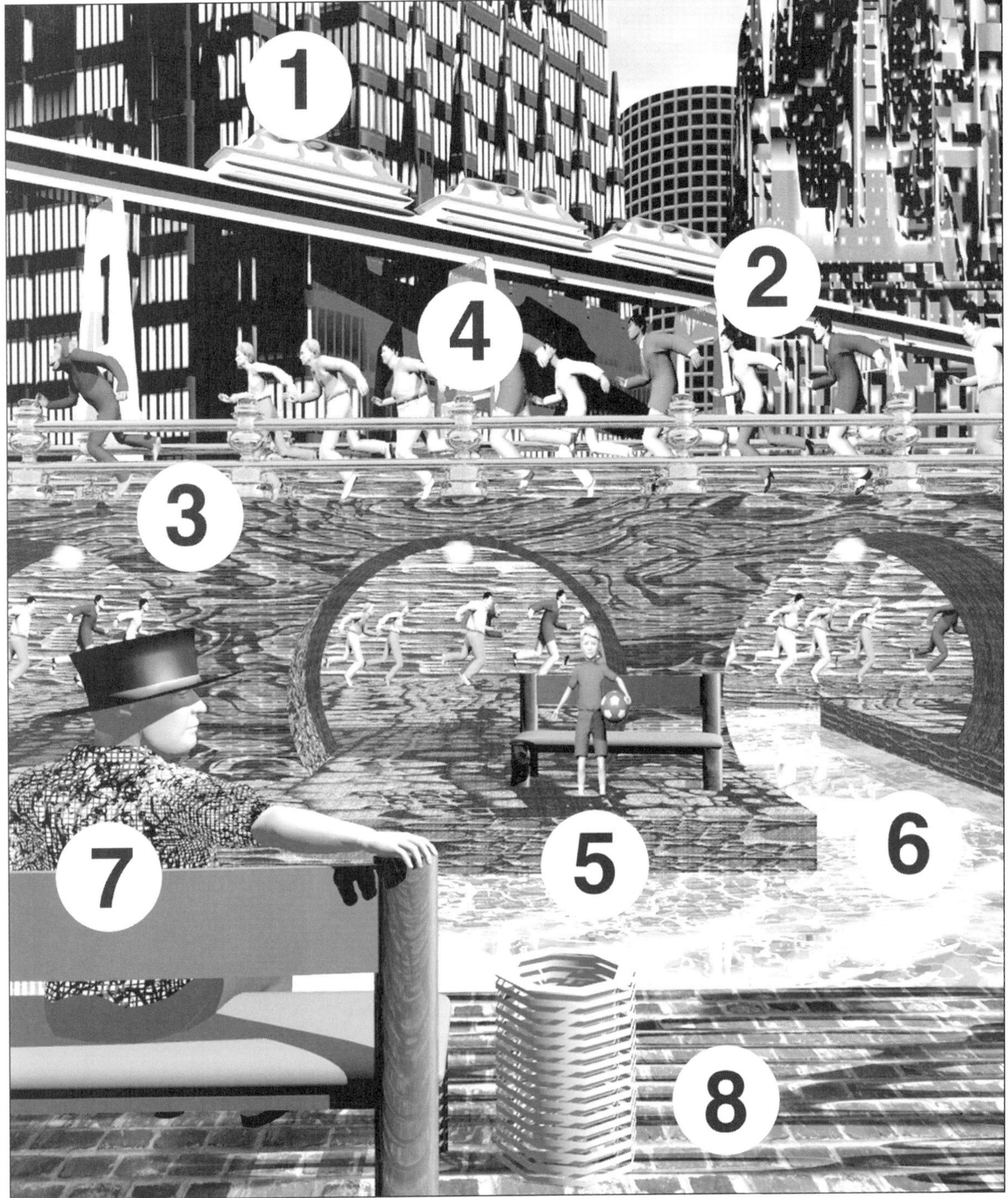

Figure 6.29

Rush Hour. (Refer to the color version in this book's Bryce Studio.) The chapter text details each labeled element.

7. The man is an actual 3D object, exported from Poser as a Wavefront object with all parts saved separately. This allowed me to paint the parts separately in Bryce. I imported the top hat from the Texture CD-ROM created by Baumont Enterprises; this collection includes a wide selection of props for Poser figures. I created the bench by importing a LightWave chair into Bryce and elongating it along its X axis.
8. The ground is textured with Old Brick, one of the new materials contained in the Material folder of this book's CD-ROM.

"Art Gallery"

The art gallery theme is a favorite among computer artists. This one includes interesting variations. This project file occupies 10MB. Refer to the numbers in Figure 6.30 as you read the following explanations:

1. The ceiling, complete with beams, is made from cube primitives. The ceiling covers the entire scene, so no sunlight lights anything. Instead, four ceiling lights illuminate the space. These lights are all Volume Visible Radials with an intensity of 30, set inside Six Sided Hollow enclosures (from the Imported Objects presets folder). The entire room is bounded by a ceiling and four walls with no windows, so the illumination provided by these lights is all there is.
2. The paintings are examples of my previous work. I simply mapped them to flattened cubic primitives, constructed a frame from other cubic primitives, and grouped the frame with the paintings. You can change paintings at any time just by mapping new bitmaps.
3. This character is the baby Sumo from the Zygote Poser collection, mapped to a 2D plane.
4. The background figures are more Poser bitmaps mapped to a 2D plane, the Heavy Man and the Young Girl.
5. This seated figure is a true 3D object exported from Poser and ungrouped for painting and texturing in Bryce. I used an array of textures to map the figure. A wig object rests on his head.
6. The image includes two tables; one in the foreground and another is farther back. I constructed them from three resized and grouped cylinders. I mapped the tables with the Clown Collar material, but I changed the colors to red and yellow in the Deep Texture Editor. The mapping is Parametric with a Frequency of 12.5.
7. The bench in the foreground is a simple grouping of cube primitives. A basic red material maps the bench legs, and a Warped Wood material (from the Simple & Fast presets) maps the top slats.

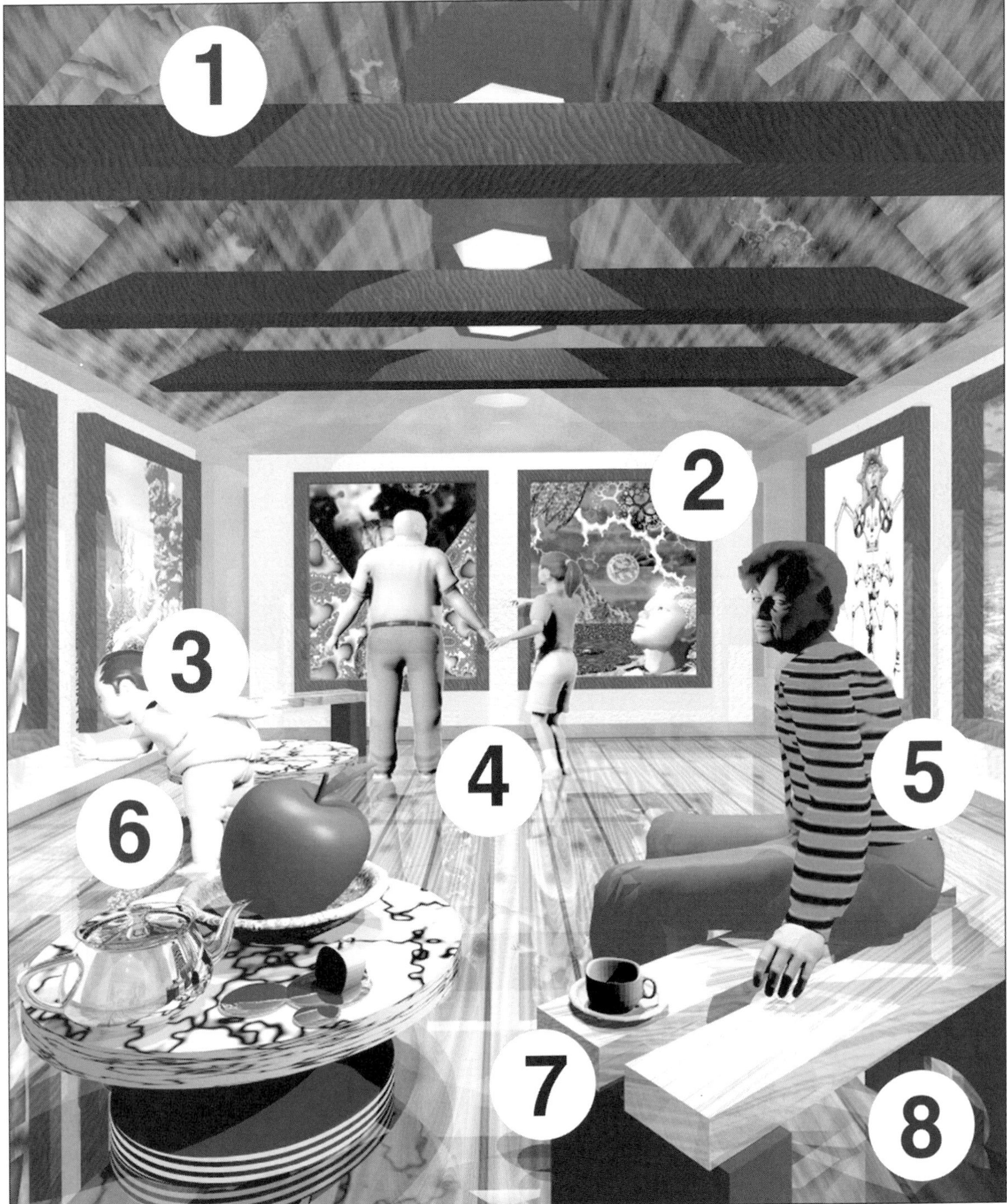

Figure 6.30

Art Gallery. (Refer to the color version in this book's Bryce Studio.) The chapter text details each labeled element.

8. The floor reflects many of the items in the scene. It uses the Plank Wood material with a Parametric mapping and a Frequency of 116. The Reflection is set to 41.

"Tea And A Good Book"

A monastic environment (and a sprinkling of surrealism) shapes this image. This project file occupies 55MB. Refer to the numbers in Figure 6.31 as you read the following explanations:

1. The stained-glass window is a cube primitive mapped with a bitmap texture created in Photoshop (using the Mosaic Tiles filter over a multicolored surface). I constructed the window frame in Bryce from cube primitives.

2. This doorway artifact was created from a scan of a plaster relic called "The Green Man," an image prevalent in ancient European civilizations. To create this object, I used the scan as a height map in the Terrain Editor on a Symmetrical Lattice.

3. The monks are composite objects. I created the robe in Amorphium. The figure is a standard Poser naked-man figure imported into Bryce. I removed the head and replaced it with a Symmetrical Lattice object height mapped with an image of my face. There is a lot of detail in the figure, including a separate belt on the robe and a necklace. The figure holds a candle (a LightWave import), which has a sphere on the top that acts as a flame. The lens flare mapped to the sphere was created with the Knoll Lens Flare Pro plug-in.

4. This scene includes a complete back room and hallway. You can see another stained glass window, placed in a spherical hole cut by Boolean operators. You can also see two duplicate monks walking towards the right in the room.

5. This dog is imported from Poser and mapped in Bryce with a Wave2 random texture with heavy Bump mapping. The result resembles fur.

6. The foreground table is replete with a collection of goodies. On the left, a Bryce book (created by mapping an image of the Bryce documentation on a Cubic object) sits on another book. More candles rest on the table. A teapot (imported from LightWave) sits at the center of the table. A cup, bowl, and spoon—all LightWave imports—are also visible. A small picture of our cat, Minky, rests on the table edge, and a framed picture of my wife, Diane, graces the far edge.

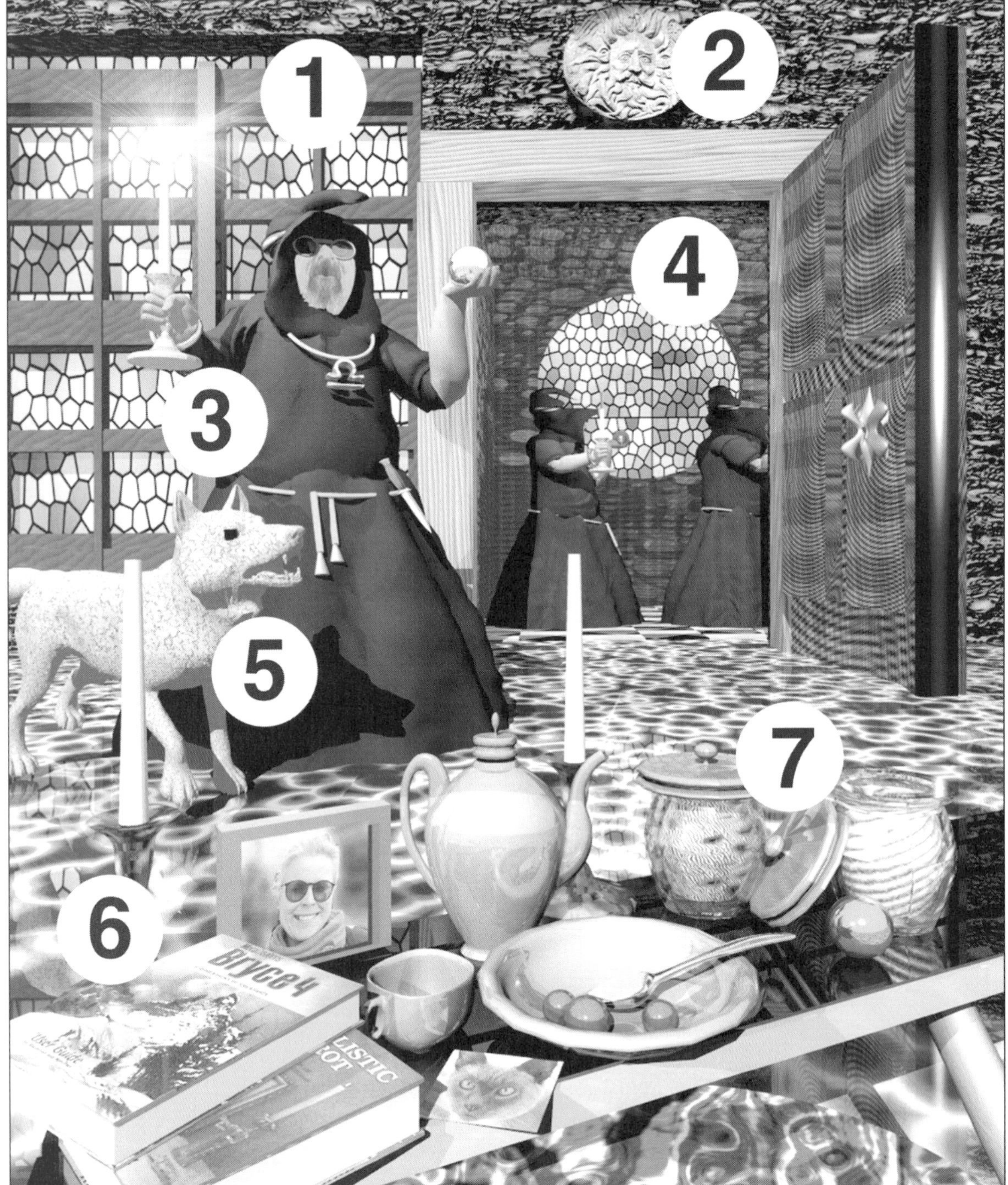

Figure 6.31

Tea And A Good Book. (Refer to the color version in this book's Bryce Studio.) The chapter text details each labeled element.

7. The two jars are special objects. Constructed in Bruce with transparent glass, they add more rendering time than anything else in the scene. They contain two of the materials you'll find on the CD-ROM: PCock and Electro Spring.

Moving On

In this chapter, the creation of the color plates in the gallery section was examined closely. I hope this provides you with insights into the creation of your own Bryce works. In the next chapter—the last chapter in the book—I'll present a collection of projects you can explore.

7 Project Paradise

In this chapter, I'll show you a number of unique projects that you can create with Bryce. The project files and related tutorial elements are contained on this book's companion CD-ROM.

A Creepy Insect

Here's a project that will leave your audience itching and looking over their shoulders. Using the information provided in this tutorial, you will be able to use the Terrain Editor to model your own creepy creatures.

Insect Reference

I refer to a specific source when I model insects: *Insects: A Peterson Field Guide*, by Donald J. Borror and Richard E. White (Houghton Mifflin Company, 1970). This small paperback describes insects in America north of Mexico. My creepy insect is a composite of examples from this reference work. This project uses only Bryce tools for modeling; no external models or model elements are imported for this project.

Bryce Tools

Some computer graphics users who don't like Bryce fault the software for its lack of modeling tools. At first glance, this seems like an accurate appraisal. Bryce provides only a limited variety of primitive shapes, and it includes no real tools for deformation, with the exception of scaling. Bryce supports Boolean operators, so you can use one model to reshape another, but it looks like that's about it. So how can we model an insect of any interest using only these limited modeling options? You'll find the answer after you master another of Bryce's tools: the Terrain Editor.

The Terrain Editor

You've worked through the Bryce documentation and this book's tutorials, so I assume you already know how to use the Terrain Editor and how to move among the three tabbed areas that contain the Terrain Editor's tools and options. See Figure 7.1.

All the creepy insect's appendages make use of the Terrain Editor. The balance of the model uses a variety of Bryce primitives mapped with a number of Bryce materials. You can animate this model fully.

Modeling The Head

I'll begin with the insect's head, a body part based on the components that are not modified in the Terrain Editor. Base the head on a sphere elongated along its Y axis. Click on the sphere primitive to add it to the workspace, and resize it so its X, Y, and Z dimensions are 20, 26, and 20, respectively. See Figure 7.2.

From the right view, rotate the elongated sphere (which I'll just call "the head" from now on), 22 degrees on its X axis. See Figure 7.3.

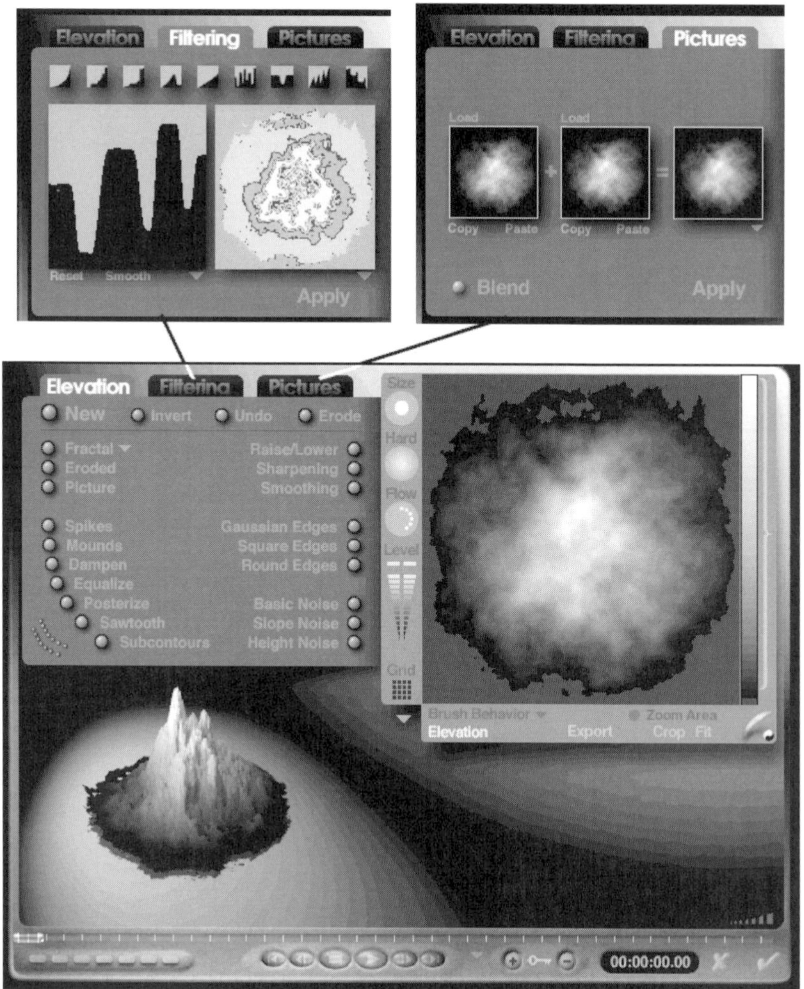

Figure 7.1

The Terrain Editor features three tabbed areas.

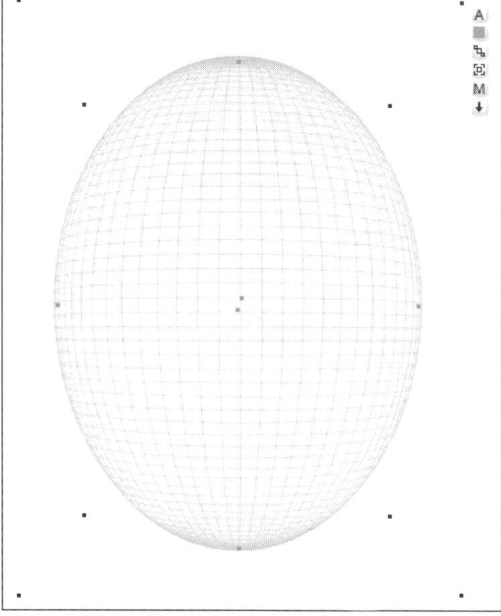

Figure 7.2

This view shows the sphere after it has been resized as described.

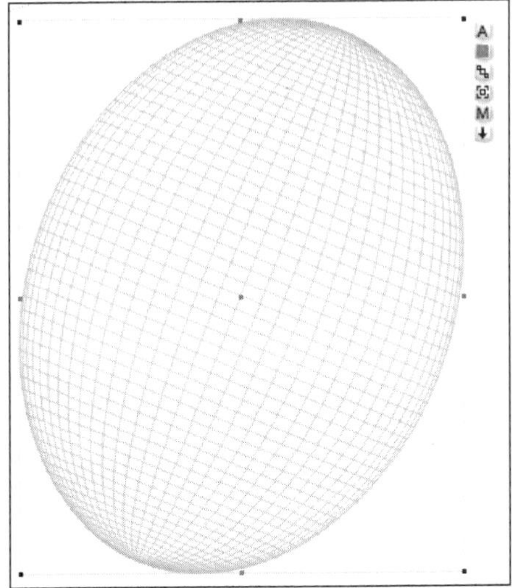

Figure 7.3
Here the head is rotated 22 degrees on its X axis, as seen in the right view.

Now I'll create two eye sockets. Create another sphere, and resize X to 13, Y to 15, and Z to 13. Select Negative in the sphere's Object Attributes dialog box. Click on the head, and select Positive in its Object Attributes dialog box. When the spheres are grouped, the smaller sphere cuts a hole in the head. Go to top view and place the cutter sphere about half way inside the head, and then duplicate the cutter sphere. Place the cloned cutter sphere on the other side of the head. Group the head and the two cutters. Name this new grouped object BigHead_1. See Figures 7.4 and 7.5.

Now for the eyes. Create a sphere, and resize X to 10, Y to 12, and Z to 10. Center the sphere in the right socket, and name it Eye_R. Duplicate the sphere, and set the duplicate in the left socket. Name the duplicate Eye_L. Link (not group) both eyes to the BigHead_1 object. See Figures 7.6 and 7.7. Use the Terrain Editor to develop the rest of the elements of the head.

The Mandibles

Create a Symmetrical Lattice, select it, and go to the Terrain Editor. Click on New to erase the Symmetrical Lattice, and use the Elevation Brush to paint the shape shown in Figure 7.8. Reduce the shape's height to about 25 percent, and click on the check mark to write the mandible object to the screen.

Set the dimensions of the mandible—X to 11, Y to 0.6, and Z to 11—in the Objects Attributes palette. In the Object Attributes Palette under the General tab, rotate the mandible (X is -76, Y is -60, Z is -44 degrees) and reset the Origin Point at the top of the object in order to animate it. (Be sure Show Origin Handle is selected in the Object Attributes dialog box for each mandible; this allows you to place the Origin Handle at the

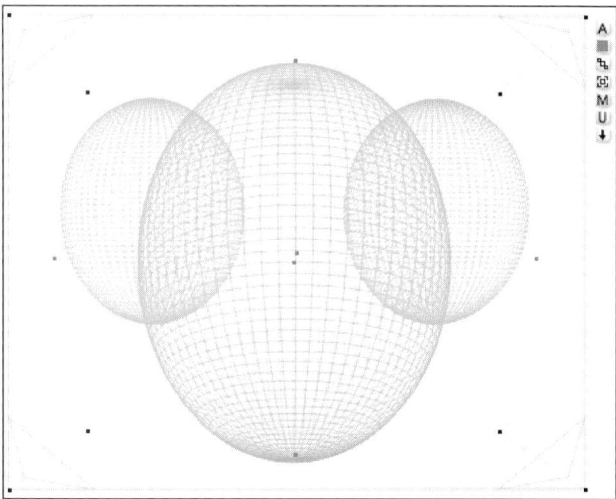

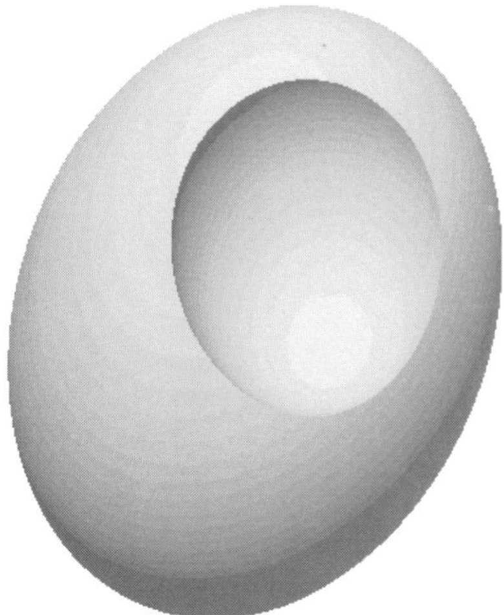

Figure 7.4
(Left) As seen from the front view, the two cutter spheres are now grouped with the head.

Figure 7.5
(Right) From the right view, you can see how the cutter sphere creates a depressed area as a home for the eye.

top-center of this body part.) Repeat this procedure for the left mandible. Then, link both mandibles to the BigHead_1 object. See Figure 7.9.

Although I used *Insects: A Peterson Field Guide* to guide the general construction of this creepy insect, this creepy insect is an original concept. It is not really a grasshopper, ant, or even a scorpion: It is my own customized insect model.

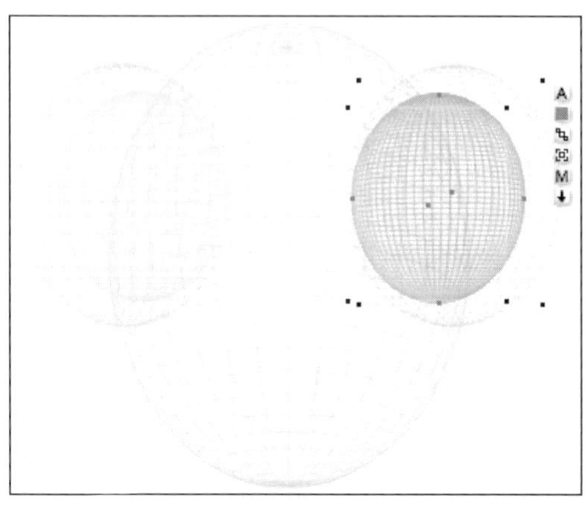

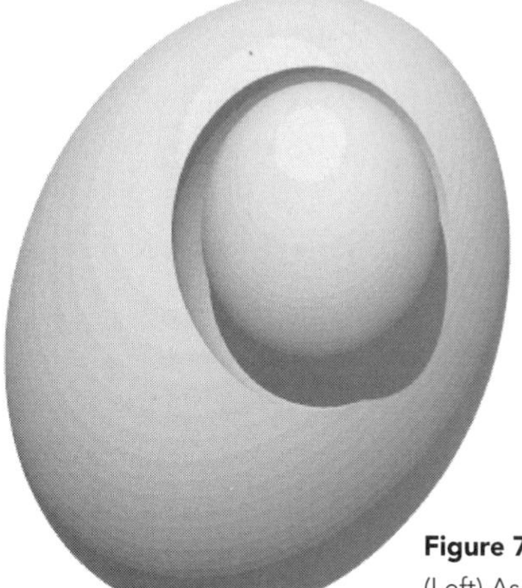

Figure 7.6
(Left) As seen in this camera view, the two eyes are placed in the sockets.

Figure 7.7
(Right) In this rendered right view, you can see that the eyes fit in the sockets while showing just a bit of the depressions on all sides.

Labium

The labium is the lower lip, set back on the head. Build it by using a Boolean operation. Two Boolean spheres—one positive and one negative—are grouped in order to create a smoothly curved surface. The size of the positive sphere is X at 16, Y at 21, and Z at 16; the negative sphere is X is 19, Y is 21, and Z is 16. Move the negative sphere so that about one-fifth of it extends to the front of the positive sphere. The result, when grouped, is a

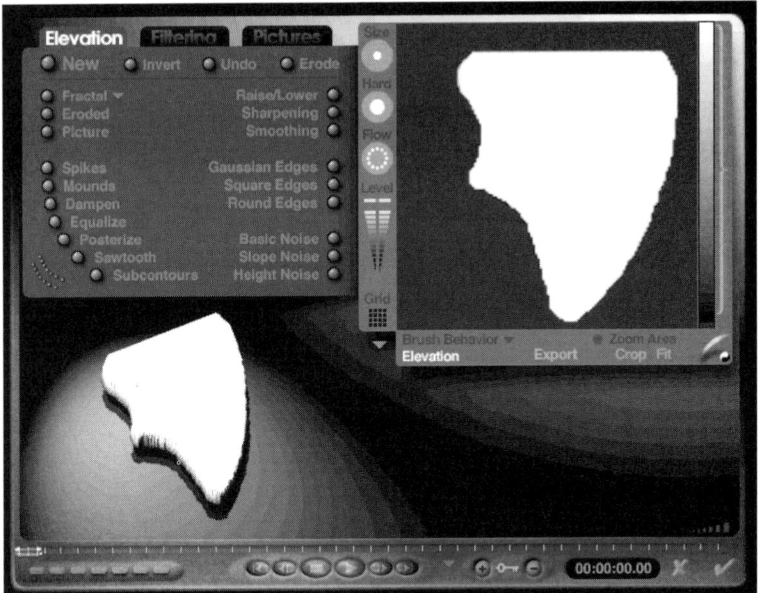

Figure 7.8
Draw the mandible object as illustrated here.

lip-like crescent surface. Move the Origin Handle so that the labium is hinged at the upper-center. Reduce the labium group to about one-half. Move the Labium into place, and link it to the BigHead_1 object, as in Figure 7.10.

The Coronal Suture

Create a cylinder with X set to 20, Y to 0.5, and Z to 17. Place this thin cylinder inside the BigHead_1 object so that it protrudes just a bit from the front of the head. This protrusion is the coronal suture, or "head split." Link it to the BigHead_1 object. On real insects, the coronal suture is a depression, but I decided to make it protrude from my insect. See Figure 7.11.

Using The Terrain Editor For Organic Modeling

Bear in mind two important considerations when developing organic elements in the Terrain Editor. First, remember that objects developed in the Terrain Editor always contain some anomalies (observable as small spikes). Although you can use the Terrain Editor's Smoothing operation to smooth out the spikes, this works better for developing machine parts. It is *not* what you want to do while developing organic elements. These small irregularities—and even any enhanced irregularities you might add—contribute to the natural look of organic components. Second, *always* develop non-terrain components—organic or mechanical—by beginning with a Symmetrical Lattice and not a terrain. The Symmetrical Lattice has no flat plane at its base; a terrain does. Elements that you use to create a composite model should not have a flat plane attached. After using the Terrain Editor to develop the Symmetrical Lattice object, you might want to substitute a terrain for the Symmetrical Lattice in Bryce's substitution options. Substituting a terrain for a Symmetrical Lattice removes the Symmetrical Lattice's mirror effect on the Y axis and compensates by making a Terrain object twice its normal size on the Y axis. If this sounds confusing, just do it a few times to get an idea of how it works. Never create mechanical or metallic looks when you develop organic objects in Bryce—or anywhere else.

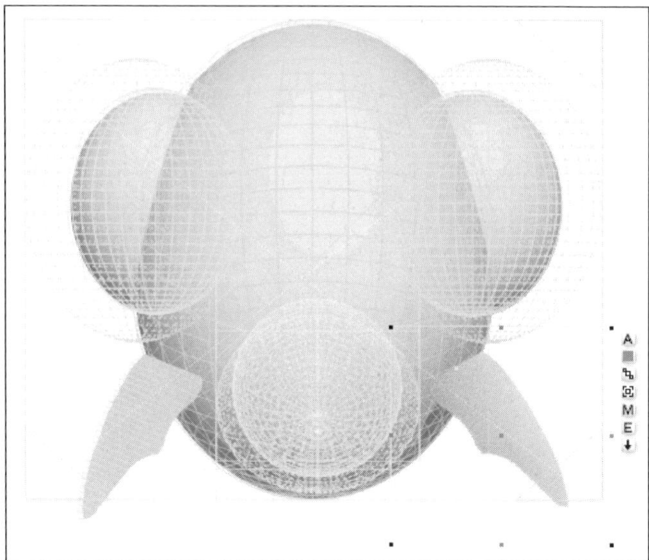

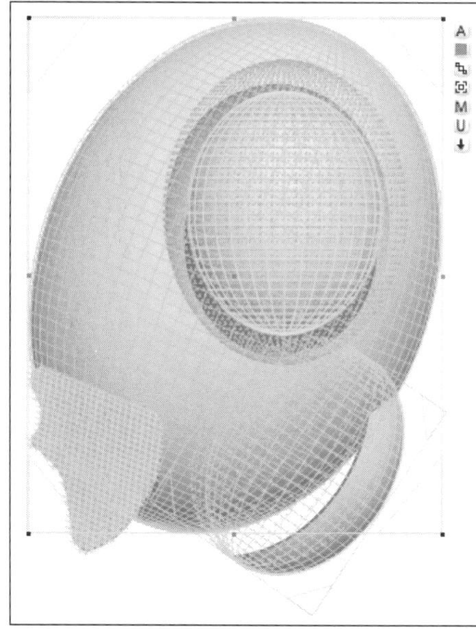

Figure 7.9

(Left) In this front view, the mandibles are shown in place, linked to the BigHead_1 object.

Figure 7.10

(Right) In this overlay preview render (right view), the labium is moved into place and linked to the BigHead_1 object.

Palps

Palps are the small, arm-like appendages found on either side of the lower head. Make the palps for this insect larger than normal, to create a more menacing look. Follow these steps:

1. Create a Symmetrical lattice, open the Terrain Editor, and click on New to create a new object.
2. Use the Elevation Brush to create the shape shown in Figure 7.12.

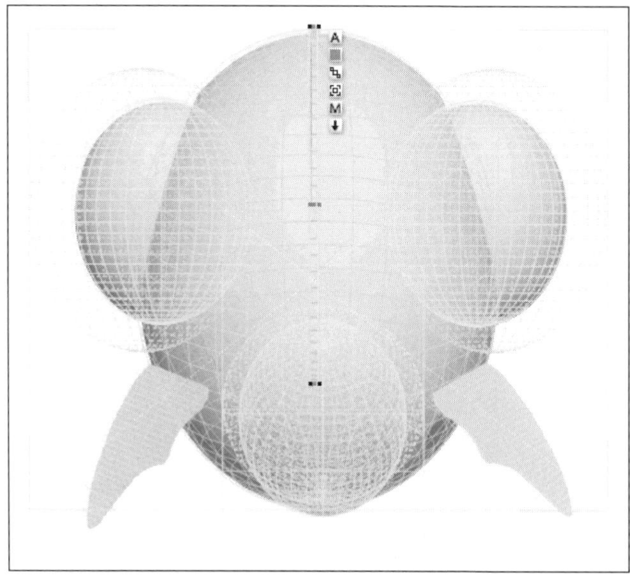

Figure 7.11

The coronal suture shown from the front view in an overlay preview render.

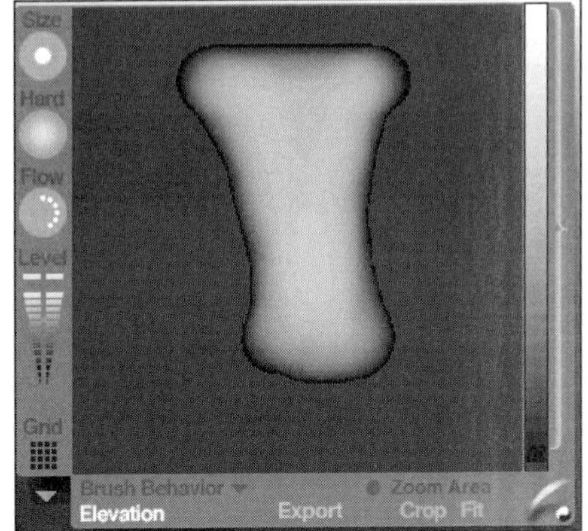

Figure 7.12
This shape is a section of the palp created in the Terrain Editor from a Symmetrical Lattice. The finished object looks a bit like a dog treat.

3. Click on the check mark to write the object to the workspace. Substitute a terrain for the Symmetrical Lattice, and resize the terrain's Y-axis height to 1.
4. Resize the entire palp element until it is about half the height of a mandible.
5. Name the palp object Palp_1, and make sure Show Origin Handle is selected in its Object Attributes dialog box. Move this palp element's Origin Handle to the top center of the object. Duplicate the element twice, and link both duplicates to each other in succession until the final palp resembles a finger (which it is). Make each descending element a bit smaller than the preceding one, as in Figure 7.13.

Now it's time to add four palps to the BigHead_1 object. In the right view, place the first pair just in front of the labium and a second pair (about 50 percent larger than the first) closer to the front of the head. You can easily create all the duplicates by selecting the top palp element. Now link all four palps to the BigHead_1 object. See Figure 7.14.

Ocelli (Simple Eyes)

In addition to their compound eyes, many insects also have ocelli, or simple eyes. Give the creepy critter three ocelli by adding three linked spheres. See Figure 7.15.

The Proboscis

Insects that draw the nectar from plants have a proboscis, or sucking tongue. This often suffices for lips and a mouth, but this creepy insect will have both—the better to bite you with! Take a look at Figure 7.16. This proboscis was created in the Terrain Editor from a Symmetrical Lattice. Add some spikes by painting them in the Terrain Editor, and shorten the object's

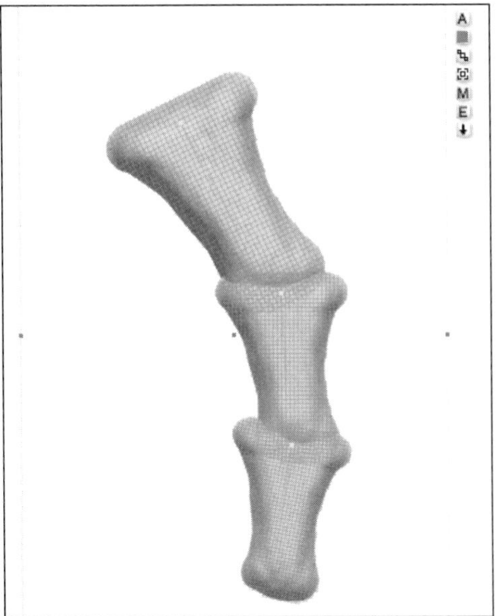

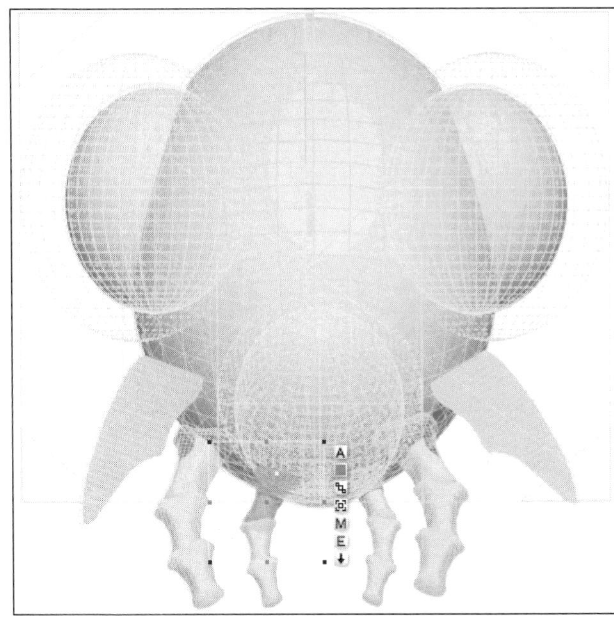

Y axis until it looks right to you. Then, add the proboscis to the head just inside the open mouth, and link it to the lower mouth. See Figure 7.17.

Figure 7.13
(Left) The final palp has all its parts linked so they can be rotated like finger joints.

Figure 7.14
(Right) The four palps are moved into place and linked to the BigHead_1 object, as shown in this overlay preview render.

The Last Head Element

The last item to link to the head is the antennae. Instead of constructing them from scratch, use the palp element to create the antennae. Simply duplicate one of the palps, and for the moment, unlink the duplicate from

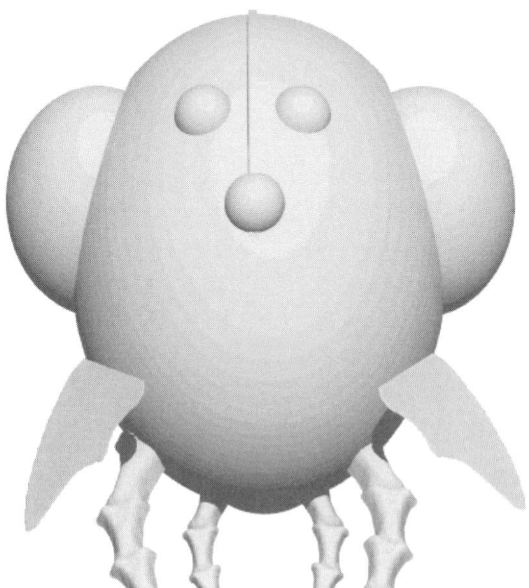

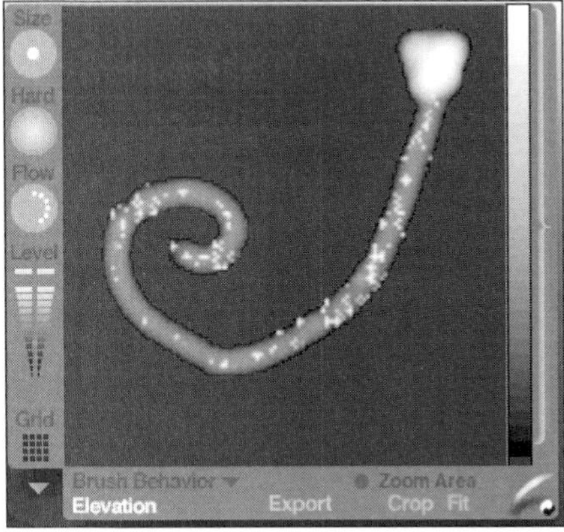

Figure 7.15
(Left) Three linked ocelli are added to the head.

Figure 7.16
(Right) In the Terrain Editor, use an Elevation Brush to paint the proboscis and to add spikes.

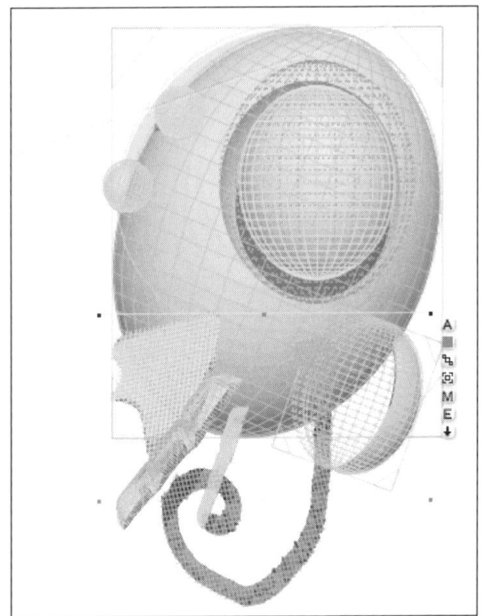

Figure 7.17
The proboscis is placed inside the insect's mouth with its spiky tongue protruding and ready for work.

the BigHead_1 object. Move the duplicate to a separate workspace, and duplicate the parent section four more times. This duplicates the entire three-part palp. Now build an antenna by linking all the descending parts to each other. By using this method, you can curve and animate the antenna in an infinite variety of positions and curls. Antennae act almost like eyebrows when creating an insect's expressions. See Figure 7.18.

Time to make the insect even more creepy and menacing. Create an elongated cone primitive resized to emulate a spiky hair, place four of these elements on top of the head, and link them. That's better. See Figure 7.19.

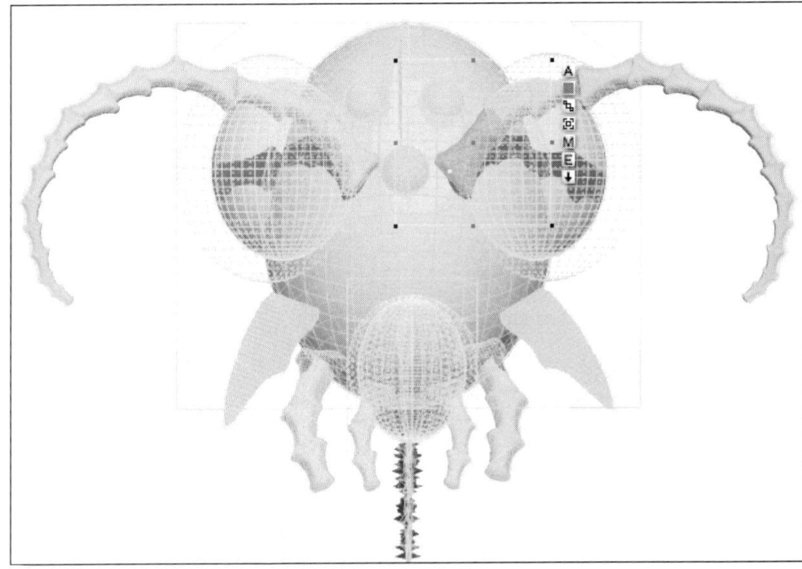

Figure 7.18
One antenna is constructed from a string of linked palps. Then the antenna is duplicated, and both antennae are placed in position. Finally, both are linked to the BigHead_1 object.

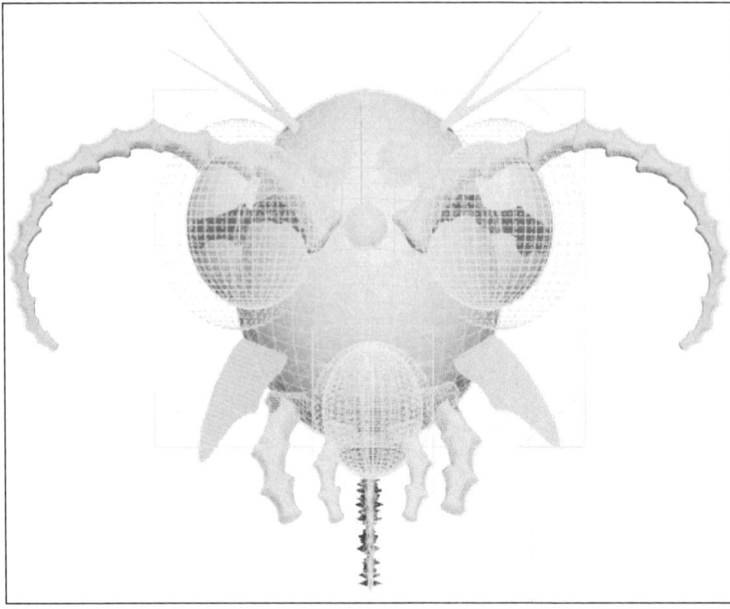

Figure 7.19
The final touch—a quartet of spiky hairs—is added. If you like, duplicate more hairs for the head.

Thorax

Set the head aside until later, when it's time to add some textures. Now it's time to develop the thorax—the part of the body to which the head and legs are attached. Create a Symmetrical Lattice and go to the Terrain Editor. Click New, and use the Elevation Brush to paint the form shown in Figure 7.20. To add cracks and other anomalies, select the Erode Brush, and paint around the edges. Add Spikes by sliding the Spikes control to the right. When you are satisfied with the look, click on the check mark and write the thorax element to the workspace.

By resizing and rotating three duplicate thorax elements, as shown in Figure 7.21, you have created an organic looking thorax. Link the BigHead_1 object to the finished thorax.

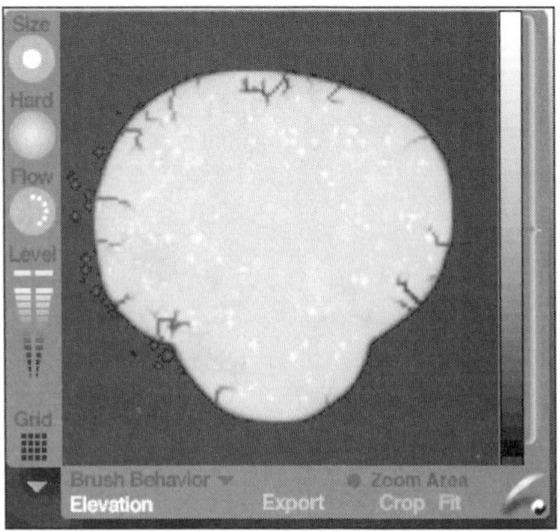

Figure 7.20
The thorax element is developed in the Terrain Editor.

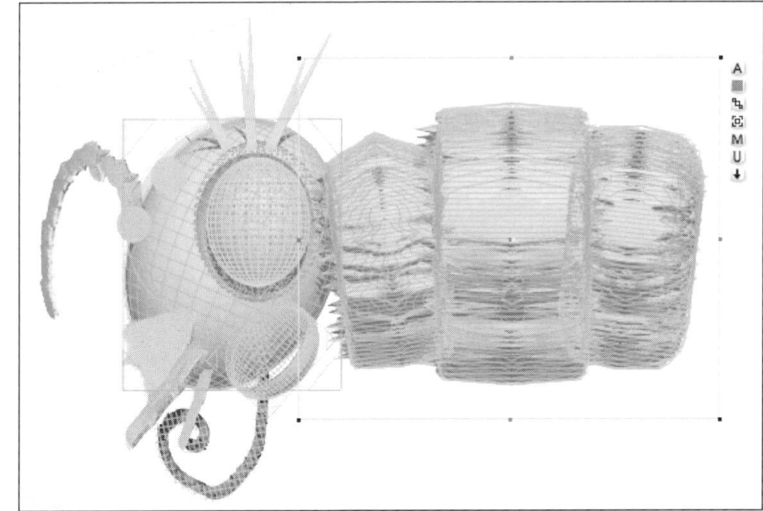

Figure 7.21
As shown in this overlay preview rendering, the final thorax is constructed from three thorax elements.

The Abdomen

The construction of the abdomen is the next task. Don't be concerned if you don't understand why the abdomen is modeled as indicated here. That will become clear when adding textures later. Follow these steps:

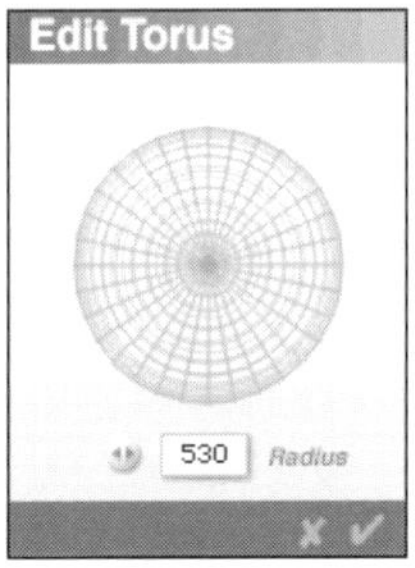

Figure 7.22
Use the Edit Torus dialog box to close the hole in the torus.

1. Create a torus. Click on the *E* (or Edit) button, and click and drag the mouse to the right to close the hole in the torus. The numerical indicator should read 530, as in Figure 7.22.

2. Duplicate the torus, which places another torus inside the first. Resize the duplicate to about half the size of the source Torus. Resize the duplicate again to make it just as deep as the source torus (that is, to give it the same Z-axis dimension). Name the source torus "Outside_Ab" and the duplicate "Inside_Ab". Group the tori, naming the group "Torus_Section".

3. Duplicate the Torus Section until you have seven. Link them in descending order, resizing and rotating as you go, until the abdomen is complete, as shown in Figure 7.23. The stinger on the end is a resized elongated cone linked to the last Torus Section.

4. Move the abdomen into place, and link it to the thorax. The model should now resemble the one shown in Figure 7.24.

The Legs

Time to give this creature the capacity for locomotion. You need to model only one leg. The others are duplicates (resized and rotated versions of the initial construct). The leg has three components, all modeled in the Terrain Editor from a Symmetrical Lattice, with some Spikes and Erosion added to make them look less mechanical. The three parts are then linked so that

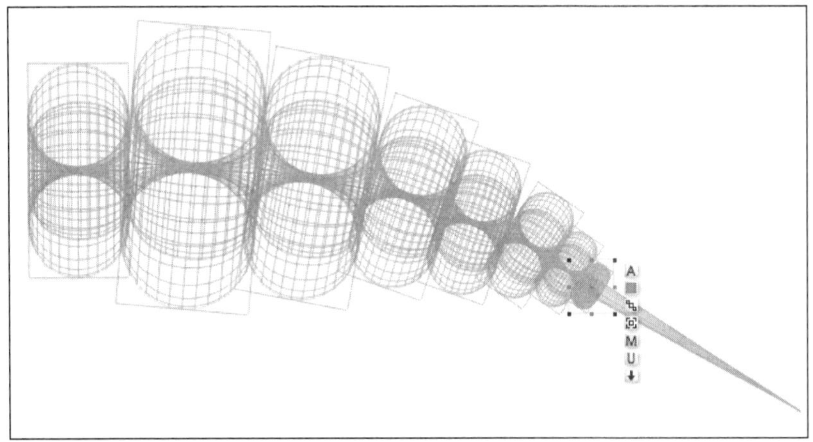

Figure 7.23

The completed abdomen should resemble this wireframe preview render, as seen in the right view.

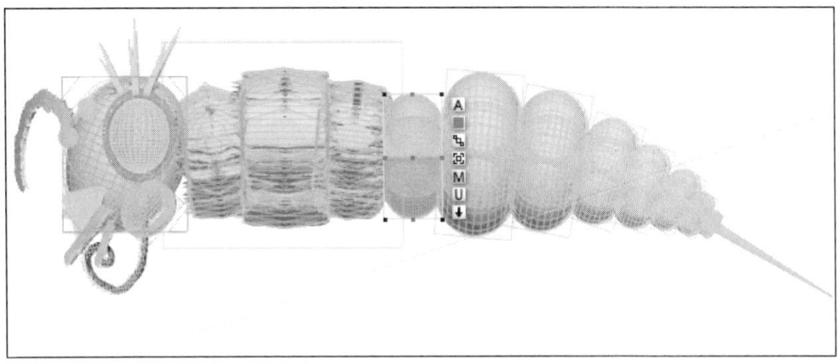

Figure 7.24

The abdomen is moved into place and linked to the thorax, as shown in this overlay preview rendering.

they can be rotated correctly. Obviously, their Origin Handles have to be moved to the top-center of each leg part. See Figures 7.25 to 7.28.

After you're finished with the root leg, it's time to create three pairs of legs for placement on the thorax. Note that each pair is attached (linked) to one of the thorax sections, as seen in the right view (Figure 7.29) and the top view (Figure 7.30).

Wings?

A "creepy" insect is not limited to creeping: It can also flutter around with wings, increasing its potential to invade your space. In my mind, "creepy" means something that makes me feel creepy when I see it—something I hope doesn't come any closer. For that reason, I'll give this insect the power of flight, making it more threatening. Follow these steps:

1. Open Photoshop (or any other bitmap image editor), and draw a wing shape with the freehand marquee. In the Filters menu, select the Stained Glass option from the Textures list. Set Cell Size to 4 and Border Thickness to 2. Light Intensity isn't required. Click on OK, and a pattern of lacey hexagons is written to the inside of the shape.

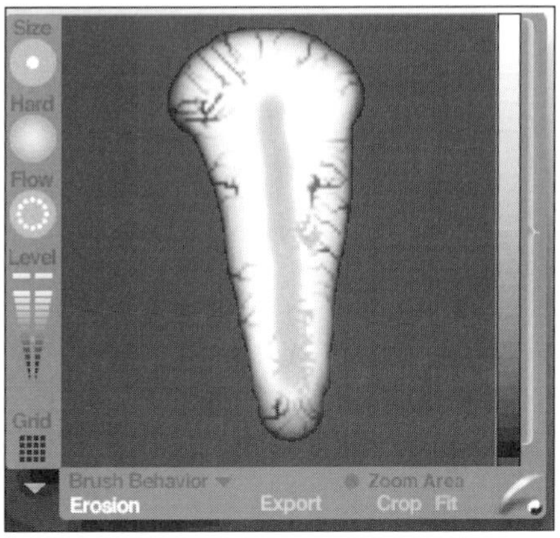

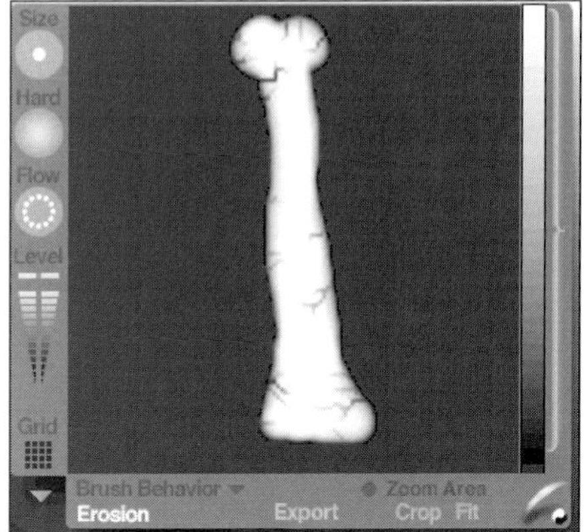

Figure 7.25
(Left) The top leg section as modeled in the Terrain Editor.

Figure 7.26
(Right) The middle leg section as modeled in the Terrain Editor.

Select Edit|Stroke, and add a two-pixel Stroke to the inside of the shape. Save it as Insect_Wing_1. See Figure 7.31.

2. Now, make a white silhouette of the wing shape on a black background, and save it as Insect_Wing_2. Go to Bryce, place a Symmetrical Lattice in the workspace, and open the Terrain Editor. Import Insect_Wing_2 into the Terrain Editor as a picture file (under the third tab). Decrease the Y axis to 0.5 to create a very thin wing. See Figure 7.32.

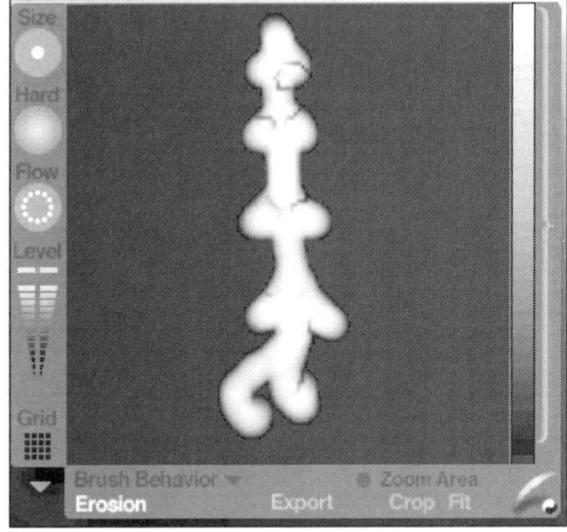

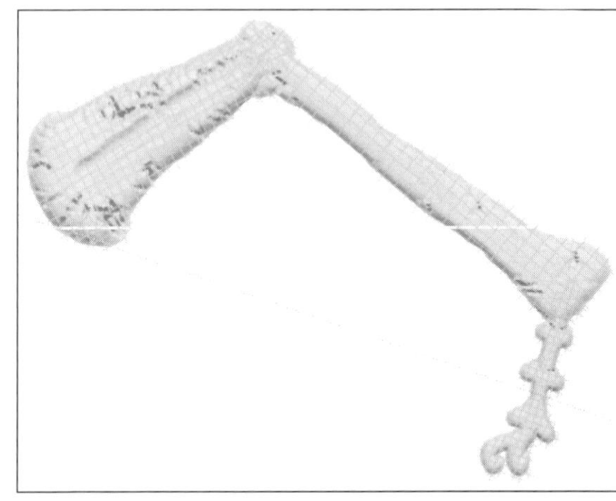

Figure 7.27
(Left) The lower leg section as modeled in the Terrain Editor.

Figure 7.28
(Right) The completed leg, with the three parts linked and ready for placement.

3. Place the wing at the top of the thorax, and link it. Duplicate the wing and flip the duplicate on the X axis to create the other wing. See Figure 7.33.

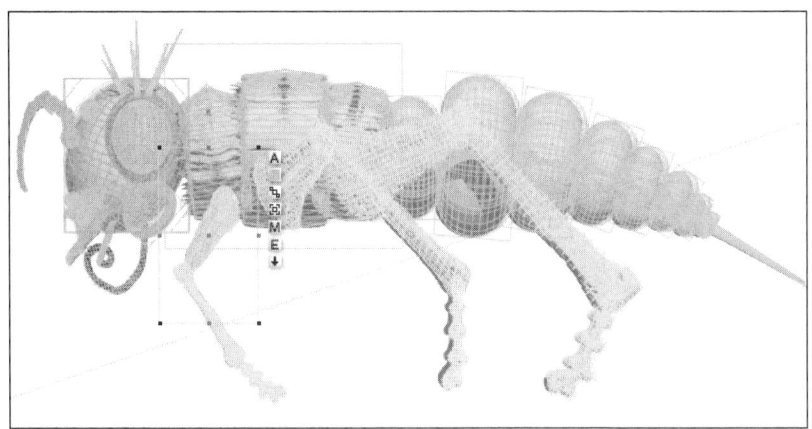

Figure 7.29
The right view of the leg pairs after sizing, rotation, and placement.

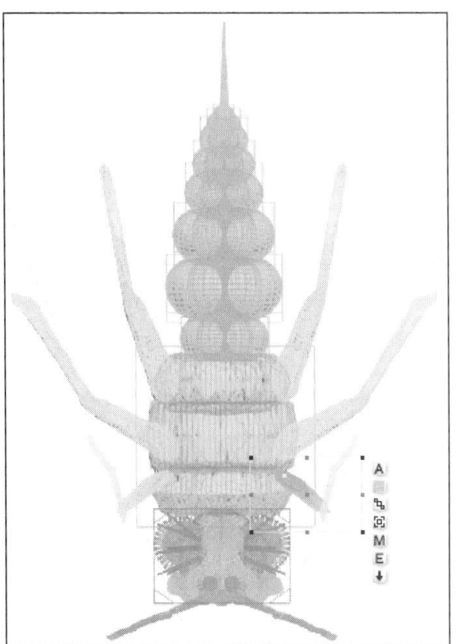

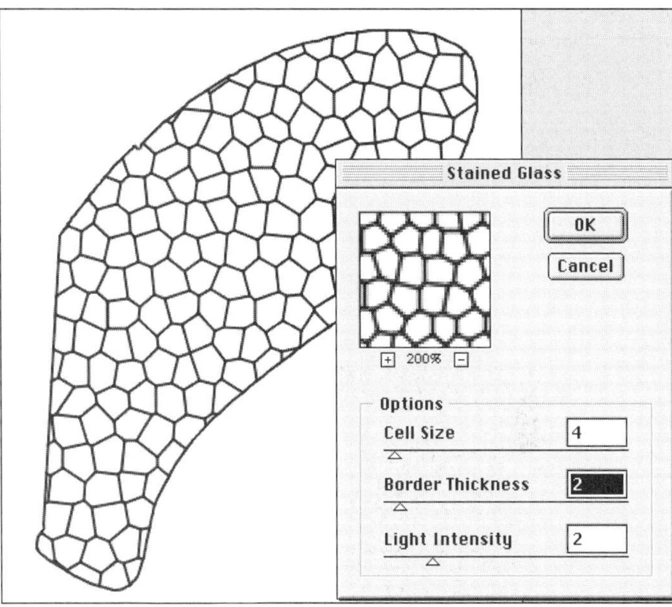

Figure 7.30
(Middle left) The top view of the legs after sizing, rotation, and placement.

Figure 7.31
(Middle right) The Stained Glass pattern is written inside the shape enclosed by the marquee. The shape is saved as a bitmap for use as a picture map in Bryce.

Figure 7.32
(Bottom) The Wing_2 silhouette is imported into the Terrain Editor as a picture, which creates a 3D shape.

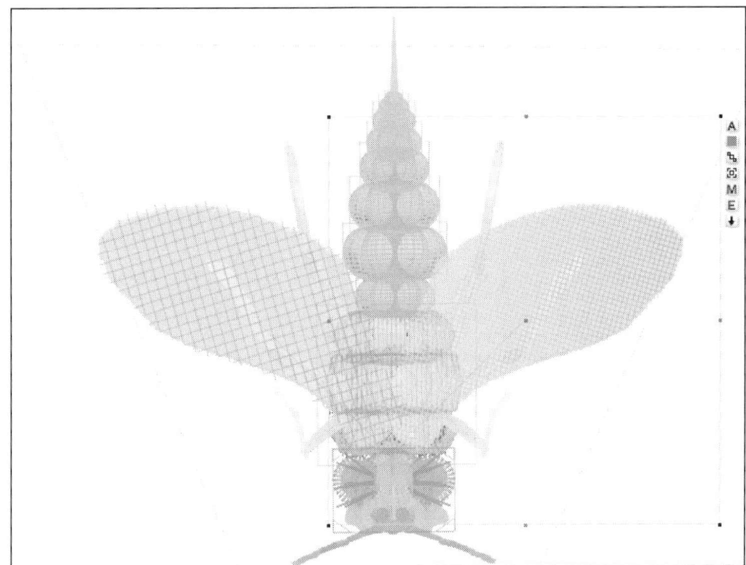

Figure 7.33
Both wings are now placed and linked, as shown in this overlay preview from the top view.

Texturing The Creepy Insect

Textures and materials give personality to a model. Begin by deciding who the creature is and how it acts, and textures will follow of their own accord.

Texturing The Wings

The wings have a special bitmap texture created in Photoshop. As described previously, the Photoshop Stained Glass filter was used to create this texture. In Bryce, apply the texture as an image map, using a size of 0 percent with Object Top mapping. Use a green Diffuse color, with only the Transparent color and Transparency Optics relating to the image map. The Transparency Optics are set to 80 percent, so the wings have transparency.

Colors

Many of the elements of this creepy insect are textured with color alone. The lower feet segments of all six legs are colored a non-reflective black, as are the antennae. The eyes are a special black. They have a Specular Red halo, so they always seem to glow. I also shut off their ability to Receive Shadows in the Materials Lab, so they always dominate in any view.

A Special Material

I used the Materials Lab to create a special material based on the Autumn Leaves Procedural (with Object Space Mapping at a frequency of 25). I plugged this texture into the Diffuse and Ambient color channels at settings of 97 and 19, respectively. I didn't place the texture in either the Diffusion or Ambience values. A Specularity value of 78 makes the texture gleam a bit, and a Bump Map of 10 also gives it some body. The result is a material that resembles mottled skin. I used this Texture for the head, palps, mandibles, thorax, upper and middle leg parts, stinger, and the internal torus elements of the abdomen.

The abdomen's outer torus segments were mapped in another way. The only procedural used was a Beveled Tile in the Bump channel, random mapped at a frequency (using the Edit Texture Scale Tool) of 7 percent (Bump Height -60). Everything else is color dependent, with a light gray Diffuse color and a light blue Ambient color. Value settings were Diffusion, 100; Ambience, 23.5; and Specularity, 90. The most important component was a Transparency value of 55. What is the result? The outer torus segments of the abdomen look gelatinous and semitransparent, allowing you to see the organs inside. It's a very eerie effect.

A Last Minute Decision

The labium and proboscis didn't look threatening enough for my purposes after I rendered the model, so I set them both to Hidden in their Object Attribute dialog boxes. (They are still there if I ever decide to render a less aggressive model.) What I did instead was copy a section of the abdomen (the section with the stinger attached) to the head. This created a proboscis that resembles a hypodermic needle—something I am deathly afraid of. Talk about creepy: *This* did the trick. See what you think of the finished model in Figures 7.34 and 7.35.

How big is this Bryce project file? The fully articulated creepy insect is 3.5MB.

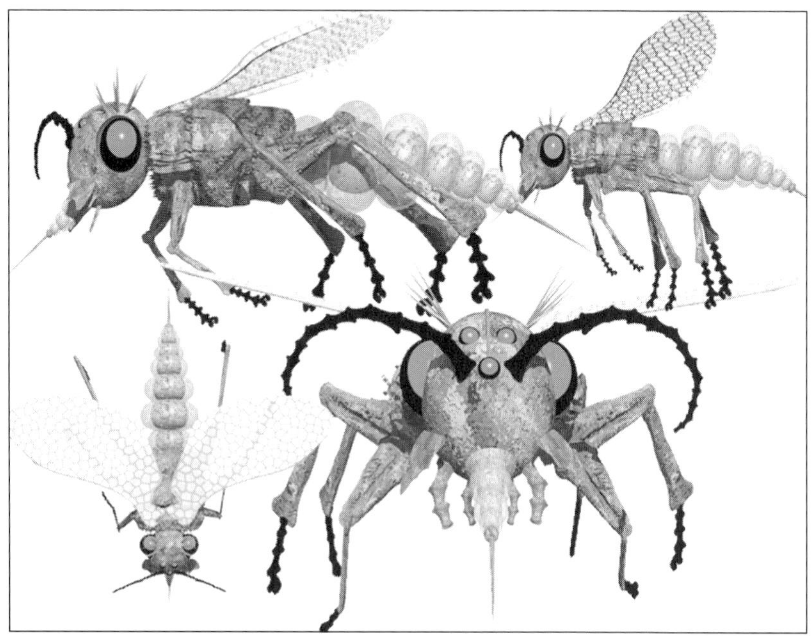

Figure 7.34
The finished creepy insect, modeled entirely in Bryce.

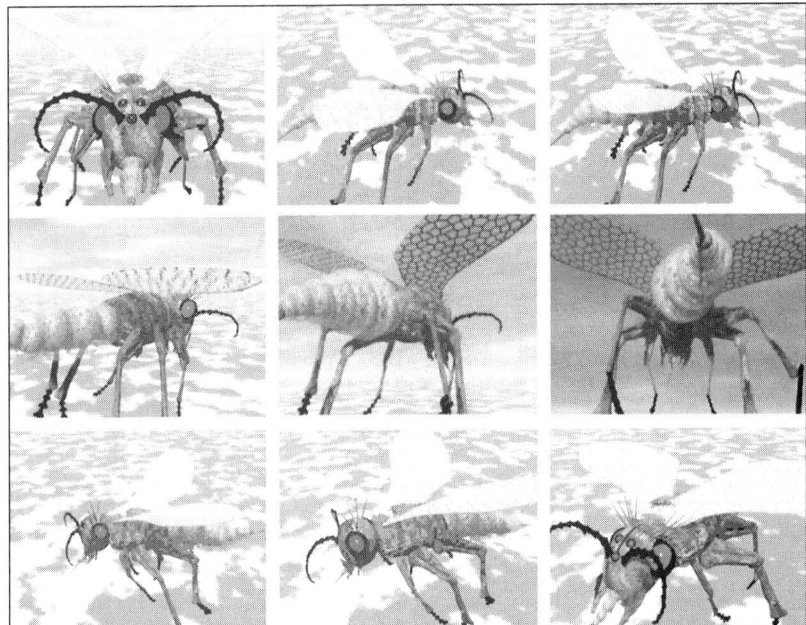

Figure 7.35
A selection of frames from the Insect.mov QuickTime animation on the CD-ROM.

> **Note:** *Be sure to check out Flite1.mov—the finished QuickTime animation for this project—on the CD-ROM.*

A Light In The Dark

This project details one of the neatest effects you can create in Bryce: shining an animated light in a dark room. You should remember two very important things when you design a project that uses this effect. First, be sure to turn the sun off in the Sky Lab. Second, make sure that all the objects in the environment have Ambience set to zero in their materials channels. A non-zero Ambience setting causes the object mapped with that material to glow in the dark (which is, of course, always an option if that is what you want an object to do). When a material's Ambience setting is zero, the material is visible only when a light shines on it.

You might use this effect to shine lights from an undersea vehicle on strange fish swimming under the sea, to shine a spotlight on a thespian on a darkened stage, or for any of a thousand different scene ideas. In this tutorial, I'll design a moving flashlight that illuminates the walls of a dark tomb.

Parts And Pieces

> **Note:** *Obviously, when you are familiar with the way this technique works, you can design a dark room with very different objects than the ones we are using here.*

This project requires the design or importation of a working flashlight, a wall, a column, and items to hang on the wall. I'll show you each one in turn and tell you how it is designed or where it is imported from.

Flashlight

The flashlight is the most complex object in the project. This is the object that contains the light in the scene, so wherever it moves, the light

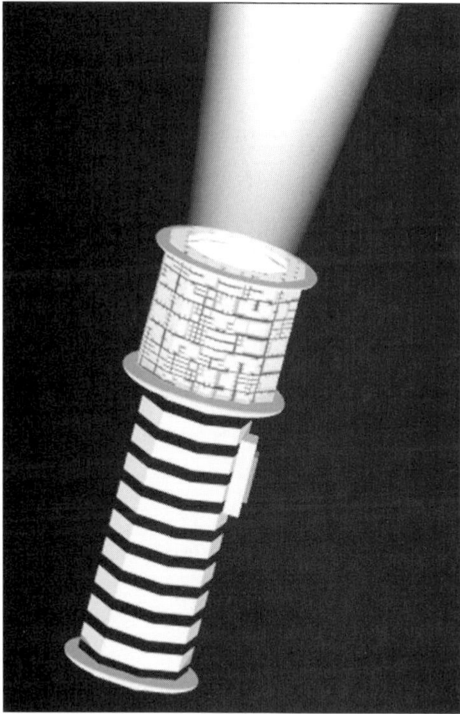

Figure 7.36
The finished flashlight is made up of a variety of components.

moves with it. This flashlight design (shown in Figure 7.36) is just one of an infinite variety that you can create, but it demonstrates the principles involved.

The flashlight is constructed from several components:

- *Shaft*—The shaft of the flashlight consists of an Eight Sided Hollow Column, which is found in the Imported Object presets directory. I wanted to use a shaft that showed some sharper edges. This object was sized X to 16, Y to 45, and Z to 16. The material used is the Worker Bee Stripes from the Wild & Fun materials presets. The material's frequency is set to 90, and it is mapped to the shaft using Object Space. This pattern allows the stripes to show the object's sharp edges. The most important material attributes are the Diffusion setting of 100 percent and the Ambience setting of 40 percent. This allows the shaft to be seen in the dark. If I hadn't done that, the light itself would have been the only thing visible, and I wanted the viewer to see the flashlight moving.
- *On/Off Switch*—The switch is made up of two grouped cubic primitives, resized to look more rectangular. The switch uses a red texture, and the switch housing uses a yellow texture. The switch protrudes a bit from the housing. Both textures have Diffusion settings of 100 percent and Ambience settings of 45 percent. This allows them to glow in the dark along with the rest of the flashlight.

- *Head*—For the head of the flashlight, I used another resized Eight Sided Hollow Column. I set the X, Y, and Z dimensions to 20. Then, I set the head on top of the shaft to hold the glass and to give the flashlight a more interesting shape. The material is what really defines the head. I could have used a solid color with enough Ambience to make it glow in the dark, but I decided to search for a unusual look. I finally settled on the BasicSin19 texture, mapped in Object Space, with a Frequency of 50. This created a flashlight head that looks like it has circuitry embedded within it. Diffusion and Ambience are set to 40 and 4 respectively, with a Bump Height of 100.
- *Holding Rings*—If you look closely at the flashlight depicted in Figure 7.36, you see that it has three holding rings. Two are at the top and bottom of the head, and the third is at the bottom of the shaft. All are the same, resized and duplicated from a torus. The size of X is set to 19.5, Y to 19.5, and Z to 1.6. This creates a flat ring, perfect for use on the flashlight.
- *Glass*—You can't really see the glass, but it's there. It mutes and spreads the light just a bit. The glass was created from a Horizontal 2D Disk and placed at the top of the head. It is mapped with a light yellow Diffuse and Ambient color, with 100 percent Diffusion and 60 percent Ambience. Transparency is set to 80 percent.
- *Spotlight*—A Spotlight is placed inside the shaft and pointed so that it aims perpendicular to the glass and parallel with the head. In the Spotlight's Edit dialog box, I chose a light yellow hue, 100 percent Intensity, 15 percent Edge Blur, Volume Visible, and a Linear Falloff. But even with a Volume Visible light, you still can't see the cone of light the way I wanted it to be seen. That's where the cone comes in.
- *Cone*—Using a resized cone primitive as a false light cone proved to be the solution I needed. The cone is resized to X is 50, Y is 200, and Z is 50, creating an elongated light cone. The material is a light yellow Diffuse and Ambient hue with a Diffusion of 0 percent and an Ambience of 100 percent. The most important aspect of the cone's material is that it is set to Fuzzy in the Material Options list, with all shadowing options off. This creates a visible light cone that adds to the flashlight effect against a dark backdrop.

I grouped the flashlight shaft, head, switch, glass, and rings. I linked the Spotlight and the cone to the grouped flashlight. I saved the resulting object to my User Object's Preset library, so now I can place it in any scene in which I need a flashlight.

Wall

For a wall, I used a cube primitive, resized to X is 20, Y is 370, and Z is 650. I used these dimensions because I wanted a wall that filled the entire view as seen by the camera. You may find that your wall needs different dimensions, depending on the camera's placement. For the material, I used the Easter Egg Dye #2 from the Wild & Fun presets. I used the material as is, with Parametric mapping. You could explore any of the other presets of course, or you could use your own materials. The wall shouldn't look too fancy, however, or it will detract from the items placed on it.

Column

I placed a column in the scene to break up the consistency of the wall. I placed the column at the left end of the wall as seen in the camera view. I imported the column from the Objects presets in the Boolean Objects directory and resized it to X is 50, Y is 300, and Z is 50. I mapped the column with the Blue Marble texture with a Frequency of 15 percent and an Object Space mapping.

Accessories

I hung two objects on the wall so that the moving flashlight would "discover" them in the dark. The first was an object I manipulated in the Terrain Editor. The object consists of a few lines of text written in hieroglyphs and edited in Photoshop. I used a hieroglyph font developed by Deniart (**www.deniart.com**). Deniart creates stylistic fonts that emulate the characters of ancient alphabets. I saved the Photoshop file and imported it into the Terrain Editor. There, I used it as a Height map on a Terrain Object. See Figure 7.37.

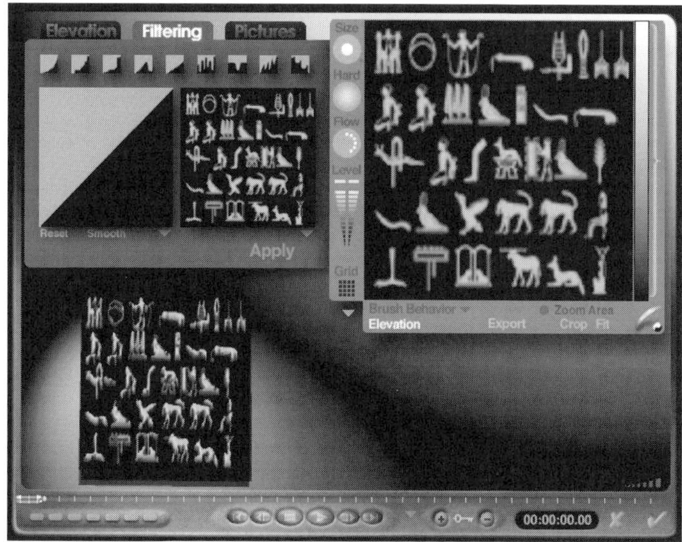

Figure 7.37
The hieroglyphic bitmap was imported into the Terrain Editor to create a 3D object.

I reduced the size so that the resulting hieroglyphs had only a slight depth, and then, I exported the new object to the scene. Next, I embedded the object in the wall within view of the camera and grouped the object with the wall.

The second object I used was a sculpted head, created in Amorphium from Play, Inc., (software that no Bryce user should be without) and saved as a DXF object. After I imported the object into the Bryce project, I duplicated the head and placed one above the other, both embedded on the right side of the wall. I textured the heads with two materials: Copper Bump and Oily Bronze, both from the Complex fx presets. I used no Ambience for either object, so the heads remain invisible until revealed by the animated flashlight.

When everything was finished and in place, I created an 8-second animation at 30 frames per second (FPS). I keyframed the flashlight to start at the top of the column on the left. From there, it moves so that the light illuminates the column from top to bottom. Then, the flashlight moves to the right (to the bottom of the hieroglyphs) and up to the top. The last movement begins at the top of the two heads and stops with the illumination of the bottom head on the right. It is quite effective. See Figure 7.38.

Remember to take a look at the finished QuickTime Flite.mov file in the Anims folder on the CD-ROM and to play with the Flite tutorial file in the Projects directory.

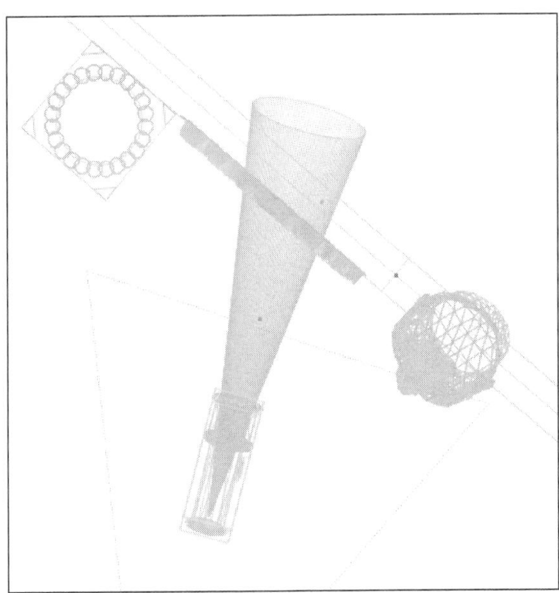

Figure 7.38
The top view of the wireframe scene shows all the elements in place. The flashlight is pointing to the hieroglyphs on the wall.

The Booley 2000

The Booley 2000 is a vehicle constructed entirely (well, 99 percent anyway) from Bryce primitives, many of which use Boolean operators to create composited elements. If you worked through the insect project, you have a good understanding of how to use the Terrain Editor to create objects. If you work though this tutorial, you will be on your way to mastery of the Boolean operators in object creation.

Sections Of The Vehicle

The Booley 2000 is composed of five design elements: roof, main body, doors, fenders, and wheels. You can see these in the exploded view shown in Figure 7.39.

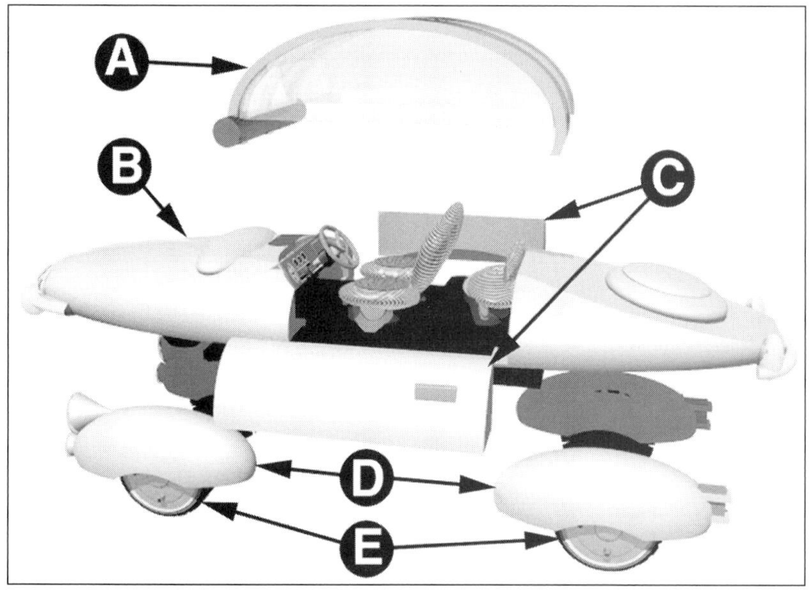

Figure 7.39
An exploded view of the Booley 2000: A. roof, B. main body, C. doors, D. fenders, and E. wheels.

Creating The Roof

After exploring several roof variations, I settled on this one. The vehicle's overall design is rather futuristic, so I wanted a roof that complimented that characteristic. I constructed the roof from a cylinder, and then mapped it with glass material with an 85 percent Transparency and a blue-green hue. As you construct the roof, don't be concerned with its overall size. You'll resize the roof to fit the rest of the vehicle as the last step in putting everything together. Refer to the wireframe drawing in Figure 7.40 as you proceed.

As shown in Figure 7.40, the roof is composited from a collection of elements: core glass enclosure, reinforcing bars, and hinge. I'll show you how to create each of these elements in the following paragraphs.

Note: *You'll find this model on this book's companion CD-ROM. Look for the Booley_1.br4 project file in the Projects folder.*

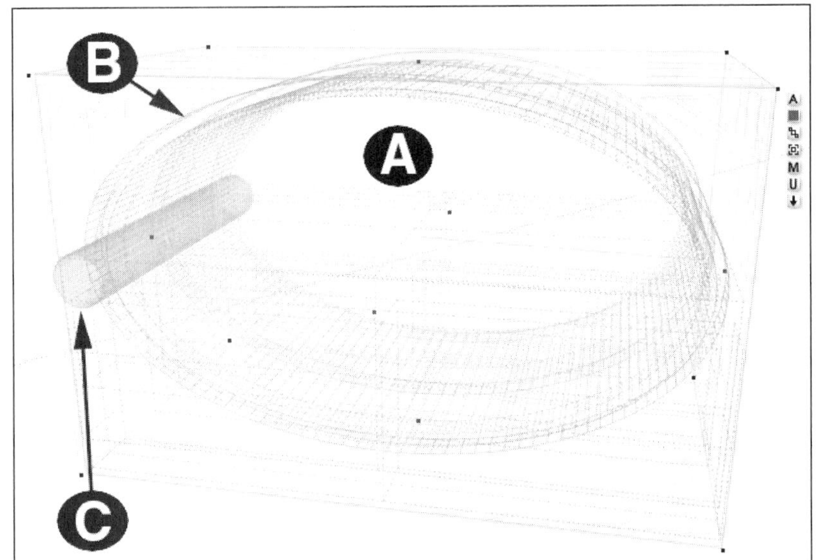

Figure 7.40
This wireframe rendering of the roof shows all of its parts: A. core glass enclosure, B. reinforcing bars, and C. hinge.

To create the core glass enclosure, follow these steps:

1. Create this element from two intersecting Boolean cylinders. The positive Boolean cylinder is sized at X is 60, Y is 30, and Z is 33. Remember that you will have to tweak the final size according to the rest of the model's requirements.
2. Construct the negative Boolean cylinder by duplicating the positive cylinder and resizing X to 56, Y to 28, and Z to 32. This places the negative cylinder inside the positive cylinder, creating a thickness for the glass.
3. Apply a Standard Glass material (from the Glass Texture presets) with an 85 percent Transparency to both cylinders. Use a light blue-green hue for the Diffuse color. Give the glass a Reflection of 25 percent.
4. Now, before grouping the elements to activate the Boolean cuts, you have to slice off the bottom of the cylinders. To do this, drop a cube primitive onto the screen, and resize X to 65, Y to 20, and Z to 40. Make the cube a negative Boolean, and place it so that it extends over the bottom half of the cylinders. Then, group the cylinders and the resized cube, activating their Boolean operators.

The three reinforcing bars guard the glass enclosure in case of a sudden impact. To create the bars, follow these steps:

1. Create a cylinder whose dimensions are 65, 40, and 7. This is the outside dimension of the reinforcing bar. Make the cylinder a positive Boolean. Use a resized cube as a negative Boolean to cut away the lower half of the reinforcing bar.

2. Create another cylindrical bar by duplicating the first one, and then resizing X to 60, Y to 30, and Z to 10. This allows the bar to fit snugly over the glass enclosure. Make this bar a negative Boolean and group it with its positive counterpart. Map the bar with a Chrome material preset.
3. Place the bar over the glass enclosure at one end, and duplicate it twice. In the top view, move the bars so that they cover equal parts of the glass enclosure. Link the three bars to the glass enclosure.

To create the hinge, follow these steps:

1. Drop a cylinder primitive onto the screen, and resize X to 5, Y to 40, and Z to 5. Map the cylinder with a Pale Blue Metal preset.
2. Place the hinge at the left end of the glass enclosure, overlapping the bottom of the reinforcing bars. Link the hinge to the rest of the glass enclosure. See Figure 7.41 for the finished roof.

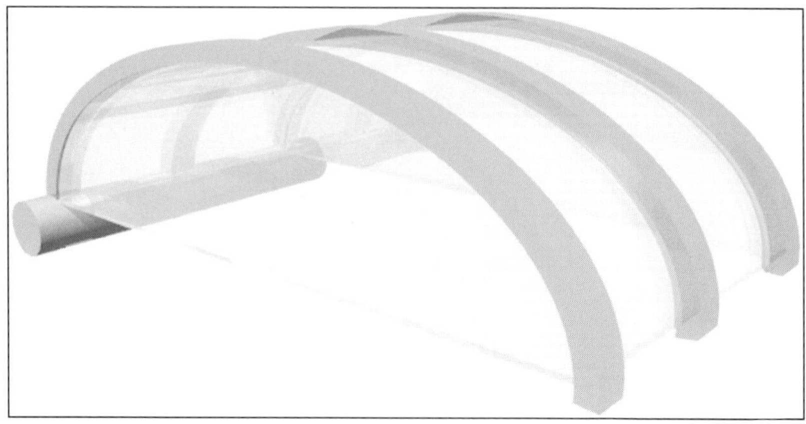

Figure 7.41
A rendering of the completed roof.

Modeling The Main Body

The main body is by far the most complex part of the Booley 2000. It is a composite of a group of separate components, each shown in Figure 7.42.

As shown in Figure 7.42, the following components make up the main body:

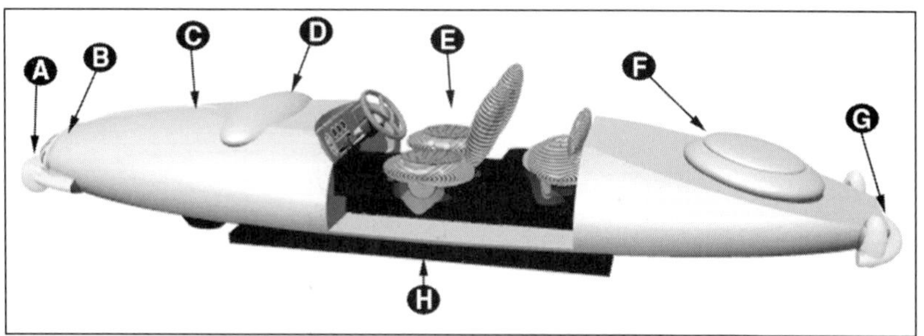

Figure 7.42
The main body of the Booley 2000 consists of many components: A. front bumper and license plate, B. grill, C. body, D. air scoop, E. cab, F. spare tire well, G. back bumper and license plate, and H. the undercarriage.

- *Front bumper and license plate*—These are two separate items, with the license plate linked to the bumper. The bumper is a Boolean construct consisting of four objects: a torus, two elongated spheres, and a cutting cube. See Figure 7.43.

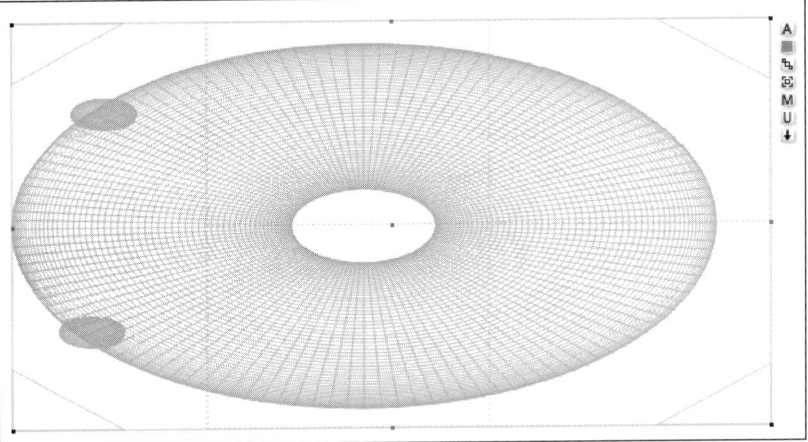

Figure 7.43
A top wireframe view of the bumper.

The torus has X set to 65, Y to 32, and Z to 4. The torus is sliced in half by a negative Boolean cube along its X dimension. The radius of the torus is set to 410; this shrinks the hole at its center. Two elongated spheres with X and Y set to 6 and Z to 3 are placed inside the torus at its left (as in Figure 7.43) and linked to the torus. These spheres are vertical components of the bumper.

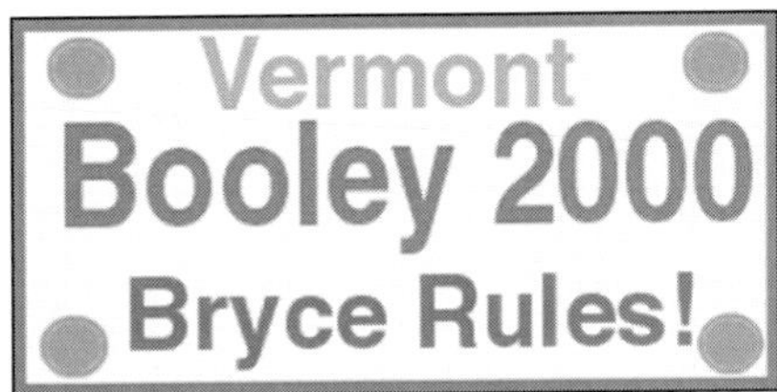

Figure 7.44
(Left) Use your favorite bitmap editing application's text capabilities to create any license plate you want, and then save it as a bitmap for use as a texture in Bryce.

Figure 7.45
(Right) The finished rendering of the front bumper with the license plate attached.

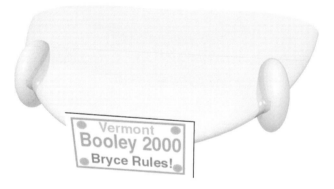

The license plate is a cube primitive with X set to 8, Y to 5, and Z to 0.5. The bitmap was created in Photoshop and mapped to the primitive using Parametric mapping. Then, the finished license plate is linked to the bumper torus. The finished bumper—with the license plate attached—is linked to the body. See Figures 7.44 and 7.45.

- *Grill*—The grill is a special part of the overall body design and deserves special attention here. The grill is a pure Boolean construct that uses a series of angled cubic primitives to cut slots in the front of the body. The example in Figure 7.46 uses fifteen negative cubes to do the trick, with some next to each other in order to vary the widths. The X dimension is set to 40, Y to 20, and Z to 0.5. The Z dimension, 0.5, is the thickness of the cut. The negative cutters produce a cut at the needed angle, and the angle is something you can vary according to the look you want. Obviously, you could also use non-cubic cutters and create a fancier grill design. See Figure 7.46.

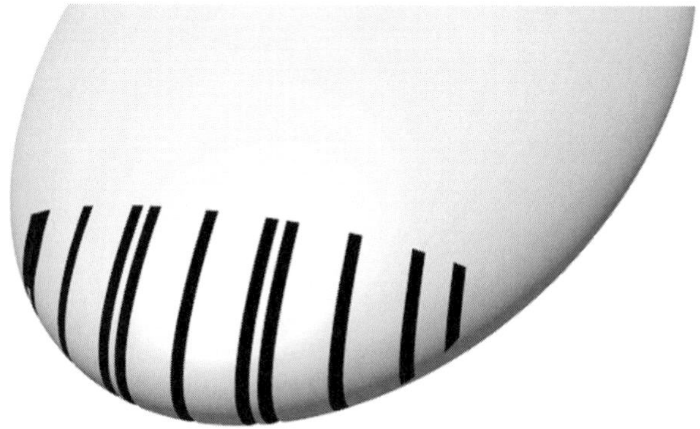

Figure 7.46
The rendered grill, showing the effect of the Boolean cutters on the front of the body.

- *Body*—The overall body design of the Booley 2000 is based on an elongated sphere (a positive Boolean) sliced by three negative Boolean cubes. The body has X set to 163, Y to 25, and Z to 47 and is mapped with the Pale Blue Metal preset. The first cube is placed just in front of the X axis midpoint at the top of the body. That cube's dimensions are X equals 32, Y is 23, and Z is 43. The cube cuts away the middle of the body with the exception of a small "floor" element. Another cubic primitive slices off the upper one-fifth of the body, and a third cuts off the total underside at about midway. See Figure 7.47 for reference.
- *Air scoop*—I owe thanks to my daughter for this feature. Upon seeing the model in progress, she commented that its speedy look demanded an air scoop on the hood, and so I added one. The air scoop is designed with a Boolean construct consisting of two sphere primitives. The positive component has X set to 14, Y to 24, and Z to 7. The negative component has X set to 13.5, Y to 21, and Z to 6. The negative component is placed inside the positive component, as displayed in Figure 7.48, and the rendered results are shown in Figure 7.49.

  The scoop is eventually embedded about half-way in the top of the body, just in front of the cab cutout area.

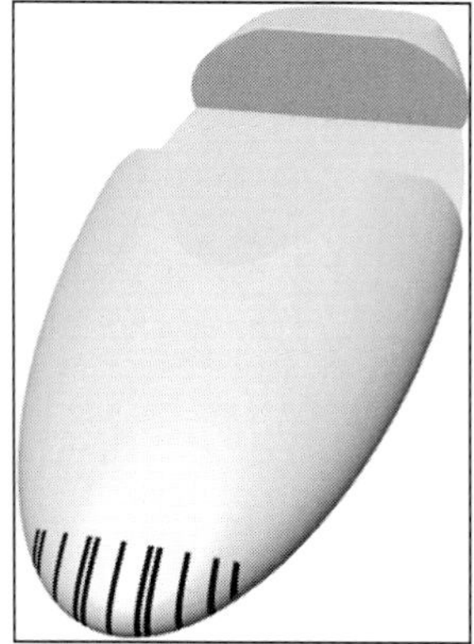

Figure 7.47
The finished body is sculpted by three negative Boolean primitives.

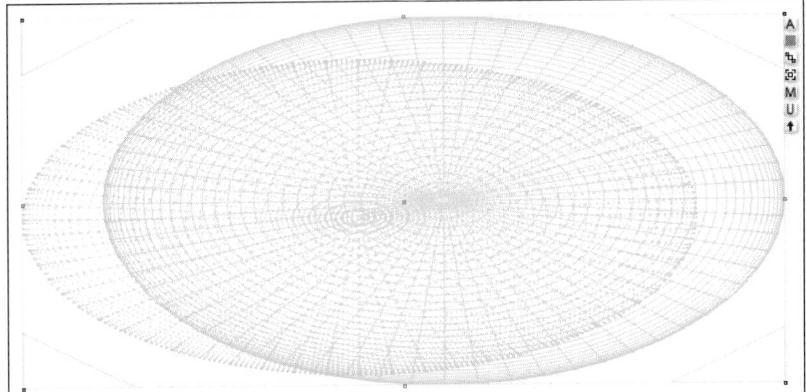

Figure 7.48
The scoop is created from two Boolean sphere primitives.

Figure 7.49
The rendered scoop.

- *Cab*—This is the most complex part of the body because it involves more than one object. You can of course use your own design ideas instead of what I have used on this model. Because the cab is so customizable, I am not going to discuss dimensions or the exact way these elements interact. You can intuit a lot just by looking at Figure 7.50. For instance, you can see that the front seats are duplicates of

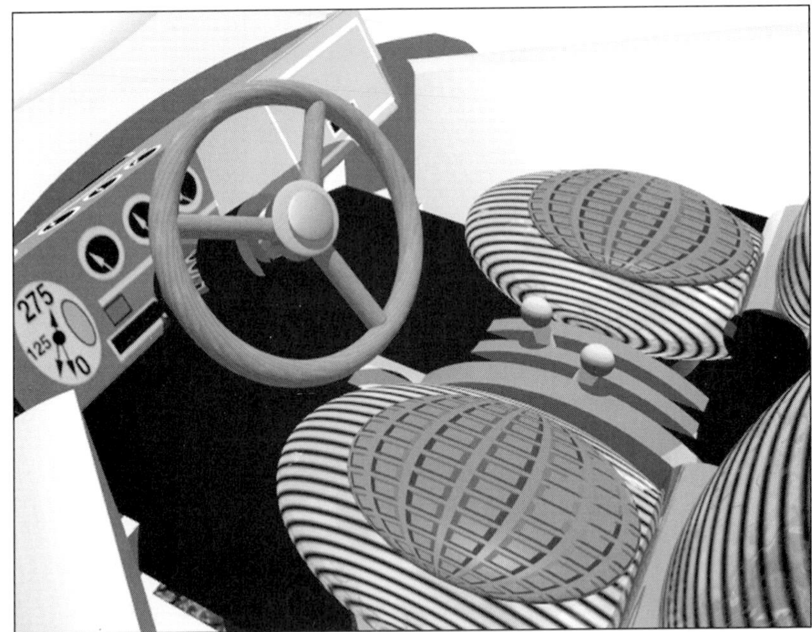

Figure 7.50
The components that make up the cab create the necessary realism if you intend to open the roof or the doors to see inside the Booley 2000.

each other. The back seat is an elongated front seat. The dashboard features a bitmap mapped to a stretched cube, and the steering wheel completes the arrangement. Open the Booley_1 project on this book's companion CD-ROM if you want to investigate the specific components further. All the elements are linked to the body.

- *Spare tire compartment*—Create the spare tire compartment (shown in Figure 7.51) by grouping two customized tori. The top is a smaller duplicate of the bottom. I tried using cylinders for this initially, but the flat sides just didn't feel right. The tori have a radius setting of 800, which completely closes the hole in the center. This produces a smooth, button-like object. On the large torus, the X and Y dimensions are set to 24, and Z is set to 6. On the smaller torus, the dimensions are X and Y equal 18, and Z is 3. The tori are placed on the back of the body and linked to it.

Figure 7.51
The finished spare tire compartment.

- *Back bumper and license plate*—The back bumper and license plate are just duplicates of the front bumper and license plate, reversed and resized to fit the back of the body.
- *Undercarriage*—The design of this element is left up to you. It can range from a simple cubic shape to a detailed undercarriage element. If you never see the undercarriage except as a shadowed element, there's no use for a detailed object.

Sculpting The Doors

The doors (shown in Figure 7.52) are basic Boolean constructs. Cubic negative Booleans cut away parts of a positive Boolean cylinder so that only one-quarter remains. The doors are resized so that they fit in the holes on the side of the cab. Move each door's Origin Handle to the back of the body so that the door can open correctly.

Designing The Fenders

The fenders are constructed by combining three resized sphere primitives in a Boolean operation: One sphere is positive and two are negative. One

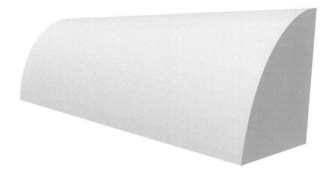

Figure 7.52
The doors are created by cutting away three-quarters of a cylinder primitive.

of the negative spheres hollows out the fender, and the other cuts away at the positive sphere from the side. The dimensions of the positive Boolean sphere are X equals 21, Y is 41, and Z is 12. This sphere is duplicated, resized to 20, 40, and 12, and then placed inside the positive sphere to hollow it out. The second negative sphere (X and Y equal 27, and Z is 19) intersects the positive one from the side, creating a scooped area (as shown in Figure 7.53).

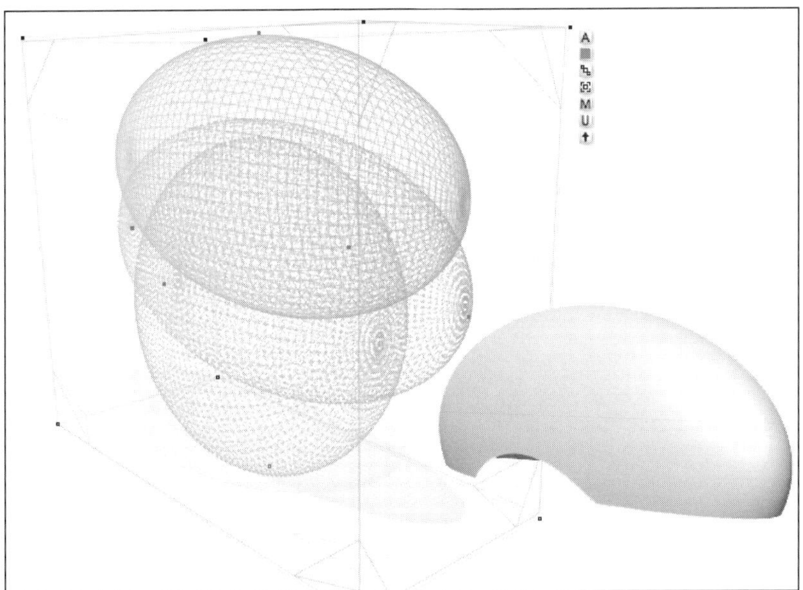

Figure 7.53
The fender's wireframe composite on the left with the rendered version on the right.

Crafting The Tires

Let's face it, there's so much detail in this model already that you could easily get away with using a compressed cylinder with a black hue to simulate the tires. But, I had other things in mind. I wanted to design a tire that I could save in the Objects library for use with other models. I also wanted to explore the use of Boolean operators to create tire treads. The tire model shown in Figure 7.54 is the result of these explorations.

Note: *You can add headlights to the fenders by linking a hollow cone. You can link a Spotlight inside the cone for use in night scenes.*

I had to spend some time exploring the angles to use in order to create the treads. I settled on a cubic primitive with X set to 1, Y to 20, and Z to 7. I placed the cube inside the tire from the top view, penetrating the tire just slightly. In the front view, I rotated the cubic cutter to -90, 26, and 160 along the respective X, Y, and Z axes. I duplicated the cutter and flipped it on its X axis. This resulted in an *X* shape. I duplicated these two cutters as many times as I needed in order to complete the perimeter of the tire. I made all the cutters negative Booleans and grouped them with the positive Boolean tire. See Figure 7.55.

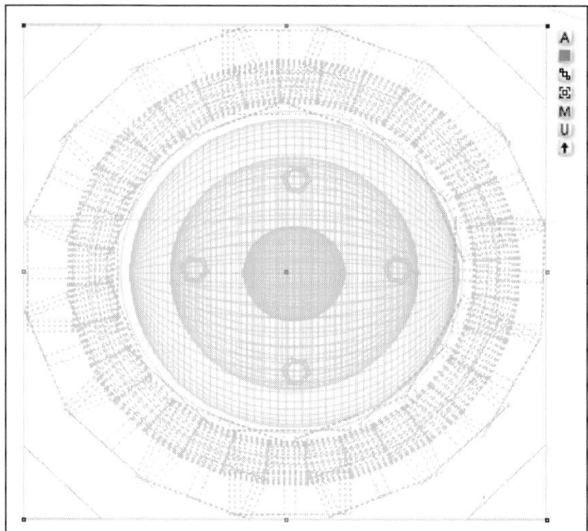

Figure 7.54

(Left) This complex tire model features cut treads and a hub cap arrangement.

Figure 7.55

(Right) The top view shows the complex wireframe that resulted from creating the negative Boolean cutters for the tire treads.

I used two squashed cylinders (with the same dimensions as the tire) to add a whitewall look and a squashed sphere to add the hubcap. I imported the four hex nuts (visible in Figure 7.54) from the Imported Objects presets (the Six Side Hollow object), and resized them to fit.

One Final Addition

I could have created a Boolean composite to act as a hood ornament, but I cheated. I couldn't resist designing a pose for the Horse model in Poser and exporting it as a 3DS model. It adds the finishing touch, as you can see in Figures 7.56 and 7.57.

The Garden

There is something magical about flowers. In the presence of flowers, all of our cares and anxieties seem to quiet down, at least temporarily. Bryce offers no way to populate a world with flora, but there is a way to use other software to prepare floral content for a Bryce world.

Figure 7.56
The Hood Ornament is an imported Poser model.

The Perfect Flower Engine

MetaCreations' Painter offers a way to create flowers that are more than 2D but less than 3D: more than 2D because the bitmaps exist in a 3D environment, but less than 3D because the flowers are mapped to planar surfaces (so the flowers can be appreciated only from the front). But this method allows you to simulate a 3D look for your planar maps. You can move the camera around the scene. The effect can be quite hypnotic, so I'll get right to it. (You need to have Painter on hand, and you need to know how to use it.)

1. In Painter, select File|New, which opens the New Picture dialog box. Create a new 400-by-100-pixel picture at 150 dpi. See Figure 7.58.
2. (This step assumes that you know how to use Painter's Image Hose.) Click on the Brush tool, and then on the Image Hose. Using any flower nozzle in your library, spray flowers on the image, as shown in Figure 7.59. Stay away from the top of the image. Use any other nozzles you prefer for greenery or other flower types. When you're finished, save the image as a PICT on the Mac or as a BMP in Windows.
3. In Painter or your favorite bitmap editing software, import the image you just created. Use the Magic Wand tool to select the white background (in Photoshop, choose Selection|Select Similar). The entire background is selected. Invert the selection. Now everything but the background is selected. Fill the selected area with a solid RGB Black (RGB = 0, 0, 0). Now you have a two-color image: a white background and a black silhouetted flower group, as shown in Figure 7.60. Save the image with the same name as the original, but put a "G" at the end of the name. (Again, use a PICT for Mac and a BMP for Windows.)

Note: *If you like, you can place a family of Poser models in the cab and set them on an animated journey.*

Figure 7.57

A series of views of the complete Booley 2000 model, which is also in the Projects folder on the CD-ROM that accompanies this book.

4. Open Bryce, and place a cylinder primitive in the workspace. Open the cylinder's Materials Lab. Load the color bitmap you created into the first image area and the black and white silhouetted bitmap into the second image area. Hit the reverse button above the second image area to create a white silhouette on a black background, as shown in Figure 7.61.

5. Click on the check mark to return to the Materials Lab's main screen. Place a button in the first channel for Diffuse, Ambient, Transparent color, Diffusion and Ambience Value, and Transparency Optics. Select Parametric mapping with a frequency of 0. Look at the

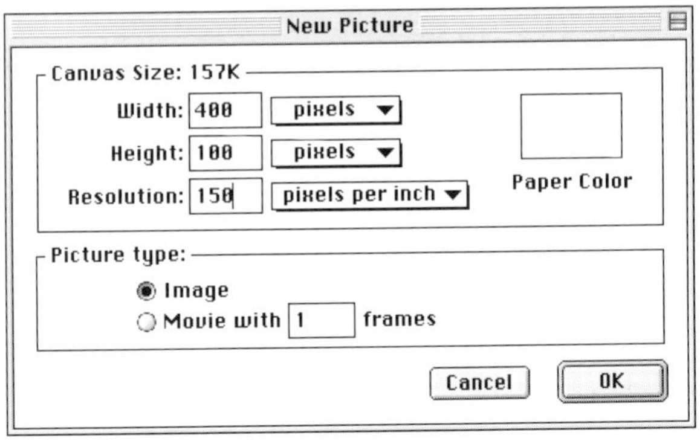

New Picture

Canvas Size: 157K

Width: 400 pixels

Height: 100 pixels

Resolution: 150 pixels per inch

Paper Color

Picture type:

Image

Movie with 1 frames

Cancel OK

Figure 7.58

(Top left) Create a new canvas of 400 by 100 pixels at 150 dpi.

Figure 7.59

(Top right) Painter's Image Hose makes it easy to create a group of flowers.

Figure 7.60

(Bottom left) A new image is saved, showing the flowers as a black silhouette. This will be used for our Alpha channel content in the Bryce Picture Editor.

Nano Preview and you'll see the flower bitmap (with its background transparent) mapped to the cylinder, as in Figure 7.62.

6. Duplicate the cylinder about 12 times. In the top view, arrange the cylinders to create random overlaps and variations in size, as shown in Figures 7.63 and 7.64.

7. If you animate the camera along only the Z axis (that is, into or out of the screen), this clump of 2D flowers works fairly well as a 3D construct. There is enough variety and overlap to fool the eye. Place

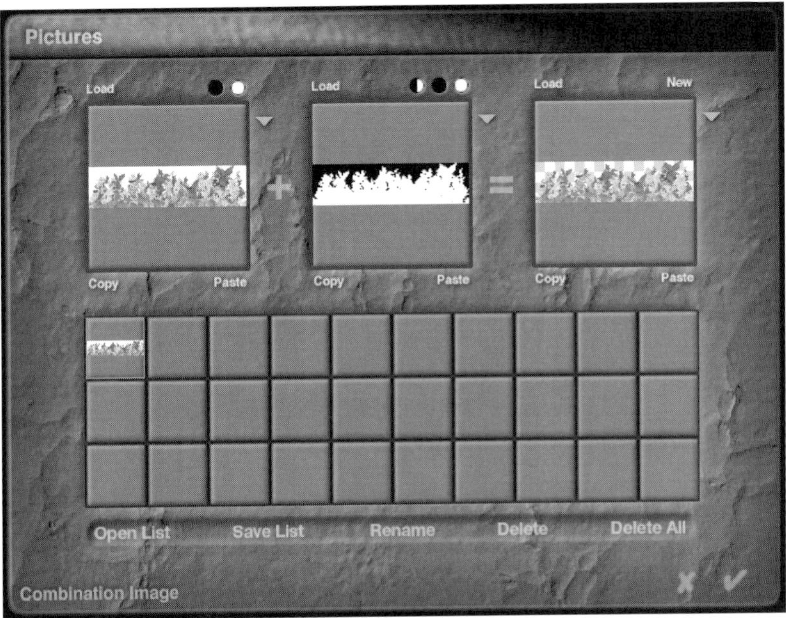

Figure 7.61

The bitmaps are loaded into the Picture Editor module of the cylinder's Materials Lab.

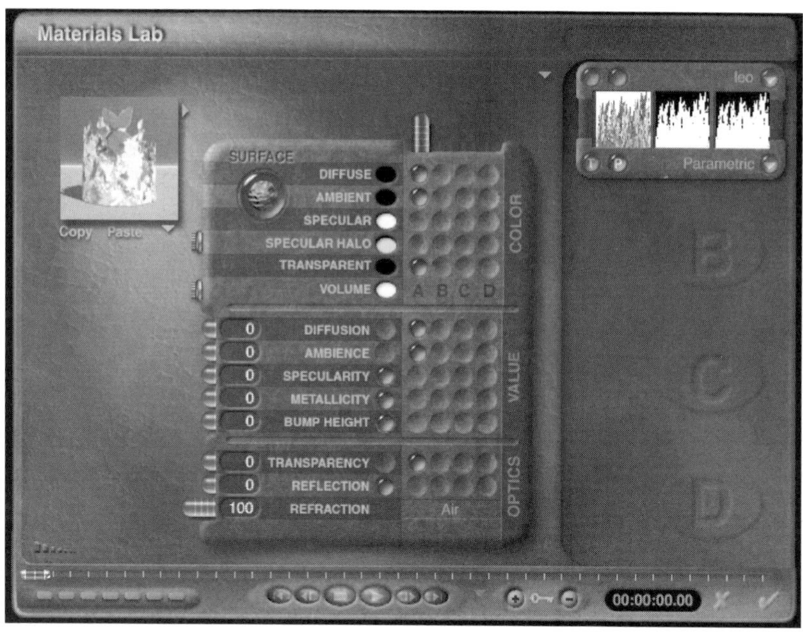

Figure 7.62

The bitmap and its Alpha channel are applied in the Materials Lab.

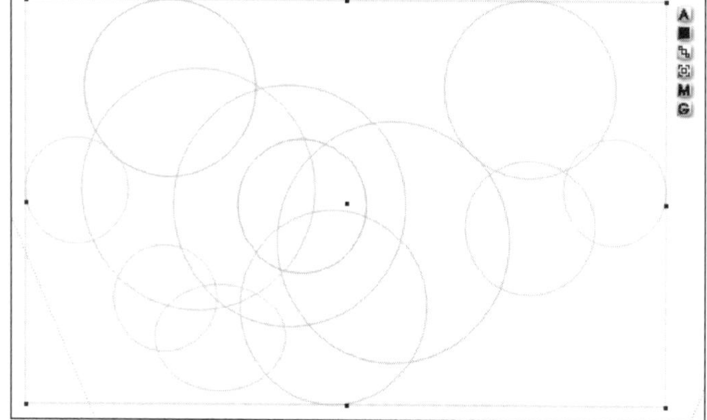

Figure 7.63

The top view of the group of mapped cylinders.

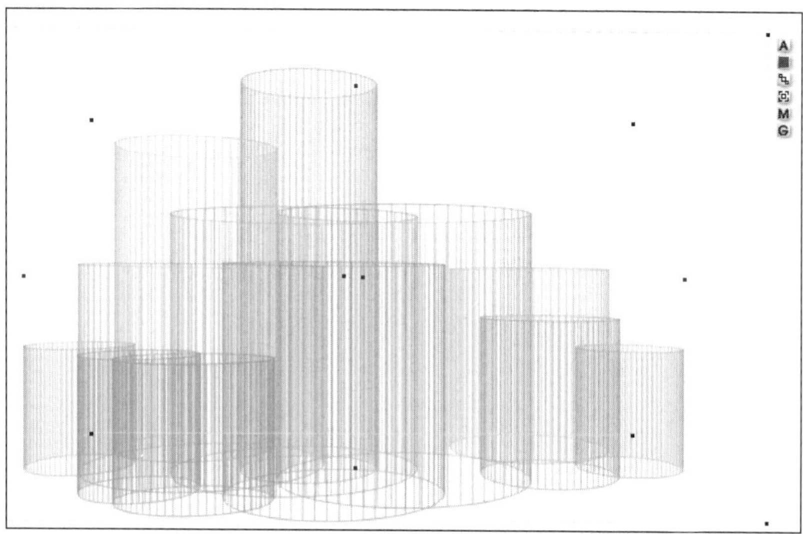

Figure 7.64

The same group of mapped cylinders, as seen in camera view.

Figure 7.65
The rendered scene with the mapped cylinders. Some well-placed rocks and a 3D plant in the background help blend the 2D content into the image more effectively.

some 3D rocks on the ground and add a stream and a sky, and you have created a Bryce scene populated with flora. See Figure 7.65.

Wild Ride

This is an animation project. You'll find the finished QuickTime animations—Wildride1.mov and Wildride2.mov—in the Anims folder on this book's CD-ROM. Follow these steps to create the project:

1. In Bryce, import the Between 8 And Mobius ribbon path (shown in Figure 7.66) from the Paths folder in the Objects Library.
2. Now it's time to create a simple air car. You can customize the car for greater complexity if you like, but I'll use just the simple version in this tutorial. The car is composed of two resized spheres in a Boolean operation. Create a sphere with X set to 50 and Y and Z set to 20. Make this sphere a positive Boolean. Create another sphere whose dimensions are X equals 28, Y is 20, and Z is 18. Make this second sphere a negative Boolean and place it inside the first sphere, as shown in Figure 7.67. Group them to activate the Boolean operation. See Figure 7.68.

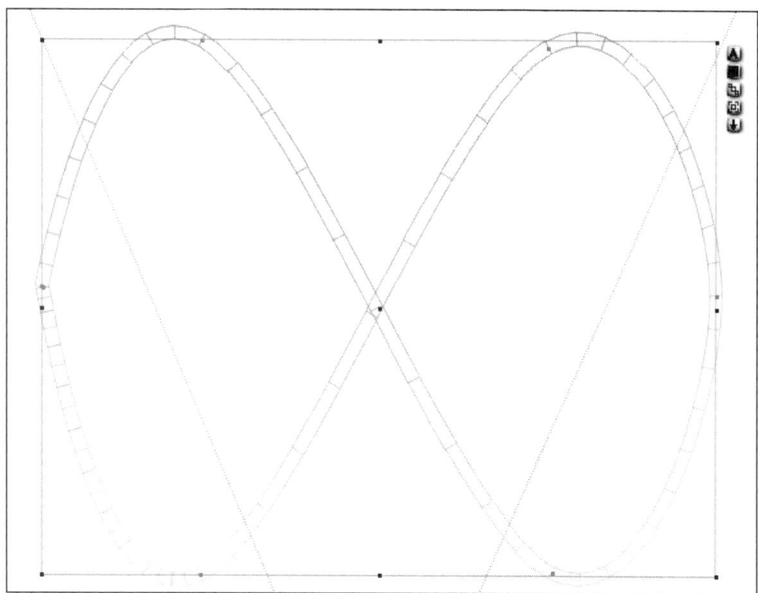

Figure 7.66

The top view of the Between 8 And Mobius ribbon path.

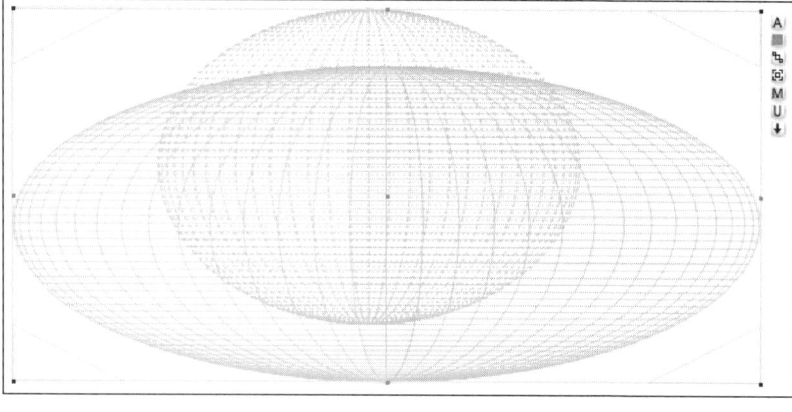

Figure 7.67

A wireframe view of the Boolean car.

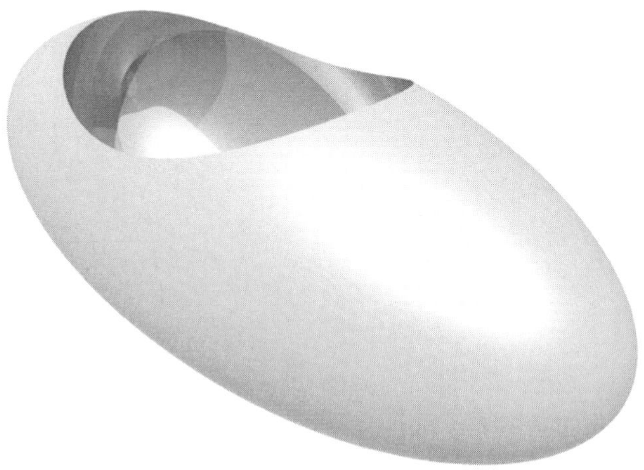

Figure 7.68

The rendered car, mapped with a Yellow Gold material preset.

3. With the car selected, link it to the path. It will snap in place. Don't use the move tool to move the car on the path. Instead, click on the car and drag it with the mouse. This moves the car on the path in either direction, and freezes it when it comes to the starting and ending points.
4. Create a 12-second, 30 FPS animation for this project. Leave Alignment off. Some objects align themselves in a bizarre manner, so it's best to tweak alignments with keyframing. Move the car to the start of the path and keyframe it for the first frame. Move the Timeline lozenge to the last frame, and move the car to the end of the path. If Automatic keyframing (Auto-Key) is on, the car will be keyframed accordingly. Otherwise, you'll have to click on the Add keyframe button to keyframe it.
5. Go to the top view. When you move the Timeline lozenge along the Timeline, the car should move as well. You have set only two keyframes so far, the first and the last. Now it's time to align the car so that it turns on the path's curves. Still working in the top view, move the lozenge until the car is positioned just ahead of the first curve. Rotate the car on the Y axis until it lines up with the path correctly. Hit the Add keyframe button to keyframe it. Move the car to just beyond the first curve, rotate, and keyframe again. Do this before and after every curve on the path.
6. If you like, place a human or animal model in the car, and link the model to the car. In my Wildride example, I used the Zygote Chimp model from Poser, configured to sit in a meditation pose. I exported the model as a 3DS file and imported it into Bryce. You can use whatever model you like for this purpose, or you can simply animate an empty car.
7. In frame 1, move and rotate the camera so that it sits slightly above and to one side of the car (either side will do) so that the entire car and its contents are visible in the camera view. Using the camera's Attributes dialog box, set the Camera Tracking to the car. Now, no matter where the car moves in the scene, the camera always looks at it.
8. At this point, the rest of this project is up to you. You can add any objects of interest you want, but make sure that nothing intersects the car's path. Bryce doesn't have object detection, so anything placed in the way of the path is rendered as a black series of frames until the car moves beyond the blockage. You can, however, create

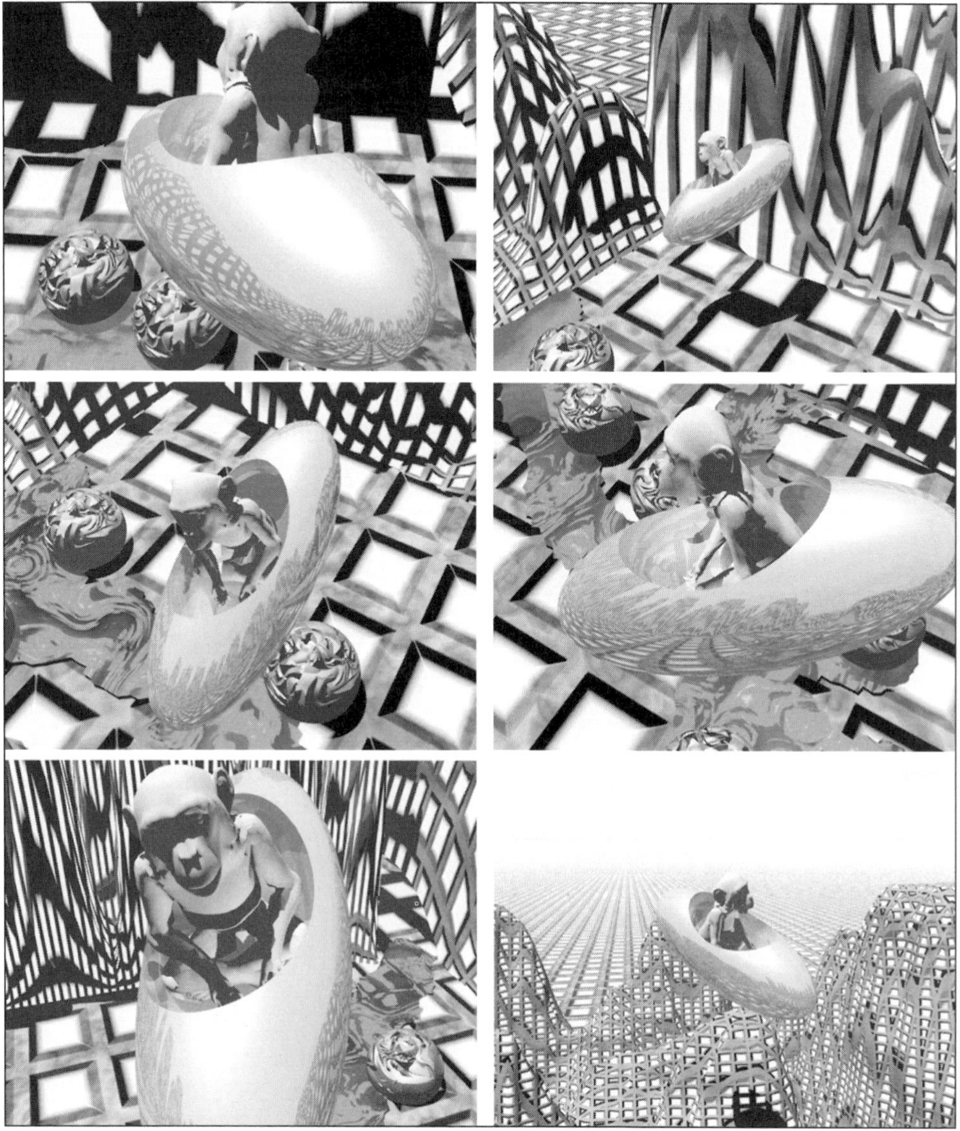

Figure 7.69
This series of frames from the Wildride animation shows how I configured the Bryce content for the scene.

tunnels or other items of interest. When the scene is complete, preview the wireframe animation from the camera view, and then render and save. See Figure 7.69.

Canoma

This final section of the chapter is not a project tutorial: It offers a look at a new MetaCreations application that you must have if you are a devoted Bryce user. Called Canoma, it is an example of the latest technical wizardry. You can use Canoma to turn elements of 2D photos into actual textured 3D objects for placement in Bryce. In a few easy steps, and with no need to apply textures in the Materials Lab, Canoma creates true photorealistic content.

How Canoma Works

Canoma makes ingenious use of applying 2D information to perspective structures. Using a new "intelligent" technology, Canoma guesses how and where textures should be applied to a 3D object derived from a 2D source. This makes it possible to speed up the creation of your Bryce world content dramatically when compared to internal Bryce methods. By using object primitives and altering their control points, Canoma's 2D bitmap texturing data fills in the planes of selected 3D constructs. All of this takes place with the aid of an interface that looks and feels very much like Bryce's (see Figure 7.70). If you know Bryce, you already have a good working knowledge of Canoma.

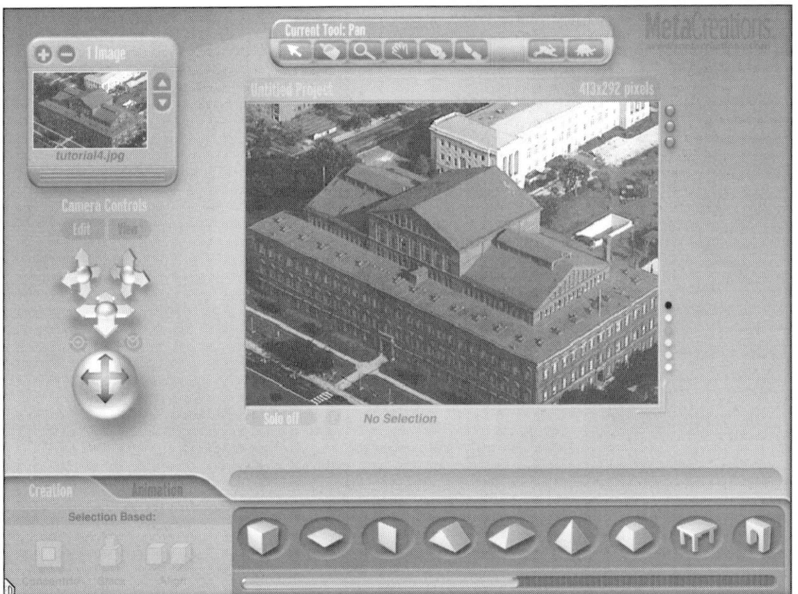

Figure 7.70
Canoma's interface is very much like Bryce's.

As you can see on the bottom of Figure 7.70, Canoma offers a number of primitive shapes. You place these wireframe constructs over object areas that have a similar shape. Then you alter the wireframe by moving control points until it matches the bitmap area underneath, and texturing is set in motion. Once completed, you have a real, 3D textured object that you can manipulate. Canoma also features "texture stealing" that allows the object's invisible faces to borrow textures from the visible areas. You can also use multiple images to texture an object and create QuickTime animations. You'll want to export Canoma objects as Wavefront OBJ files for use in Bryce worlds. The 3D Canoma models enter Bryce as grouped objects. Ungrouping them allows you to use Bryce textures on any or all the parts. See Figure 7.71.

Figure 7.71

The building depicted in Figure 7.70 was outlined in Canoma and saved as a Wavefront OBJ file. Imported into Bryce, duplicated, and resized, the model becomes the basis for a village by the sea (Bryce materials have been applied to the roofs).

Expanding Bryce Export Options

Although Bryce 4 can export objects as different formats, this works only with Terrain and Symmetrical Lattice object types. You can't, for example, create a textured cubic primitive and export it to Poser with its texture intact. But if you use Canoma, you can do just that. Here's what to do:

1. Create a model in Bryce whose elements resemble one or more of the Canoma primitive structures (the simplest would be a cubic object).
2. Use the Materials Lab to apply whatever texture or material you like to the object.
3. Rotate the object so that you can see two sides and the top.
4. Render the image. Use a white backdrop (with no sky), and remove any Ground Plane. Use High Antialiasing when you render the image.
5. Save the image, and open Canoma (if your system has less than 64MB of RAM, you may have to quit Bryce first).
6. Use Canoma's File|Add Image command to select the image you just saved from Bryce. The image appears in Canoma's preview window.
7. Use the appropriate Canoma wireframe structure to define the edges of the 3D object you are about to create by manipulating the wireframe structure's control points.

Note: *It's a good idea to heighten an image's contrast in an image editing application first before working with it in Canoma. This helps pop the texture out of the object when you use it in Bryce.*

Note: *This makes many of your textured objects in Bryce (in addition to the Terrain and Symmetrical Lattice objects Bryce can create) available for export to other 3D applications.*

8. Make sure Texture Stealing is on. Select Apply High Quality Textures from the Canoma Textures menu. Preview the object by rotating it in space, and save it as a Wavefront object (.OBJ).

Three Canoma-Bryce Project Ideas

Here are three project ideas that demonstrate a range of uses for a Canoma-Bryce partnership.

Paintings In 2D For 3D

Create the 2D bitmap of the object in perspective in your favorite bitmap application. Then, export the bitmap into Canoma, where it can be made into a 3D model. Why would you want to do this?

- You have much more control when you create a bitmap to your specifications than you do when you try to create the same texturing effect in Bryce by using Procedurals.
- You can avoid using the Picture Editor in Bryce to place textures on the finished 3D object because the textures are automatically applied when the object is imported (provided the object was saved as a Wavefront OBJ).
- You can apply multiple textures to the object that will later be translated into 3D, or create different textures to alternate object parts. These actions are not possible in Bryce.
- When working with the object types supported by Canoma, it is much faster to create those objects in Canoma than it is to create the same objects in Bryce using grouping or Boolean methods.
- Canoma offers more object primitives than Bryce.

See Figures 7.72, 7.73, and 7.74.

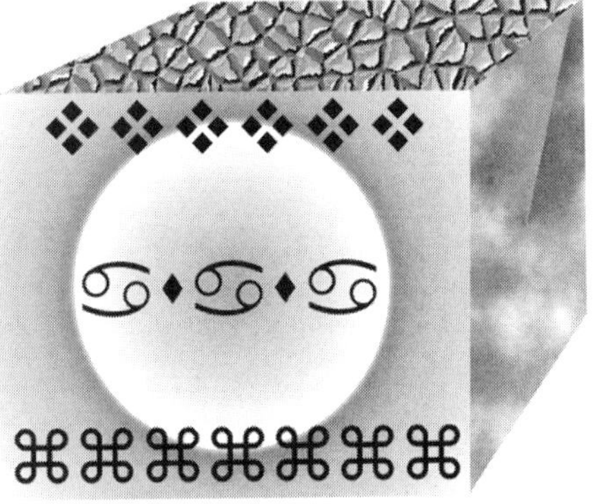

Figure 7.72
A "fake" 3D image, created in Photoshop, that simulates a 3D box.

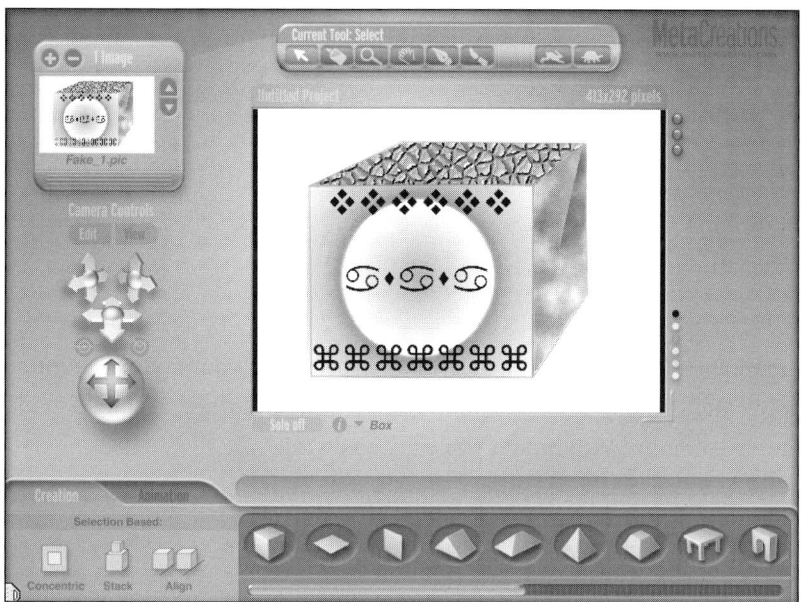

Figure 7.73
The image is transported to Canoma for 3D transformation.

Figure 7.74
Now the image is a real 3D object (shown here in a Bryce environment).

The Library

If you're looking for another fun way to explore Canoma and Bryce, use a digital camera to take a picture of a volume of an encyclopedia. Capture a perspective that shows the front, top, and spine. Save the image and import it into Canoma. Process the image as a 3D object, save it as a Wavefront OBJ, and import the object into Bryce. Create some shelves, and duplicate the volume fifty or more times to populate the bookshelves.

Turn some of the volumes in a random fashion. This image occupies very little RAM and renders very quickly. You can use it to simulate a library that animated figures can browse through.

DigiTown

If you go to a hobby store that sells electric train sets, you will find hundreds of kits for building model buildings, allowing you to create towns featuring all of the expected building types. Using Canoma and a digital camera, you can populate your Bryce worlds with all of the buildings you need. Just build the model of the house of other structure from one of the kits. Use your digital camera to capture a perspective view of the structure. Then, use Canoma's 2D to 3D conversion capabilities to transform the digital image into a real 3D model, ready for placement in your Bryce environment. Nothing could be simpler or more effective. Do this with several scaled models, and you have a walk-through town.

In Closing

I hope you have enjoyed these excursions through the wondrous realms of Bryce, and I hope that this book has enhanced your learning. Bryce remains one of the most open-ended and versatile creative digital tools on the market, and future versions will add even more capacities for creative design and astounding effects. Stay tuned.

Appendix A: Bryce 4.1 Update

Bryce is continuously being updated. This appendix refers to version 4.1, which was released as this book was going to press.

Just as this book was being readied for press, MetaCreations released an updated version of Bryce 4. Much of the following description of the update is extremely technical, and none of the updated features affects this book's information or tutorials.

Bryce 4.1 Updater Content

With the introduction of Bryce 4.1, MetaCreations has added a number of features and fixed a number of problems:

- Converted the new texture engine to double precision in order to avoid quantization errors.
- Made the PICT Sequence movie plug-in append the .pct extension to each image file name, rather than the .p extension. Also, a bug was fixed to ensure that there is enough space to append the additional text to the file name.
- Fixed a Mac bug that prevented images with a .p extension from loading in association with a scene.
- Fixed a bug that caused Bryce 3D scenes saved with the Volumetric World (Fine) setting to be loaded using the new planet Sky model. These images now load with the proper settings.
- Improved the conversion of the Sky model's Atmosphere Off mode in scenes created with versions of Bryce earlier than version 4. Old scenes—such as the Simple White Background Sky preset—are now converted to match the original more accurately.
- Fixed a long-standing problem with the Windows version involving Sky presets. Since the release of the original Bryce 2 for Windows, some Sky presets were saved without the proper flags set.
- Fixed a bug in the OBJ importer that prevented objects with an empty group statement from being recognized on the Mac. This update also improves Nano handling by allowing changes to the document (either through New Document or Document Setup) to interrupt the Nano rendering. Now the operations occur immediately rather than after the Nano rendering finishes.
- Added a mode to Movie Preview that displays movie frames with drop shadows.
- Fixed a small bug in which the check mark next to the Movie Preview menu's Storyboard option appeared even when the option was disabled.
- Fixed a bug that could have caused a crash if an error occurred during the rendering of a Movie Preview.

- Fixed a bug in which Movie Preview frames were rendered off-screen if the document was too big to fit on the screen.
- Made the default Movie Preview playing mode use the main animation Play mode rather than the Repeating mode.
- Fixed a bug that sometimes caused the Cumulus and Stratus clouds to be turned on while adjusting cloud cover and height from the Sky & Fog Palette, even if one of the cloud layers was turned on already.
- Fixed a bug in which the user interface was not updated after using the Find File dialog boxes within the LightWave OBJ importers.
- Fixed a bug in which the wrong date stamp was applied to a file that was saved over an existing file.
- Made text-based importers and exporters always use a period as the decimal point.
- Updated the Help file: The Help Topics option in the Help menu now reads "What's New."
- Added a control to BryceTalk to disable the Talk button, and changed the Links menu to the Internet menu.
- Fixed a bug that corrupted file extensions when using the Export Image or Render To Disk functions.
- Lengthened the fade-in time for the opening credits.
- Removed all Axiom virtual memory usage on the PC.
- Fixed a bug in which scenes that had spaces in their file or directory names did not respond properly when double-clicked on or dropped onto the program.
- Fixed a bug in which scenes did not resume rendering properly if they were loaded with the Load Image With Scene option disabled. (The resumed rendering was usually filled with a pattern of white dots.)
- Made the Windows version display a detailed error message when plug-in loading fails.
- Added a control to randomize the starfield in the Sky Lab: Hold down Option or Alt when turning on the stars or the comets.
- Fixed a bug in which the sun and moon icons failed to update when a numerical altitude value was entered in the Sky Lab.
- Fixed a bug in the Windows version in which Bryce 2 scene files were loaded as Bryce 3D or 4 scene files, crashing the program.

- Made a number of significant enhancements to the way starfields are handled. In previous versions, the starfields were never copied into the skies used for the Bryce's Nano renderings. This meant that in many cases, the stars changed from rendering to rendering. The setting in the Sky Lab's Intensity, Stars, and Comets controls are now persistent. Selective changes made to stars or comets no longer change the entire starfield.
- Fixed a bug in which the AVI movie plug-in showed the wrong compression settings after those settings had been altered.
- Allowed the path to the resource DAT files to be customized for both the main and plug-in resources.
- Fixed a bug in the Windows version that caused a crash if you changed the AVI compression settings, switched to the QuickTime movie plug-in, and then tried to render a movie.
- Changed some of the sky Timeline descriptions to match the Sky Lab's interface more closely.
- Added a control to the Edit Light dialog box: You can now manipulate the range value used by the Ranged Falloff option. Hold down Option or Alt, and then click on and drag in the Nano preview.
- Added a drop shadow to the Edit HTML dialog.
- Improved the LightWave and OBJ importers' Find File function so that the function learns more from the files it finds. The new method requires far fewer instances of file finding per import. One is sufficient in many cases.
- Fixed a bug in which clicking the Movie Preview's Play button did not use the current play mode, even when the Play Using Mode option was selected.
- Made exporting Symmetrical Lattices to some exporters—such as OBJ and DXF—no longer cause crashes.
- Fixed a bug in which all available image maps were saved with exported terrains, regardless of the image map selections in the Export Lab.
- In the Macintosh version, changed the color of the border around the wireframe display from black to medium gray.
- Modified the RaySpray cursor so that it has little spray particles coming out of the nozzle.

- Made the current-time indicator on the Timeline update while generating and playing a Movie Preview in non-storyboard mode.
- Fixed a bug that caused RaySpray to malfunction when the rendered image was larger than the wireframe image or when the rendered image was panned or zoomed.
- Added a Bryce4 Help item to the Mac version's Help menu; the localized version now launches a PDF help file.
- Made the random application of a material to newly created rocks, terrains, and Water or Cloud Planes more random. (Previous versions always followed the same order of randomness.)
- Fixed a bug in which a floating-point value entered through a text edit sometimes resulted in the wrong number on some non-U.S. locations.
- Fixed a bug in which the multiplex text was stale after edit operations (cutting, copying, pasting, duplicating, replicating, and multireplicating).
- Fixed a bug in which pasted objects had their creation count incremented by two.
- Added a system for the creation of user-defined keyboard shortcuts. This allows the localization of key commands, such as *D* for Don't Save, ~ for Director's View, and so on.
- Fixed a bug in which the use of Spherical Clouds could cause a crash. (This was the cause of some of Bryce 4's crashing problems.)
- Made a small modification to Axiom's key handling (on the PC) to accommodate plug-in user interface tests.
- Added enhanced error-checking to the Axiom routine that swaps the file names of two files. This process was failing on some Windows 98 machines, causing saved files to "disappear."
- Added new text strings to describe the selection of one or no objects. (The interface no longer says "0 objects" or "1 objects.")
- Fixed a bug that caused the key indicator to flash wildly when playing an animation in one of the Labs (Material, Terrain, Sky, or Advanced Motion).
- Fixed a bug that caused the cached Movie Preview in the Material Composer and Sky Lab to be reused even if the animation had changed outside the lab.

- Fixed a bug in which the zoom command (Alt+Space+click) did not zoom in on the cursor's location. In addition, the cursor now correctly remains a magnifying glass when this command is used.
- Changed the Terrain Editor's Cancel All Changes command from Command+Option+N to Command+Shift+N (from Ctrl+Alt+N to Ctrl+Shift+N on the PC). This never worked on the Mac.
- Fixed a bug in which the Sky & Fog palette's controls were not refreshed after evaluating an animation.
- Fixed a bug in the Edit Light dialog box that caused gels assigned within the dialog box to be persistent across different lights.
- Fixed a bug in the Edit Light dialog box in which the Material Presets dialog box (used when applying a texture gel) was not initialized with the current gel.
- Fixed a bug in which a full redraw took place when the current-time indicator was clicked, even in the absence of a time change. This made it impossible to double-click and get the Edit Time dialog box if the scene was large and took a long time to redraw.
- Fixed a bug that caused a user interface update problem if the Export Terrain process was canceled while creating the image maps or writing the object data.
- Added an updated menu and keyboard shortcut handler to the Mac version.
- Fixed a bug that caused visible lights to lose their material settings if they were edited through the Edit Light dialog box after they had already been made visible and edited through the Material Composer.
- Fixed a bug in which the Reset Views function failed to reset banking.
- Improved the error handling in the AVI movie exporter: If the file can't be opened, a normal error message now appears.
- Fixed a bug in which altitude renders and the rendering of altitude-sensitive materials or textures was incorrect if some objects were soloed out or hidden.
- Removed many hard-coded strings to improve localization.
- Modified ImageIO to allow for localization of the resource DAT file's path and of various menu item strings.

Appendix B: Contributor Biographies

This book features the work of some of the best Bryce artists around. Here are their biographies.

Kuzey Atici, "Melbourne, Australia"

I completed the advanced certificate in Art and Design at the Royal Melbourne Institute of Technology, and then I went on to receive a bachelor of arts degree in fine art (also at R.M.I.T.) in 1996.

During this period, I got into photography as a hobby. In 1993, I was a finalist in the Felix H. Man Photographic Prize and Exhibition. The exhibition was held at the National Gallery of Victoria before touring the state of Victoria the next year. My entries in that exhibit won other awards and were parts of other festivals. In 1995, I received an arts grant to photograph the intellectually disabled. I have been using a computer for less than two years, and I continue to learn.

Sandy Birkholz, "Dusty Nebula"

I live with my husband in Portland, Oregon, in the dramatically beautiful Pacific Northwest. There was a time when I didn't consider computer-generated artwork "real art." However, times—and minds—change, and I've enjoyed a personal rebirth as an artist using the computer. What began for me as a way to relieve the stress of my job as a veterinary technologist in a research facility has become a full-blown second occupation. Now newly retired, I am looking forward to putting my energies into my first love, studying and creating art.

I've found that my interest in science influences my artwork—often to a profound degree—depending on the piece I'm working on. I can't help but believe that the advent of computer art programs, such as Bryce, has led many people to discover their hidden talents as artists, as well as launched many traditionally paint-and-canvas artists into a new and exciting realm of computer-generated art. It is, indeed, a renaissance in the world of art, and a welcome one at that.

Bruce "HangTime" Caplin, "Digital Tavern"

A programmer at heart, I suffered from an extreme lack of talent for many years. But I found myself suddenly able to create beautiful pictures on my Macintosh after I purchased the first version of Bryce the week it was released. I still can't draw, paint, or model with clay, but I have created hundreds of pictures with the tools provided by Bryce, Bryce 2, Bryce 3D, and now Bryce 4.

Having designed, built, or run online forums for a number of years (on GEnie, AOL, and currently Delphi), my current pet project is the Bryce Forum on Delphi (**www.delphi.com/bryce**). The Bryce Forum is available without charge to anyone with an interest in 3D art. The forum offers help to beginners as well as to "Masters of Reality," contains tips for users of any level, and offers live chats most nights of the week. If you have any interest in Bryce, you owe it to yourself to check out the Bryce Forum on Delphi. With nearly 100,000 hits, tens of thousands of messages, and a friendly atmosphere, the forum has quickly become the Number 1 Bryce resource on the Internet. If you stop by, you'll see why.

Lannie Caranci, "Treasures"

I was born in Southern California and grew up with a passion for art. My family finally settled in Iowa. My art has moved through many stages: oil painting, airbrush art, stained glass, pottery, welding, stone sculpting, bronze sculpting, and finally 3D art. I find that this medium is constantly a challenge. Most of the other art forms I've experienced amount to learning the techniques and then repeating them. With 3D art, I have to think in all dimensions and create in all dimensions. And best of all, there is a certain thrill in getting a computer to do more than add a column of numbers in Excel.

The number of techniques useful to 3D artists seem limited only by one's imagination. I am constantly surprised at the results of my efforts. I have not had much formal art training, though I studied bronze sculpting (my first love) at Bellevue University for three years. Currently, I am working in Bryce, Poser, Ray Dream Studio, Paint Shop Pro, Photoshop, and other applications. I haven't truly mastered any of them, so it seems that I will be doing this for some time to come.

Lee Chapel, "A Friendly Game"

I first started working with personal computers in 1978 with a couple of computers that used a 6502 processor: the SYM and the KIM. Over the years, I went from a TRS 80 clone, a Radio Shack color computer, a variety of IBM PC clones, to the home-built Pentium II 400MHz machine I now use. During that time, I wrote and sold computer games for the various machines I owned. It has been several years since I've written a game that I felt was good enough to try to sell.

I'm not a professional artist. My regular job is working as a computer information consultant at the Illinois Environmental Protection Agency. I got into 3D graphics three or four years ago with the purchase of VistaPro 3. Early in 1998, I spotted Bryce 3D and Poser 2 at reduced prices and decided to experiment with them. Since then, I've obtained Poser 3 and Ray Dream Studio 5 and created a number of graphics. You can see a gallery of some of my better work on my Web site at **members.aol.com/leec279241.**

Robert Cross, "In Praise Of The Best Seller"

I have worked at *The Ottawa Citizen* daily newspaper since 1988. Since 1997, I have been nominated for two National Newspaper Awards for work in design and graphics. In February 1999, I received an Award of Excellence from the Society of Newspaper Design. In 1996, I taught courses in Photoshop at Algonquin College in Ottawa, and I won second place in the Alias Research International 3D art contest in 1992. I first produced graphics for the newspaper on a Mac Plus with a 20MB hard drive, 4MB of RAM, and a black and white monitor.

Martial Fauteux, "Promenade dans l'île"

I am 51 years old and live in the Montreal area (Quebec, Canada). I have a master's degree in urban studies and have worked in an urban and regional planning office for some 25 years. After my family, my greatest passion is for computer graphics. I began my computer life with an Atari St1040 in 1986 (16 colors, 320-by-200 pixels). My favorite applications are Painter 5.5 Web Edition, Bryce, Poser 3, and Ray Dream Studio—all MetaCreations applications. I also work with an Ultra Slate graphic tablet. I have always loved to draw, and it remains the one artistic endeavor that I enjoy more than computer art. Creating art on the computer is secondary to creating art with a pen and paper, but all my skills are beginning to translate to my computer art as well.

Andrew Paul, "Bonsai"

My involvement with the arts began during and after high school and involved painting, film animation, silk screen, and other more traditional media. I left this behind to pursue a job in optics that has kept me busy gazing into lenses and prisms for the last 11 years. My involvement with computers began three years ago, and I began to look into computer graphics—and Bryce in particular—in December 1998. Raised on the east coast of Canada, I currently reside on the west coast. Graphics is a hobby/obsession of mine to which I will happily lend a lot more time in the near future. I have a family that has offered unconditional support for my hobby. My wife and daughter have always been a wellspring of inspiration, strength, and unfortunately, criticism—which I have to listen to!

I am one of the many users who became immediately bewitched after seeing Bryce for the first time. The ability to create, explore, and share new worlds is something that amazes me and makes graphics so engrossing. The immediacy and ease of a program like Bryce really appeals to me, and its depths and possibilities are something I am just on the brink of exploring. I hope with time I can move into more advanced modeling and work with greater, more complex images. Bryce has been the first stepping stone in the discovery process for me.

Jeff Richardson, "Almost Eden"

I have a solid background of formal art training along with photography, but getting into 3D work was a complete accident. Since I was at secondary school, I've been artistically inclined, through O and A level art and design courses at the local polytechnic, and eventually going on to work in a photography studio and with digital imaging. But my favorites were "ye olde fashioned" pen and ink or airbrush work for personal enjoyment. Then I stumbled across a demo of Bryce 2 on an old *Computer Arts Interactive* magazine CD-ROM. After a couple of weeks of playing with the demo, I went whole hog and bought Bryce 3. I have to admit Bryce has become an obsession now: I use it every day without fail. And Bryce 4 has renewed my enthusiasm all over again; I'm like a kid with a new toy.

I think my background in photography helps a lot when I try to visualize how a Bryce scene should look, how it will be composed and lit. But Bryce has to be one of the easiest 3D applications around, and it makes me want to experiment—to push things a little bit further each time I create something. Some dismiss Bryce as a "gimmicky" application, but it has some incredibly powerful features once you start to delve a bit deeper into the separate areas. Admittedly, the Deep Texture Editor still baffles me at times, but one day I'd like to think I'll get the better of it. The challenge is always there. I never sit down and wonder what to do next. Bryce makes you want to create, and Bryce 4 opens up yet more possibilities for creating your own personal worlds.

Mark J. Smith, "Creada" And "Thor"

I have been a professional digital artist and animator for the past 15 years, and I have been in the industry for 20. I am an original *paintmonkey* (a term I coined that found it's way into *Wired* magazine and hopefully the popular vernacular). My obsession with the digital realm has led me to an array of media, including film, television, books, software, and magazines. In addition to consulting, I write on the subject of computer graphics for any magazine that will listen. My company, Digital Drama, has created visual f/x for such companies as MCA/Universal, HBO, Showtime, Fox Home Entertainment, SABAN, Trimark Pictures, Gramercy Pictures, Concorde/New Horizons, and others. I hope to finance a 40-minute short, called *Organix*, in the near future. My home is nestled in suburbia between

New Jersey's famous turnpike exits, where I live with my wife, Nella, our children, Franco, Marco, and Caterina, and two cats, Darby and Kramer. I can be reached at **mark@digitaldrama.com**

Celia Ziemer, "Forbidding Hands" And "Environment"

I jumped from non-objective painting and pen and ink drawing to the computer several years ago, finding it was my "Magic Anything Box." I work on both Mac and Windows with 3D Studio MAX, Ray Dream Studio, Bryce, Photoshop, Poser 3, Painter 3D, and I have recently added Nendo, Organica, and Amorphium to the box. The last two have caused me to back down from a former position that the only way to model was vertex by vertex. Although I have done "right down to the moss blooms on the rock" realism for scientific illustrations and museum projects, I also have a great necessity to roll my own worlds. My 3D work allows me to climb right in, manipulating the on-screen world of the imagination to tell my story—or watching the story unfold. I want to mess with your head.

INDEX

D

E

F

G

H

I

J

K

L

M

N

O

P

Q

R

S

T

U

V

W

X

Z

Colophon

From start to finish, The Coriolis Group designed *Bryce 4 f/x and design* with the creative professional in mind.

The cover was produced on a Power Macintosh using QuarkXPress 3.3 for layout compositing. Text imported from Microsoft Word was restyled using the Futura and Trajan font families from the Adobe font library. It was printed using four-color process and spot UV coating on 12-point Silverado Matte Cover.

Select images from the color studio were combined to form the color montage art strip that is unique for each Creative Professionals book. Adobe Photoshop 5 was used to create the individual special effects.

The color studio was assembled using Adobe Pagemaker 6.5 on a G3 Macintosh system. Images in TIFF format were color corrected and sized in Adobe Photoshop 5. It was printed using four-color process on 90-pound Silverado Gloss text paper.

The interior layout was built in Adobe Pagemaker 6.5 on a Power Macintosh. Adobe fonts used include Stone Informal for body, Avenir Black for heads, and Copperplate 31ab for chapter titles. Adobe Photoshop 5 was used to process grayscale images, lightening them an average of 5 percent from the original files to accommodate dot gain on 90-pound Silverado Gloss text paper. Text originated in Microsoft Word.

Imagesetting and manufacturing were completed by Courier, Stoughton, Mass.

WHAT'S ON THE CD-ROM

The *Bryce 4 f/x and design* companion CD-ROM contains elements specifically selected to enhance the usefulness of this book, including:

- A demo of PlantStudio (Windows) from Kurtz-Fernhout Software. This application allows you to develop an infinite variety of plant types, perfect for your Bryce worlds.
- A demo of ArtMatic (Macintosh) from Eric Wenger, the originator of Bryce. ArtMatic, which runs on system 8.x, is a texture creation application that creates images and animations of customized fractal graphics.
- A demo version of LiveArt98 for Windows from Viewpoint Datalabs. LiveArt is an image utility for Word.
- More than 300MB of Bryce project files related to the color plates in this book. Many of the project files contain objects that can be saved to your User Objects folder for use in other projects. The project files also contain new materials, skies, and more.
- Full project files for the animation projects detailed in this book. These project files contain new objects that can be used in any of your future Bryce projects.
- Dozens of new Bryce materials. All of these materials are detailed in the book regarding their use for specific effects.
- A collection of new Sky presets, including many that use the Deep Texture Editor. These Sky presets create effects that range from natural phenomena to abstract and experimental looks.
- New image files to apply as either backgrounds or bitmap texture components in your Bryce creations.
- New objects created in 3D applications that can be imported and used in Bryce. The objects include a number of organic elements, such as body parts and flora.

System Requirements

PC

Software:

- Windows 95, 98, NT4 or higher
- MetaCreations Bryce 4
- MetaCreations Poser 3 or 4, Painter 5, Ray Dream Studio 5, and Canoma, as well as Adobe Photoshop with the Knoll Lens Flare Pro plug-in may be necessary to complete the projects detailed in this book.
- Useful accessories to Bryce 4 include Amorphium from Play, Inc.; Organica from Impulse, Inc.; LightWave from NewTek; and 3D Studio MAX from Discreet.

Hardware:

- An Intel (or equivalent) Pentium 200MHz processor (300MHz processor recommended)
- 32MB of RAM (128MB recommended)
- Bryce 4 requires approximately 50MB of disk storage space (200MB recommended)
- A color monitor capable of 24-bit color

Mac

Software:

- System 7.6 or higher
- MetaCreations Bryce 4
- MetaCreations Poser 3 or 4, Painter 5, Ray Dream Studio 5, and Canoma, as well as Adobe Photoshop with the Knoll Lens Flare Pro plug-in may be necessary to complete the projects detailed in this book.
- Useful accessories to Bryce 4 include Amorphium from Play, Inc.; Organica from Impulse, Inc.; LightWave from NewTek; and 3D Studio MAX from Discreet.

Hardware:

- A Motorola G3 200MHz processor (300MHz processor recommended)
- 32MB of RAM (128MB recommended)
- Bryce 4 requires approximately 50MB of disk storage space (200MB recommended)
- A color monitor capable of 24-bit color